# SCARLETT
## Inheritance

### Christine Taylor

Grosvenor House
Publishing Limited

The right of Christine Taylor to be identified as the author of this
work has been asserted in accordance with Section 78
of the Copyright, Designs and Patents Act 1988

The book cover is copyright to Christine Taylor

This book is published by
Grosvenor House Publishing Ltd
Link House
140 The Broadway, Tolworth, Surrey, KT6 7HT.
www.grosvenorhousepublishing.co.uk

A CIP record for this book
is available from the British Library

ISBN 978-1-80381-214-4
eBook ISBN 978-1-80381-215-1

# INTRODUCTION

*"The heroine galloped in the sunrise, the robbers were closely following her, the strong rays of the sun blinded our protagonist. Her eyes squinting, trying to get some vision, as the road began to clear before her, she noticed that she was heading for a chasm, it seemed too wide to succeed and get through alive. Her blood began to cool in her body. But she had no choice, if she didn't risk it, she would be captured by the bandits, not in any case she wanted to give them that pleasure, so she drove her horse and jumped... They successfully crossed to the other side, getting rid of the evil people. She looked back calmly. But when she nailed her head, she saw the...".*

-Scarlett! -Anne approached interrupting her.

-Now my tale is told! -She clapped her palms.

-Oh! -The children began to sigh.

-Oh, dear Scarlett. You're pushing the boundaries again.

-Why what's wrong with dreaming? -She jumped up from under the willow tree, leaving the company there, and walked after her sister.

-There's nothing wrong with dreaming of real things, but dear Scarlett, you're telling impossible things to kids, three innocent children who aren't ready for the hardships of life yet. The only thing you run away from, is nothing but problems, you are embracing your dreams while you are trying to get rid of the real life. But listen here, your skirt will get dusty if you cross the road, not cleaner.

-What do you mean?

-If you are not dealing with problems, they will not get solved on their own. So, get into the house and do your housework.

-Why would I even ask if you have dreams... -She raised her voice sullenly, then her voice almost dried in her throat as they entered the house and saw a soldier. The house was tiny but nice, the furniture was old but clean and tidy. It had two doors, one at the first entrance, and another on the side of the house about twenty steps from the willow tree. Their gaze didn't change from the gentleman, so he was forced to take off his hat and move closer to the ladies. He was wearing a military outfit, but he looked too young to be a soldier. The girls already knew him, they went to the same church every Sunday, although they weren't baptized, only their parents.

-Who are you? -Scarlett asked- Did you come to ask if my sister wants to marry you? -An evil grin sat on her face, for which Anne became embarrassed and poked her.

- The gentleman is Mr John W. -Their father said, leaning against the table.

-Well thank you for your answer, Sir, I'll see you at the camp. -Then, lifting his hat passed by the girls.

-What does that mean? -Scarlett asked in horror.

-The French are recruiting their forces.

-And? What do we have to do with that?

-Oh, dear Scarlett... -Her mother sighed in a crying voice in her chair.

She went out of the house upset, back to the hilltop under the tree.

-Dear good husband, please tell me, what do I do with this stubborn girl while you are there?

-Give her in marriage. -He says in a low voice.

-Scarlett is a good soul, but she's still a child to understand this all. -Anne said, then went out to comfort her.

-Dear good husband, father of my children, you are so wise. Now that you leave me alone with our children and only heaven knows when you will return, tell me please, what to do. Next year in the spring, this child will also be an adult, should I tell her the truth or wait for you, my dear?

-Woman... I can't dictate. If you listen to me, do what you think is good.

-But still, my dearest one, what would happen to Scarlett, if her sister would not be with her anymore? She is her support, the only person she trusts, the one who encourages her, the one who gives her reassurance.

-Scarlett must grow up for heaven's sake! -He growled at her.

BOOK ONE

# *NEW LIFE*

# CHAPTER I

It was already difficult for their father to prepare, knowing their destination and destiny. One of the lines of a military oath was in his mind *"Give your life in exchange for your country, your wives, your sons, and your God"*. -For your sons, huh? -He coughed. -My sons are all going to die for this political nonsense... When it came to classifying his youngest son, the messenger interrupted that it was not his decision and unfortunately, he could say nothing in their favour. Everything was already decided. -The rich, of course... they pull themselves out of this as well. -The man murmurs- The life of a rich is simple. They are important, their life must be left. Nor do they care if the child they are calling in is only sixteen years old. It was a shame to waste my legacy... but no longer matters.

The boys were enthusiastic about this little outing. Certainly, they have been excited when they had never been at war before, nor could they have any idea what it really was like. The pages of books, however, do not always reflect reality, as not everyone becomes a hero, not everyone survives and not everyone's life counts.

The boys chattered all the way, they were worse than the old women on the little bench, the topic was uninterrupted about war and power show.

-I can't wait to finally get a gun and serve my country. -Said the biggest boy- My wife and children will treat me like God after we win the war.

-I'm sure it can't be that hard to use those weapons. If I learn to use them, they will recognize my abilities and surely like me so much that I will also receive an award. Just imagine what kind of father that child will have. I will be the only person he looks up to, I will be his role model, the man for whose footsteps that child will starve. If he follows my path, he will have a good life. -Said the middle one.

-Shut up, you don't even know if it will be a he or a she.

-Or maybe you don't know if you will become an aunt or an uncle. -He said pointing seriously.

-You are such an idiot. Did you know that? -The eldest looked at the silly boy. -And even why do you think it's that simple? With those skinny arms, you will hardly be able to hold that gun. -He began to laugh- And you, little Bloom, what do you think the future holds?

The boy arose from the side window of the rattling carriage on which he was lying and touched the company with a word, *"Darkness"*, then there was silence among them for half a minute or so, then the two older boys began to bully each other again. Their father watched them wordlessly, why would he have said anything? Why would he take away that little drop of hope from them? After all, they have only this, in the present situation. He knew his youngest child, Aydan, was right, they had reason to be afraid and if they had a little bit of mind, they would try to mingle between the other soldiers rather than stand out, because everyone knows they would be sent out to the front, the mouth heroes and troublemakers who stand out of the line.

*

When the carriage arrived in front of the camp and they got out of it, the two older boy's mouths dropped open by seeing the many dirty, sick and truncated people. They stood silently in front of the entrance for a few more seconds, then the whip of the carter brought them back from their thoughts as he slammed between the horses.

-It is not going to be a bed of roses. -Their father said, then they headed to the entrance, where a one-eyed man was waiting for the newcomers with a list in his hand.

-Names? -The one-eyed asked. After they introduced themselves, the man looked at the list and scribbled something. -We've been waiting for you. Turn left at the third column, they'll get your equipment there. -The four men/boys did so. They began to get discouraged by the many strangers and truncated people, they felt a kind of bad feeling, they realised that not even half of it was a joke. On the way, as they reached the second pillar of the tent, Aydan looked to the right, where nurses were caring for wounded men, he stopped. Among the wounded was a man who was pressed hard to the bed and resisting.

-No! Nooo! I beg you, please don't do this to me. - There was fear and pain in his voice at once, the doctor holding a funnel in one hand and a saw in the other.

-Please understand, Sir, that there is nothing else I can do, this is the only way to survive, you have already lost way too much blood. -The doctor spoke in a raised voice to be able to speak beyond the roaring man.

The man was still trying to object, saying he would choose death rather than live his life as a cripple, but in spite of the opposition, the doctors did not even wait for the anaesthetic to take effect after he poured it into his mouth through the funnel, he began to saw the foot of that poor man. Why would he have waited when there were as many wounded people as the sieve hole, and one more. The clotted blood was wiped off the man's leg by one of the nurses with a damp cloth, then under the small saw a layer of skin began to gently separate and open in two, fresh blood just spilling out of the open wound. Aydan shivered, the cold ran down through him, then a hand lay on his shoulder.

-Come on, son, let's move on. -His father said.

At the third column, they turned left, where a man was sitting at a table, uniforms, hats, and weapons all along the table. After handing them the equipment and weapons, he took out a paper. *"Another list…"* little Bloom rolled his eyes. Then began to list.

-Mr. Elliot Bloom, you can go straight into the third wing, among the trained soldiers. Mr. Elliot Bloom Junior himself goes into the second with Aydan Bloom. And you… -pointing a finger at the middle boy- go to the fourth.

-It's an injustice, why can't I stay with my brothers?

-This is not a wish show, soldier! -The sergeant said in a resentful voice.

-I'm not moving a tread until you're directed to the other wing.

-All right, -the boys began to smile at each other, but in a blink of an eye their smile disappeared as the sergeant continued what he had to say- you could go to the seventh then. Instead of the soldiers waiting to be trained, you can go to front-line training.

-Please, Sir… -Their father tried to intervene, but the sergeant would not let him continue.

-This topic is closed here, go to the designated place soldiers!

The father looked at his sons in despair, then nodded as he said goodbye. The three boys, still standing there for a while, the two boys patted reassuringly on the back of the middle one and then said that everything will be fine. He himself set off for his designated place leaving his brothers.

# CHAPTER II

*"My dear diary, I feel like my life is starting to get more and more unruly, everything has changed since my father and three brothers were enlisted. Even the neighbour's cat moans differently since then, not to mention my sister, who was just marrying the messenger who informed my father of the war, but what could the hapless girl have done when that screwy got her pregnant? The child was born, not only in order to bring unrest into my life, but into everyone else's as well. Besides, I'm afraid my mother has a lover, more and more letters are coming since that old man came here. I feel so lonely, I wish, I could have a friend with whom I could discuss everything, although I have no reason to complain because my time with the children is a little comforting, but I can't tell them about my troubles for heaven's sake, they wouldn't understand... at least I can describe it all."*

-Scarlett, have you seen the knitting needles? I was convinced I had put them back in the wool ball. -Anne's face showed fatigue, no wonder the child was crying day and night and the poor thing didn't have a minute of rest. She was worried about what would happen to them, the sudden marriage and becoming a parent brought an unexpected turn into her life, her husband is in the army and heaven knows when the war will end.

-I last saw them on the mantelpiece. -She replied.

When it was about to get dark in the evening, Anne, like a stump, threw herself on the bed, causing her to fall asleep from one minute to another like some enchanted princess from some tale. Scarlett was thirsty and tried to leave the room in silence, it was not an easy task. Nobody cannot even imagine how difficult it is to sneak out in such a silence that the baby next to Anne's bed

7

would not wake up, this dull little creature, had nothing to do but always wake up at the worst time. It was a curse for Scarlett that all three of them were in the same room. Who would have thought that it would have such a rebound effect to look down on someone because of their misfortune? Poor Anne, didn't know how much she despised her for all that had happened to her, since Scarlett had never really shown it, she felt it in part, but she thought that such things could never happen to her.

As soon as she reached the stairs, she heard that her sister-in-law, her eldest brother's wife, had arrived. She stopped abruptly, before she started down the stairs, old, faded, worn stairs that should have been renovated at least ten years ago. Scarlett was afraid that some steps will squeak if she suddenly steps on them. So, she took a deep breath before setting off, when she reached the third step of the stairs, she was forced to move again, hearing her sister-in-law and mother talk.

-Everything happens at the worst time, dear Mary... -Mrs. Bloom sighs.

-Don't say like that, everything has its own blessing, you know there is always a rainbow after the storm.

-You cannot know about these darling, because you're still young, you still have so much time to live to see things differently. -Then she took a sip of the cup. -At least this girl wouldn't have brought shame on the family, what would we do now if that feeble-witted man had not married her before he joined the army?... -She sighed.

-My dear mother-in-law, you know what young love is like. -Mary tried to protect Anne.

-Youth, nonsense... Then now they're all going to die. We have to take care of everything for our existence as a women, men are all stupid, they only understand criticism, war, and politics.

-Enough of this, mother! -Scarlett turned up from behind the door. -Yet why did you lose your faith, why do you say they won't come back? Everyone knows we are having a better situation at the war. -Then she started to walk towards the front door. -And as for Anne, please don't say that, because she's trying to satisfy you all hours of the day, she's watching out for all your wishes, it's not her fault that the thing ended like this. The war has been going on for a whole year now. Of course, everyone is waiting for it to end and the men to finally come home. -Turning up her nose she walked away, through the door straight to the willow tree, where she began to cry, at the place where no one can see or hear her weakness. She is a stubborn girl, but full of love.

Meanwhile, Anne looked at her sister from the window of their room. The most painful thing was that she was idle, as her mother was right, if she hadn't been so naive and in love, now at least there would be one less problem in the house, she regretted it and she didn't her thoughts. Who wouldn't love their own baby? She knew if it hadn't happened, she wouldn't have this beautiful child now, Aliona, but if it hadn't happened either, it wouldn't have been so hard to feed another mouth. Anne didn't understand what had happened, because there was never a reason to complain, there was never food missing from their table, they always had everything, they weren't rich either, but they didn't lack anything. *"This filthy war"*, she thought, yet what else would she have thought in the present situation? Everyone is pointing everything to the war.

Listening to the further conversation, Anne just wished that if fate sought to separate her from her sister, then all she taught her would be to Scarlett's advantage. The pain she felt knowing that one day they would be torn apart, was indescribable, she felt stabbed in the heart. Her chest filled with such a stabbing pain that she could not breathe, Anne just silently shed her tears.

-Mary, dear, if you knew how much a mother's heart had to go through without letting it split into two. If Anne would know that she will lose her sister, in a month too... The two girls always looked like they were growing together as one, they always supported each other, I have no idea what will happen after that.

-What do you mean *"her sister too"*? Who else? -Mary was shocked.

-Mary, dear, I'll tell you the truth, the reason I called you here at this late hour... My dear, beloved husband... -Her eyes filled with tears -Today I received a letter informing me that my beloved husband and son-in-law, Aliona's father, had passed away.

The young girl, with her navy-blue eyes, just stared at the sobbing woman sitting in front of her for seconds, couldn't speak, then finally moaned her question. -What are you talking about?

-Mr. Bloom had been shot, three weeks ago. I didn't tell the girls, not to worry them, he wrote that he was already feeling completely well... -The woman took out her handkerchief and began to wipe away her tears more and more frequently.

-His wounds were starting to heal, but he caught some nasty infection, the doctors said it was probably after careless attendance, there are so many wounded people, they cannot all be treated in time. And my son-in-law died two weeks ago, according to the letter, he got a bullet in his neck. I have no idea how to tell the girls... -She admitted.

Mary was silent, because what could she have said in this situation? The news shocked her so much that she couldn't even comfort the woman in front of her. So, she just changed the subject quickly.

-What happened to Scarlett? What did you mean by *"the girls would be separated soon"*?

# CHAPTER III

*"Dear diary, the days are starting to merge so much, another year has passed since my last birthday, even faster than the previous ones, all because of the war. The pain I feel due to the loss of my father is indescribably deep, since he is the first person, I knew from my family so well who passed away. My mother, whose marriage spanned twenty-one years, was affected to such an extent that it nailed the strong woman I once knew, to her bed. Anne, on the other hand, had never cried before me in the last month, she was always busy diverting her thoughts. Taking care of our mother and the child. All this has taken all of our time and energy so much that I am ashamed to admit it, but I can't wait for it all to end. I'm trying to take the example of Anne, the only one I can rely on during these difficult times. She will always be the only woman I will look up to for the rest of my life, she is the one who gives me strength during the difficult hours. I am ashamed to admit how much guilt I have for looking down on her for what happened back then, she is a heroine that everyone can follow, I wish I could be as strong as she is."*

-Happy birthday little sister! -There was a sudden voice behind Scarlett and as soon as she heard this, she closed her diary and then looked behind from the armchair. When she saw a small gift box in her hand, got up and turned to Anne.

-Celebrating when we need to mourn, don't be foolish! If one of the neighbours hears this, my dear good God... -Mrs. Bloom sighed from her chair, and the baby immediately began to cry, because of her grimly speaking.

Scarlett was offended all the way and left the room with the small box in her hand. Mrs. Bloom looked at Anne incomprehensibly, who sighed and then answered the woman in the armchair who was covered from head to toe with a blanket. With her wrinkled face and little scarf on her head, she looked like a caterpillar starting to become a cocoon.

-You know, Mother, that we won't see her for long, why did you have to talk to her in such a derogatory way? -Then Anne hurried after Scarlett, leaving their mother in the darkened room with the crying baby in her arms.

-Anne, wait! At least take this little screaming child with you! -But she shouted in vain, it found deaf ears. Even if Anne could hear it, she wouldn't.

Anne, just as she had guessed. She found Scarlett under the willow tree, where the memories of their childhood tied them to the most.

-I remember when I first wanted to teach you how to climb trees. -Anne laughed.

-Yes, I had a great fall, I never wanted to climb since then. -Scarlett smiled, turning the small box in her hand. -Why did she never like me?

-Who? -Anne wondered, then leaned down next to her sister.

-You know who I'm talking about. It always seemed to make a difference among us. When I fell out of the tree, for example, she just yelled at me to stop bellowing. If it was about Aydan or any of our other brothers, she ran to them with a bandage and disinfectant, even if it was only a splinter in their finger.

-You know Scarlett, there are many things in life for which you only get an answer by time. -Then smoothed her hair out of her face to see it. -Do you want to open it? -Anne asked, looking at the box, Scarlett just nodded and opened it. The box contained a beautiful three-rows of pearls with a blue shell-shaped gem in the centre and other small stones on the rows among the pearls.

Scarlett was stuck for words.

-Would you like me to? -The girl nodded wordlessly. The jewellery fitted her beautifully, it gave a very good contrast to her red hair and blue eyes. -I kept that for the time you were getting married, it would have been my job to prepare you for everything...

-How do you mean that... -Scarlett couldn't finish her question, a gentleman showed up at the entrance to the house near the tree. He was dressed quite elegantly and had a nice carriage. He took off his hat when he saw the girls.

-Miss. Scarlett Bloom?

*

-Do you want some coffee, Mr.? -Anne asked with the coffee pot in her hand.

-Owen Thaker. - The old man replied, the girls were both waiting for the man's words with interest. Their mother was in a deep sleep in the other room, and Anne took the baby to her room when the man arrived. They had no idea what he wanted, they believed it was something important with such an appearance, like he was going for some significant event or something. For his age, the man looked very good, his sea-blue eyes were glowing when he looked at the girls, especially at Scarlett, his completely white hair was shorter at the sides and on the top was worn longer, combed to the right-hand side. He could have been at least fifty years old or so.

-Miss. Bloom, to the best of my knowledge, you had turned eighteen today.

-That's right. -Scarlett agreed.

-According to the order I have, if you accept, I will have to take you to your aunt's property to fill out the inheritance documents.

*

13

-I don't understand that. -Scarlett expressed herself- Sir, you're trying to tell me that my aunt, who had never seen me before and who has been dead for a decade, has left me all her fortune, which I would have to manage? She didn't give it to my father because he had his own inheritance and gambled it on cards and this is how we lost our wealth? That is why we have become impoverished and we are destined to have little to eat? And if I refuse, we won't get anything because Aunt Miranda is only bequeathing that property to me, and it will be auctioning off and we won't see even a shilling of all of this and I can't even overwrite it for someone else's name until I get married? Do I understand all of that correctly? -Scarlett barely had a few seconds to process it all, gasping for air and looking into the corners of the room, she was trying to stay calm.

-Yes. -The gentleman replied briefly.

-I still don't understand that. Why me? I have three brothers, two of them are married, they have a family, the oldest has two little daughters and the other has a son, the youngest is unmarried but still he is a boy. By the way, here is Anne, who also has a family, and my mother. Of course, my father is dead, but she couldn't know about it. Besides, I would have to leave my birthplace, I cannot take my mother with me in her condition, and Anne cannot come with me because she has to take care of her. Yet I cannot leave them alone in such circumstances. All this is so unfair. Why? Why? -The girl continued confused.

-I can't accept it! -She declared, to which both stared with surprising round eyes. Then she replied once more with the same answer.

-As the little woman wishes. -He replied, then got up from the table -But if you change your mind, you have two weeks to appear at the address on the contract. -He nodded at the paper lying on the table, then put on his hat and left.

14

-Miss. Scarlett Miranda Bloom, why do you think you're rejecting such an offer? -Anne finally said after the man closed the door behind him.

-Please Anne, understand. I can't. What would our brothers say when they heard it? This is so unfair.

-Scarlett, I was by your side to raise a soldier of a woman of you. -Anne got up from her chair -Is that what I taught you? To flee? Such opportunities are gifts, you have to seize them, and by the way in Cornwall... You'll be stupid if you don't take advantage of this offer.

-I admit the truth, Anne, I'm not going because I'm needed at home, I know it's a great opportunity not only for me, but for the whole family, but I'm afraid Anne, what if everything doesn't go the way I want it to? I've never done such an important thing before; I don't want to disappoint. -Scarlett was so confused that she didn't know what to say or what to do. -You knew it, right? You knew it all along. That's why you gave me this gift too. -She pointed to the necklace.

-At first, when I found out, I was scared. -Someone said, from the door. -No, I was more envious, than scared. I wished you didn't know about it, because your father was Miranda's brother after all, he would have to receive all the fortune. But I realise you are the person who deserves this opportunity. I have heard the conversation and the love and loyalty to your parents and siblings has penetrated my heart. I've always treated you differently, I see that now, you have no idea how sorry I am. Go try it. If something goes wrong, we will always look forward to seeing you back. -She held out her arms, hugging her, then whispered in the ear. -You have such a good soul, girl.

# CHAPTER IV

*"My dearest diary, it was so hard to make that decision, but I did it at the request of Anne and my mother. I don't know what I'm going to do without them, because they'll be so far away. I can only count on myself. I am looking forward to the moment to find out what magical treasure I have inherited."*

-Scarlett come, the breakfast is getting cold! -Anne shouted, she put her diary in the luggage, it was the last thing she packed, then she locked it up and walked down the stairs. Which squeaked noisily after each step.

-I'll miss that sound... -Anne smiled at her- How much I like it when I don't have to make breakfast. -Anne playfully picked up the jug of water and then splashed Scarlett down a little.

-Girls don't play with this. -Said Mrs. Bloom with the baby in her arms. -The stagecoach will leave in three hours; Scarlett can't be late. -She continued, then sat down at the table.

*

The farewell was difficult, but it happened.

The rider of the stagecoach said out loud, *"Last call, boarding!"*

Scarlett hugged the two women tightly and then got in. Along the way, she wrote scenarios about the adventures ahead, trying to prepare for all the good and bad that awaits her. Scarlett set out for a trip to Cornwall from a small village in Bath. Mrs. Bloom extols the ocean she had seen in her youth, Scarlett was looking forward to seeing it herself as well, but the poor girl had to travel for days for it, the people around her were constantly changing, she felt that she will never arrive.

# CHAPTER V

A sudden jolt made Scarlett wake up from her most beautiful dream, and then she almost hit her head on the door when the carriage suddenly stopped.

*"Ladies and gentlemen, we have arrived in Truro."*

They stopped in front of the town hall; the carriage driver started unloading. After receiving her luggage, she only admired the city for a few minutes. She had never been to the capital, and even very rarely to the city, she was a country girl. Not many things took her to the town, but she never bothered about it. She didn't know where to go so she stopped a woman to set her on the road. She was a kind lady explaining everything to her in detail. She grabbed her luggage and the little basket, then set off. Scarlett tried to do everything the way the lady said, turning left at the first street, then left, after that right, and left again, but so many streets led to so many others that she was at once confused and no longer knew where to turn left or right. So, she set off according to her intuition until she reached a narrow alley. She paused for a few seconds and began to think when the bell had just struck noon, then she took her first steps.

Scarlett reached the centre of the alley as a crowd approached her, she had to stop when she saw that many dirty people heading toward her, she wanted to turn back, but the crowd caught up. Lots of people, one by one dirty, skinny and smelly men. They couldn't pass the girl without a word, there were those who whistled, those who spoke to her, and those who touched her. Scarlett attempted to give way and get rid of them as quickly as possible. As less people passed her, Scarlett straightened up and looked after the passing men. Suddenly someone grabbed her arm from behind and started tugging her towards him, *"What is a beauty like you doing in here?"*

Scarlett began to object, but the man pulled her more and more closely, the girl dropped the basket from her hand, which contained the food for the trip. The man was about to kiss her when someone appeared suddenly out of nowhere and grabbed him by his shirt. He was a tall, very handsome man, his skin was amazing, for the first time in her life, Scarlett had seen a man of coloured skin. The man looked deep into the white man's eyes, who was two heads shorter than him, then pushed him away, saying, *"Get lost!"*

The man ran away in fear. She was trembling with fear, not knowing what the consequences would be if she stayed there with this man longer, she could have run away, but she didn't. The man bent down and picked up her basket and handed it to her. Scarlett recognized this gesture and nodded, with thanks.

-What is such a sophisticated lady like you doing here Ms.? -He asked respectfully.

-Miss. Blo... call me Scarlett! -She corrected herself, she was not used to being called Miss, before that no one did. Scarlett then held out her hand, the man grabbed it and then began to lean to kiss it, but she shook hands.

-I'm going to my aunt.

-It would be wise, if at this hour you wouldn't come at this place, every worthless bastard, is leaving their job at this time, they are taking their lunch break. Do you know the way, Miss?

-As a matter of fact, -Scarlett wasn't sure if she could admit that everything was completely foreign to her and she was here for the first time in her life, but did -I'm not sure.

-Come, I can accompany you to the end of the alley if you want.

She just nodded and then they set off. When they reached the end of the alley, a huge building stood there, it seemed like a dead-end at first, Scarlett was hesitant, but the alley continued to turn left, at which point she sighed deeply. Staring at the building, she saw a young man looking at them grimly, he was a handsome man, but his face reflected seriousness, cruelty. Seeing the end of the alley and the busy street, Scarlett paced faster and faster and took a few more steps on the busy street, but she noticed that her partner was no longer following her, so she turned back to him. The man watched the many people walking on the street, and like a beaten dog, he didn't want to take a step out of his little nook.

-Can you accompany me for a while? I'm not entirely sure yet... -then it occurred to her -You have lunchtime... Don't worry, I will not hold you back just for a minute. Just tell me what I owe. -She reached into the little basket for a moment -I don't have much money, but...

The man interrupted refusing. -I can't accept money for such a small thing.

-What? Do you think that was a little thing? You must have a family...

-I have a daughter. That's why I know how important it is to value women.

-Accordingly, you are going home to her at lunchtime. And I am holding you back...

-I can't. I just stay for 20 minutes on my break, not like the other men.

-What are you talking about? After all, you deserve a break just like the others.

-Look at me, miss, just look at me, people like us are glad to get a job at all.

Scarlett was ashamed of herself. Looking at her basket, she noticed that the man had nothing.

-Please accept this, -then she handed out the basket -there is fruit, bread and more.

-I can't do this, for me it is...

-I insists!

The man finally took it. Then Scarlett walked away.

# CHAPTER VI

-George, my dear, are you joining us for lunch? -An old lady asked the man standing in front of the window, stopping at the door.

-Not now, Aunt. I have a lot of things to do.

-I see... -She said sarcastically, then walked over to him, leaning on her walking stick. -I understand everything now, you'd rather look at pretty girls from a distance than find yourself a wife.

-Aunt, please don't come with this again... You know that my career is more important than a wife right now.

-I never had a child of my own. So, I have to deal with you... With a stubborn careerist. -She said with sarcasm again. -At least don't be careful in brothels and get one pregnant. Otherwise, I will never live to have a grandchild.

He kissed Miss. Salvatore's hand and then added: -You know I'm not going to places like that. -He said with a smile.

-And what about pretty ladies like her? -She asked, nodding at the red-haired girl walking down the street.

-Don't be silly. Just look at her, she walks in a dark little street at noon, she's touched by all sorts of dirty workers, not to mention her attendant... Just those people didn't have her, who didn't want to. I will never have anything to do with a person like this. Her parents must be proud of her...

-Georgie... you always find excuses for everything. You never know what the future holds, child. It could even be, that woman will be your wife. Or worse... the ways of the Lord are unfathomable.

21

# CHAPTER VII

*"My dear diary, if I don't write it down, I will still remember for the rest of my life, the first day I arrived in Gracewith. My trip was quite adventurous, I got lost several times when I got here. The city is huge, crowded, I have never seen so many people at once and I have never seen such a brave and helpful man as... To tell the truth, I forgot to ask the name of the gentleman, but without his help, I would not have gotten this far and not only because I got lost. I would never have thought that such evil people existed, uneducated and unclean, I had read of the people who were destined for this life, but I would never have thought that I would nurture such immeasurable hatred for them. Although, my family was never rich and there was no maid in the house, my parents never backed away from teaching us or keeping us clean. But not just their image has been distorted in front of me. I am afraid to get to know the nobles in advance. I saw a man today, albeit from afar, but he looked down at me from the window of his luxurious suite. A handsome young gentleman with dark brown eyes, dark hair, dressed in an elegant outfit, but judging by his posture and his look, I will never want to have anything to do with that man.*

*I had come a long way and I am not just talking about my carriage ride, but from the city to Gracewith. I walked for hours to get here, not to mention the heavy luggage I carried; at a moment I was thinking about leaving it there in a hedge. But since I don't know the place, I probably would have left it there forever.*

*When I arrived at Gracewith I was completely shocked by the so-called "heritage". I arrived at a palace. When I knocked on the door, an old lady of coloured skin opened it. As soon as she saw me, she crossed herself. Her face was completely shocked, she couldn't speak, she didn't even invite me in until I asked if I could.*

*I'm not completely aware of the names yet, but I think her name is Doris. She is a kind person, she was happy to lead around, showed everything and explained the policy nicely, introduced me to the staff, which consisted of a kitchen maid and a butler. The house was a bit old, inhabited only by the staff who still live here. Four wings were locked, declared as dangerous due to the decaying walls, including the ballroom. Doris said there were memorable balls held here while my grandfather lived. I got a huge room, Doris says it's one of the biggest rooms in the building, my grandparents' room. Everything was preserved from the previous inhabitants in the room, even their paintings hung on the wall. Until now I didn't know that my father looked exactly like the never seen grandfather of mine, although I couldn't put my grandmother's face anywhere. However, Grandma, on the other hand, could have been a very kind lady, she had a pleasant radiance, a kind face, while apparently, Grandpa couldn't smile even for a portrait. I have an appointment with Mr. Owen Thaker in an hour. So, I have taken the moment to describe it all. I'll be back soon with news."*

-Miss. Bloom, Mr. Thaker is here! -Doris knocked, then opened the door when she got no answer.

-Doris, -she smiled kindly- just call me, Scarlett.

-You can't ask me that, but not from anyone! -She growled.

-Why can't I?

-Never do it, it violates etiquette, you can only be called that by those who are family members or in a close relationship with you. It would be indecent to do so. Did you not learn anything?

-As a matter of fact, no one has ever taught me that.

-CHh-chh-chh... -Doris kissed her teeth. Then she wanted to walk away, leaving Scarlett with her thoughts, but she called after Doris.

-Doris, are the workers here my servants?

-The three of us stayed here because Mr. Bloom, then his daughter, Miss. Bloom and now you, Miss. are our owner. We are the slaves of the young lady, ON PAPER. -She stressed.

-Does that mean I don't have to pay then? Because after all, if I have to, I don't have a budget for it, at least for now.

-Don't worry, young lady. Slaves have no free choice; we are unable to go elsewhere to work. We are owned by Miss... Scarlett, until you free us or give us English identity documents. -She said kind of offended.

-That's nonsense. Humans cannot be objectified. How would you be my property?

-Only a white man can't be Miss. -She said, then closed the door behind herself.

*

Mr. Thaker was waiting for the girl at the bottom of the stairs. The stairs at first ran in a straight line to the middle (meeting point), then split into two branches. There was a portrait on the wall of the meeting point, the man was looking at the picture, so immersed in his thoughts that he didn't even notice Scarlett until she reached the front of the painting. The man shuddered for a moment as if seeing a ghost, no wonder, Scarlett looked eerily like the lady in the portrait. Although she was about the same age as her, she wore her hair halfway back, just like Scarlett. The only difference was that the woman in the portrait had dark hair and dark brown eyes, while Scarlett's hair was vibrant red and her eyes were lighter than the sky.

-Mr. Thaker, are you feeling well? -She asked, then looked behind herself, she was noticing the painting for the first time, although she had already walked past it, but it avoided her attention, the only thing she could say when she saw the picture was "*Ohh...*"

Then they retired to the library.

-Well, I suppose you changed your mind... -She just nodded. -I am happy to see you here. You made a great decision. Please sign here.

-Tell me something, a woman, as my aunt... How could she assert herself in the company, with so much power and opulence, without a husband?

-Do not think it was easy for her. She had a nice dowry, but she never saw that money. As you know, Mr. Bloom had only two children. You already know the fate of the boy. But Miss. Bloom... She was a marvellous person. She didn't get married, as you know. However, there were suitors... -The man paused for a few seconds. -She was picky. Her father did not give her the dowry, which was meant, he rather gave money only to his son and as I see your papers Miss, you have no dowry either. Your father didn't leave a single shilling for his family, so as soon as the homeowners run out of the money they saved, they become paupers. -Scarlett's gaze revealed she didn't know anything about it. -The money slipped out of your father's hands. I do think that is the reason why he couldn't buy himself out of the military, he had no choice, he couldn't show evidence about being an important member of society.

She was very disappointed to hear these words.

-I found transactions that suggest Miss. Bloom transferred money to her brother's account, very large sums, once a year, every March 15th. They started a few years before she died and then in her last year she asked for my help to continue with all this. By her entrusting me, I am now here with the inheritance documents in front of you.

-But that's my birthday.

-That's right. Just Miss. Bloom knows its reason. Well, going back to the subject. Your aunt was shunned by society. Although nowadays, it is not a real problem if a woman is handling the money. But a decade ago, it wasn't an easy thing to do. Men are proud, they don't like if a woman exceeds them. Mr. Bloom could not leave his daughter with nothing. Just before his death, I received a note from a doctor that he was unable to continue to run the farm, due to his illness. So, everything was inherited by Miss. Bloom, the estate and those who and what comes with it.

-You mean, Doris, Matilda and Nivek?

-So, as you see Gracewith is huge, and I dare to bet you haven't seen the whole estate yet. Nearly 342 hectares (which is 845 acres): of which 181 hectares (447 acres) is arable land, 34 hectares (84 acres) of the village, and the other 43 hectares (106 acres) of meadow, 39 hectares (96 acres) of the farm, eight hectares of smaller forest and then the remaining 37 acres (91 acres) of Gracewith. Your aunt gave homes to 173 families in the village, of whom hardly 32 still live here. She provided them work and homes, from which she profited as well.

-But... I don't understand... -She said.

-You mean, Miss. Bloom, you don't understand how could a woman handle that fortune, don't you? -She nodded- That's why I'm here, I've always had a good relationship with your aunt and vouched for her finances. But now the farm is ruined. The sowing lands dried up and weeded in. And people left the village. Unemployment, famine, and frustration affect people like a disease.

Doris entered the room with a letter in her hand. -It's for you Miss.

-What? What is it? -Scarlett unfolded the letter, which was an invitation to a ball, she read it aloud, but she looked at the letters in shock as if she was looking but not seeing.

26

*"Dear Miss. Bloom,*

*I've been notified about your visit to Cornwall, I hope you are enjoying your time here. I would be delighted to invite you to my ball, which will be held in Penvenwirth on Saturday night. It would be a pleasure if you would visit. Society is waiting to meet you.*

*Your sincerely,*

*Norman Quas."*

-I don't understand, how could they have known I was here? I just arrived a few hours ago.

-Well, this is a small town, Miss. Bloom, people love rumours. Be careful to whom you talk and what you say. Because the people here are far different from the ones you know. Now if you'll excuse me, Miss, I'll let you process the news. Thank you for making the decision so quickly.

-Please wait. -These words were difficult, but she had no choice- I don't know these people.

-You'll get to know them soon. -He stood up and headed for the door.

With shame in her eyes, she spoke softly as the man passed the armchair. -I had not yet been introduced to society. -The man stopped, he was speechless for seconds, then spoke again.

-I see. You can count on me, Miss, I'm sending a carriage for you on Saturday.

-I can't accept the invitation, I barely arrived anyway. I have a lot to do. I can't go.

-If you change your mind, Miss, you'll find me in the bank, Monday to Friday from the morning until noon.

# CHAPTER VIII

In the morning, Scarlett couldn't sleep from the excitement, so she got up earlier. She decided that a morning walk would not hurt so she set out to explore the countryside. She had many things in her mind, most notably deciding to write to her family as soon as she got home. Then she will start to renovate deeply some corners of the house. Her land was large enough for other people to pass through it freely, so there was no need to make a detour. She watched the passers-by, excitedly as she passed them in one of her meadows. High grass grew in it, it seemed unused, she saw neither a cow nor a horse grazing on it. However, she saw plenty of wildflowers. Making a larger bouquet along the way, she was just leaning down to pick an English bluebell when she saw a man on horseback. At first, she didn't recognize him because of the distance, the man stopped and looked at her from far away.

Scarlett tried not to notice him at first, but she felt very frustrated after a while. As she moved on, it finally appeared that the man who was watching was none other than the aristocrat who also watched from the window. She smiled at him, but the man didn't return her smile, just raised his hat and yanked the reins as he cut off. Scarlett rolled her eyes and walked on. When she looked around again, she saw a small village, Scarlett decided to visit it. In the morning, she thought that if there were workers living there, they would have been at work. An engraved milestone marked the village with the inscription *"Welcome to GracewithHenry village"*. She felt very ironic that her inheritance name was changed and a part was cut off, but she went on. Some children played with a dog at the entrance of the village, all were girls. She divided the bouquet of wildflowers into as many bunches as there were children and gave them all a bunch. A woman was walking to the river with her clothes in a basket to wash them when she saw Scarlett, and the girl looked at her, she threw down the basket full of clothes and ran away screaming. The kids just laughed amusingly.

*"She's alive! She's alive!"* she shouted to the villagers. Everybody who was at home ran out into the street to see what was happening. They didn't understand what the noise was. *"Our Mistress! She's alive!"* she shouted, no one understood what had gotten into her.

As Scarlett walked through the village, she caught everyone's eyes, some people crossed themselves, some prayed, and there were those who shouted, *"Witch!"*. No wonder, she was a complete image of their mistress who had been dead for a decade. Most people were just speechlessly amazed at the apparition. Scarlett tried to cover her fear, she just walked past the people who were staring at her, like she would be a bloody rag. Once a woman escaped from the crowd and said, *"My mistress, please give food to the hungry souls. Give us jobs again, as you did before."*

Scarlett was very frightened, so, she ran away. People didn't go after her, they just shouted *"Help us!"*.

When she got back to the house, Doris was already waiting for her.

-Where did you go, Miss? Are you feeling well? -But she didn't say anything, she just passed by. -Breakfast is ready! -Doris said again.

-I'm not hungry, give me some clothes. -Doris turned towards her- I don't want to get dirty in my best clothes.

-What are you up to? -She was puzzled.

\*

She began by cleaning the east wing, where some of the doors and windows were covered with nailed planks to keep the wind from entering. Scarlett took them down, choosing Matilda to help her.

Matilda was a woman in her sixties who had been serving the house for a long time. She was a woman with a pleasant radiance, but she didn't seem confident enough judging by her demeanour.

After cleaning the house for hours, she finally reached a beautiful room.

- Miss. Bloom's room! -Matilda remarked.

The patterns on the wall and the curtain were gorgeous in red, and the furniture gave a perfect contrast to the deep red space. Scarlett looked around, taking down the planks in the window, then opened it, she started opening the drawers and wardrobe doors, which contained old dusty clothes, but time was relative, the clothes were still in perfect condition. She was passing by the dressing table, where she saw a silver comb and its mirror, when she turned it over, she saw Miranda's name engraved on it, she looked at her reflection on the back of the comb for a while, then caught her attention a portrait of Miranda, behind her on the wall. She turned to take a closer look at the portrait. As she got closer, the rustling sound of the wind moved the curtains.

Matilda, as if she saw a ghost asked: -Can't we go, Miss? -When she was right at the picture, Doris ran in and they both got scared, Matilda even screamed then put her hands in front of her mouth.

-Mr. Salvatore is here to see you!

-Scarlett looked at Matilda, waiting to be told who the person is, then they left the room. In the hallway, by the time she had actually wanted to ask who it was, the gentleman entered the door through the hallway door.

-George Salvatore, at your service, Miss! -He introduced himself, bowing, ready to kiss her hand, but when he saw Scarlett's dirty hands he hesitated. She wouldn't let him refuse to kiss her hands, so she jerks it away. -I'm sorry for my morning immodesty. I didn't have a chance to introduce myself.

30

-I think, you, Sir, already know who I am, so it's unnecessary to introduce myself. -She said raising her head.

-Yes, that is right. Of course, not thanks to you. -He cleared his throat- Lord Quas, wants to know if you will be present at Saturday night's ball or not? Because you haven't messaged him yet.

-And who are you? His messenger? -She tried to look at the man as contemptuously as he did when he saw her hands.

-No, Lord Quas is a friend of mine, I was just visiting him when he mentioned that you elected not to answer yet. -Said the man, who then looked at the woman, Scarlett's former light blue dress turned grey, her hair shone from the dust and her headband was torn. -Let me add, even if I were a messenger, I don't think I should be less ashamed of myself than you should be with this look. -Then he pointed at her look.

-Do you think I'm less of a gentlewoman because I'm not afraid of work? -She asked trying to forget how ashamed she was of her appearance, but a little it was felt of her voice.

-No word about it, I appreciate hard work, I only don't think it's worthy of you!

-Please tell me then, yet what is worthy of me? Should I put myself in a cage and beautify myself all day?

-I think you're already trying to close yourself in a cage. You don't think you'll fit in with society. Are you trying to isolate yourself from where you've lived in before? Let me say something: Birds born in a cage think flying is an illness.

-What do you expect me to do? To dress up, put on my wig and giggle all night at the corny jokes of aristocrats like "the other ladies"?

-Honour me with a dance, that you are not afraid of new things.
-The man's provocation triggered what Scarlett feared the most.

-Tell Lord Quas, I'll be there on Saturday night.

With this satisfaction, the man said goodbye and left with Matilda.

-Honest hands might not always build big but what they build is always strong. Do never be afraid of work.

-I'm not afraid. I was never afraid of work. -She took off her apron and pressed it into Doris's hand. Then went out into the garden. In one of the most beautiful parts of the garden of the huge house, the flowers were already budding, only a few had already bloomed. A willow tree adorned the garden, next to which was a pond with water lilies.

-Say, what do you expect from me? -She looked up at the sky.

# CHAPTER IX

Early the next morning, Scarlett hurried to the town to have a word with Mr. Thaker. She stormed into his office and started pacing up and down in there.

-Good morning to you as well, Miss. Bloom! -He said looking at the nervous girl.

-Do you remember telling me to let you know if I change my mind regarding the ball?

-So, after all, you're asking for my help?

-No, I'm not asking for anyone's help, just to introduce me at the ball. -She said firmly.

-Until you say a word, you are from head to toe a copy of your aunt.

-A lot of people say the same. -She replied, then took a seat.

-I did not mean exactly that. -Then he watched in surprise as she sat down. -Can I help you with something else?

-Call it whatever you want. -Then she bit her lip. -I just want to know how much money my aunt left me beside the property.

-I understand! Let's see, there is no more than £8,000 on your account.

-What do you say, is that enough to get the villagers to work?

-Do you want to start the farm again?

-Is it too late?

-You are just in time, if you find workers within two weeks.

-I see...

-Tell me, how many people do you want to hire?

-I was thinking of a hundred people.

Just as she said it, Mr. Thaker took a sip of his cup, but as soon as he heard he spat it out. Scarlett pulled back as a result of the action.

-I wouldn't have dared to mention even 20% of that...

-I know, but the land is huge. So, help is needed.

-Miss, it is impossible to pay so many people unless you can find partners to share the profits with.

-How do you imagine? I do not share. Those are my lands and my workers.

-Then you have to handle money wisely. That's my only suggestion. You still have to buy goods, seeds, animals and all other equipment. And prices are starting to rise sky high as a result of this misery.

Scarlett nodded and left. As she stepped out the bank door, she saw Mr. Salvatore who was just going into a brothel to meet a friend. The ladies looked at him longingly, then greeted him gently. Soon one of the ladies of pleasure, who was more desirable to the eye, passed by him. She shook her upper body with her deep cleavage then lead him into the building, keeping her hand on the man's back. Scarlett rolled her eyes and moved on. She set off again on the road where she got lost in the alley last time, which was almost next to the brothel. Then she stopped and said to herself: "No, not this time!"

-Did you get lost again? -A familiar voice asked.

-Me? Of course, not. I know where I'm going. -She turned with an ear to ear smile.

-Is that so?

-Yes. -She replied proudly.

-It doesn't seem like that to me.

-You caught me. I really got lost again. -She admitted.

-Just go around the building and you'll find your way.

After George Salvatore had finished, he left the brothel contentedly, then began to release his horse from the fence next to the drinking trough. So, he overheard the conversation against his will. Meanwhile, the rain clouds began to gather. And the people on the street began to disperse.

-Please tell me your name. In the turbulent situation and rush of the past, I failed to find out.

-Kwaw. Thomas Kwaw. But everyone just calls me Kwaw.

She nodded contentedly. -Have a nice day, Mr. Kwaw! -She then turned around and set off.

Mr. Salvatore also set off, but he took his journey on the same route as the girl on the street, so, he kept his distance properly.

-Miss, please! -But she didn't hear it, so he called again. -Scarlett! -At this call both walking parties stopped. Scarlett turned back, but George didn't, he watched the girl in front of him as she began to walk back to where she had left. But she didn't have to go far as

Kwaw also walked towards her. -You left it in the basket, I think you forgot in it, last time we were immersed in the... -But the man fell silent as he saw George's gaze still watching them. -I just thought I'd give it back to its owner. -He said, then handed over the small money purse and went on his way.

After taking it, Scarlett turned to continue on her way as she made the turn, she faced Mr. Salvatore.

-Do you have nothing else to do? -She asked proudly, not letting this embarrassing moment embarrass her any more.

-I do have. But I was unable to decide if the man was harassing you and you need help or you just liked to have a dalliance with such a man in public and bring shame on your name.

-What do you mean, with such a man? How is he different from others?

-Did you forget where your place is, or did you never know, Miss?

-Asks the man who was escorted into that building by two "honour" ladies who had more plaster on their faces than their own faces. By the way, you came out, Sir with such satisfaction that six men together do not feel that way. -She declared indignantly.

-I don't have to explain my business to a person who has already contaminated her own name on the third day! -He said indignantly, then began to arrange the saddle of his horse so that he could sit up and ride away.

-You're so wrong to think you've been able to know me after two encounters. You don't know anything about me. -She said angrily, then took a deep breath and tried to finish calmly. -You are very prejudiced.

-So are you! -The man closed the subject and sat on his horse.

As she looked up at him, a drop of rain fell on her face. George looked at her as well, as he watched her kind face, he admitted his prejudice. He wondered how he could think something about a woman with that kind of radiance. The rain was getting heavier.

-It looks like it's going to be a storm. -He declared, looking up at the sky. -How will you get home?

-I came here by mail carriage! -She confessed. She was already ashamed to add that Doris had explained to her how to get from point A to point B. As she uttered her answer, she bent her head down, looking at the small purse.

The man swallowed the dumpling, or rather his pride from his throat, then asked: -Do you want to come in for a tea while the storm subsides?

Scarlett's answer was hidden in her smile.

*

Later, in the man's apartment, sipping hot tea by the fireplace, there was jolly giggle.

-So, you're saying you can get lost so many times? -He laughed.

-Yes, but I'm not complaining. Mr. Kwaw saved me pretty much. So that's how he had my purse.

-I apologise, for the prejudice. But you really have to be more careful, there are a lot of mean people in the world waiting to make a little trouble. Many times, it is those who we would least expect.

Scarlett sipped from the tea and pursed her lips. Her pride would never allow her to say something like, *"Your right,"* *"I need help,"* or *"Thank you."* She learnt as a child that she can't expect much in life. While her parents always made a difference between their children, she couldn't count on anyone in her life, except her sister. They just dreamt about seeing the world, visiting cities, or going to a ball. As a child, she knew only the path from the house that led to church or the market. She didn't spend much time with people, in her spare time she escaped to her books and lived through as many stories as she could read.

-So, was the business successful at least? -She asked curiously.

-Yes, we could say like that. -He said, closing the subject. If he would want to, he couldn't have reported more thanks to his aunt, who had arrived in the room with a strange noise that made both parties feel embarrassed.

-Georgie, could you... -But she couldn't finish, as soon as she saw that their guest was a lady. It calmed her heart, and even her voice became calmer. -Aren't you going to introduce me to your guest?

-Yes, of course, my aunt. -He said, then both of them got up from the armchair. -My aunt, the lady is Miss. Scarlett Bloom! Miss. Bloom, this is my aunt, Edith Salvatore.

-I'm glad to meet you, ma'am! But if you don't mind, I still have a lot to deal with, luckily the storm is gone. -She bowed politely, then walked away. After passing them, she turned again to look at George. -And I'm grateful for the hospitality and the tea. -Then finally left.

As Scarlett left, she looked at George with a wide smile on her face, as if to say *"Pretty Girl"*.

-Don't start again. -He said, walking toward the window.

-I didn't say anything. -She apologized- She seemed so familiar from somewhere. It's like I've seen her before. -She didn't know where to place the girl, but George didn't dare admit that she was the girl they had seen out of the window a few days ago. He just watched silently as the girl went out of the gate and then turned the corner to the right until she completely disappeared from his sight.

# CHAPTER X

Scarlett got home late in the afternoon, the butler, the kitchen maid, and Doris were already starting to worry, but the worry disappeared when the girl popped in the door. Each of them excitedly asked, what could they serve her with. Scarlett didn't ask for dinner, no cake with tea, or a hot bath. She left the room wordlessly, wondering what to do, as she had only been informed about the rules of etiquette from books. She had never been among aristocrats, she had never had to behave like one of them before, and the worst part was she couldn't even dance. She was afraid that she would make a bad impression. She wandered aimlessly around the huge building. She was so immersed in her thoughts that she did not even notice that she had entered the territory of the once locked wing. Passing beside one of the rooms, the cold wind blew through her long skirt, forcing her to step back a few steps to find out where the cold had come from. It was the red room where she forgot the window and door were open when she stormed out to meet Mr. Salvatore the other day. After closing the window, Scarlett took another look at the painting before deciding to leave the room.

"*Creepy*" she told herself. Then she started towards the door. It was then that she noticed that one of the drawers on the dressing table was open, which she had probably left open when she noticed the comb and the mirror, these items had distracted her, so that she no longer looked into it. It was a brown leather-covered booklet, rotated it in her hand for a while, then opened it, she realised that it was actually her aunt's diary, who had been dead for ten years.

She sat down on the edge of the bed and, in the light of the full moon, began to read the first few lines.

*"My dear diary, I have to admit that this is the first time I have written down my feelings and thoughts. I received you from a dear friend on the occasion of my eighteenth birthday.* -The first few lines looked very interesting already, so she continued- *O.T considers it worthwhile to describe all this. On the one hand, because it reassures our souls, many times we cannot tell our feelings or thoughts to people. Most people would not understand, others would criticise and some would judge. And secondly, as we get older, it will be easier to refresh our memories and tell your grandchildren when they are curious about, what has happened to us in life, what experiences we have.* -This also looked interesting for her, these were just the same thoughts as she had about her diary- *But how can I expect them to understand? Because if they do not experience the same thing, if they don't get through the same story, they will never understand the other person, because that is how we are.*

*I'll be attending my first ball soon, my dad is already counting the hours, proud to finally be able to introduce me to society.* -She felt that it was meant to be for her to find this little book. -*Luckily, E. has been at many balls already, she's been my best friend since we were kids, she told me a lot about parties, and she also reported that I will have to take care of the young men. She said, quoting her words, "They really like fresh meat!". I don't even know what to think of it, or what to do to keep myself busy until then. I'm so excited that I got in trouble at lunch, my mom nagged me to eat at least a bite, and Dad was just amused by how excited I was, not to mention my brother, who was about to make the biggest mistake of his life by taking that horrible woman as his wife. I'll rather neglect them. I'm just trying to point out that this is a big event in my life, Doris will be the one who will prepare me, because who else could do this task better than someone who has been serving and preparing my mother for years. I will be back with details."*

Reading these lines, she shut the book and stormed out. Doris was sitting at the table in the huge kitchen with a steaming mug in her hand. When she burst in, she jumped up in fright.

*

-Does the Miss. ask me for help? -She asked in surprise.

-No. -She corrected- I just want you to prepare me for the ball.

-So, you commanding me to, then? -She asked teasingly.

-Will you do it or not? -She asked, losing her patience.

*

Later in the salon, Doris taught the girl some steps. She walked to Doris with three books on the top of her head, then when she got there, she tried to bow politely, but they fell a few steps ahead of the goal.

-I've been trying this for at least a tenth time... -She said desperately.

-You can do it, just try again. -She tried to encourage.

Scarlett tried again, but the books ended up on the ground again. After a deep sigh, she fell as well to the ground, her arms folded on her knees and her face slammed inside.

-Do you think these are the most important etiquette rules of life? Then you are mistaken. Dear Miss. Scarlett, let me tell you the five most important things you need to know in life. They are the following: First of all. Before you pray for something, you have to believe. Second, before you spend, make sure you earn. Third...

-Why do you think it's going to work, I don't even know where my place is... Where was I meant to be...? Why I came here at all... -Interrupted Doris, who also interrupted the girl.

-Before you speak, you have to listen. The fourth rule, before you quit, you have to try, my dear. -She finished her sentence.

-And what would be the fifth? -She asked after a few seconds of pausing, after she was sure Doris wouldn't resume.

-I'll tell you when the time comes. -She replied.

Scarlett just smiled and said: -Do you think they'll accept me? Will I fit in? I think we both know what kind of life I've lived before and I'm sure other people know also.

-People love rumours. But don't be intimidated by this, show them who you really are. The world is going to judge you no matter what, so live your life the way you want to. Be honest all the time, not only to others to yourself as well. Be yourself all the time, my dear.

Scarlett stood up, smiled at Doris, and walked toward the door. Leaning against the door jamb, she turned back and said: -I'll need three workers to start tomorrow at noon. Let's fix this dusty nest. Starting with Aunt Miranda's room, where I want to move in within three days. -Doris just smiled.

# CHAPTER XI

*"My dear friend, I promised to write after the ball. I had a fabulous evening. O.T the son of the late accountant of the bank was also present. I would give it my all to go back in time and dance with him again. Lots of men wanted to enjoy my company, as E. said. If I would be able, I wouldn't have had the opportunity to reject them, since O. was always in my company, so the other men all got away from themselves. We went out for a walk in the garden, most of all I wanted to report this moment. About the big moment. About the first kiss. He was very attentive to me all the way, he always listened and responded kindly. As a kid, I didn't think to ever look at him like that. The moment he handed me the diary yesterday, the gentle smile on his face, his dear voice. But at the ball, I really realised that he was the man my heart was beating for. My dear friend, I think I have to admit to you that I fell in love against my will."*

-Promising. -Scarlett said to herself, then turned on her belly, it was only about an inch not falling off the bed -If she could do it, then, so do I.

At noon, Doris reported that the three men had arrived and were ready for work. Scarlett herself went to greet them and then explained what to do. After the men thanked her for the opportunity, they went to work. There were three thin men, one of them was amazingly tall, at least seven feet tall. When Scarlett first saw him, she had to swallow the surprise down her throat so that it wouldn't come out as *"wow"* from her mouth. The other two men were about the same height, the age difference was the only thing, it appeared to be a father-son pairing as they were very similar to each other.

-Can we trust them? -She asked, watching with her eyes a very valuable bureau as the men put it away.

-Do you ask if they are not red-handed, Miss? -She asked indignantly- They are my family, tiny Aalim, Uncle Clevon and Dad Chike. How can you assume that?

-Don't be mad, I just don't know them. But if you trust them, you need to know that I trust you. The fruits of their works are yours as well, just as the consequences of their actions affect you also. -Upon hearing these words, Doris's mouth remained open in surprise, it took a few seconds for her to gather her thoughts. Scarlett patted her, on the shoulder and retired to the library.

After she left the room, Doris frowned and looked after her, "If only she would have known... she couldn't deny the truth."

*

*"My dear friend, I tell the most horrible day of my life with teary eyes. I'm sorry I haven't written so far. Even my brother become a father, my sister-in-law surprised him with twins, two gorgeous and healthy boys. But how would I have done it when I spent all my free time with my only love. In the heat of happy moments, I was unable to put what had happened on paper, because when I wasn't with him, I thought about him or I just wrote to him. It's been a year since my first ball, and I've attended more than seven balls since. O.T at one of the balls, became jealous when he saw one of the richest heirs in the county, (though, if you believe me or not, we just exchanged a few words), he later said he couldn't wait and risk someone else doing it before him, so he asked for my hand in Mr. Gorth's garden. And this morning he came to do it from my sweet father too. But Dad refused, saying he was just a dowry hunter and that I deserved more than a small tenement house in Truro. When I said I didn't want more, he came up with the fact that O.T was too old for me, and in his almost thirties he was having a hard time getting a young wife like me. He said that I am just needed to give birth to offspring for him, then our discussion degenerated and I said I would be proud to give him offspring. Then he forbade me from him and said if I don't look*

*for a better party for myself then he will do, "Love is not an option in life!" he told me. Oh, my dear diary. I wish you could talk and give me some advice. I have no idea what to do!"*

All-day long on Saturday, Scarlett tried to tie down her thoughts to her aunt's diary, afraid that if she didn't, her thoughts would overcome her about the ball and intimidate her. She read for hours about her aunt's horrible days, how she lived through those days, heart-breaking stories, and tear-jerking emotions. She didn't even notice when Doris had walked in the door to tell her it was time to get ready or she was going to be late for the ball. As soon as she saw Doris, Scarlett hid the diary under her pillow.

-What are you reading, Miss?

-Nothing interesting. -She replied- There is no such thing in a woman's life that she is late, everyone else arrives too soon. -She quoted a part of Miranda's diary. -Did you clean my aunt's dress, which I asked for? -Doris rolled her eyes and said her bath was ready.

After that, Scarlett started the preparation. Following her bath, she put on some make-up and perfume, then Doris dressed her. She tried to ask about her plans when pulling the corset, Scarlett didn't want to answer because she didn't even know what to do, so all she had to say was to pull the corset tighter.

-But then you won't get any air...

-Do not worry about it. I'll know how tight I want it. -The woman did as she said. Scarlett took a sudden breath from which she let Doris know it is tight enough.

-People say, "You have to suffer for beauty". No wonder why... -She added ironically as Scarlett admired her thin figure in the mirror.

*

Mr. Thaker waited in front of the carriage, complaining to the driver that the women were always late. When he saw Scarlett, his word stalled. Her hair was pinned in a bun adorned with a ribbon full of black beads. The string of pearls she received from her sister matched her deep burgundy dress perfectly. Her steps were sophisticated and elegant, matching a real lady's look. Her eyes were smoky, which highlighted the colour of her sky-blue eyes. She painted exactly the same image as a young lady born to an aristocratic family.

-You look amazing Miss. Bloom.

She bowed politely as soon as she got there, then asked: -What do you think, will I fit in the company?

-You'll be too good for them. -He replied, then helped her up to the carriage.

-Tell me how I can express my gratitude for your kindness. -Scarlett asked.

-Promise me a dance, Miss. -Said the man smiling.

-If you dare to risk being injured at the beginning of the ball, then with pleasure. -They both started chuckling.

\*

At the door of the building, there was a footman stated who had announced each time someone entered. When it was their turn, the footman spoke aloud, *"Mr. Owen Thaker and Miss. Scarlett Bloom."* Everyone turned their attention to this announcement. Scarlett smiled nervously, which rather was snarls, Mr. Thaker reassured her confidently, *"Everything will be fine, darling"*. He introduced the girl primarily to the host and the company around him, which was formed by a nearly four-member man and a woman, the wife of the host. Everyone stared at her with interest and tried to converse with her.

-Gentlemen, -and then he took a look at Lady Quas -and my lady, -he nodded politely -Let me introduce a dear friend's niece, Miss. Scarlett Bloom.

Scarlett bowed politely, then looked around the small group with her head raised. The lady smiled, it could have been one of her aunt's contemporaries, Scarlett saw that Lady Quas was looking at her as she would be familiar to her, and then asked: -Wasn't Ms. Miranda Bloom your aunt?

-She was, Madam. Did you know her? -She asked.

-We could say we used to be friends; we've known each other since we were kids. My first house was almost next door to hers.

-Do you hunt Miss. Bloom? -An older man asked, a handsome gentleman was standing next to him, tall and sophisticated. Unable to take his eyes off the girl, Scarlett thought his interest was too obvious.

-No. -She replied with some confusion in her voice. -You know, I sympathize with foxes. -She joked, everyone in the company laughed, finding it interesting and humorous.

She was an attractive person. The tall man, though with some seriousness, but laughed. Scarlett was watching the laughing company as Mr. and Miss. Salvatore arrived. The man, as usual gloomy, accompanied by his aunt holding his arm, walked in. When he saw the girl, he nodded politely from a distance, then passed away without joining them.

-I'm glad you came, Miss! -He said, kissing her hand -Evelyn, my dear. -The host addressed his wife, then opened one arm pointing the way to his wife and they left to greet the other guests.

-Tell me, Miss, where did you live before? -A man with a moustache asked, judging by his emphasis, and his palm-climbing gaze, something suggested that the question had some kickbacks. -I mean before you got the inheritance.

-In a small village on the east of the country, called Penworth.

-Isn't this "little village" -he stressed- in Bath?

-It is, Sir. -She agreed.

-I heard the neighbourhood is very poor. How many peasants live in that area? -He asked, raising his eyepiece to his eye. The increasingly interesting conversation was followed very carefully by everyone, especially the tall man.

-Most people are deficient in nothing, but there are  exceptio...-

-And you miss? -He interrupted, unable to answer in the embarrassment, the man asked his question again. - Did you miss anything? Ever? -There was silence for a few seconds, she stared at the ground, Mr. Thaker had already opened his mouth to speak, but someone had preceded him.

-I heard is a very nice neighbourhood. I plan to go to visit the city one day. Tell me, do you have a favourite place or have an idea of what to see there? -The tall man asked, with an American accent.

-Well, um, indeed is a nice place. -She said.

-I suggest if you go to visit, visit the town hall in any case, it has been beautifully renovated. And Pulteney Bridge is breath-taking. -Mr. Thaker suggested. The other two men looked down at Scarlett.

-How do you like Cornwall Miss. Bloom? -Asked the third man, who had been silently watching the conversation so far.

-Splendid! -She replied, still a little nervous, -Although I have to admit I have had seen more hungry mouths in one week here than I have in Penworth in my whole life.

-Hmm... -The man who asked about the girl's life muttered.

-Mr. Salvatore! -The older man called when he saw George.

-Gentlemen! -He greeted the men, then looked at Scarlett -Miss.

Scarlett nodded silently.

-I'm glad to see you again, Mr. Thaker, like we haven't met in a thousand years. -The man only agreed with a forced smile - And yet what did I miss? So far?

-Oh, before I forget, Mr. Salvatore this lady is Miss. Scarlett Bloom. -Mr. Thaker pointed at her, smiling.

-Yes, we've already met. -He declared with great seriousness, Scarlett couldn't help her smile at the situation, she was trying to hide the tiny grin on her face. When she looked at the company, everyone was looking at the new member who joint them, except one person.

-We just talked about how much poverty is in Cornwall. Miss. Bloom said it is worse than it was in Bath. -The moustache man said, putting the girl in an awkward position in front of the man. After all, everyone knew that she was only talking about the village and not the city.

-Well, compared to that, the city has flourished in marketing for so long and that it is the commercial centre of the country, the number of unemployed has greatly increased and God knows how many will get on the streets. But I doubt Bath has fewer people in a similar situation. This war is ruining everything.

-I heard, Bath, is bathing in a pool of blood. Maybe the young lady will be right and there will be fewer poor people because there are few who survive. -The moustache said again, laughing at his own joke.

-What are you referring to? -She asked angrily.

-Didn't you hear it? The French occupied much of Bath and plundered it. -The older man said again.

The conversation continued dully in Scarlett's ears about politics, but her attention was completely overwhelmed by her thoughts. She stepped back from the small group in slow steps. The tall man followed, the others deepening in conversation no one, except George noticed that the group two other members split from them.

Scarlett took a glass from the tray of one of the waiters walking past and took a deep sip.

-I can see you like politics. -A voice said from behind her with some irony, she was so frightened, almost swallowed aside, but there was only a momentary alarm as she saw the person standing beside her.

-Not really my world. -She declared.

-Neither mine. -He whispered- I'm sorry, I haven't introduced myself yet, I'm Leonard Wolowitz.

-A pleasure to meet you! If I'm not mistaken you are American.

-Indeed, I am.

-Honestly, I've never met people overseas before I got here. But I'm not surprised to meet an American after... um... -she tried to express herself, but somehow, she couldn't. She didn't have experience with a wide variety of people yet, she didn't know who and how to talk with, to give due respect and not to insult anyone. It was one thing she had been practicing every day since her arrival.

-Are you referring to coloured people? Well, there are many things, that you have to get used to. We need to move with the ages and accept change.

Scarlett felt tense when she saw a group of women looking at them and starting to laugh out loud. Her chest began to tighten, and her breathing grew deeper and deeper.

-Apologies, I'm not feeling very well. I think I'd rather go out into the garden to get some fresh air.

-Can I accompany you?

The girl just nodded in agreement, and together they headed for the exit that led to the garden. Before they reached the door, someone called after the man and handed him a message on a tray, which he opened with quick movements, and read it.

-Pardon me, Miss, but I have to leave you alone for an urgent matter. But I want to make up for this evening. Please promise to give me a chance to propitiate. -Scarlett bowed, the man raised her hand and then kissed it. -See you soon.

-What a pity, he is so young... -A voice said from behind her. As Scarlett turned, she saw Miss. Salvatore standing there.

-Oh! I didn't notice you, Miss. -She took a step up the stairs, next to Edith, to not keep her back to the woman. There was silence for a few seconds, then she spoke again.

-For sure, his mother called him. She's been sick since she heard the rumours about her child...

Scarlett was curious, but she was ashamed to ask what she was aiming for. She never loved rumours, they always showed the dark side of people and never told the whole truth. So, she thought it was better not to know about it. She knew that she would look at Mr. Wolowitz with a different light then. Scarlett wanted to know herself as he was, not after some rumours.

-Aunt! How do you like the ball? -George came among them. Miss. Edith Salvatore was a lady in her late forties, if you gave enough attention, you could see the slightly wrinkles on her face, her hair already starting to discolour and her eyesight could be terribly poor, judging by how hard she was squinting as Mr. Salvatore approached them.

-Yes, my dear. But, tell me, would you escort this young lady out? She's not feeling very well, her companion had to leave because of an important matter...

-Oh, it's really not necessary. -She replied, then quickly picked up her fan and began to fan herself, feeling herself blush in embarrassment, so, she tried to cover it up.

-Certainly. -He replied to his aunt. He was embarrassed as well, so he was happy to get rid of his aunt at the same time. He let the girl go forward and followed her out the door into the yard.

Edith Salvatore smiled to herself, then remarked *"She's so familiar!"*

\*

They walked silently side by side for a few seconds, then George spoke, breaking the silence.

-How do you like Cornwall?

-It's a pleasant place.

-Do you plan for long term or you just stay temporarily?

-I think I'll stay for a while.

-I saw a few people working around the house. Are you restarting the farm?

-Well, I can't tell you yet. But they are actually renovating the house. As you saw there was a tower back then, which destroyed the east wing of Gracewith after it decomposed.

The conversation died for a while until Scarlett realised she didn't inquire anything at all about the man.

-What do you do for living, Mr. Salvatore?

-I run a cotton factory. The factory is located in the same building where my apartment is in Truro.

-Oh, really? I'm surprised I didn't see your workers when I was there last time.

-They use the back entrance, everything related to the company takes place there, you must have been noticed that part of the alley is more spacious. There is the loading and there is the entrance. The factory covers three floors below the ground floor as it is so far from the exit, so I had to build a platform to make it easier for my people to transport the product.

-Oh, that's interesting. I haven't heard of such before. Ingenious. -The girl appreciated the idea.

-Why do you think so?

-First of all, you don't have to go far to work. And second, you handled the delivery so cleverly.

-I wish I could be as positive about the development of my company as you are. Instead, I feel just ashamed.

-Why do you say that? -She asked, fearing that she had said something wrong.

-Most of the people who work for me suffer from lung disease. -Scarlett's expression showed that she didn't fully understand what the man was talking about, so  he continued. -Before it is woven, the cotton, looks  like the feather that has broken down into a million pieces, which is easily imbibed by a person during inhalation, so it is deposited in the lungs. Due to the closed space, the room is not ventilated at all, so it is guaranteed that the people working there will get sick. Including children.

-You just give them a job, which they need so much right now. If people are aware of the consequences, then there is no reason to blame yourself.

-You think so? In your opinion, when I've lost my two best workers in the last month... There is no reason? -He asked indignantly, when he saw her face he tried to calm down. Scarlett blushed completely as he growled at her. -Excuse me. You can't understand this... -The man said, then started to walk forward, leaving Scarlett behind.

-Mr. Salvatore. If I said something offensive...

-You don't have to apologise. -He said cutting in her word, when turned back toward her.

-I didn't plan to. -She declared -I just wanted to say that you shouldn't talk to me like that.

-Indeed, I really shouldn't have.

Scarlett smiled, leaning against the fence they had just passed. She asked about his occupation, trying to distract herself from the malaise. The air was leaving her lungs and her body felt as if it was boiling in a cauldron. Her vision also began to blur. But she tried to hold on. She tried her best, to focus on what the man was saying.

-Well, what can I say? I have to travel to India soon, for a trial. India is one of our most advanced co- owners, after America of course. And the alliance with it will be strengthened after the visit... -When he looked at Scarlett to see the girl's reaction, she was already unconscious on the ground. The man rushed over to her and called her name, but there was no answer. He sent a passing lad right away for his carriage and a doctor.

The carriage took them to Scarlett's home, as it was one of the closest places to them, so this way they didn't have to disturb the party. When Doris saw the man bring her almost lifeless body into the house, she screamed "*Miss*! *My miss*! *Died*!" she cried out loud.

George began to silence her and then asked her to drive him to the nearest room. He reassured her that the doctor was already on his way and then explained to her that he doesn't understand what had happened either, she had trouble breathing, but he thought she was upset because of what he said and then fainted, he explained as he checked Scarlett's pulse.

-Breathing problems? -She asked in shock.

-Yes. -The man didn't get to finish his one-word speech, Doris picked up the girl and asked the man to keep her. Then she began to undress and untie her corset, but as it took a long time, she took a leaf-opening knife from the drawer and cut the lace.

-How do you think to do this, just like that in front of my eyes...? -But his word got stuck again as soon as he heard the girl gasping for air in his arms. - Miss. Bloom! -He laid her back on the bed, then pulled on her dress, which began to slip off from her shoulder.

When Scarlett opened her eyes, George's face was the first thing she'd seen, there had never been a man so close to her. The worry was undeniably on his face, as was the joy of seeing the girl waking up. Scarlett hadn't noticed just how deep black eyes George had before. The bushy black eyebrows stood like a puppy writhing between joy and sorrow. A tiny, curved line sat out in the corner of his mouth as he watched the girl wake up. Scarlett's tiny hand was lost between the man's huge hands, the heat she felt through it penetrating her entire body and warming it up.

55

-Dear good God in heaven! -Doris said in delight. Then she heard sharp bangs from the front door. -Probably it is the doctor! -She said, then muttered to herself as she started to walk out, but as she walked away her sentences faded, all they understood was: "No wonder this girl doesn't get air near such a man... That's the breath-taking love, huh? She wanted to be prettier... I told her, there is no point to make it tighter...

-I didn't know that I was so boring. -He joked.

-Even more boring. -She cut back.

# CHAPTER XII

She read Miranda's diary to learn more about running the farm, but instead, she penetrated into her aunt's private life. Miranda described that she was preparing to escape with the love of her life, the exact date and time. The fact was that she gave herself to the man she loved the most in a brothel and that she was not at all ashamed because she would be soon his wife anyway. This cannot be avoided in any matter. The only person who knew about it, was E., her best friend, with whom she shared everything, she also described in detail how much E. was against it. The only person she trusted and shared this top secret with.

She was reading these pages of Miranda's story when Doris knocked on the door.

-Mr. Salvatore came to visit.

-Tell him I'll be downstairs. -She replied, then smiled from ear to ear while looking into the diary.

-Miss. Bloom! -He greeted the woman coming toward him.

-Mr. Salvatore, did you come again to get me bored? -She asked sarcastically.

-I'll do my best. -He replied, unable to hold back a smile.

-Good luck then! I have to tell you I dozed off last night very early thanks to you, and I slept enough. So, you don't have much chance for that.

-In that case, would you come for a walk with me in order to get tired?

-Gladly! -She replied with a wide smile on her face.

-Have you ever seen the ocean?

-No, I haven't had a chance yet. Only from a distance. -She pointed to the landscape, which showed the distant blueness as it merged with the colour of the sky.

-Would you like to ride with me over there? -The man asked as they walked in the yard.

-I don't have a horse. At least for now. -She replied uncomfortably.

-I think we'll fit on a horse. -He smiled, then jumped on his horse after taking the reins from the butler and held out his hand to Scarlett.

-Sir, -she bit her lip, winning a few seconds, not knowing how to express herself, but she realised she had nothing else to say except the truth -I've never ridden a horse before.

-Are you scared?

-Me? I am afraid of nothing. -She declared shrugging.

-Then what are you waiting for? -George asked provocatively.

-Are you just saying, you don't actually know the person who claims that people easily judge and we need to make sure we keep our name clear?

-Ohm... No, not at all. -He shrugged. - Maybe he was wrong and we should not care what other people think of us. We should enjoy our life with our own rules. What do you think?

-Own rules? What those would be?

The man shrugged again, then added: - Maybe we should create some.

Scarlett didn't say anything, she went closer and let George help her get up on the horse's back, the man bounced back behind the saddle and put the reins in Scarlett's hands. Her trembling hands clung very tightly to the reins. They were out of the gate in an instant. Doris watched as they walked into the distance, as they reached a junction after the gate, where they turned left. *"She's just getting in trouble..."* she murmured. They had barely left when a coupe carriage turned in from the right. As soon as it got to the building, a tall man got out of it. Doris was watching in amazement as he approached her, muttering to herself again before he could get there, *"That's what I was talking about!"*.

-Greetings! I'm looking for Miss. Bloom.

-Miss. Bloom is out of the house. -She declared looking over the man.

-And tell me, please, when will she return?

-I'm not a fortune teller. -She replied condescendingly -She just left recently. -She pointed to the gate.

-You want to tell me that the woman on Mr. George Salvatore's horse was Miss. Bloom? -He asked angrily.

-No, I don't want to say that. -She replied, and began to close the door in front of him.

-Tell her, that Leonard Wolowitz was looking for her. -Upon hearing this, Doris slammed the door so suddenly that it hit the wall and returned, slightly hitting her side.

-That Mr. Wolowitz? -She asked in astonishment.

-Why how many are there in the city? -The man asked with irony in his voice, then turned around on his heels and left.

-I'll keep her informed, by all means. -Doris said to herself, then watched as the carriage left the yard.

*

-This is amazing! -Scarlett marvelled at the sight.

-Do you want to get closer? -The man asked, standing behind her.

Scarlett nodded, then headed down the hill to the shore. George followed her as soon as he secured the horse.

-Did you talk to Lord Quas? He visited me the other day, and he asked about our sudden leaving.

-He wrote a letter, but I haven't had time to reply yet... I really don't know what to write. -She confessed- He was wondering what had happened so that I had left so suddenly, he was afraid I wasn't feeling well at the ball, but he had also heard rumours of my malaise.

-And his intuitions were true at least? -She looked confused- Regarding how you felt about the ball. -He clarified- Already considering that Mr. Anderson and Sir Limsenham were pretty substantial about what made them curious.

-Not in the least. -She raised her gaze proudly- It was an indecency to mention the circumstances in which I grew up. But I can proudly say I had a happy childhood.

George didn't know what to say, so there was a mute silence between them for a few seconds.

-Scarlett, does it have any meaning? -He asked, after a few seconds of pause as he look at the girl's gaze turning toward him.

-Bright Red. Maybe I got it because of my hair. -She laughed cheerfully.

-Your parents had a great sense of humour.

-Maybe my aunt. -She replied sounding depressed.

-Pardon me...

-Nothing happened, you couldn't have known. Although I have never felt her loss, nor her presence. -Embarrassed she started fumbling with her fingers and then continued -She gave me my name, my fortune, and quite her look. Then she ceased. Her name was never mentioned in the family after her death. Maybe guilt ground my father's soul or maybe her loss hurt him so deeply. But we may never know this. -Then she watched the play of her hands again, George grabbed the girl's hands and stroked them, Scarlett blushed completely.

-Maybe you'll get to know her better than when she was alive.

Scarlett smiled, then looked at their hands. She jerked her own, unable to look into the man's face to say what she wanted, looking at the ocean, she said: -Maybe it's time for us to go back.

*

After a long time, when the moon and stars lit up Gracewith, they returned home. As they entered the door, amidst a fun laugh, Doris cleared her throat to change the mood, but in vain she stood in front of them with her hands on her hips, the smile was steady on their faces.

-Dinner is served! -She declared.

-Are you staying for dinner? -Scarlett asked.

-I can't, it's too late. -He replied, looking at the serious expression on Doris's face.

She nodded understandingly. Then they bowed to each other and said goodbye. After the man left, Scarlett asked if anyone was looking for her. She waited for important letters, on the one hand waiting for a reply from her old home to her letter, and on the other hand, discussing the subject of the land and the workers with Mr. Thaker.

-There was no one! -She replied with a quick word to close the subject and left.

# CHAPTER XIII

*"Dear Anne,*

*I am now writing my second letter since I am living here. I don't know when you have received my previous letter or if you got it at all. After all, there is the possibility that it was lost or you will get it late. I want to tell you what happened at my first ball. I'm sure you are interested, because you've never been to a ball before."* -Then she lifted her pen from the paper, sat silently for a few seconds and stared at the letter. She folded it and threw it at the other end of the room, arranged the clean, blank paper on the table and started to write again.

*"Dearest Anne,*

*Only after a week, I can tell you, I miss you so much already.*

*The ball was interesting, although I didn't attend it for a long time unfortunately, but I was still pleased with myself that I didn't run and took the courage to go among strangers who know the story of most of my life. The host was a very pleasant man, Lord Quas is a judge in the Truro People's Council and a member of the House of Lords where he declares his visit to the rallies every month. And his wife is a picture of a truly sophisticated woman, a model of femininity. Compared to her age, Lady Quas' skin is as tight as someone's of my age, and her attire is overwhelming.*

*And Mr. Salvatore...* -Then she raised her pen to the sky again, looked at the letter and smiled- *is a real gentleman who promised me a dance but didn't keep his word.*

*There were a lot of burdens on my shoulders that I sometimes try to ignore so as not to suppress my mind's harmonious thinking ability.*

*I have no idea how to restart the farm and in an unexpected way I found out that my fortune is not enough for it either. I wish you could be here to tell me with your kind smile and optimistic look, "Surely you can figure something out!"* –She had to raise the pen in her hand again, suddenly an idea of something occurred to her. Just at that moment Doris entered the door and said: "Miss. Scarlett, I hope you know very well, that you are wasting your time, I have to say regarding the farm, it's almost the end of the month. It's time to start the work."

-Doris call a courier as fast as you can. -She said fiercely. Doris stormed out. After the woman left, Scarlett just sat and smiled and then returned to her letter.

*

Confident footsteps were heard as they walked on a one hundred year old floor. When they got into the library, they fell silent. It was owned by Mr. Thaker, the small old man with a hunched back, who felt much more like a foster parent of Miss. Bloom than a notary, banker, and a confidential person beside her.

-Do you have any idea why you have been called here? -The red-haired woman asked, looking at the man in the reflection of the window.

-Not really, but I guess you got something in your head. -The man replied, pulling the chair towards him and taking a seat.

-Indeed! -She remarked, then turned to him. -Brandy?

-Will I need it? -He asked curiously, raising one of his eyebrows.

Scarlett just smiled, then went to the drinks cabinet and poured the drinks.

-You find it impossible, to give a hundred people a job with that much money.

-Impossible, I wouldn't use that word. Rather, I don't think it's possible. I mean without a co-owner.

-And if I say it is possible? -She asked, leaning closer to him relying on her thighs.

-I'd say, ... -He searched for the words, but he didn't really find anything appropriate, so he just rotated his tongue in his mouth until something finally came out: -I'm glad.

-Ask it. -She said, raising her eyebrows smiling.

-You'll tell me anyway. -He said, then took a sip from his glass.

-That is true. Didn't you say that the villagers were renting out those houses? Couldn't we ask them for an advance?

-Yes, that's right. But the famine is increasing, you can't do that to them. There are plenty of people without work and plenty on the streets already. In fact, they have to be paid enough to make a living and pay the rent. Usually, they will receive a part of their salary from which the rent comes out. So, the money does not circulate as many times. Of course, this is in case they rent your property. Your aunt hadn't said anything before she died, so most people stayed there. I think they waited until a new owner arrived to make a decision, and in the meantime they freeload. So, it's up to you, Miss, how you want to get along with them.

-I've never done this before. But do you think I could ask those who still live there to work for little money until the harvest?

-Probably. Yes. There's a chance. And how did you think that would be achieved? -Is anyone who fails to pay your bills penalized?

-She rang the bell as Doris burst into the room. -Bring the diary. -She told the woman.

-I am afraid I do not fully understand. -He replied, leaning with interlocked fingers looking toward the girl, who then began to lean back with a proud smile on her face, then held out her hand for the black leather-covered book which Doris handed over.

-I asked Nivek, my butler, to list the tenements which are occupied, along with all the families who have lived here since my aunt is dead. Personally, the names are given. The plan is to make posters and display them in a few places in the village announcing work. Then send them letters describing their rights and the infringement, how they can repay and what their responsibilities are in detail.

-That's what you think?

-It's called *"trespassing"*. -She replied, returning the book to Doris, who had left afterward.

-I didn't mean that. What do you do with those who already have a job? With regular payment?

-I doubt there would be a lot of them, and if there were any of them. There must be someone in the family who is unemployed. All I need is for the people who live there to start working for me again, and if it is to reach the law for it, then let it be. At least one person from each house must start working in order to be able to repay their debt. They will receive 20% of their salary and the remaining 80% will go to this month's rent and repayment.

-This is impossible to achieve with a scribbled paper or invitation.

-Why do you think that?

-These people never held a book in their hands. They never learnt to write or read.

-Oh... I didn't think about that. -She said thoughtfully.

-What I don't understand still is why do you think that a family, let's say a family of five or six will be able to make a living from that much money? You still have to figure out something else. Maybe you should talk to them in person. -The girl then shuddered and stared at the man sitting in front of her. -Or are you afraid of them?

-Me? Of a couple of peasants? -She asked humming.

-I can see that you are starting to fit in the aristocratic society... -He said sarcastically, hearing how she talked about the villagers. -Then we can leave whenever you ready.

-You mean right now? -She asked again, treating the man with the same respect as before. -I'd still have to get changed, and I haven't collected my thoughts yet, I have no idea what to tell them.

Then the man stepped closer and squeezed her shoulder. -I'll be with you! -He said, smiling at the girl in front of him.

*

The carriage drew attention to them, a couple of villagers just looked at each other or just talked about it, and some of the children ran around the carriage, giggling cheerfully. As they reached the centre of the village, a couple of people watched as they got out of it. After Mr. Thaker helped the girl out, Scarlett began to arrange her pheasant feather hat.

-And now what? -She asked, leaning toward the man.

-Do you see that big bell there? -He asked, pointing to a bell about five feet high in the middle of the large empty room that hung from a headboard. -Pull it! -She just nodded, hesitated for a few seconds, then stepped beside the bell and pulled it. In just a few minutes, the whole village gathered there, from small to large, from young to old.

-Good morning! You must be surprised to see me here. I came in order to... Ohm... -She tried to search for the appropriate words, but she was unable to find the ones that fit here. What could she say? I come to dispossess you. To take the remaining little savings. That you will run out of food? But by the time she started saying, a couple of villagers started shouting: *"Miss. Miranda, help my family!"*, *"She came to help us!"*, *"Miss. Miranda, our saviour!"*, *"She will put an end to our misery."*

Scarlett swallowed the lump in her throat as she looked through the skinny, sick, dirty people, most of them in torn clothes, some unable to decipher the colour of their hair because they were so dirty, their skin wrinkled with thinness and covered in blisters. She looked around then she said: -Although my middle name is Miranda, I'm not my aunt. My name is Scarlett Miranda Bloom! And I came to help you. But I would need help for that first. I want to start the farm again! -Then the villagers started a great jubilance and the merriment overwhelmed them. -Although I have some bad news. Over the years, you were aware that my aunt had passed away, but you had not moved out of the properties. I offer a job, but in order to get paid in full, you have to get me to trust you. -Then people's faces became serious. -You will receive 30% of your salary, so the rest will cover the past rent which has not been paid and the present rent. Which I calculate, it will pay off in full in the next seven years. -People started to *"Huu,"* "Don't rob our time! Rather, return to your comfortable little palace. You won't see a shilling from anyone!" a little man shouted. Scarlett took a deep breath and walked towards him, opening the black-leather book in her hand -All right it can be resolved otherwise. -Then she started to list: -Gareth's family, Wilskow's family, Enderson's family, Mr. Meadow... -Hearing this the short man started to shake -Mr. Widow and his sister Ms. Widow -These are just five families from the last ten years who have not paid even a shilling for rent but have lived here all along. On my land! -She declared then closed the book. -They lived in a place on another's estate without permission, which means nothing more than committing a trespass for more than ten years. By law, these families are sentenced to a maximum of eight years in prison. -The eyes surrounding her become rounder and rounder. -Well, to avoid that, I would ask the people here to show up in front of my house on Thursday morning so we can start work. And for whoever I see striving and working decently I will be willing to let go of the debt as well. -Then people began to yell cheerfully again. -Once again, only when I see that they are working diligently.

-Of course... -Mr. Meadow murmured, then spat on the ground and then turned his back.

# CHAPTER XIV

-Georgie! Georgie! -Miss. Salvatore ran into the room in horror, as soon as she saw her nephew reading on the couch sitting by the fireplace, her breath recovered and she was no longer gasping for air. -I thought I was late and you were gone. Tell me, what happened that you're not looking for your unfortunate aunt anymore? We live under the same roof, but we don't even see each other.

-What are you talking about, Aunt? I'm still here before your eyes.

-You know I'm not talking about that. As if it weren't you... You got so cold these days. You're not even talking to me. You're completely aloof.

George closed the book in his hand and then stood up to put it in its place, back to the bookcase, which was opposite him, on the other side of the room. At the waist-height of the bookshelf, stood a well-designed chest of drawers with a whisky decanter that looked like crystal glass on a tray with two glasses.

-My dear aunt. -The man shook his head. -You know that I have a lot of things to deal with. Market values are rising. And India sounds so foreign.

-Maybe it would be best to get married by then to have a familiar face with you on the trip. -She said with a half-smile at her nephew, who had just filled two glasses of whisky and handed over one of them to his loving guardian. -Although I know how reserved you are, how timid you are, and how much you love being alone. You love to control your life yourself, which is obvious. But next to such a young man, who is also handsome, at least a bride would fit. Otherwise, you will end up like me. You stay a bachelor for the rest of your life. Edith grinned, then stared in the opposite direction. George just turned to himself and laughed.

-Aunt, aunt. It just hurts that you don't have a grandchild yet, right? -He asked jokingly.

-Yes, that is one of the many reasons. -She replied suddenly -A lot of sophisticated young ladies' lust after you. And you're wasting your time. Or maybe... -She asked in shock, pausing with an open mouth because she couldn't find the right words -You have already a crush on someone? -George just laughed in confusion, then looked at the glass in his hand. -Noo! Is she the little red rose? That... What was her name?... I can't remember her name... -She put her fingers in front of her mouth like someone concentrating on something so important that she must remember as if her life depended on it.

The man's serious gaze was fixed on the woman. There was no faint sign of his smile as if he had completely forgotten the meaning of joy, the essence of what the word happiness encompasses. He looked at his glass again, then smoothed its side with one of his fingers, then put it down on the table. He leaned towards his aunt, kissed her on the forehead, and said only a few words to reassure the woman who had helped him all his life to become who he was now: "There is a full year until my journey to India" then he left.

-What was her name? -She was confused by the gloom of ignorance. -Red rose full of thorns. -She chuckled to herself.

# CHAPTER XV

*"Dear Diary,*

*Sitting in my prison window, I pour my feelings back on you again.*

*I received a life sentence from my dad for what I did. He said I stigmatized my family's name, that I brought shame on everyone who bears the Bloom name, and if he still knew what awaits him... Dad will never talk to me, it could be even a denial from the family. E. was it. That damn E. The person I trusted the most, who knew all my secrets. She betrayed me. I will never forgive her. It was her, it could only be. No one else knew about our plan with O. My only love, the man for whom I would give my life. The one who provided comfort in the darkest moments of my life. He disappeared from my life forever. We were already standing at the altar, it seemed like the happiest moment of my life. We were dressed in simple clothes. I didn't hold a wedding bouquet instead I had a red rose in my hand that I received from him. There was not a single guest present. There was no wedding that most girls dreamt of. There was just him and me. It was the wedding I dreamt of. The perfect wedding. We should have just said the big YES and now we could be with each other until death parts us. But my father showed up before we said it. Like a hurricane, he broke into the church with two other dogs of his, who had dragged me away from the only meaning of my life. But in nine months, nine wonderful months, my life will take on a new meaning. The only thing in my sore heart that turns the dagger every time I think about it, is that the only man I ever loved will never know about it.*

*I am thankful, at least for you, for the little simple item made of a lot of paper."*

-She was with child? -She asked in a whisper.

-Come on, Miss., out of the bed it is almost noon. -Doris burst into the red room so she could pull out the darkener, Scarlett quickly hid her diary. -Or shall I call you Miss. Laziness? You still have a lot to do. What are you waiting for? It is Thursday in two days and people don't have tools.

-Doris, tell me... Was my aunt Miranda ever married? -She asked curiously.

-No, never. -She declared, then close the subject and left hurriedly.

Looking at the painting on the wall, Scarlett pondered what a mysterious woman was her aunt.

*

-Nivek! Nivek! -She shouted down the hall as she picked up her riding hood on the way. The butler appeared in front of her eyes in half a second. -Tell the three men who are renovating the house that I have a more important task for them. Which can take days.

-Yes, Miss. Tell me, what would the task be?

-Here's the note. -She handed Nivek a piece of paper that included a long list. Quantity and price are indicated for all agricultural tools, animals and all goods. -Go with them and get it all. Here's the money for it. I'll award the reward after completing the task. -She said, handing over a little purse of gold, then putting on her hood, she left.

-Will you be, for long? -The man asked curiously the young lady.

-Until I will see clear. I have to know from what kind of family I am from.

*

It was a huge castle before her eyes. At least five times bigger than her modest little shelter. She had to walk at least ten minutes from the gate through the front garden to reach the front door. As soon as she got there, the host was waiting for her. Two butlers and two maids were waiting on either side of the door, in a male-female pair, including in the centre of the entrance a woman who was the embodiment of perfection, compared to her forty years, she looked like a contemporary woman. Her hair looked silky soft, even though it was covered in gel to make her perfect bun stand even more perfectly. Her breasts were as tight as two honey melons. And her shape was more perfect than Venus's.

-Miss. Bloom! What an honour!

*

The salon was huge. Until now, she thought her house was a palace, but it was far from what she was meeting now for the second time. She couldn't comprehend, how she hadn't noticed it all, the last time she'd been here. Is it possible that the malaise would have distracted her so much? Or was it society that caught her attention so much?

-Your home is just amazing! -She declared in amazement.

She just smiled and then shook the bell.

-Do you want a cup of tea? -She could barely finish her question, the moment she put the bell back in its place, a maid was there. Scarlett just nodded, then looked around again.

-And tell me, why do I have this honour? -She asked curiously.

-I didn't reply to your husband's letter, I thought I'd rather come in person to tell you how wonderful I felt at the party and also to apologise for disappearing so suddenly. Unfortunately, the change of the environment physically wore me out. Scarlett said, then looked around again like she was looking for someone. -And if I already mentioned your husband...

-He is out of the house! -She replied, leaning back comfortably on the couch, squeezing her cup.

-We can talk at least more comfortable. Like women. - Evelyn, smiled and then sipped from her cup. -You said you knew my aunt. What kind of woman was she?

She smiled at her silently for half a minute, then replied: -She was marvellous! -She took a deep breath and continued -She was a beautiful woman, and she was headstrong to the core. She achieved everything she wanted. -Scarlett smiled, then thought about objecting to this woman being wrong, maybe she wasn't able to achieve everything. Maybe she had weaknesses, which she never shared with the world and showed only her strong side. She was unable to achieve that, to soften her father's heart and become the bride of the man she loved. Or was she wrong about all this? She didn't get to the end of the story yet.

-I've known Miranda since I was a kid, we practically grew up together. I know, about her most embarrassing secrets, which her favourite book was, her favourite work of art, or her favourite flower. The first trip to London. Even about her childhood love. -She laughed. Scarlett stared at the person sitting in front of her, in shock. -Of course, she had secrets she never shared with anyone. Just like me. -She said kindly. Scarlett kept realizing that she was close enough to decipher that who was the mysterious E. and what secrets Lady Quas might have thought of. From her thoughts, a laughing man brought her back to the real world.

-The most beautiful wife in the world, Evelyn! -Lord Quas stepped in, then leaned over to kiss his wife, but she was just holding her cheek with a forced smile. -Miss. Bloom! What a pleasant surprise! -He said cheerfully, then kissed her hand.

-As a matter of fact, I'm just about to leave. It was good to see you! -As she walked through the garden, she wondered what had happened to her aunt's child and why she had never heard of him/her. Who can be that mysterious person? And if he's alive, how could she contact him? She thought about giving the wealth she inherited back to him all to a shilling. But she had first to find him.

# CHAPTER XVI

Scarlett was standing on the porch of her huge house at exactly 7 a.m on Thursday morning. Not a single soul came from the villagers, so her worries grew every minute. Doris brought the girl a poncho against the early morning cold.

-You're reminding me of her. She, too, was always standing here in the morning when she was assigning tasks. She was a real leader.

-Do you think they're coming? -Scarlett asked anxiously as she watched the back gate entrance.

-Never let it shake your confidence. Not for a minute. -She said as she pulled the slippery material over her shoulder to protect it from the sharp spring cold.

-Can I ask you something?

-Did anything stop you so far from finding out what you wanted? -She laughed sarcastically, while Scarlett smiled.

-Did my aunt ever had a child? -She asked now with a serious expression.

Doris, just forced a smile. -You read her diary, did you?

Scarlett lowered her head in shame, then looked up at the sky. -It's awkward, I know. But I felt I had to know her. -Doris nodded in agreement. They watched the approaching crowd as they entered the gate one after the other. More and more people gathered. Some laughed happily and some whispered softly. Scarlett waited a few more minutes to see if anyone else arrived. The last man was Mr. Meadow, who was already drunk in the early morning. At first, he just leaned against the gate, then after finding his balance, he slammed the gate with such force that the people shuddered at the noise. Scarlett closed her eyes for half a moment to regain her calm state of mind again before speaking.

-The world we create is a reflection of what we become. -Doris said softly, then took a deep breath.

After a while, Scarlett began to speak.

-Ladies and gentlemen. It is a pleasure to see you in such large numbers here this morning. First of all, I would like to present my butler, Mr. Nivek, and the three men who procured all the supplies, animals, and goods on time, which took no less than two full days, they deserve special praise. Applaud them!

Most people started applauding happily. The four men began to smile with pride, and waved gratefully as a king would from his carriage to his people.

-Now I would like to list those who are present and then assign the duties, please. Whoever hears his name raise his hand. -Then she started reading the list: -Matthew and Angelina Curtis, Andrew Mooron, David, John, James and Ken Frame, Lilian and her sister, Lea Anderson, ... -and it continued until the end of the list- I ask the ladies to stand on one side, and the gentlemen to the other so that I may begin to assign tasks. For these tasks, the workers change every other week so that the monotony is not present for a minute (except for some, such as the shepherd). There are a total of 100 sheep on the farm, for which they are supposed to need a shepherd. I would ask Mr. Andrew Poldem to accept this task. -Then she marked him on the list. -For the forty-three cattle, I would like to see a couple of brave volunteer candidates from among the ladies for pre-producing milk (milkwoman), sweet and salty cheese, soured cream, and many other goods and three men for feeding and watering. Then I would like a man for the task who chooses the role of the herdsman (which again cannot be changed, just like the shepherd). -Doris could barely take notes. As soon as she got them, people started again to scream their names for the roles, it wasn't an easy task for her, especially since the names they shouted weren't always clear. -Twenty-six goats and a buck with the same task as cows. Next to our hundred hens and ten roosters, I wish there was someone every morning and evening to pick up the eggs, feed and give them water. Eighty ducks, along with gander all together, the task is the same as with hens. This can be done by the same people. Thirty-eight pigs and two boars will wait every morning and noon to get fed and their sheds will need cleaning. There are a total of seven horses, including two over the age of twenty, which is now considered old. That means these two horses will not be used for farming, they will be kept for my leisure activities and for transport. This means that the three wagons and the carriage, which is in the hay barn, need to be refurbished. I would also like to ask for five candidates for this job, this job can take no more than a day and a half. I wish we could sell already on the market on Monday morning. I would ask Lilian and Lea Anderson to take on this job, of course, if you can count and handle the money. I know your mother is used to the market life.

The girls start nodding. -I also want a couple of women for the orchard department, I know it's still spring, but I want them for pruning the trees and want them to be organised, they are already starting to bloom. So, I want you to report to me when you've done with them. Luckily, most of the tools required , Miss. Miranda Bloom left it behind, so they just need to be repaired and sharpened. Is there a blacksmith among us?

An older man raised his hand, right next to him, a young man as well. -Do you have a workshop? -They started nodding, they were father and son, as they said, so they had the honour of taking the tools and taking them under their hands. -Men who don't have the tools to start the work, will help the women out around the house and farm until everything can be settled. In the barn, women will also find the equipment necessary to produce cheese and butter, you have to take them to the kitchen on the farm, which must be cleaned before the production, and you have to clean the tools as well. In the kitchen you will find everything necessary for it, I have already taken care of that. The kitchen is located about 160 yards from the hay barn. Tables, knives, buckets, cloths, churns, strainers, and cans have already been carried into the kitchen. Last but not least, agriculture. Mr. Nivek is aware of everything and will choose a man who will carry out stock control: the tools, seeds, animals, the production of goods, the work on the land, and many more tasks. Are there any of us who can write and read?

-One of the men raised his hand holding a Bible in the other. Scarlett was concerned, more than likely that he was a Methodist. -As I see there is not much choice... -She whispered to her butler. -Mr. Nivek will explain everything to the men who will be working in the fields.

-Then the man started down the stairs to the workers, stopped halfway, and sighed. -I would like to ask those still present not to be late. -Scarlett tried to look as confident as possible, though no one noticed, she felt her voice tremble a little. -I can't tolerate a minute's delay. For anyone who is late or not showing up, I want to hear a compelling reason. Appear here every morning at 7 a.m. for the roster.

The farm was no more than three and a half miles away. Scarlett watched calmly as people began to leave. With the exception of a few women.

-Maybe you are unsatisfied with something? -She asked, being a little afraid of the answers.

-Not at all. -Declared one of them in a quick word, they seemed a little afraid of Scarlett's austerity. -We hoped the mistress would be so kind that maybe...

-Allow...

-That... -the three women alternated. Then the fourth spoke up, gathering all of her courage.

-You'll allow Miss. so that our children can come to work too.

Scarlett was unable to speak. She didn't understand. So, the first woman who had lost weight until she was just skin and bone, a wrinkled woman in her torn dress, spoke again. She bows, then the scarf on her head covered her face, so Scarlett couldn't see her facial expressions.

-We know there are few job opportunities and our debts are high, you don't have to pay them. Only deduct from our debts for it.

-Why aren't the kids in school? -Scarlett asked in surprise.

-To school? Miss., our kind, do not go to school. The only thing that benefits us is the work. So that we can make a living from one day to another. We had to learn this as children. -Said the braver one, who was a fuller woman, not very tall, but it showed that she had worked in her whole life. She had a figure like a man, with her muscles, which would put many men to shame.

-I'm hiring a kid from those who are here. They can arrange the hens and ducks. -The women just smiled and started talking- But they must all be over ten years old. -She interrupted the merriment- Doris writes down the names so they can start tomorrow. -Then she turned and disappeared behind the door.

# CHAPTER XVII

*"A glooming peace this morning with it brings. The sun for sorrow will not show his head. Go hence to have more talk of these sad things. Some shall be pardoned, and some punished. For never was a story of more woe Than this of Juliet and her Romeo."*

*-William Shakespeare*

-What are you reading, Miss.? -An unknown voice asked. She looked up from her armchair in surprise, not expecting guests, so the surprise stepped up to the roof when she saw who the voice belonged.

-I've just finished. -Scarlett said, closing the book in front of her, then stood up to put it in its place. The man turned his head curiously to peek at the cover of the book, then smiled deeply.

-And what is your opinion? -He calculated the pause, while he gained her attention, then continued- I mean about the end?

-In my opinion, being able to give up everything for love is amazing. -She stopped and thought for a few seconds before pushing the book in between the others. -Correcting myself, they gave up on it. They died for each other so that they could be together in the afterlife. -The man just looked at her silently -Why I'm telling you all this since you have probably read it. -By that time the man smiled with a forced smile.

-Do you think it could happen in real life also?

-Well, I give a chance to the idea that people are able to put love in the first place.

George laughed, this time out loud. Then stepped closer.

-Isn't that how you see it, Mr. Salvatore? Do you think we can't give love a chance in our lives?

-In a world where there are more marriages of convenience than those which were born of love? You had never asked me why I was a bachelor. -Scarlett frowned, by giving an answer to her doubts. -Well, I think love is relative. We have a lot of other things to put in front of it in life. Out of love, man does not make a living, it is not vital.

-So, you mean you don't believe in love?

-I wouldn't say that, but there are times when we have to hide love in a deep and dark hole in order to satisfy our needs and happiness.

-I have decided not to accept your opinion. The consciousness, that love will find me too gives me hope.

-You are a real daydreamer, aren't you? -He smiled as Scarlett raised her head proudly. -We have a nice weather out there. -He said. She looked out the huge window beside her, which George was looking at.

*

-Tell me, how does the farming go? How much time has passed since you started it? -The man asked.

-I've been operating for two weeks. It's bumpy, but every start is the same. -She did not dare to admit that her efforts may be in vain, one day the real heir may show up, and she may lose everything. She didn't even dare think about it, because it means that Miranda's child shows up once and everything she started to build during that month will be lost. Not to mention that Mr. Salvatore will be quite right and she will have to marry an aristocrat in order to help her family. The war brought cruel poverty to the country and it is feared that these are only the first steps leading down.

-And the farm? Did you manage to provide customers?

-There are no suppliers yet. So, unfortunately, most of the product's will spoil.

-I can help with that. -She looked at him in surprise, then watched wordlessly -I have friends in marketing who deliver to the surrounding villages and towns. I would like to mention it to them at the next meeting.

-It would be great! -She exclaimed. -Tell me about your trip to India. I read that there is a competition between cotton and silk. What do you think, will you have a chance to convince them to raise the prices? -The man was completely taken aback by these questions.

-I didn't know you were so in the swim with market prices and business. -He said with a smile- I confess you completely shocked me.

-Do you think as well that business isn't for women? -She smiled.

-I'm not a feminist. In my opinion, no matter what your background is, it only matters to have knowledge about what you do. There are a lot of businessmen who go bankrupt because they just don't understand it. -Then he looked at Scarlett to see her reaction, but her gaze was neutral. -Returning to your question, now that silk is thriving so much in the market, there's a chance I'll fail. But there is still plenty of time until next April. Until then the dice could turn.

-I trust you will succeed. -She said, looking at the man, who was smiling, so they continued their walk in the garden. The man was so handsome that day, so it took Scarlett's attention for a moment and she didn't notice that she had stepped into a mole hole and she stumbled.

-Are you all right, Miss. Bloom? -George asked anxiously as he reached for Scarlett to help her up.

-Well, I was just careless. -She said, sitting on the grass.

-Let me help you. -The man helped her up and then bent down to look at her injured ankle -Can you walk? -Scarlett tried to take a few steps, but collapsed. Luckily, George was there to catch her.

-It seems like I need to rest for a few days. -She said, laughing at her own misfortune.

-And how will you keep your promise like this? -Scarlett looked at the man's dark eyes in confusion- The truth is that the purpose of my visit would be to bring the invitation myself, so you can't escape with an excuse. Miss. Scarlett Miranda Bloom, would you do me the honour of coming to the ball on Saturday? -Then he took the invitation from his inside pocket and handed it to her.

-Ohm... -She smiled as she picked up the envelope. -Yes, I will.

-But? -He asked the thoughtful face.

-There is no 'But'.

-Do you think you'll be able to recover by then?

-It seems I must. -She laughed. Mr. Salvatore held out his arm, Scarlett thought about accepting it for half a second, but finally clung to it. So, they continued their walk.

Doris watched them from the window. She took a deep breath and shook her head. She stepped closer to the fireplace and threw some paper into the fire, looking at the flames, she said:

-You will try loving less, but it will hurt just the same.

# CHAPTER XVIII

*"Dear Diary,*

*I can only be delighted with my condition, sometimes it wears me out and full of pain I think I can't take it anymore, but then I began to think again and I'm sure I wouldn't change my life with anyone, no matter how much hardship it brings in the future. It is a pleasure to see the process. I can't wait to get to know the man who will give new meaning to my life. O.T. showed up one day, I didn't miss his company at all."*

-I don't understand her... Has she forgotten how much she loved him? I thought she was looking forward to seeing him again. -Scarlett whispered, then continued reading. *"I found out that he came at my father's request to ask for me in marriage, and later it turned out that my father had offered him a lot of money in addition to my dowry. But I have known O.T. for a long time, yet I refused him. I could not marry a man I do not love."* -I don't still understand her... How does she mean she doesn't love him? What has changed she was melting for him so far. -Scarlett flipped back a few pages to her aunt's entry a few days before, where she wrote *"I'll love you O.T for the rest of my life."*

Scarlett was still puzzled for a few more minutes, then folded back to the current pages to shed light on the truth. *"I didn't regret my decision because I know he would have taken me only because of the money. He said he wanted to save souls from eternal damnation in this world. A few weeks later, the Pope inaugurated him as a reverend of the Catholic Holy Church in Truro. Although I'm out of favour, in Dad's eyes, I refused my only chance to get married and pretend nothing had happened. But that didn't bother me, the only thing that bothered me was that my mother had lost consciousness so many times in situations when I was arguing with Dad. Not even the news that my brother's third child has been born helped my mother's condition... The doctor said she was suffering from nervous exhaustion, prescribed some medication, and suggested her rest, after which she was in bed for days. Oh, dear O.T., why did you disappear from my life?"*

Scarlett lost the meaning of the entire text reading the last sentence. She read the pages in confusion, hoping to find answers. Doris took a tray of tea to Scarlett's library and put it down on the table in front of the couch where Scarlett was just resting. The girl addressed her.

-Doris, do you know a pastor who had a close relationship with my aunt?

Doris staggered; she couldn't dare tell Scarlett the truth. Scarlett motioned for her to join her for tea. Doris took a seat and then poured the drink with zigzags steams.

-So? -She repeated.

-Mr. Otto Tamayo was known by your aunt from a young age.

-Do you know if there was any attachment between them?

-All I know Miss. Scarlett is, that Mr. Tamayo wanted to marry her before he decided to become a servant of the Lord.

Scarlett was seemingly unhappy with the answer, but she knew she had to make it through.

-Milk? -Doris asked, reaching for the small milk jug, Scarlett lifting her palm toward her, as an answer. Pondering so much that she didn't even notice that Matilda had entered the room. Doris was instantly aware, she knew the girl was upset and needed peace of mind, so she gestured for Matilda to leave. -Why are you wasting your time on stuff like that? You will be attending a ball soon. Do you know what you're going to wear? Did you practice the dance steps?

-You might be right. -She said, returning to the present and her cup of tea.

-Sugar? -Doris asked with the cube of sugar bowl in her hand.

-What do you flavour your tea with? I've never seen you use sugar before.

-With honey, Miss. Scarlett. It is much healthier and provides a sweet taste just like sugar.

-With honey? I've never eaten honey since I've lived here. Can I have some too?

-Of course. -She declared, putting down the sugar -Honey heals all wounds.

-Someone really loves honey. No wonder I barely get some. -They both started to laugh.

# CHAPTER XIX

"People who have never fought for their homeland, who have never sacrificed their lives to serve a cause that doesn't really serve the peasants, will never understand what the soldiers are going through. Standing out at the front and being shoot in front of your brother's eyes may sound heroic, but that's just sheer nonsense. When you watch your father with what he goes through for weeks because of his infected wounds, and then when he becomes completely under its control, he gives up the fight against it, when he falls into an eternal dream in your arms, is not a feeling that could make you stronger, but one that will break you. Then you start thinking about: "What am I doing here? Would I really have no choice? Do I have to choose death?" The fire-trenches are, they said, to be for cowards who dare not fight on open ground. I think this is a chance to survive. Maybe it's a little safer after all, than to run into the head of the enemy and be the diversionary operation. The pits filled with rainwater to the knees, in which people has to stand for days, are not a dream, most of the soldiers catch a cold, deaths are increasing in this area. Everywhere on the battlefield you look at corpses every metre or in piles. The mud is so large, that you can barely take a few steps without slipping. Disabled or limbless soldiers in the tents, not to mention how many they are unable to save. The war, in a word, is 'Terrible.'"

# CHAPTER XX

*"Dear Diary,*

*I'm in my sixth month now, Dad forbade me to move my feet out of the house, I can't even go to the yard. I cannot talk to anyone except the servants, I can't even write a single letter... It's not like I'm writing to anyone, no one was looking for me. O.T. didn't even write a farewell letter. I wish I would know what was going on in his head, where he was going, and most importantly, how he was.*

*I almost forgot to tell the story of my father's cruelty while I was daydreaming about O.T. One of our maids muttered to another that I was pregnant, so by accident in the presence of family, including Dad, she asked me how my condition was and how long I have left. Although I did not feel it bothered me. I mean her question, in fact, the interest fell particularly well. Dad was unable to leave the case without retaliation. He wondered how she knew about this information, because it was appropriate to know that this servant was one of the villagers who did not know about my blessed condition, and my clothes or positions always hid my beautifully rounded belly. I was often in need of hiding it even in the good weather conditions, likely I got bigger in the cold season. While I was sitting in the library, for example, I had to hide with a blanket my little melon. Or I was hiding in my room for days when the family came to visit, with such lies that I was taken ill. Essentially, Dad crossed the border. Both rumoured parties were so punished that for weeks, purple and dark spots covered their skin and they were unable to straighten their backs. The pain was completely on Matilda's face, I could see how much she was suffering on a daily basis, I was unable to show my feelings for her, even though we both suffered from different things from the same person's torturing.*

*I can also say that it wasn't just me who brought shame on my family, much to Dad's annoyance. My brother had also. Just a few years after marrying that horrible woman and his family was almost complete, since two beautiful twin sons and a beautiful daughter were born and after receiving his wealth. He was able to put his passion above all else and he played on cards with almost all of his inheritance. Making his wife and children almost paupers. He begged me not to tell Dad while he tried to fix the things. But it would have leaked out sooner or later anyway, and what would make me happier now, in my darkest hours, than to see suffering the man who tortures me too?! My father."*

-I can't believe this woman, after around six months writing which means at least 220 pages. She writes nothing about the real heir, just about her suffering and vituperation of my parents. -Scarlett murmured to herself.

Then she got up from her bed to look out the window to see who was coming, the galloping of the horses clearly indicated that an unexpected guest was coming to her again. As she was still recovering, she swayed slightly because of her injured ankle. She took strength and limped to the window. She clung to the huge dark curtain, though she knew that if she depended on it, the curtain would not be able to hold her weight. She saw a coupe carriage with two footmen standing on the accompanying ramp at the back of the car. The driver drove in front of the entrance, bypassing the fountain that adorned the front garden, and then stopped.

The footmen got down and went to the carriage door to help out the person or persons sitting in it. Scarlett didn't know who to expect, the car was a closed coupe, so she couldn't see who had arrived. She hoped  Mr. George Salvatore would come to visit her, though she knew he usually rode alone with his own horse, yet she did hope. Her wide smile, on the other hand, faded when a tall man came out, wearing a black, even higher-than-usual hat, his hair tied with a ribbon at the back, and his hair had been supposedly raised for a long time, not to mention his beard. But while Mr. Salvatore was always used to wearing under the knee buckle boots, dark trousers, a sailor hat, and a white shirt that was usually well-tucked into his pants and covered his shirt with a waistcoat on his upper body, Mr. Wolowitz's appearance was not particularly pleasing to her, even if it was more modern and elegant. He wore ankle-length short-heeled shoes that usually corrected men's height, but he didn't need them. He was wearing long hose, which was continued to cover his muscular-looking legs with shorter-legged trousers.

He looked up at the window of the room Scarlett was in as if he knew someone was staring at him. He raised his hat and walked to the front door. Scarlett stumbled quickly to the dressing table and reached for her perfume. After a few minutes of preparation, she walked down to receive her guest.

The man was already in the library when Scarlett walked in. He got up from his armchair to greet her, he was twisting his hat in his hands in confusion. Doris stared nervously at the ground, unable to look at Scarlett like that, then left the room.

-Miss. Bloom, I'm sorry to arrive uninvited.

Scarlett silently pointed to the armchair, suggesting that the man could take a seat now. Understanding the gesture, he sat back down.

-Brandy? -The red-haired girl asked with a smile. Leonard just nodded.

-The purpose of my visit is to find out if you resent me, Miss?

-Why would I do that? -She asked as she filled the glasses.

-I didn't get an answer to my letters. I thought there might be a compelling reason for this.

-What are you talking about? -She asked uncertainly as she handed over the drink.

-I sent countless letters, but still did not receive a reply. I just want to know the reason, and you will not see me here.

Scarlett was unable to sit down, completely shocked by the man's claim. So, she walked up and down in the room, with fluctuation a little. Mr. Wolowitz showed contempt for her injured leg, not even interest in it. It was an inability to decide if it was because he didn't want Scarlett to feel uncomfortable because such an aesthetic problem was easy to spot or simply because he didn't care.

-Maybe I exaggerated. I'm sure that's what you think. That I sent so many letters after a single ball, or that I want to see you so much. Maybe you think I am too pushing.

-For how long have you been sending letters?

-Since my visit. I know I should have announced it in advance even then, but I didn't expect you to be outdoors. Not to mention that you were cut off in the same saddle with your suitor, just after a few days you came here. -Scarlett's eyes widened at this sentence, she tried to hide her annoyance, only hoping not to show it, as there was no mirror in the room and the window was completely in the other direction, her confidence swayed even more, but she successfully hid all such gestures and mimicry, which would have suggested that the man was able to plunge her into an awkward position.

-Posts hardly get here. -She spread her arms like she was waiting for an explanation for this problem. -You know I've been living here for two months almost and I haven't even received a single letter from my family.

-I understand. I'm sorry, Miss. if I harassed you or you felt I slandered you. Nothing like that was in my mind. Although it is interesting that the letter does not get this far from the neighbour, especially since I sent it with my own courier.

-No insult, don't worry. But if you'll excuse me now, I still have a lot to do.

The man stood up, then nodded understandingly. Scarlett grabbed the bell and shook it twice. It didn't take long for Matilda to appear, her ageing wrinkled face always painting a worn-out image as if she was angry with the world. The man bowed politely, then began to follow her to the door, stopping next to a bookcase which was neighbouring the door and a dresser, he turned back to Scarlett.

-Then see you at Mr. Salvatore's ball! I suppose you will be present. -Then he looked at the bottom of the glass to the brandy left in it, after which he set down the empty item on the tray on the dresser, and left.

Scarlett smiled proudly at him until he disappeared from her sight. Then after a deep sigh, left her disobedient body to fall into an armchair. Doris, who had entered the room after Matilda, watched Scarlett silently as she fell, then stared at the floor in shame.

-Tell me, why didn't you say he was here? -She asked Doris motionlessly, who was just picking up the glasses from the dresser. The person with her back to her didn't even look back when she asked the question.

-It totally went out of my head. -She declared troubled.

-The same day, I asked you, that particular day, if someone was looking for me. -She rose from her chair, turning to Doris.

-I remember it now, Miss Scarlett.

-And the letters? -Scarlett asked angrily- Where are the letters? -But still no answer- Where are the letters? -Scarlett shouted nervously this time.

-I burned them. -Doris whispered.

-You did what? -Scarlett didn't believe her ears, she hoped if she gave her a second chance, the answer would change, but it didn't turn out as she hoped, Doris's answer was the same "I burned them".

-How could you do that?

-He is not suitable for the young lady. He is a terrible man, he is considered distasteful, a sputum.

-Who are you to decide who I can talk to and who I can't? -The flame of Scarlett's anger grew flammable.

-Miss Scarlett...

-Don't call me like that. I am Miss Bloom to you, so for every other servant in this house! And the letters from my family? Did you remove them too?

-No, Miss. Bloom -She shook her head.

-Do not lie to me! -She shouted.

-I'm not lying Miss. Bloom. No mail was received from your family.

Scarlett could barely breathe from the anger, she walked toward the window. When she saw her reflection on it, the girl who looked back at her was unknown. She tried to calm down, then said, *"You can leave now."* Doris listened to her without a word she walked out of the room.

After closing the door behind her in tears, she said to herself: -Oh Doris...You fool. You should never let your feelings get too deep; people can change anytime.

# CHAPTER XXI

*"Dear Anne,*

*I'm trying with another letter. I don't know why I haven't heard from you so far, but you need to know I'm fine and I miss you.*

*I am preparing for another ball, this way I will be present at the invitation of Mr. Salvatore. The excitement I feel is indescribable. I don't know what clothes to wear yet, luckily our Aunt Miranda had a lot of nice dresses.*

*Doris isn't going to help me get ready now, I was so cruel. I said terrible things which I regret...*

*Dear Anne, I wish you were here..."*

She lifted her pen from the paper placed on the book on her lap. Wet the paper with her tears, she annoyed herself, dropped the book and the letter from her lap, then hugged her knees and sank her face into it. The wind blew pleasantly, it wasn't cold, but it wasn't too hot either. It was beautiful spring weather, the trees were blooming and the birds were chirping. Scarlett watched everything around her, the tendrils of the willow tree swaying gently in the wind. A small buzzing little creature landed on her hand, which lifted from her melancholy mood. When she looked up, the tiny little bee landed on her knee. Her hairy little striped coat was full of flower dust, her little black eyes were gleaming in the sunshine as she looked at the girl and her sweet little antennae stood to the sky.

-Oh, Hello there! -She smiled at the bee, wiping away her tears. When it left, Scarlett took strength and got up to finally start preparing for the evening. She didn't dare think what it would be like. She decided it was better not to think about it. Because she also knew that over-thinking was a disease.

*

Doris arranged the table, bringing fresh flowers into the vase. She found a jug of honey in the middle of the table. "-*What the...*" she asked herself. Next to the jug stood a small note with her name on it.

-Once a kind person told me that honey heals all wounds. -A voice said behind her. As she turned to see who this lovely, silky voice belonged to, Scarlett glanced at her, leaning against the door jamb. Laughing, Doris burst into tears, then walked toward her and hugged her.

-Doris, I'm very ...-

-I know! -Doris declared. She didn't let her finish the sentence. She always knew what she was feeling without words. -Where is the beautiful dress, Miss? That way you won't get to the ball in time! -She declared motherly, then yanked her away so she could prepare her, to get there in time.

*

Mr. Salvatore was waiting for the guests in the doorway, his aunt knew by the time what kind of game went out, George had never held a reception class before. Rather, he was just mysteriously lost in the crowd and then came up and exchanged a word or two with people. Miss. Salvatore stood next to him and said: -Aren't you waiting for someone, Georgie?

-I'm just welcoming the guests, Aunt. -He said, then shook hands with a man to greet him.

-Does it have anything to do with that girl? -She chuckled.

Scarlett's horse-drawn carriage arrived at the entrance as the conversation took place, and George looked at his aunt and said: -Mrs. Elson was looking for you, Aunt would you be nice and look after her?

-Oh, it's not that easy to play around with me, boy. Did the Miss arrive? -She asked, looking at George. Scarlett walked slowly up the stairs with elegant steps, her mustard dress with a silver necklace hanging around her neck looked perfect together. Her red hair was held in a perfect bun and her blue-sky eyes gleamed at the elegant man in front of her. -Tell me, is she approaching us? I would give anything to have my old eyesight again. -She said, holding the man by the arm.

-Miss. Bloom! What an honour to have you here.

-Miss. Bloom... -She said to herself as both sides looked at her. -My memory, like my eyes, bad as a barn door. Tell me, dear, did you travel well? -She yanked her through the door, urging her to speak. Scarlett glanced at George, who was left in the doorway to receive the other guests, with a kind of "save me" gaze, as the man thought for a few seconds to go after them.

Miss. Salvatore took Scarlett among the other ladies who were just debating whether or not it was appropriate to buy a new dress for each ball. A familiar face appeared among them, Lady Evelyn Quas.

-What do you think Miss. Bloom?

-I think it only satisfies the ego every time we show up in a new outfit. But in keeping with the symbol of morality, the new dress is just a tool that appears in the company of ladies who have no other subject to discuss. It's just about finding out who's in your company with whom you can talk about people you don't like. And right now, let's clarify, I'm not exactly the person you need in this group.

Scarlett lifted her dress, bowed, and moved on. Lady Quas smiled contentedly at her, while the other ladies furiously gossiped. Miss. Salvatore was amused by what happened until she was called upon to do something important. Scarlett found a chair to rest on, immersed deeply in the harmony of the dancing people's footsteps and the soul-warming song of the rhythmic music. A man walked slowly past her, trying to draw attention to himself as he was unable to shake the red-haired girl out of her dream world, he decided to take a seat next to her.

-They say we are able to show our current feelings by dancing. -He said beside her, finally noticing the girl next to him, who was sitting in the chair humming in harmony with the music and swinging her body, she only touched him with a smile and then returned to her thoughts until she was jerked out again. -Would you like to dance with me? -Mr. Wolowitz asked.

-I'm sorry, I promised my first dance already to someone. -She said with regret, not knowing for sure if the one who promised would come to ask.

-And where is this mysterious person, who has just left you here alone? -Scarlett was about to answer when someone showed up next to them.

-He's already here. -George said loudly to be heard from the music. Leonard stood up. There was such a fire burning in the eyes of both of them, that almost their flames scorched each other. George's gaze made Leonard leave. -Are you all right, Miss? -He asked the slightly embarrassed girl.

-Yes, it's just a little too warm in here.

-Let's go for a walk. -He said, his eyes still on the leaving man.

*

-I can provide good news. -Said the man, now walking in the yard, together with Scarlett, who was quietly waiting for the man to continue. -I had talked to my friends, about what we were talking about last time. They are willing to buy your products so they can continue to sell them as their own in many markets. I dared to send them a letter with your contact details. They will probably be contacting you soon to agree.

-I'm grateful. -She said not too enthusiastically, then took a deep breath.

-Did I say something wrong? Or didn't you expect that?

-That's great news. -She stopped. -I just don't understand your dislike for Mr. Wolowitz, nor many other people's feelings towards him.

-Miss, Mr. Wolowitz is not who he shows himself to be. There is a lot of talk about him.

-You think he's a man worth keeping your distance from. - The man just nodded wordlessly -But you still invited him to your ball.

-This is politically useful. As you know, Mr. Leonard Wolowitz is a very influential man with a prominent role in the world of the market. He himself is a merchant who has travelled to innumerable places and countries, including India.

-And I think you hope to learn more about India in his company, which will benefit you. Am I correct?

-You see through me, Miss. -He said with a smile, the music was sounding less loud on the side of the garden where they were, in competition with hundreds of crickets chirping into the night. People did not walk in this part of the garden as there were plenty of roses there and they were afraid they would get caught on them in the dark. Their faces were lit by the light of the moon and stars, and George knew every corner of his house, as well as his gardens. This country house was one of the most beautiful properties in the county. And George loved it very much, he spent most of his childhood here. -Well, you'd like to dance with me, Miss. Bloom? -He held out his arm to the girl.

-Here? And now? -She asked in surprise, but she saw that he was serious. -Gladly! -She declared to the man collecting the promise. Then they started dancing. George put his hand on her waist with a gentle touch, then held her hand with the other and controlled it confidently. He knew that seeing them could seal their good news. But he didn't care. All that mattered was the way he danced with the one after whom he had been waiting all week. She can't be wiped out of his thoughts not even for a minute when she's not with him.

Miss. Salvatore watched them from a balcony. The pleasant cool breeze permeated her dress, endowing her with new freshness. A man appeared beside her; she certainly didn't recognize him due to her poor eyesight. But she must have known he was one of Scarlett's suitors.

-Sometimes you have to create your own happiness. -Edith said, then walked away, leaving the man watching the dancing pair with piercing eyes. The tall man sipped from his glass and then turned his back to them, then walked away from the balcony.

# CHAPTER XXII

-Miss. Bloom! What a pleasant surprise. -The short, completely grey-haired man declared as he rose from his chair to greet his guest.

-Mr. Thaker, I hope I didn't disturb you. -She said, walking toward the man, pulling her gloves off her hands with slow, calm movements.

-No, not at all. Please have a seat. -He pointed to the chair opposite his desk.

-I'm sure you are surprised to see me here. But I need professional advice.

-And how do you ask for my advice? As a friend or as a customer?

-Maybe I'd take advantage of both if you don't mind. -She said, taking a breath between her teeth.

Mr. Thaker smiled. -This here... -Scarlett picked up a brown-bound booklet. -Is my aunt's diary. -Mr. Thaker's smile froze to the bone on his face, but he didn't say a word -My aunt wrote a few entries, and I jumped forward a few pages because I needed some information about farming. But she did not write in detail. So, I thought maybe you could fill in the missing parts.

-Miss. Bloom... what you did is...

-I'm well aware that I pried into someone's private life. But I need to know where to start. I took the first steps. Before sowing and planting vegetables, the fields were ploughed three times to soften.

It was also enriched with enough manure. But I don't know what to do with cereals.

-Then what did you learn from that diary?

-Not much. -She replied shrugging.

-Do you know what a crop rotation is? -The girl just shook her head silently -This plant exchange in the fields. This is to allow the remaining seeds to be replaced in the ground, the rotten and potted seeds to disappear. In a nutshell, crop rotation is the practice of planting different plants in succession on the same land to ameliorate soil health, optimize soil nutrient content, and control pests and weeds. Thus, the fruit of the next sowing will be more successful and we can maintain the soil health.

-Would you mind if I took notes? -She asked, reaching for a piece of paper on the table, the man silently pushed towards her ink with a pen.

-The question is, what do you want to sow?

-Barley, Oats, Wheat, Corn, Rye, Lucerne. Everything that is used to maintain a farm.

-You need to know one thing, Miss. This is a region further away from Europe, not a Mediterranean region. The weather is unpredictable. That is why there are only a few people working in agriculture in this country. But if you do it smartly, you can make a big profit. Do you know what you will be using your farm for? Do you know about the varieties of wheat? Or about harvest periods?

-No, sir. That's why I visited you. To share your knowledge with me.

The man nodded silently and said: -There will be plenty to note. -He prepared the girl -Well, the autumn sowing mainly are barley, wheat, and rye. But since the lands were not sown last year...

-Yes, cleaning and ploughing can take weeks, but I thought I'd send them in two teams so we wouldn't waste so much time. While one cleans up, the other group can sow afterward. Since there are some lands already prepared, we will be ready for sowing, so we will have an easier time. -She interrupted the man as he swallowed the dumpling from his throat, she realised how silly she was, that she had talked over him. Shamefully Scarlett lowered her head.

-This, well... It's a very wise thought. -Mr. Thaker remarked as Scarlett regained her confidence. -But note that these forages are autumn type. Of course, it can also be sown in the spring, if you have prepared the land, so you bring in some backlog, and your animals won't starve, you won't have to buy hay and straw when the time will come.

-And for the summer, the weeds from the lands, which my men had cleaned up, I had dried up. They can be useful to us in some form, right?

-Well, it will be good for nothing more than a nest. -The man laughed, and Scarlett was ashamed again, but this time she was blushing. -Didn't you come to study, Miss? The nest is needed also under the animals, just like you need a fluffy bed during the night. So where were we? Ah, yes. They also have their harvest time. Wheat should be sown in spring from late March to early April and autumn in early October to early November. It has to be harvested from the end of July to the beginning of August. It also need to be threshed, so that the grain can be ground in the mill. There are two types of it that are not recommended to mix into the same field, there is the fibrous and bald head. I mean there are six in total, but these are the most common, and the easiest to identify. I enumerate them if you wish so: Hard red winter wheat, soft red winter wheat, hard red spring wheat, hard white wheat, soft white wheat, and durum wheat.

-I've got a question. -Scarlett raised her hand, as if she were in school- What is threshing?

-Threshing is the process by which the edible part of a grain or other crop is loosened from the straw to which it is attached. This is the step of preparing the grain after harvest. You have to know as well that threshing does not remove the bran from the grain.

-I also wonder what the difference is between that many kinds of wheat.

-Well, in simple words, hard red winter and hard white wheat are mostly for bread with the same content of protein, hard red spring is also for bread but it contains more protein, if I am not wrong around 13% or 13.5%. Soft red winter is for harder cookies, while soft white is for groceries that made softer cakes and the last durum wheat is for pasta.

-Got it! -She said making a quick manoeuvre with her pen as if making a dot at the end of the sentence.

-The point is, now Miss, you will have to sow the seasonal wheat, but I could accompany you to the market if you wish.

-That would be great.

-Back to our topic, the stem will be hay. Also, you should be aware that when sowing, the spreading is done by hand, and you should always spread it where you step, for example, if you step to the left, spread on the left, and if you step right then spread to the right. But your people know for sure, you don't have to worry about it. Barley is also like wheat; it is spring and autumn. Autumn sowing is most abundant. This should be threshed in the same way as the wheat and the eyes sprinkled on animal feed, such as pig's swill. It can also be sown at the same time as wheat or in the autumn from mid-September to early October. Oats, horse feed, should be sown from late March to early April. This should be mowed when the green head is thrown out, at which point it should be cut off for fodder hay and also threshed for horse's food. Alfalfa, this should be sown from late March to early

April. This should be mowed when buds are visible before it blooms. Otherwise, it dries out and you can put it under the animals... in the middle of May, it should be mowed for the first time and then every six to eight weeks. There is usually a lot of rain in early May so the first forage collection is in the middle. The rye...

-Pardon for interrupting you. But I missed most of the spring sowing. In this case, what should I do?

-Things are always in the fine print, aren't they? The best way to succeed is to identify with who you want to be. If you want to become a master, you have to learn all the ins and outs of things. First and foremost, you need to know how to think in accordance with the weather. Once you have it you will be a professional trader. If you think about the weather of the last month and look at the hardness and moisture of the earth, you will realise that this year favours you. And a little slip will fit in, with this kind of weather.

-So, this means that I can start sowing? -She asked in surprise, the man in front of her just nodded smiling.

-We kept with the rye. It is an autumn fodder, cereal-like wheat and barley. It is used to make bread and alcohol. The rye is dependent on the weather, this plant needs to be bitten to find out if its ripe, if its cracks you can start harvesting. It most often occurs on the day of Peter and Paul. The corn, you see Miss. Bloom, you are still in time to plant, it should be sown from mid-April to mid-May. We distinguish two types of this. There is a 100-day, if the rainy year is good, after barley, it can already be cut down by the end of October, and there is a pioneer corn (perje diploid), that can be picked in early September or October. I almost forget to explain. -The man said after a short pause- The clover, this is sown in the winter to get into the ground with snowy water. It can be sprayed on the lands where you have sown winter wheat or barley. If the crop is good, it can be cut up to twice a year.

-I'm grateful for the amount of information you've provided.

-Grateful or thankful? -The man joked, since he never heard the girl thanking for anything. -You said your visit has two reasons. One is more confidential. Tell me, how can I help? -He asked the girl, who turned her back to leave.

-Maybe. -She turned back, clutching her paper. -Is there any chance another heir will show up?

-I don't know about that, Miss. Bloom hasn't appointed any other niece or nephew. Only your name came up.

Scarlett felt reassured for a second, but couldn't hide the thought that was still bothering her in some form. She didn't understand then, where could Miss. Bloom's child be and why didn't he apply for what rightfully belongs to him. The thought arose that maybe her aunt might have lost the baby, it could also be the reason she had left them at such a young age. With this horrible thought, she was startled. Scarlett bowed politely and left Mr. Thaker's office. In her haste, she didn't even notice Lady Quas approaching her, so as she stepped out the door into the street, taking a few steps she collided with Evelyn Quas.

-Oh! I didn't notice you. -She said, trying to hurry away, feeling her chest start to tighten, unable to think of anything but to get home and find out what had happened to Miranda Bloom's child. But Lady Quas held her up.

-What a pleasant surprise Miss. Bloom. Wouldn't you want to join me for a walk?

-What? -Scarlett asked, not registering the woman's question.

-Only in the market. We could shop or just watch around to see what is there. -She comes up with ideas- Let's say, we could buy new clothes. -She laughed sarcastically. -Only the other dames should not find out. -She winked at Scarlett, who didn't really care. She tried not to take her into consideration, hoping she would leave her on her own, but Lady Quas didn't.

-Please Lady Quas, I don't feel able today, I am not very well. I want to get home as soon as I can.

-I know you don't like shopping and what you think of new dresses, but still...

-Lady Quas for heaven's sake! -Scarlett said nervously, for which the woman fell silent- If you think we can be friends, you're very wrong. I know what you think of my family. I also know how much you loved the man who you could never get. And what you did to my aunt, too. So no, I'm not asking for your company.

-How? -She wondered.

-I'm asking for nothing else, just leave me alone. -She said and set off on her own journey. The people on the street were all watching them. Lord Quas arrived at his wife's side, who was about to hurry after Scarlett to question her. But her husband's presence held her back.

# CHAPTER XXIV

*"Dear Diary,*

*I am unable to express my gratitude for being here for me. A lifeless object that means a lot more to me than a flesh and blood man. I can always say my grief and you are silently listening to my words. Today was filled with moments of joy and sorrow. My mother, my dear mom, the mistress of this house. The woman who gave me life has passed away from us forever. My father, who I can't call like that anymore. The monster who did terrible things to me during my pregnancy that I can't talk about and even think about. Henry was by her bed for hours in her final minutes. The doctors said in vain that they could do nothing for her anymore and her body cooled to ice, all the corridors of the house vibrating with his voice. He was unable to let go of the woman he loved. He fought all day with the maids and doctors not to have her body taken away. The only thing that tore him apart was when he came to see his new-born granddaughter. Yes, that is true. Today, March 15, the one who gave me new hope was born. It is a joy and a sorrowful day because the one who could give me the most happiness has been torn from me. My little girl with rusty hair, the fruit of my love, the little rosebud, Scarlett."*

Scarlett fell into the couch in shock as she read this. She couldn't believe what she was reading. She was unable to comprehend the words written on the paper. The truth about who her mother really was. She was unable to realise that her life so far had been a lie, everyone had lied to her, and the greatest pain came from those who knew the truth and did not tell her. She looked ahead in front of her for a few minutes, staring at her chair with wet eyes. She was angry, angry at all the objects around her, at all the people, and especially angry at the world for being so unjust and cruel. She nurtured hatred against the man who, though he no longer lived among them, had torn her apart from her mother, against the man who knew the truth and yet had not spoken for so many years, and ultimately hated the man who could have visited and raised her as her own. Miranda was the one in whom her hatred was deeply rooted. Why didn't she go for her? Why didn't she visit her daughter? Why don't they have a common memory? Why don't she remember what her mother looked like? If she hadn't seen paintings of her she would never have known what the woman who gave her life was like. She stood up angrily and shouted down the hallways with Doris's name. Doris hearing her in the kitchen, took out two cups and took off the water splashing into the fire. When Scarlett entered and saw the woman's calm face, she became speechless for a few seconds. She sat down weakly on the bench next to the table.

-All this time long you knew who I really was. -She said weakly.

-My darling, Miss Bloom. I was the one who helped you come to the world while the household mourned Mrs. Bloom.

-And you haven't said a word about it.

-You would have found out sooner or later. It was more important to find yourself than for someone else to actually tell you who you are.

-To find myself. Huh? -She laughed.

-Yes. But, not as the child of the mistress of this house. You Miss. Bloom are more than you think. -Scarlett raised her eyebrows and looked away ironically at what the woman in front of her said. -When you arrived, you were a child, and in just a few months you became a real woman without anyone's help.

-Doris, you don't know what you're talking about.

-But I know. You found yourself, Miss. Bloom. Once upon a time, you were an oppressed child who never received maternal love, tossing among the foam of the seas doing what others tell you. You lived your life unknowingly, without self-knowledge. Then you came to Gracewith to get to know yourself. Becoming a strong, independent woman, whom no one commands. You created the impossible. It has revived Gracewith, given jobs to the unemployed and given a new purpose, a purpose of life to its household, to those who believe in you. -Doris grabbed Scarlett's hands, which lay lifeless on the table. -Miss, you are a real miracle.

Doris got up to fill the teas, then pressed in front of her, leaning on the table, saying: -Now go and prepare that barn, the people want to have fun for the evening, show those who still doubt, who you really are.

*

After a few hours, Doris went out with a hot drink to Scarlett, who was done with the decoration. She climbed down a ladder when Doris appeared. The barn was huge, as it was still mainly empty, Scarlett was sure her workers would fit in the room. The seats were made up of tied haystacks or logs, although there were not many tables or they were unable to assemble more in time, so there was only a huge table lined up from many tables, to operate as a self-service place where the food and drink were placed. Then everyone will take as much as they can eat. Although the table was still poor, most of the food was still in the kitchen, and its seating was cramped, radiating a kinder atmosphere.

-Did the goods arrive? -She asked the woman.

-Yes, they were recently unpacked in the kitchen.

-Don't you think it would be too cold tonight?

-Yes, the sky is pretty clear. But if the evening will be a great success, no one will be cold. You know dance is warming our souls and bodies. -The two women smiled.

-Could you please tell me what happened that night?

Doris took a deep breath and walked slowly toward the huge doors. She looked up at the stars and said: -Once I promised I would never talk about it. But this is an exceptional case now. -She said with a smile on her face. -Miss. Bloom, Miranda. Everyone in her family condemned her, except her mother. She supported her daughter all the way. On the afternoon of March 14, terrible news arrived. Mr. Bloom Junior carded all of his assets, with his father's investors, confidants, and friends. His father expelled him from the family, embarrassed to send away his only son, who would have been his heir after his death, with nothing. There was a lot of fuss that day, Miss. Bloom decided to give her income to her brother so as not to become an earth runner. Mr. Bloom didn't want to agree first. Miss. Bloom insisted as she wouldn't need that money because she would never get married. Their father, even more angry, said he would only give half of the sum on the condition that he move a good distance where no one knows him. That's how they got to Bath. They were ready to leave the next morning. Mrs. Bloom, from the pain of losing one of her children, collapsed on the spot as soon as she realised it. Just when she was starting to recover. -Doris cried. -Mr. Bloom broke down and completely lost his head when the doctors told him they were unable to save his wife. He was by her deathbed all along. No one could convince him that the Mistress was no longer with us.

-Then it was not Miranda who told their father about her brother?

-Noo! She could never tell on her brother, maybe it would be a good feeling for her, but she didn't, even if she knew. A man wrote the letter, writing about the day Mr. Bloom Junior lost the inheritance on cards and about other debts.

-What happened next?

-Then for hours, the only thing he was able to tear from his dead wife's body was the "*birth*". -She said at the same time as the girl. -When you were born, you were phenomenal, you had

116

snow-white skin with rusty red hair. Miss. Bloom and I shared the joy as if we had seen some miracle. It was hard for me too, but it could have been much more painful for Miranda when her father broke in. She could hold the child she had carried under her heart for nine months for barely five minutes. He took you from a woman who had just given birth. You were torn from Miranda's arms as a five-minute-old baby. Your mother sobbed helplessly for hours in bed until she cried herself to sleep. I thought we would lose her too. She didn't eat for days, didn't talk, didn't smile. She just lay there waiting for death to reach her too. When her mother's funeral arrived, it was the first time she got out of bed. She combed, dressed, and walked out of the red room with a full demeanour. Everyone thought she was mourning her mother so bitterly, but anyone who knew her, knew that her child was the one she really missed.

-In the diary, after this page, I only found entries about sowing and harvesting. She wrote no more about her feelings. So far, at least I haven't found anything.

-Don't blame her. She was completely shattered. She was as if she had become a completely different person, as if she had been replaced after what had happened. Especially the difficulties that followed...

-And what happened to her father?

-He was locked in a room for years, it was unpredictable. He often hurt us, one of the maids was beaten to death. Miss. Bloom promised she would never let anyone hurt us from now on. She took control into her own hands. She ran the farm for years. Keeping her father in check, cut off from the world. Until his last hours arrived. The possessions were put in the name of his daughter, but until then there was a long and difficult way.

Time has passed with the conversation. So, people started to drift in slowly. More and more people came and looked at the poorly set table in surprise, and everyone agreed and was very angry. Many had already turned to leave the room when Scarlett stood up on a smaller podium.

-Dear workers. I'm glad you came to attend this evening. -People were still loud and talking, some shouting *"what kind of fun is this"*, *"where is the food"*, or *"what kind of poverty is this"*. Scarlett continued undisturbed. -As I said this morning, I am grateful that so many diligent hands are working in my lands, and I have acquired such devoted people. I hope this year will be a year full of abundance. Now let the fun begin! -She exclaimed, and as the music began, on the other door, the servants came in a row, holding huge, plentiful trays in their hands, with all sorts of food on them, there were meats, sides, desserts, vegetables, and fruits. The villagers had never seen so much food in one place, most attacked the food first, many started drinking, and some started dancing. There was consolation there, everyone ate as much as they could manage, and they feasted in abundance and drank in abundance. They yelled at the host and had fun like never before, from little ones to grownups. Many even brought their families.

Scarlett set off after a while to get some fresh air, no one was happier that the evening went so well as she was. She saw the young girl in the doorway again, who was looking at her in the yard without blinking in the morning. She stood in front of the door like a statue just like she did in the morning, not taking her eyes off Scarlett even for a moment, so she walked over to her.

-How do you like the evening?

-The mistress is overly generous. They are very happy; I mean the people. No one has done this for us for a long time. -She said, bowing.

-Do you work on the farm too?

-Yes, I milk the cows. -She declared, as Scarlett almost choked on the sipped water.

-I haven't seen you before. What's your name?

-Daphne Jelon. -She said with a mischievous smile.

Scarlett just nodded and then headed for the exit. But something was making her feel she was watched by someone, so she turned back at the door. Her instinct was good, Daphne was still looking at her with the same flawless smile. She took a deep breath and walked out. A small child was present, closing the doors next to hen houses.

The little boy walked by the well. The lady who stepped next to him, he didn't know. Looking at the bottom of the well, he said: -Wouldn't you draw me some water, Miss?

-Why aren't you going to eat first? Everyone's having fun inside.

-I want to drink first, we always do it this way at home. Then you know, I'm not going to be so hungry and I don't eat that much, so it is enough for everyone.

Without a word, Scarlett sat on the edge of the well and then drew water for the seven-year-old child.

-I've never seen you before. Tell me, what do they call you?

-I'm Matt.

-Like Matthew?

-Not just Matt. I have been serving here since the beginning.

-But that is impossible, I do not employ children, only over the age of ten. I mean they don't. -She corrected herself.

-Yes, but Mom has a lot of debt and I'm her biggest kid. -The child said as Scarlett began thinking. -Hmm, this water is so delicious, I've never drunk like this before. It is much different from the water of the pond. -Scarlett frowned at the child.

-Are you talking about the pond that is next to the village?

The child nodded with a smile, then put down his bucket and joined the party in the barn.

Despite the cold, Scarlett stayed by the well for a few more minutes.

# CHAPTER XXV

-Miss. Bloom. You called for me! -Declared a man approaching with confident footsteps, speaking to the young woman standing by the window, holding a book in front of her and gaining the light from the last rays of the sun to read.

-Have a seat. Can I pour a little heart booster? -The man took a seat without a word, while she walked past the chest of drawers, waiting for no answer, she reached for the glasses on the dresser.

-I heard, you had a big feast for your workers.

-It went well. But where did you hear it?

-Are you joking? The rumours of the great Miss. Scarlett Bloom, what they spread is heard all over Truro. The helper of the poor. The most successful Miss. Business in Cornwall. Unbelievable what you built in just a few months.

-The news may be a little exaggerated. My profit is really bigger than I expected at the very beginning, but I am far from getting what I targeted. -The man could only smile at her modesty, but he did not argue.

-When you call me here, Miss, I always feel like you're struggling with something. -He leaned on his walking stick while sitting in the armchair. His old trembling hands vibrated the stick. -Tell me, what can I do for you?

-I'm glad you asked this question. It is true that I did not invite you just as a guest. -She said with two full glasses of heart booster in her hands as she reached over, handed one to the man, then took a seat on the couch opposite Mr. Thaker. -The truth is, I called to discuss my investments and the amount in my bank account.

-Certainly. What would you want to know about it?

-I would like to open a separate bank account under my company name. So, if I ever decide to get married, I don't want my partner to have access to that amount. Since men handle their wives purses, I decided not to give him access to it at all. Since the company would be in my name, I know only the owner can manage it and the appointed CFO (Chief financial officer) for which I would like to appoint you, Mr. Thaker.

-Miss. Bloom... -The grey-haired man searched for words, looking at the person in front of him with an open, trembling mouth.

-Are you not happy with this position? You can boost the bank budget and make the investment yourself. I do not know a more suitable person.

-No, Miss. Bloom. I am delighted with this appointment. But I don't understand. Are you engaged? Or what are this fuss and hurry for?

-It's personal, Mr. Thaker.

-I thought I was your friend.

-Yes, but you might not understand that. After all, I don't even understand myself, everything happened so fast. It was the ball that changed everything.

-What kind of ball are you talking about?

-About Mr. Salvatore's ball.

-Did you engage each other? -The man asked in shock. -Mr. Salvatore is one of the most sophisticated, best businessmen, most trustworthy and resilient gentlemen I have ever known.

-I think you misunderstood. There is no engagement. Yet. Mr. Salvatore was just asking permission for courtship. I haven't authorized it yet, I've written a letter to my family, but since my father... Mr. Bloom is dead, there would be no one else to ask for permission other than the person who raise me, outside of him. He himself wrote them a lot of letters. But since I haven't received a response from my family so far, I don't have much hope for his letters either. I will have to answer myself. He said he proves his intentions are serious. But I still have to think it over. Oh, Mr. Thaker, I'm so confused. -She said, standing up to walk to the window, staring at the gorgeous sky lit with the colours of the setting sun.

-You are facing a difficult decision. -He got up from his seat, leaned on his walking stick, and walked slowly toward her. -How long has there been no answer from your family?

-Since I got here, I haven't received a letter. Why are you interested? Do you know something? -She turned suddenly again to the half head shorter man than her.

-Something is wrong... -he whispered- The county of Bath was at one time under French rule. But I haven't heard from them in a very long time. I know no one was once allowed into the area until they were beaten back two weeks ago. Plenty of villages was set on fire and looted.

Scarlett had to sit down hearing those words. The fear and anxiety that saturated her body had almost completely taken over. But she fought it, she couldn't let Mr. Thaker see her cry. She put her hand in front of her chest as if it could curb the pain and help her breathe again. She was thinking about that man from the ball, so he was serious and didn't want to stab her side.

-I'm sorry you have to hear this, Miss. But I will do my best to find out something about your family.

Scarlett nodded silently for a while as she felt the feelings inside her and she decided to suppress them. To prevent the inevitable, she decided to change the subject.

-I want to withdraw money from my account. At the village party, I met a kid. -She said, recovering, but avoiding eye contact with Mr. Thaker. -He said they drink water from the lake I want to surprise them with a well in the middle of the village. Next to the little bell.

-Are you sure it is necessary? -The man asked.

-We are talking about hungry people who drink water to quench their appetite before eating. They drink from the lake in which they wash their clothes, where they bathe, and wash the dry faeces of sediment from the cow's buttocks. Do you think they don't deserve clean water? -Scarlett raised her voice. Completely losing control. She didn't even notice Doris appearing in the doorway, in the company of a man.

-Miss. Bloom. Mr. Wolowitz has come to see you. -Doris declared softly. Scarlett stared wordlessly at her reflection in the window pane. Which was now clear because of the contrast between the light inside and the darkness outside, which had become like a mirror. She raised her head, then swept away the lock of hair hanging into her face.

-Excuse me, Miss. Bloom. Come to me when you are available so we can take care of your affairs. -He said, bowing and putting his hat on, then walked out of the room, waiting for no answer.

Scarlett took strength, then, following Mr. Thaker's example, walked toward the door where the guest and Doris stood.

-I'm sorry. But I think we'd better make time for this meeting another time. -She said, stopping beside the man before walking away.

-I see you are being too busy with the poor's life and other business matters. Maybe it would be best if there will be no other time. -He said, squeezing the envelope in his hand, looking at her with a goodbye nod, trying to hit the fireplace in the room with the paper crumpled into a ball, but it bounced back off the grate to the floor, then put on his hat and left upset.

Scarlett didn't care, just sighed, then turned to walk up the stairs, raising her right hand over her shoulder in a *"Do you think I care?"* or *"Doesn't matter anymore"* way.

# CHAPTER XXVI

*"Can a person hate a nation just because his family is slaughtered for political reasons? If you meet a French soldier after a war, can you look at him like a man or will you look at him like a slaughterer? Do they think the same as we do? Do they want the end of this war as much as we do? Do they just want to go home as we want to? If they still have a home to go to, if there is a person in their family who is still waiting for them to go home.*

*Do they feel just as forced to kill, as the English soldiers? They close their eyes in tears every night for the lives they have taken cruelly. Do they also count how many people's lives were spilled or did they do it with cold blood, with pleasure?*

*Can we ever forgive each other?"*

# CHAPTER XXVII

Next to Scarlett's footsteps, the two little spotted creatures were constantly there, following her with every footstep she took. After a while, almost no one was allowed near the girl, not even the usual maids.

Doris greeted Scarlett with tea in bed one fine May morning. As she enters the room, the dogs at both feet of the bed grumbled at the greying woman, who almost dropped the tray frightened.

-Miss. Bloom, you have to curb these beasts, for Judas's sake. They will tear me apart when they grow up. -She said, avoiding the dogs in a big arc.

-Shhh-shhh-shhh! -She whispered, laughing at her dogs, leaning against the edge of the bed, stroking their cheeks. -Not if it's up to me. -Then stretched out while sitting in bed.

-They grew incredible in a couple of weeks. How big will these be in a year? -She rounded her eyes at the dogs. Scarlett was still sitting in bed laughing. She looked out the window where the rays of the morning light illuminated and warmed her skin.

-Has Nivek brought the morning report yet?

-I do not know about it. -Doris replied, pouring water from the jug into the washbasin.

-What is today's programme?

-Mrs. Kent arrived in the morning, she said she wanted to talk to you, she probably wanted to get one of her kids to work. A letter was received from Mrs. Quas. -The girl just noticed the letter next to the cup and then opened it. -And you have a meeting with Mr.

Thaker at noon. -But as soon as Scarlett caught on reading, it was as if she was submerged, the voices were muffled and she seemed to be in a completely different world.

*"Dear Miss. Bloom,*

*I don't know how informed you were of what was going on between me and your aunt, Miranda. Not even how much you know about me and the man I once loved.*

*I am currently in London, but as soon as I return, I will write.*

*It could also be that my letter will arrive after the ball. We will probably meet at Mr. Wolowitz's ball in the meantime.*

*I would like to clarify this disagreement.*

*Kind regards,*

*Mrs. Evelyn Quas"*

-Miss. Bloom. Did you hear what I said?

-Ohm... What? -Scarlett returned to this world. -Of course, I did.

-Then pinch yourself, until Truro, it's a long way! -Cried the woman already halfway down the hall.

*

Scarlett went down the stairs, grabbed her hat off the rack, and headed for the exit door. When she half-opened it, something occurred to her, after a deep sigh she closed the door and headed to the library. It was the fifth day that she had not been in the room. Her daily activities were completely busy, people arrived on a daily basis begging for work, with a sore heart but unable to offer all of them work, no matter how much she wanted to. She was unable to deprive them of the hope that they would have an honest job and food on their table again, so all she told them was to notify them. She searched in a pile of letters on the desk when she found what she needed, Mr. Thaker's letter. As soon as she pulled it out a flyer fell. Scarlett leaned over to pick it up, but before putting it on the table, something hit her eyes, raising it closer to herself, the flyer read in capital letters *"THIS YEAR'S COMMON MASS WITH OTTO TAMAYO AND THE POPE."* -Does the Pope come here for mass at Pentecost? -She morphed. She shook her gaze and dropped it on the table. As she walked towards the door, she walked past the fireplace, kicked into something through her inattention, she didn't want to consider the small object at her feet for the first time, after being upset she remembered what it might be, so she picked it up. Scarlett unwrapped the crumpled letter and read it. It was an invitation to a ball in block letters, but not just any ball, it was a masquerade ball. There were even masks drawn in the lower right corner of the letter. Mr. Wolowitz hosted a masquerade ball for his mother's fiftieth birthday. She remembered how foolish she had been that night when Mr. Wolowitz visited her. Scarlett was flooded in shame of warmth. She fanned herself with the paper and looked at it again, the date being June 17th. She sighed, then hurried out of the room, visiting Doris. Doris was just cleaning the hallway, training the new housekeepers Scarlett had hired not so long ago.

-Well, how are they doing?

-Great, they're learning very fast.

-Very well then. -She counted to herself until five, when Doris turned back to continue what she had started, Scarlett spoke again. -What did you say, what was the pastor's name who wanted to marry my mother? -After hearing these words, the student housekeepers looked at her. -I want to say to my aunt. -She corrected herself.

-The five-second rule, you are a fast learner. -She pointed with a chunky index finger in warning. The five-second rule is used when someone does not want to be too intrusive, leaving a five-second break between questions, and is usually used when they want to ask about a sensitive topic. Doris had once taught this rule to Scarlett. She just smiled that Doris recognized the trick. -Otto Tamayo, why are you interested?

-Just like that, it occurred to me. -She said, stroking Doris's shoulders. Scarlett was about to question when Nivek came in their direction. -Oh, Nivek! It's good to see you. Did you manage to arrange everything I asked for?

-Of course, Miss. Bloom.

*

-Tell me, Miss. Bloom, do you really think it's a good idea to spend the money you barely earned after investing in the farm to renovate your village houses? -Mr. Thaker asked in his office the girl sitting in opposite him.

-Of course, not all of them. -She declared- Only those which are in a very poor state. There are plenty of houses, on which their roofs have been damaged by the storm.

-Hmm, that's going to be expensive. Including  work coverage. Much more than the amount you wrote here.

-The amount only covers the price of the materials. The work will be done by the tenants. They are given a day off until the work is done. So, it comes out much cheaper. The houses that have not been inhabited so far and are in a worse condition will be completed by Doris' relatives, those who have been renovated in Gracewith. We have already negotiated their salary. Lately, a lot more production and hatching has been profitable for us, every single egg that was under the nesting hens hatched, so the price of the hens we lost that night, has been recovered. And the dogs are doing a great job too, not a single fox has appeared on the estate since then. With this, I would like to say that we are not in minus.

The man just smiled, shaking his head.

-Miss. Bloom, you can always surprise me. -Then he laughed tastefully -I write a receipt for you and I'll get the amount right away. -He then got up from his chair with great difficulty, barely able to straighten his old, hunched back.

-Oh, and please don't forget the amount for the well we discussed last time.

-No way. -He said from the other room.

When he returned, he came back with a cradle and a paper in his hand, he set it down on the table in front of the girl.

-Until I forget. I have written several letters to the Bath office. The answer to all of them was that they didn't know anything about your family or the address on the letter- They also said that they don't have time to go after the case, because after the French occupation they had a lot to do, I was advised to try it in a few months. -Scarlett became very sad -Until now. -The man continued, Scarlett looked up hopefully -From the cathedral in Bath, I received a letter regarding: Miss. Riley and Miss. Julia Bloom, Mr. Jared Bloom, and even Miss. Aliona Bloom. -He had a hard time reading the last name -They had confirmation of these names, and I was given an address where they were. Any of these names is familiar?

-Yes, they are my nieces and my nephew. -She said in confusion. -I've been thinking about leaving for days anyway, now I know at least where they are.

-No, miss. It is dangerous, even the French, had not retreated completely from the area of Bath and you have a lot to do on the farm anyway. If you leave now when your company demands the most attention, it could lead to serious consequences. I'm travelling there myself. -He said, leaning on the table.

-I can't ask you for that, you've already done so much for me.

-You didn't have to ask. -He said with a smile.

*

After leaving Mr. Thaker's office, she accidentally saw Mr. Wolowitz, who was shopping in the market, just watching a horse.

-You're not trying to show interest nowadays in a new horse, right sir? -She asked, stepping softly behind him.

-What else can I do? The only one I was interested in, knocked me down. She treated me like air. Why would it make sense to keep hitting the wind?

-Maybe I just needed a storm to open my eyes and finally see you, Sir. -The man finally looked at Scarlett at that sentence, who smiled flirtatiously.

-Let's take a walk. -He offered, raising out his arm. Scarlett put her arm around it.

-It's really uncomfortable that we've been separated like that in the past. -Of course, what else could such a whimsical lady say? After all, she's not going to apologise -The events of that night were really upsetting. -She said, pouting her lips.

-I noticed it, too. -He said, but he was a proud man himself too, he had no intention of apologizing either. -What would you say if I make it up to you?

-But how?

-With a ball. -He replied, unaware that the letter had not been destroyed.

-What kind of ball? -Playing as she too doesn't seem to know about the invitation.

-My mother's fiftieth birthday masquerade ball. I would like to see you there.

Scarlett just smiled flirtatiously. A man in a tall hat walked over to them unexpectedly. His confidence almost radiated. But from his anger, he was almost boiling.

-Mr. Salvatore, what a surprise. -Leonard said, squeezing Scarlett's arm, who blushed because she felt the gravity of the situation.

-The joy is mine. -He bowed with a smile, trying to hide his dislike. Which was a bit forced, but it worked. Then he left.

Scarlett said goodbye, with the excuse that she had to hurry home because she still had a lot to do. The man just says, "Then at the ball!" then flicked his hat. As much as she was in a hurry, she couldn't catch up with the man, and then she lost track in the large crowd. Thinking he had gone home, she hurried to his apartment. Miss. Salvatore opened the door, and greeted her with great pleasure.

-Miss! What a pleasant surprise. Didn't you just come to visit the old girl to discuss the wedding?

-How? -She looked in surprise, gasping for air.

-I'm just joking. -She said with a laugh, then began to gesture inward with her hand. -Come on in, dear. Let's have a tea.

-I'm actually, looking for Mr. Salvatore.

-He's out of the house now, but he should be here soon. -She said as she directed her to the salon. As soon as they got in, a maid arrived just a few seconds after the bell rang. -We'd like to have a tea party with my nephew's future wife. -The old lady said jokingly, Scarlett just laughing with her as she adapted.

-And tell me in what matter are you looking for George? Maybe not wedding invitations need to be discussed. -She leaned in laughter, laughing so heartily that she could barely breathe, Scarlett was afraid she would get a stroke in front of her eyes because then she wouldn't even see the unplanned wedding. -Of course, there will be a lot of grandchildren, right? -She continued the almost insulting joke as if she just wanted her nephew to take her as a wife to have "*grandchildren*". -And how do you plan? Whose name will it be in front? Because you know it's been so fashionable lately that women's names are on it first. -She was so undisturbed on this subject, that it embarrassed Scarlett. -Forgive me, what did you say your full name was? My name memory is so bad. Let's just say it's no worse than my eyes, but still. -She added.

-Scarlett! Scarlett Miranda Bloom! -She said, completely confused by the subject. She felt that Miss. Salvatore had crossed that certain border and she would not have nerves for long to take it anymore.

-What did you say? -She asked with a frozen grin on her face.

-Scarlett Miranda Bloom. -She said, a little reassured, taking it back from her voice, knowing that it wasn't Edith's fault that she had become so irritated. After what happened in the market now, she thinks it would have been better if she had gone home straight away and didn't try to explain. What could she achieve with it? Maybe it's even worse. If George hasn't overthought about it before, he'll be after it.

Edith took her eyepiece from the book on the coffee table and held it in front of her eyes, slowly leaning into her aura. Scarlett leaned back as far as the backrest would allow, while the woman suddenly stopped and froze. She blinked a few times and sat back in her armchair. Then she just stared silently at Scarlett without a word.

She felt uncomfortable, sure she had offended her future mother-in-law with her raised voice, so she stood up.

-I think it's time for me to go. Maybe it wasn't such a good idea to come here in Mr. Salvatore's absence. -With that, she left.

# CHAPTER XXVIII

-Have been digging that pit for days, what do you think they want with it? -One peasant woman asked the other.

-I do not know. -She stretched out her neck to see if she could see what was going on there.

People worked diligently to improve the village. Together, they repaired the houses that had been destroyed by bad weather. And those that were destroyed at the time were taken care of by Doris' relatives, and let them see what precise work they had done. The empty houses were almost collapsed, and with the help of these men and sometimes, of course, women, they were completely refurbished. Scarlett was immeasurably satisfied with their work.

*

-Tell me Nivek, how the work is progressing? -She asked the man walking down the hall.

-Everything is as planned. We have already reached water. We will have another success soon.

-Don't forget that the edge of the well must be high, there are plenty of kids in the village. -She remarked with a smile. - Doris! -They turned to the woman not to lose sight of her. -Don't forget, I'm getting ready for Mass tonight.

-I won't forget, Miss. I just don't understand why the church in the village is not enough for you. Why do you have to go to Truro for a mass?

Scarlett just smiled.

-Did you take my dress plans to the seamstress? Of course, I'll be visiting soon so we can discuss the cut and take off the size as well.

-I did it. Of course, everything you asked for. Again, I don't understand why it's so urgent. Mr. Wolowitz's ball is still so far away.

-Dear Doris. -She stroked the beautiful dark skin of the woman in front of her.

# CHAPTER XXIX

-My aunt! Why are you so gloomy lately? You are like it as you had seen a ghost. -The man joked. -You should be happier, share happiness with me. They delayed my trip to India because the prices on the market started to raise and the cotton price is equal to the silk's. Spring time, I will get on the water at the end of the next year.

-And are you taking anyone with you? -She asked, turning to George by the window.

-I'm planning to take my future wife with me. -He sat down and clasped his fingers, leaving only two of his fingers free, with which he played nervously. -I know we haven't talked about this yet. And I've been a little angry at her lately, but I guess I had unnecessary worries since Mr. Wolowitz isn't that kind of person. I'm planning on asking for Miss. Bloom's hand. -Edith undeniably showed dislike for the thing. -I love her, aunt. I've never wanted anyone as close to me as she, ever. Although she is stubborn and wilful. But she is the woman with whom I envision my future.

-Love? Yet what do you know about love? It's just suffering.

-Yes, it is. That's exactly how I feel when she is not next to me. Emptiness. And I'm sure the feeling is mutual.

-What makes you think that?

-I just feel it. -He said with a smile.

-You don't know what you're talking about, son. That woman wants only your fortune.

-I doubt that would be the case. She has her own.

-And she wants more. -Clicking the spoon continuously over to the side of the cup. -She knows you wouldn't take from her what's her property, maybe she had already done it against you to keep her possession untouchable. But one thing you can believe me, that woman longs for more and more money. -She sipped into her cup as she stared out the window at the people in the market.

# CHAPTER XXX

*"²Thus saith the LORD the Maker thereof, the LORD that formed it to establish it, the YHWH\* is His name: ³·Call unto Me, and I will answer thee, and will tell thee great things, and hidden, which thou knowest not. ⁴·For thus saith the LORD, the God of Israel, concerning the houses of this city, and concerning the houses of the kings of Judah, which are broken down for mounds, and for ramparts; ⁵·whereon they come to fight with the Chaldeans, even to fill them with the dead bodies of men, whom I have slain in Mine anger and in My fury, and for all whose wickedness I have hid My face from this city: ⁶·Behold, I will bring it healing and cure, and I will cure them; and I will reveal unto them the abundance of peace and truth."*

*(Jeremiah 33:2-7)*

### \*YHWH/ יהוה /JHVH/Jahve/Jehovah:

*=i.e. the so-called tetragrammaton (Greek: τετραγ ράμματον -(the) four letters) is the four-letter Hebrew name of God, the name of the God of Israel in the Old Testament. Judaism traditionally does not pronounce the tetragrammaton, but uses surrogate terms such as Adonaya (Lord) or ha-Shem (the Name), which are translated in the form of Eternal or Almighty. Its pronunciation(s) and/or translations within Christianity are highly dependent on and distinct from worldview and denomination.*

The Pope read aloud. -These are answers to your questions so far, my children, which may have been raised with us during the war. Why are all these evil things happening to us? Why did we deserve this? The answer is in the Bible. Just as Judah and Jerusalem were in his hands, so now we are in his hands.

140

Scarlett wondered how he could talk such nonsense since we are at fault, these are all the consequences of our actions, not some Divine plague. It is not in vain that she does not go to church, she is not even Catholic. But she was curious about something, better said, at someone. But this someone was not the Vatican Pope. But Otto Tamayo, the pastor of Truro, whose eyes were as blue as hers, and even if the colour of his hair was no longer visible because of his discoloured old age. She traced his origins to his beard, which was red.

*"No temptation has taken you but such as is according to man's nature; and God is faithful, who will not suffer you to be tempted above what ye are able to bear, but will with the temptation make the issue also, so that ye should be able to bear it."*
*(1 Corinthians 10:13)*

Continued Otto Tamayo, pastor of the city. Scarlett's brain was ceasing to be in the right place, or just groping in the dark. All signs pointed to him. The description of the age, the genetic traits, and even the proud look indicated that Otto Tamayo was none other than Scarlett's blood father. Miranda's great love. The man who promised her his life there forever, but did not send a single letter after their breakup. Could it be because of Henry, her grandfather's tyranny? Did he blackmail him? Or was he unable to decide whether to choose a woman of love or his profession? Or maybe there was a completely different background to the matter? She only knew that she had to get to the bottom of it all. The man her mother had been waiting for all her life, the monster that had broken Miranda Bloom's heart, was now standing in front of her and she was unable to add any good thoughts to him.

*"I have strength for all things in him that gives me power."*
*(Philippians 4:13)*

It was read aloud by both of them. Then Mr. Tamayo spoke again alone: -Let us take our faith in the Lord, my children, for He is the Saviour, He is the One who gives us strength and we are comforted in these difficult hours! Now let's sing Psalm 51:14. In closing, our beloved Pope says a farewell prayer. -Everyone stood up except Scarlett, so stuck in her thoughts that she was unable to comprehend what was going on around her. She couldn't think for a minute other than her parents' secret. Does Otto Tamayo know about her existence at all? If so, why didn't he visit her? Why didn't he report, even if they should have to keep it a secret because of his call? She can keep a secret. Why did they do this to her? Scarlett thought about unanswered questions from the point that she realised that her assumptions were most likely true. If the Lord really only rolls obstacles that we are able to overcome, then why is she stuck? Why can't she get to the other side of the wall to see the sun? Why is she stuck in the dark?

# CHAPTER XXXI

-Dear workers, it is my great pleasure to give this gift, the intention to have fresh, clean water in everyone's jug every single day. This gift belongs to all of you. It is also the fruit of your work. After all, it would not have happened without you.

People around her began to cheer like never before. Some began to fly away after the speech, some tasted the water, and a few talked in small groups. Scarlett looked at them contentedly.

-Don't you think Miss. Bloom, you have given them too much lately?

-I just think they deserve it.

-Yes, but you also have to think about what you will do if you don't have something to give them or pay them. They can easily revolt if they are used to the good.

Scarlett was about to speak when a couple came to her for the promised renting home. To take over their new home, which was discussed weeks ago. Scarlett was about to set off with them when a man on horseback galloped toward them, so she just guided them and sent Nivek with them.

-Mr. Salvatore! How did the wind blow you here? - She asked, the man stopped his horse but he did not look at her.

-I come from Lord Quas, I thought I would have no problem shortening this way.

-Not in the least. -She was enthusiastic. -Isn't your intention to make up for the promised time for courtship?

-My time is so short that I don't even have it for myself. -He laughed sarcastically.

-I'm glad to hear because I don't have time to waste myself either for you, Sir. -She said now less enthusiastically but confidently. Thinking, the man responds back with something more pungent. But he didn't. Scarlett realised he meant what he said. -So, Lord and Lady Quas are back.

-As you say. They really like to go to Balls and celebrate. Usually, none are left out unless there is a very serious reason for it. In this case, too, they definitely want to be here at Mrs. Wolowitz's ball, they say they put a lot of emphasis on it. -As they talked, the horse moved from right to left, and the two spotted animals next to Scarlett became more and more irritated, so much so that they began to growl.

-I'm not surprised. She's been living for half a century.

-If you'll excuse me now. -He said, preparing to strike his horses with his reins. But he couldn't finish the operation and say goodbye to the girl, as her dogs, playful and mischievous puppies were so upset at the sight of the horse that no matter how much Scarlett tried to silence them, they caused jibber to the horse and George fall off. Scarlett immediately started shouting at the butlers, one in a hurry for the rider while the other after Mr. Salvatore's horse. Scarlett leaned next to the man to take a closer look at his condition. As she lifted his head, it was noticed that a bloodstain had formed on her gloves. This meant nothing more than serious injury. Scarlett was so terrified that she almost dropped the man's head.

*

Shortly after they reached Gracewith, Scarlett put a watery cloth on his forehead. They waited for another hour, but the doctor was nowhere to be seen, and the man was still lying unconscious on one of the beds in Scarlett's house.

-Miss. Bloom... -Matilda arrived in the room, Scarlett just shook her head that he hadn't recovered yet.

-What about the doctor?

-There is no news yet. -Matilda said anxiously. -The maids began to talk and come up with all sorts of stories about Mr. Salvatore's condition.

-What? What are they talking about? -She bounced off the bed on which the man lay.

-That the gentleman died, that he will die and that it is the Mistress's fault because you couldn't restrain the dogs.

-And what did you do? -She asked now irritably.

-Nothing, Miss. Bloom. -Matilda said regretfully.

-Then go and make them quiet! -Scarlett growled at the woman, who hurried out of the room.

Scarlett knelt beside the man's bed and began to pray, holding George's hands tightly.

*"Lord, I know I am not a good Christian and I sin many times. But if you really exist and I have done good things in my life, please don't take him. I beg you!"*

-Miss. Bloom. -A voice said softly. As she looked up, George's dark eyes looked back at her. Scarlett burst into tears of joy as soon as she saw that he had woken up.

-Miss. Bloom... -Matilda opened the door. -Doctor Bing, -she announced- had arrived. -And then let the man in.

He was half bald and had a thick white moustache, if anyone would look at him, wouldn't think he is a doctor. But in his confidence and speech, he seemed to understand his profession, Scarlett hoped this time the looks will not be deceiving.

-What did you establish? Is he going to be all right? -Scarlett asked anxiously.

-It's possible to have a concussion, but as I see it is just a minor alarm. -The man reassured her. Then Scarlett left them alone.

Scarlett was waiting in the hallway when Doris showed up. She saw the concern on her face.

-The doctor said he'll be fine, but he's in such bad shape. What if it caused permanent damage?

-Never give up hope. Yesterday was hard. Today is worse, but the days after will be sunshine.

Scarlett smiled forcedly, then stroked Doris. During this time, the doctor came out of the room, but as they did not notice, he cleared his throat.

-Mr. Salvatore... Well... -He said in slow words, and the two women became more and more excited. -Is fine! -They both sighed. -I bandaged his wounds. I told him too, but I'll tell you as well, he needs to rest. It is not recommended to get out of bed as he may feel dizzy or faint. The next... -But he couldn't finish what he wanted to say because Scarlett ran into the room.

When she reached the room, she staggered past the door, watching for a few seconds as he rested. But she couldn't do it for long because he felt her presence and turned to her.

-Miss. Bloom. -He said with his outstretched hand.

-Didn't you just change your mind and still come to my property during the day to spend the evening in my company? -She asked teasingly.

-Not in any case I wanted to meet a stubborn woman like you today. -He said, pinching her. Then they both started laughing.

# CHAPTER XXXII

Scarlett got up early in the morning. She waited nervously to visit Mr. Salvatore and know he was fine. She met one of the new maids who was carrying the gentleman's breakfast on a tray.

-Give it, I'll take it over. -She said, snatching the tray from her hand.

When she reached the door of the room, she first looked at the hallway window to see her reflection. Scarlett exchanged one or two expressions and swept away the lock of hair hanging in her eyes, then opened the door. But the room was empty. It took a few seconds to realise the situation and then hurried out the door. No one would have been able to prevent her hasty steps. When she reached the stairs, she stopped. He stood there at the junction, staring at the picture of Miranda. Approaching him slowly now, she said: -I thought you were in a hurry because you had more important things to do than spend the morning with me. -The man smiled flirtatiously at her.

-I was, but I saw this painting. At first, I thought it depicted you. -Scarlett felt a little uncomfortable. -But it can't approach your beauty. -He said making her smile again.

-She would be the famous Miranda Bloom. -She said, pointing to the painting.

-I've heard a lot about her. My aunt mentioned her a lot.

-Your aunt? They knew each other?

-Yes, as far as I know. But I don't want to hold you back, your breakfast cools. I should be on my way by now. -Kissing her hand, he started down the stairs, which were now intertwined.

-The doctor... -She said to the leaving man. -He suggested you have to eat on time, to schedule it. You know, it's important because you are very weak. Either way, you have a long way to go to Truro. -She said, pretending to be worried about the man's health.

-Well, then I think I'll have to keep that advice. -He said, putting his hat back on the hanger. Scarlett could have jumped for joy, but to keep her dignity she avoided this behaviour.

After breakfast, Mr. Salvatore offered a walk before he left. -We have nice weather for a morning walk. -They talk and joked a lot during their walk. Shortly after they left, they reached the part of the garden where Scarlett sprained her ankle. They both looked at the ground and searched for the mole hole in which Scarlett stumbled. But they were not found. They looked at each other laughing.

-You have to take care of this part of the garden in my absence. -He said jokingly.

-Yes, how lucky I am that you are here now. -She said for which he watched her with an interesting look. -I walk a lot more confidently this way, I know if I fall, I can rely on you.

-It wasn't here last time, right? -He asked, pointing to a white bench under the willow tree.

-Indeed, I recently put it here. -The girl took a seat next to George -Can I ask you something? Why didn't you come to visit me after the market incident? Were you really that busy? -She asked, squinting a little at George because of the strong sunlight.

-That was a stupid excuse, I confess. I had a totally different reason.

-Then, what happened?

-If I see you with someone else, it makes me completely wild. I lost my head. Even if I know that person is Leonard Wolowitz.

-Why would there be any cause for concern? -She asked jokingly. -Mr. Wolowitz didn't even get my attention.

-Miss. Bloom. I have to tell you something. -He said as he took Scarlett's hand. -When I'm with you, my heart beats fiercely and slowly at the same time. I feel like I've been lost before in my whole life. A man who just drifted with the tide. My dreams are the colour of your eyes. Miss. Bloom, I... -He tried to express how he felt, but the gardener walked over and disturbed the moment as he greeted them.

-Pardon, what did you say? -Scarlett asked.

-I, I have to go now. -He said as he got up from the bench and hurried away.

-Every word has consequences. Every silence, too. -Doris said, stepping beside her after a few minutes.

# CHAPTER XXXIII

In the afternoon, when George got home after finishing her job, Edith hurried in front of him when she saw him.

*

Scarlett flipped through her mother's diary again to see if she could find anything interesting about how to handle her workers. But she accidentally came across a page that was not about her work, her self-knowledge. It was a forgotten letter. A diary page that depicted a sketch of a letter. But this letter was different from one of the silent words she had written so far to her father, brother, or mother. It wasn't even for O.T.

> *"My dear rosebud,*
>
> *My only beloved child! I write this letter on the occasion of your first birthday. My nurturing love for you is immortal..."*

Scarlett was unable to continue reading because something that she suspected was her mother's tears had become unreadable. So, she flipped through.

*

-You didn't come home last night. -Declared Miss. Salvatore.

-That`s right.

-What happened to you? -She asked in a serious way, pointing to the man's head as he turned his back so he could hang the coat on the pronged.

-Nothing that should get my aunt's attention. -He said, stroking her shoulder confidently.

*

Scarlett continued to read the pages. Each page that was addressed to her ended after a few sentences. Words expressing Miranda's feelings usually appeared how much she loved and missed her, the year of her birthdays, or just the dates in the top right corner, so she knew she had written a letter for each birthday until she was 8 years old. So, it was almost a decade since Miranda Bloom, wrote a letter for her daughter every year on Scarlett's birthday, which she never sent.

*

-Please say you spent the night in a brothel and fought with another man to get the attention of a pretty lady. -She said, almost begging her nephew to lie to her, even though she guessed the most horrible truth.

-You well know, aunt, that I'm not going to such places unless it's for work. I'm surprised you assume something like this when you know I have other prospects in this area. -He spoke as he walked toward the library.

-I hope you didn't visit that red-haired little woman. -George didn't answer, so his aunt had to process everything that was going on around her and accept that the near future would get even more awful.

*

Folding the pages, Scarlett came across another letter Miranda had written, shortly before her death. This letter was different from the previous ones. This letter was complete, encompassing two pages. But not only the amount that caught her attention, but also that it was a pre-written letter. That was the letter Miranda had written ten years in advance. Her mother knew she would get her hands on the diary letter. She knew Scarlett would come to Gracewith, as well as to find out the truth about everything that had happened, and who she really is.

\*

-Georgie, you know that girl isn't for you. As well as wanting to take everything away from you.

-Aunt...

But Miss. Salvatore didn't let him speak. -Not George! -She said, lifting her palm and gesturing to listen. -This woman doesn't want you. She wants only to claim your fortune.

-Where do you still get all this from? -George asked insulted.

-Why do you think she keeps another iron in the fire? Why is she meeting Mr. Wolowitz? Although my eyes aren't very good, do you think I don't recognize it when a woman flirts? Do you think the way she talked to him was ordinary at the ball? I'm sorry to say but it was obvious. She was flirting with him and God knows with how many other men we don't know about.

-She was dismissive of him. She didn't dance with the man, no matter how much he forced it.

-Just because she wants to catch a bigger fish first. You would have her as your first wife. You have no past and your name is respected. You have serious friends. This is not the first time Lord Quas has asked you to become an MP.

-I don't want to become an MP... but that's not the point. Miss. Scarlett, is not who you think she is.

\*

153

*"My dear child,*

*I am writing this letter on the occasion of you becoming an adult. You need to know I never forgot you for a minute. I live in unpredictable hours. But of course, you already know all this. Your anger I guess will never be forgiven, but to understand why I didn't meet you; I have to explain what I felt..."*

*

-You could find much richer, more upscale and sophisticated ladies if you were an MP.

-I should have to win election first for that.

-I'm sure you would win the election. After all, there is no one in this city who would not like you.

-What do you mean there are no people who don't like me? There are dignitaries, take Mr. Thomas, for example, who has not spoken to me since I withdrew his request as a co-owner of my father's factory. Mr. Elmer, who doesn't like me because I dared to express my opinion about the silly idea that the river could not flow backward, at the mouth of a mountain that is sloping. It was a silly story... -He laughed- And what about Mr. Wolowitz? He's noble and has the voting right, he's a very influential man.

-Anything can be arranged with little money. And as far as Mr. Wolowitz and the other bloated so-called "nobles" are concerned, it's just about a few people, they can't stand up to those who like you. If you didn't have bad wills or so-called enemies, it would be a bit boring, right? So at least you know you're doing something right.

-Maybe you're right, aunt. But I won't be an MP. -He said, hoping to close the topic.

*

*"When you were born, I felt that day was blessed and cursed at the same time. After that monster Henry, took you from me, I knew I had to get back on my feet in order to have you back. After all, if I lie in bed and feel sorry for myself, it wouldn't bring you back. So, I got up, put on my mourning costume, and attended my mother's funeral. I had a complete desolate period at that time. As in the lands, as in my soul. I refused to feel it, hoping it would hurt less then. But now I'm lying here, on the bed, which is probably the place in this house where I'm resting for the last time, the room I'm seeing for the last time, and the faces I'm crying and cheering with for the last time. Never forget my dear, crying is not a weakness, crying means you are strong enough to show your feelings. To this day, I have been unable to realise this, I have been unable to experience it, when we mourn someone, that gives our hearts and minds peace. Never forget when the storm is raging and you feel like there is no way out. You will be fine. Storms do not last forever."*

*

-For the last time I want to tell you, that I don't want to see that girl in my house again.

-I thought this topic was closed.

-No, it's far from over. -She was angry- Do you think I won't recognize a perverse person if I see one? I've experienced so much. You're just a game out of Lord know, among how many besides Mr. Wolowitz.

-You're talking nonsense. -Said the man, trying to keep his blood cool.

-My God, how did she achieve that? How could she fool you that way, what happened that you can't see from the colourful clouds? You and that unfortunate Jewish man.

-That's enough! -He growled at her.

-I won't be quiet. I will express my opinion if you like it or not.

-Why do you have to ruin everything? -He asked looking deep into her eyes.

-Why do you have to be so naive? You saw the first day what she was like. When she walked with that... -She took a deep breath and then broke her words - You saw her with that coloured skinned. Things happen in front of your eyes, but you still don't notice them. And now you let her play the fool with you, while secretly meeting other men. Why do you think their servants call her "Mistress"?

-Don't be old-fashioned, we are not in the 17th century anymore. Unmarried women are called Mistress as well, who can manage to run their own business.

-Or you can call someone else's lover that way.

-I said it would be enough! -He shouted, sweeping away the things that stood on the dresser, on which he had relied so far.

*

*"It taught me to mourn my beloved partner, O.T, too. Oh, my dear only daughter. Never forget my little rose, your thorns are meant to protect yourself, not to stab others with them. Life is so cruel, always be on the lookout. Especially if a person collides with the kind of people, I've encountered in my life so far. If it hadn't been E., if she hadn't told my father the secret, if she hadn't revealed it, we could still be together now, I could see you growing up. O.T, my dear O.T, my little fox, my only love. I regret the day I couldn't tell him everything when I last saw him. How much I love him that I have always loved him. I'm sorry I didn't, maybe if you couldn't have a mother, I could have given you a chance to have a dad, but he never has known you existed. That damn E. ruined everything. I will never forgive Edith Salvatore for what she did to our*

*family. That she took everything from me that was most important to me..."*

*

When the maids arrived in the room, after they heard the crash to clean up, Mr. Salvatore left at the open door next to them. Edith told them to leave her alone, so the girls left soon. Miss. Salvatore went closer to the window, looked up at the moon, and said with tears in her eyes: -You've already taken from me the one I loved, the second time I won't let, Miranda.

# CHAPTER XXXIV

When she heard the horses galloping and the squeak of the carriage, she closed her mother's diary and hurried to the door. She burned with the urge to keep reading the letter, but considered it more important to greet Mr. Thaker. She wondered what news he had received about her family. When she reached the front door, the man was waiting next to his landau.

-I'm so glad you're back. What news did you bring? -She asked excitedly after hugging him, the man wasn't the hugging type, so he just patted her gently on the back.

-You have to see with your own eyes. -Scarlett looked questioningly at the old man in front of her, who stepped closer to the carriage door and opened it. Four children peeked out of the carriage. Scarlett gladly held out her arm to the children, but they sat in horror, motionless. Jared was the only boy among them. Of Scarlett's three brothers, it was the child of his middle brother, the only one in the family who had a son and would carry the Bloom name, is also the youngest child in the family, an infant Scarlett has seen about twice or three times before, the little boy may have been a few months old when she came to Gracewith. He was held on Julia's lap, who was the very first niece of Scarlett, around the age of ten. She held Jared in one hand and squeezed the hand of her sister, Riley in the other, who was no more than six years old, they were the children of her eldest brother. Opposite them sat a maid who was more than likely one of Mr. Thaker's subordinates, holding Anne's child, the little Aliona, on her lap. Although Aliona was Annes and the soldier's daughter, after she was born her mother decided to give her the Bloom name.

-Come on! -She gestured them out of the car as soon as she realised they wouldn't jump in her arms. They got out so she was able to hug them. -Come on in. -She pointed to the door where Doris was waiting for them. At first, the children stopped, then looked at Scarlett, who nodded reassuringly, so they approached the stranger with courage. Scarlett did not leave the yard until she was convinced that Mr. Thaker had set out for the house also.

-Come on, my dear ones, eat some soup. -Doris told the children, for which Mr. Thaker's maid added that they had recently eaten. -They are all bones and skin. -Doris said grimly again. Then they disappeared down the hall behind one of the doors. Scarlett and the man continued their journey to the library together.

-Tell me, how was your journey? -Scarlett asked with a smile.

-It was all right. But I don't think Miss you are curious about this. Rather, you want to know where the children's parents are. -He said, a little depressed.

-I can't deny, I'm really interested in why they're not here. -Scarlett said, opening the library door.

-Well, that's a bit of a long story.

-But are they fine? -Scarlett asked a little nervous.

-They passed away, Miss. Bloom. -The man declared, and Scarlett's eyes filled with tears, but the news didn't break her. She wouldn't let it go through her consciousness; she couldn't let anyone see her crying. As the man saw that Scarlett could handle the tension continued- The pastor of the village took all the children there during the occupation, into the convent. So, they were protected under the threat. 80% of those living there lost their lives during this time, including your mother, sister, and sisters-in-law. Only those survived, who left the village and those who lived in the monastery, since it is a holy place and the French themselves who were Christians did not desecrate it. But because of the famine, many children and nuns also died, they could not go outside the monastery without being shot, so they ate what they found inside. It would have been three weeks after you left, if you hadn't taken that opportunity maybe now you wouldn't be here either. -The man told her, for which why she had to sit down, Mr. Thaker poured her a glass of brandy, and then he took place in front of her and continued. -But that's not all, if you can stand it...

The man clasped his fingers. Scarlett took a deep breath and nodded wordlessly, knowing if she would speak it would break her. -I think you already know about your father's death. -Scarlett nodded silently again. - Mr. Andrew Bloom, the younger of your twin brothers, passed away. Mr. Aydan Bloom the youngest is missing. No one knows if he is dead or needs hospital treatment. The soldiers are already looking for him. -Scarlett looked at the bottom of the glass. -Mr. Elliot Bloom Junior, though, was transferred to the Serious Injury Department in Bath. He got a bullet in his head, he had three strokes, the doctors say one more and...

-He will die. -Scarlett finished the man's sentence. Scarlett looked at him with teary eyes.

-That's right. -He said depressed again ,looking to the floor. -My question is, what are your plans with the kids? There is an orphanage in Truro, they would have a good place there and you could visit them at any time. The monastery where the children were housed is also raising donations, and they also want to open an orphanage.

-They are staying. -Scarlett said softly.

-I hoped you would say that. Now, if you would excuse me, I have to go. When you are ready, please visit me to arrange the adoption papers. -Then he got up to leave, Scarlett escorted the man. As they reached the front door, she paused for a moment before closing the door and then shouting his name to the man, who was already turning his back, and said: *"Thank you!"*.

-Miss. Bloom. -Doris spoke from the kitchen door. Scarlett hurried over and saw that with the help of Matilda, the kids were eating with enthusiasm.

-All is well? -Doris asked anxiously when she saw her teary eyes.

-Oh, Doris... if you knew. -She said in a crying voice -Nothing is well. And that can't even be fixed.

Doris was unable to speak, so she hugged the girl in front of her. Scarlett felt the tears flow from her eyes like a waterfall. She pushed the woman away from her, then wiped her eyes quickly so she wouldn't see her tears. She blew her running nose, then said: -Make them the bed in a room, I wish they could all be together today. And tomorrow I'll decide who will get which room.

Doris knew what that meant, so she found it unnecessary to ask. But there was one thing she had to mention: -We don't have a cradle, Miss, and as I see, two would be needed.

-I think you'll solve it. -She said, stroking her shoulder as she passed Doris and with a forced smile, she smiled at her. -And let's not forget to appoint a nanny tomorrow. Think about who would be right for this position. -Then left at the back entrance.

*

Doris has solved the cradle problem by pushing two armchairs together in no time. Matilda and two other maids bathed the children. Matilda called Doris to her and pointed to the children's condition. Riley was the one she had just rubbed with soap when she noticed the tiny stains on her body, and then she pointed out that she was so skinny that the ribs on the side could be grasped almost one by one. Doris bent down and stroked the child's face, looking at Matilda only and she said: -She's going to be all right; I can assure you; we will do our best to help them through this condition as soon as possible. -The other two maids made the bed.

As she prepared the room, Doris noticed, standing by the window, that Scarlett was still in the garden. She sat on a bench in the shade of a willow tree. Doris couldn't see her from the tall tree, but she knew for sure why she was still there.

-You cannot be strong all the time. Sometimes you just need to be alone and let your tears out.

# CHAPTER XXXV

Scarlett hadn't slept almost all night wondering what to do now. Early in the morning, after the maids had even woken up, she was already dressed in the hallway waiting for the carriage driver. Doris was just walking around when she saw her with the luggage in her hands.

-Miss. Bloom, will you leave us? -She asked in fright.

-Only until next weekend. I'm visiting Elliot at the hospital. Please take care of the kids in my absence. Advertise that we are looking for a nanny and when I return, I will interview them. I left money with Nivek that should be enough to cover the costs during my absence. I also made it clear to him to buy only cradles that are suitable for three years old children. -She said as the driver waited outside at the door with an umbrella.

-But Miss., we don't know anything about these kids...

-You'll get to know them. -She said, closing the door behind herself.

*

Jolting in the carriage, all the way she was thinking how to tell the children the truth when she returned.

The next morning, when the carriage stopped again in a small town, Scarlett got out to look around, while the driver drank and rested the horses. She passed through a marketplace to buy some food. On the way, she saw a red-haired family. It was a poor family, but they seemed very happy. Laughing, the father ran after his daughter, chasing her, who was about five years old with long red hair, then picked her up in his arms, kissed her all over, then

163

put her in his neck, then they continued on their way after the mother joined them. Scarlett was deeply affected by what she saw. This time she wondered if she could have such a happy family as well. In all likelihood, if Edith Salvatore wouldn't intervene. She didn't know if she could have hated more for what she had done or she was more pathetic for it, because she thought that if the man, she loved could not be hers, he cannot be other's either. How could she get into a convent with a priest? How could she talk face to face with Mr. Otto Tamayo to tell him who she really was and what her mother had described. Next to the fish stall, she dreamt about what the man who was most likely to be her father would receive the fact that they are related to each other and what would he do with that information.

*

While Doris was feeding the kids, someone was angrily knocking on the door. First, Doris walked to the door in fear, when there was a weeping silence near the door, she approached it with a raised wooden spoon. When she was next to it, someone started knocking again, which shook her completely. As she peeked out of the ambush hole, she calmly lowered the spoon from her hand. Mr. Salvatore burst in uninvited.

-I'm looking for Miss. Bloom. -He said, then hurried to the library.

-The Mistress is out of the house. -Doris said after him, so he turned around.

-Then I'll wait until she gets home. -Raised his hat to put it on the hanger, but he almost froze when Doris answered his question. -Where did she go?

-She won't be home until next weekend. She said something, about someone called Elliot, she said she was going to visit him in Bath.

The man nodded understandingly, then walked back from the hanger toward the entrance. There was frustration on his face.

-Do you want me to deliver any messages? -Doris asked as she accompanied him.

-Not necessary. You don't even have to report that I was here. -He said, sitting back on his horse's back, then left. After all, how could he ask her to do it when Scarlett visits other men, why would he ruin her happy hours by saying he came to confess his feelings and doesn't matter how much her aunt opposes this romance he is willing to stand up for it, even if as a result the wealth his aunt owns will never be his. He was able to give up everything, as in the story written in Romeo and Juliet. He couldn't, because he didn't even know Scarlett really wanted him, especially since he had so many competitors. And now he was unsure of what he wanted either. Could it be that his aunt was right?

-Anything and everything that belongs to you, will find you. Patience. -Doris said as watched him leaving, then closed the door.

# CHAPTER XXXVI

It was a pretty dirty and overcrowded hospital. There were plenty of soldiers there. Many of them were in a state that if someone saw it, they would say they are not going to see tomorrow's sunlight. A large number of patients with disabilities and nervous breakdowns were being treated. It made Scarlett feel like she was walking in an asylum. One of the men had to be restrained in bed while his medication could be pushed down his throat. He roared, cried and shouted why couldn't they give him a bullet in the head and kill him on the spot. Scarlett was completely horrified to see it all. The nurse stopped beside the fully-head bandaged man's bed.

-Mr. Bloom a visitor has arrived! -The nurse told the patient kindly.

Elliot's face was so bandaged up that it was unrecognizable. Barely a small hole was cut at his eyes, nose, and mouth. Elliot Bloom's head was so injured that the bullet had to be removed. And there were complications during the operation so that his wound began to become completely infected and affected every single part of his face. Because of the rust that has penetrated the bloodstream. There were also easily visible wounds on other parts of his body. Which forced the blood vessels to swell from the coagulated blood, to burst in some places where internal bleeding occurred under the skin. The doctor also prepared Scarlett before visiting, that these could be Elliot Bloom's last hours, the blood clotting could reach his brain at any time and another stroke could happen, which will be his last one and they would be unable to save him because his brain would not get enough oxygen. He also said that if this does not happen first then it will attack his lungs, although in this way a blood mass could mean that his lungs will be unable to perform their functional allowing him to survive. The man will not breathe and will die. He was a great doctor who explained everything to Scarlett in detail (perhaps too much in detail).

-Hey, little robin! -He said with a laugh drowning in coughing. Scarlett just smiled, unable to speak. She sat on his bed and took her brother's hand. -I heard what happened in the village. Is everyone all right? -He asked in hoarseness.

Scarlett always argued with her siblings that a merciful lie is also a lie. His brothers were always in some trouble, so they were forced to fib to their parents. This is what they called a merciful lie. She never thought she would get the chance once to lie to anyone. But now she's here, sitting on her brother's deathbed, holding the hand of a half-dead man. Yet which is the better way, to tell the truth, and let him suffer even more or lie and protect him from this horrible news?

-They are well. -She looked at him with teary eyes.

The man lying on a bed next to Elliot's bed lifted his head from his book and looked at Scarlett.

-My daughters? I think they're pretty big already. -Scarlett nodded with a smile. -They will be the smartest kids in the world. Would you tell them how much I love them? My poor brother didn't even live the day to see his child. Does he have a son? -Scarlett nodded silently again, but a tear appeared on her face. The man next to them had now closed his book -And Mary? My wife? Is she still just as beautiful, as always?

Scarlett covered her brother and smoothly stroked his bound face. -Relax a little, don't strain yourself.

-Is she all right? -Scarlett didn't answer, just wiped her tears. -Mary, my Mary. Is she alive? -He shouted in dismay. But Scarlett just cried, so bitterly that the people around them looked at them with tears in their eyes.

-She is fine. -Scarlett said softly.

-And mom? Will she bake a delicious sponge cake, like she used to do at Christmas when I go home? -Elliot knew what was waiting for him, but it was good for him to play with the idea that he would be in a happy family again. Scarlett just nodded again. -We'll be sitting all around the table again, singing Christmas carols and you, little robin, will be playing the piano for us, playing our favourite songs over and over again, and Julia will be sitting next to you again like she used to, learning one or two songs. She misses the keys; she hits them incorrectly in your perfect song. We'll tell stories, the kids will run and chase each other around the table, the way we did at their age. We'll say poems and laugh a lot while the Christmas turkey is roasting.

Scarlett cried more and more bitterly, unable to stop when she needed to, she was immeasurably angry with herself, but the memories her brother recalled had broken her old wounds so much that at the moment Scarlett thought she would never be able to heal again.

-Merciful lies. That's what I need now. -Said the man with teary eyes. -Thank you! Thanks, Scarlett! -His voice became duller and then ceased, as did his breath. Scarlett was unable to hold back anymore, and she flew as if a waterfall was running down her cheek, her body felt like she was standing in the middle of a burning fire, and a storm was raging in her head that would pick up all Gracewith at once. The patient on the bed next to them began to clap, causing all the surrounding patients to join in that wing. That's how they saluted Elliot Bloom.

# CHAPTER XXXVII

Scarlett always tried to seem confident, in her social life as in her private life. After all, children need another support, a person they can look up to, providing safety and peace of mind. She tried at all costs to abide by her principles, but whenever she was left alone, she felt a failure. She had so far been unable to understand what parents were going through, yet she thought her mother had been relieved of this responsibility and that was one of the main reasons they had not reunited as a family. She thought that in fact her mother secretly did not want to get her back.

After the kids ran themselves out of the room, they were escorted by the new nanny, Daphne, who looked like a very pretty and kind person, yet Scarlett felt she shouldn't be underestimated. A blonde girl with bluish brown eyes, with fuller lips than normal women have, she always looked like she was scheming in something. After they left, Scarlett was left alone with Doris.

-So, she is the chosen one.

-That's correct. -Scarlett put down her cup of tea on the table.

-Why her?

-Well, I would like to say a lot of reasons, but I can't. After I interviewed her, I felt somehow sorry for her. I asked of course, like any other candidate if she can read and write. Her response caught my attention. Her family is very poor, but still, from the money she made at the farm, she bought books, and she learnt alone to read and write. She jumped up from the chair and went to the bookshelves and took a book to prove to me, I didn't even have to ask for it. I can see that she is very diligent and more than a farmworker.

169

-She looks smart... -Doris looked after them through the window.

-But that is not the whole story. I met Mr. Meadow, he said that he heard that I hired his niece, Daphne Jelon. He wasn't delighted by the news. He said to take care with her. Since then, I have had no idea what to think about this whole decision.

-I cannot comment on this. If you think that you can rely on that man's words...

-I don't know either what to say.

For a while there was silence between them, Scarlett looked very thoughtful, for which Doris had to ask her.

-You are so far away again Miss. Bloom. -She said kindly as she cleaned the table.

-Do you think I'm doing something wrong? -She answered with a question.

-What do you mean?

-The kids are so cheeky with me. I don't feel I'm respected enough. And I try so hard. Not to mention the teachers, they will not stay until the next lesson, everyone is running away from them. Last time, imagine Riley screwed up a paper ball in class, throwing it at the teacher, when he called her to punish her by hitting her hands, with the ruler, of course, her sister, Julia, was in her defence, so he should have punished her, too. Then, when the teacher called her in advance because she responded like an heir of the throne, standing above everyone else, she said it would have consequences if he did it. Then when the teacher asked her to show her hand, she raised her head in a wordlessly proud way. The teacher said, holding out his ruler, that at one end of the ruler is a runaway, unemployed, hopeless person who is not even able to make sense of their own future. Do you know what was her answer? -Doris just looked at Scarlett questioningly. -She asked him which person at the end of the ruler? Can you imagine a ten-year-old girl saying that? -She explained as she gestured with her hands.

Doris laughed hard. -She is a very smart girl.

-And immeasurably stubborn and wilful. -She said, a little angry.

-Doesn't she remind you of anyone? -She asked, gesturing with her index finger.

-I have no idea what I should do differently. They are much worse than when they arrived. They were such little angels when we lived at home.

-Everybody thinks the children are angels until they get one. They've only been here for two weeks. Give them time, they recently found out that their parents had passed away, and they were still unable, in my opinion, to process what had happened. -Doris said kindly as she folded a kitchen towel.

-Maybe you are right.

-The Miss is very much there. Maybe you settle on them too much, give them a little distance, they're not used to it.

-I will do like that.

-Miss. Bloom, you're a good woman, who has a huge heart.

-You know there is no honey for your sweet words. -She smiled teasingly, and then they both laughed.

*

Later, Scarlett went out to the farm and did her weekly inspection routine. Matt, a younger-than-allowed worker, whom she was unable to fire, collected a basket of eggs, and then went to the cart. The basket in the hands of that tiny kid was almost as big as him, but he coped with the task.

-Can I help you? -She asked as she approached him.

-Don't worry about me, Miss. They say the pepper is small but strong. -Said the boy, raising the basket with a deep breath. Scarlett just smiled.

-How many baskets have you collected?

The little boy just put the basket on the cart, which will soon be at the market for sale, and the other will be delivered to Scarlett's customers, which can hold twice as many products as the cart that went to the market.

-I have a lot to do. -The child said after a half-minute break. -I still have to feed the poultry and I will have to clean the pen's as well.

-I understand. But still, how many eggs are in those baskets?

-Did I tell you that, you have a lot of brooders again, Miss? If you are lucky by mid-summer, there will be so many little chicks again that will make up for the loss of those that the rats stole.

-How many baskets did you put on the carts? -Scarlett asked a little impatiently.

-Did I tell you before I stuffed the holes, but the  damn rats pushed it out again? I'll fasten it stronger today.

-You can't count, right? -She asked with her hands on her hips.

Matt lowered his head and sniffed his stuffy little nose sadly, but as it didn't help, he grabbed his wool sweater between his fist-clenched fingers and smeared his mucus on it.

-Who counted them so far? That would be your job.

-Mr. Nivek, after he found out that I couldn't count, took on this part of my job. -When he looked at Scarlett and saw her surprise, he continued. -But believe me, I work for my money, and even clean most of the eggs that are very dirty almost shiny.

# CHAPTER XXXVIII

-Good morning, Mr. Thaker! -She stumbled into the man's office unexpectedly.

-Miss. Bloom, what a surprise! - The man expressed his joy to see the girl again- How do you feel?

-Excellent. This early summer weather is to my liking. -She said, looking out the window.

-Please have a seat. -The old gentleman pointed to the empty chair in front of him- Tell me, how's the farm going?

-It is blooming, surprisingly. Imagine, one day I went to see the lands myself. You were right, the weather was really good and we didn't sow those many seeds unnecessarily. All of them sprouted, many of them growing tremendously due to the good rain in May. And in fact, it was already the first mowing on alfalfa land. If all goes well, there will be more forage this year than expected. -She said enthusiastically- I'm grateful for your help. -She said to Mr. Thaker in a slightly restrained, more serious voice- I wouldn't be where I am now without you.

-I always help where I can. -He smiled.

-Thank you!

-You become a real woman here, Miss. Bloom. -Mr. Thaker said in all seriousness, and Scarlett smiled just from the edge of her mouth.

-Not enough, for that matter. -She said a little depressed- I'm having the kids for three weeks now. I failed as a guardian. That's why I haven't come to sort the papers so far.

-Miss. Bloom, I'm not urging you. The deadline is three months. Give the kids more time as well as for yourself. You should be always true and original, because no one can replace you. Work hard. Stay disciplined and be patient. Good times are approaching.

-You are such a wise man, Mr. Thaker.

-You know the proverb: "What the elders see while sitting others cannot see while standing on their toes."

-I've never asked how you met my aunt.

He clenched his lips between his teeth and took a deep breath with his eyes closed.

-She was a dear friend of mine. -He said, turning his head to the side, then opening his eyes and looking at Scarlett with his sea-blue eyes, which, filled with tears, resembled a wild sea full of deep waves. With waves that revived memories, Scarlett thought it was better not to ask.

*

After leaving the man's office, she walked through the market straight to the Catholic church. When she got there, she told one of the nuns why she had come. The nun led her to the confessional booth and asked her to wait there. At first, she wondered what to say. But she knew it was better not to think too much about things, just to let them come on their own. After a few minutes, she heard someone come to the other side. Mr. Otto Tamayo's voice spoke, saying a prayer. At the end of the prayer, he said: -List your sins, my child, your words before the Father, the Son, and the Holy Spirit will be heard, your sins will be forgiven, and your heart will be relieved under your burdens. -As she heard these words, Scarlett's first thought was that the pastor mentioned the Holy Spirit as if it were a third person. She read a lot about the beliefs of different religions and was aware that "the three main branches of

Christianity: Roman Catholic, Eastern Orthodox, and Protestant"
-worship a three-person God: God the Father, God the Son, and
God the Holy Spirit. Christian theology argues that this does not
acknowledge the existence of three Gods, but that these three
persons are essentially one. In her whole life, Scarlett believed that
the power of God, which he writes of in the Book of Acts: "filled
with the Holy Spirit upon everybody," is logically a kind of Divine
active power. She had never heard of it before being used this way,
but she also accepted that many religions believed that Jesus, the
only begotten Son of God, was the Father himself, the Lord. Scarlett
let go of what she heard.

-You know, Father, I didn't come to confess my sins. It would be
something else.

-We're all guilty, my child. You don't have to be afraid to
admit everything you're trying to hide from yourself. In life, we
have to talk to someone about the things that are pressing on our
hearts. *"Cast thy burden upon the LORD, and he shall sustain
thee: he shall never suffer the righteous to be moved" (Psalm
55:22).*

-Maybe my only sin is to fall in love with a man with whom we
may never have a future together. -Scarlett waited for the man's
reaction, but he didn't answer- Only because this information got
into the ears of a person who opposes our covenant.

-Maybe that's how it should have been. The Lord has other plans
for you, Miss, you will be called for something else. -He spoke
again, but this time in a sad voice.

-And if it shouldn't be like that? If there is a way to change our
future? -She raised her hand and placed it on the side of the booth
where Otto Tamayo was.

-Everything is written in advance in the book of our lives, the Lord
takes care of us.

-If that's what father thinks... -She said in a semi-hushed voice
-Didn't you think you could change your future, but you miss the
chance? If you could see the love of your life again and have a
chance to tell her how you feel, would you do it?

-If there is an opportunity for this, Miss, it means nothing more
than that our Father gives you another chance. Which, of course,
you can choose of your own free will. The Lord opens two paths
for you and chooses which one will draw your heart to. There is
no bad or good way. Every path the Lord reveals to us is only a
good path.

-If there was a way that a man you had never seen or knew,
wanted to be a part of your life. Do you think that's the work of
God?

-I see the chance. -He said, a little confused.

-Mr. Tamayo, I have to admit something to you. In fact, I didn't
come to talk about my own love life, much more about yours. I
found out that Miranda Bloom, the former owner of Gracewith,
wanted to tell you, but she was never able to do it. She has always
loved you, all her life. -Scarlett left the booth, the pastors with
some hesitation, did the same.

-Miranda? -He whispered when he saw her.

-My name is Scarlett Miranda Bloom, I'm Miranda Bloom's and
O.T., i.e. Otto Tomayo's daughter. -The nuns around them were
all watching them with their mouths open.

-This is a misunderstanding, Miss, I don't have children.

-I thought you wouldn't believe me, I know about your brothel
night you've spent together, that was the night I conceived. -The
nuns have now begun to whisper and be horrified. -I know it's not
some compelling memory, but that's the truth, Miranda wrote

everything in her diary, wait and look. -Then she began to search her basket.

-Say nothing more. You commit transgression and humiliate and even slander a person who is a servant of God. Aren't you ashamed of yourself, Miss? I should have known at that moment when you entered that door that you are a troublemaker. -Then pointed to the door of the church- This case violates a law in which the victim is me and only me. You wouldn't get out of it without messing up your name, Miss. And above all, the fire of hell is said to be much hotter than the fire on earth. -If something Scarlett didn't like, it was nothing more than a threat to hell. Yet who is the fool who believes in it? If there is a father who is truly as forgiving and loving as a parent, would he allow you to suffer forever in a place that is hurting you? Sure, a parent will punish you, but he wouldn't want or even hurt you that much. And more importantly, he wouldn't do something worse than passing away (death) to you.

Scarlett stopped searching without a word, knowing that if she could prove her truth, the pastor would lose his followers, pollute the religion in which he found his place, and it would ruin his life, even more, himself.

*"But thou, O God, shalt bring them down into the pit of destruction: bloody and deceitful men shall not live out half their days; but I will trust in thee" (Psalm 55:23).* -Otto Tamayo said, looking up at the ceiling as Scarlett went outside.

# CHAPTER XXXIX

She thought Mr. Tamayo was disgusting and unworthy of his profession, a man who didn't even know what he was talking about, and his knowledge of the Bible was equal to zero. She who does not consider herself a strong believer, who does not go to church and doubts the existence of God, believes that her views and logical interpretation based on the verses of the Bible are more correct than the man, who was raised up in faith before, and who surrendered himself to serve the Lord. It was the first time her confidence that she could have any relationship with this man was shaken. Otto Tamayo was nothing more than a clown, a half-hearted man who tried to convince people that God was real, that war was a blow to them, and that they would all burn in hell. He might be right in some things, but still, he is not worthy of his profession. It is always messy, if there is someone in a family who contaminates the family name, just the same Scarlett thought is with Otto Tamayo, he contaminates the religion although is a sin, many people may judge the whole religion because of a man.

She had a lot of things to do around the farm, especially as the fruits began to ripen, she struggled a lot with the kids, not to mention that Mr. Wolowitz's ball was also around, where she was more than likely going to have to face Evelyn Quas.

She walked toward the kitchen when she accidentally heard a conversation between Daphne and another maid, in which Doris intervened.

-Doris, would you put for me aside a little of the delicious cottage cheesecake the princess asked for?

-You want to say, Miss. Bloom, right? -She asked, getting closer to them. -Wouldn't you like to lie in her soft bed? To take a hot bath to lubricate your skin with all sorts of expensive soaps and creams that make your skin so soft? Don't you think you want to have dinner in bed tonight? -She asked with sarcasm in her voice.

-I don't mind. But you have to know I don't share the bed; I don't like roommates. -Daphne said, and they both laughed. -And the cream isn't like they say I smeared my hands with it last time and they haven't been so soft. -She said, as Doris wanted to ask a kind of *"How dare you?"* question, but she could only open her mouth to speak as Scarlett entered the room, there  was a deep silence, and they both jumped up from their seats. Doris raised an eyebrow in a *"Now let's see, princess how big your mouth is"* way.

-I'm glad to see that you have nothing else to do but spend your time discussing my soaps and creams. The fire was almost extinguished in the library, -she looked at the maid, who had run out the room to do her work- and if I heard right, the kids got up from their afternoon nap. -She looked at Daphne, now- And to let you know my body lotion is really as good as they say. It is just not for the hands of nannies or maids. -She said, then left.

-Is it so bad that you dare to dream? -She asked, turning to Doris.

-There's nothing wrong with dreams if you can control them and you don't forget your place. You're just a nanny in this house, who sometimes takes on the role of a maid for some extras, as opposed to Miss. Bloom who owns this house and who's our employer. Rather, be glad you found a job at all during the war.

-You want to say this house and your owner too. -She said grimly, which Doris didn't look at with good eyes, but she tried to ignore. -And if she were a real sophisticated lady, she wouldn't have set foot in the kitchen.

-And if you would respect your employer, you wouldn't be so cheeky. Rather, give thanks for not being fired.

# CHAPTER XL

-Does Miss. Bloom think this is a good idea? -Doris asked as she dressed Scarlett in the burgundy dress.

-Why not? -She asked, arranging her dress.

-Do not seek revenge, Miss. The rotten fruits will fall by themselves.

-Don't be silly, there's no such thing.

-Miss. Please, promise yourself to be so strong that nothing can disturb your peace of mind.

-I promise. -Then she turned back in front of the mirror to beauty herself further.

-You can come out bitter or you can come out better. There is purpose in your pain. -Doris said softly as she admired Scarlett in her dress, which made her even more gorgeous by the string of pearls.

*

This day has finally arrived. Mrs. Agatha Wolowitz's 50th Birthday. Celebrated with an infamous masquerade ball. Many kinds of people appeared at the ball, nobles, aristocrats, judges, MPs, all kinds of rich and wealthy people, including counts. Scarlett had never been to Mr. Leonard Wolowitz's estate before, at the mysterious man's home, so she didn't even know he was living in her neighbourhood. Scarlett didn't know how much wealth the tall and incredibly handsome man had, nor how influential he was. The ballroom was huge, the ballroom of

Lord Quas could not even be approached this. Most people wore masks, everyone wore their most beautiful galas and most wore wigs, including Scarlett.

*

A stairway leading to the ballroom was at least five metres wide. Scarlett walked down on it, holding her burgundy dress in one hand and a mask in the other, which she had now lifted from her face. The confidence she radiated penetrated the ballroom, as if Miranda Bloom herself had walked into the hall, straight from Gracewith's painting hanging on the wall. She still looked eerily like her mother, and since she had just hit her hair colour when choosing a wig and sewed for herself a dress that her mother once shone with, she stunned the nobles inside, but most of all Miss. Edith Salvatore. Lady Quas, was in the company as well, within Scarlett's horizons, but she was just smiling at her, like an old friend, perhaps she was most impressed by her ability to scandalize people who once knew Miranda Bloom. Until addressed, she reflected on her mother's reflection. As soon as she reached the bottom of the stairs, Mr. Wolowitz was already waiting there.

-Miss. Bloom, you are glamorous tonight. Tell me, as you took off your mask, who would you like to depict?

-I hid in Miranda Bloom's skin for an evening. -She said proudly.

-Don't consider me intrusive...

-Yes, she was my aunt. The famous Miranda Bloom, whose works, men did not look at with good eyes, they could not tolerate her, it was difficult for them to accept that a woman could manage better her business than they did with their own.

-It really appeared to be known. -He said, returning her smile. -I'm glad you came.

-So I am. -She said, looking at Edith Salvatore, who was in the company of the other ladies who were gossiping about Miranda and her. Stressing that this dress was already tasteless when Miranda wore it at her first ball. But Edith wasn't like the other women, rumoured left her cold, she seemed to think of another revenge, her glass was never full for a long time. Lady Quas was the other person who didn't share their opinion. Although Scarlett was rude to her, her opinion did not change towards Scarlett, she told the ladies that it was an honour for Miranda and that the dress looked really good on Scarlett. She was not far from hearing every single word that penetrated her heart. She realised how she misjudge Lady Quas.

-Let me introduce my mother, Mrs. Agatha Wolowitz! -He said, pointing to the woman approaching them. Her face was covered with a mask so she couldn't see it, Scarlett was politely waiting, but when it was time for Leonard to introduce Scarlett, the woman suddenly fainted. The people there all gathered around. Leonard and another man were soon taken out of sight, Scarlett wasn't sure, but she thought she had been taken to a room.

People all started a deep conversation about what happened or continued on their own topic. Scarlett had no desire for women at all so she thought she would try to fit in elsewhere. She targeted the company of Lord Quas, which consisted of six men and two women. But as soon as she began to approach them. Most of the men turned their backs on her, Lord Quas looked at her with regret, but he could do nothing else. He knew the truth too, that most people didn't like Miranda Bloom.

-Don't think you can fool me, Miranda. Everyone knows what kind of person you really are. You knew I loved him, and you took him from me. But I won't let you take George away from me, remember this one well. -Scarlett became completely goosebumps when she heard these words, but she didn't let Edith intimidate her, her confidence didn't waver for a minute.

-Really? Then maybe you can even admit, if you're already so immersed in the subject, that you betrayed them because you didn't want the man you loved to be someone else's if he couldn't be yours anymore. But let's face it, it wasn't up to you, because O.T. didn't love you, Miss. Salvatore, he loved Miranda. -She said all these words hoping Edith will ensure her that O.T. is Otto Tamayo or not.

-There was a time when he only saw me and only me in front of his eyes. That was the first ball, your first ball that changed everything. Damn it! -She shouted as many people looked at them, but as if nothing had happened, they tried to continue discussing their subject.

-Did he ever tell you he loves you? -She stepped closer to Edith, but she was speechless -Just as I guessed. It was a platonic love, but with Miranda... You were unable to watch their happiness. And you had to ruin it, as well as a child's life. You took everything from Miranda in a selfish way. -Edith was gasping for words, but she couldn't say anything meaningful, she couldn't make a single excuse for her actions. -And do you know why you were never happy in your damn life? Because you have no heart. -Scarlett said, then turned away because she could no longer look into the eyes of the woman who ruined her whole life. She left pushing through the people gathering there, including pushing Evelyn Quas aside.

Miss. Edith Salvatore began to cry in front of the company. As Scarlett tried to escape the place where she was hated by half of the room who didn't even know her, someone grabbed her arm. It was Mr. Leonard Wolowitz.

-Are you feeling well, Miss? -Scarlett looked silent, not wanting to let the man down again, so she hesitated to leave. When she looked to the right, Lady Quas approached them, and when she looked to the left, Mr. Salvatore moved every step closer to them. Neither of their company she really wanted, so she pretended not to notice them and looked at the man in front of her again.

-Let's dance! -She said, but didn't expect an answer, she grabbed his hand and pulled him straight into the crowd on the dance floor.

The women stood side by side and the men in front of them in a line. As soon as the music started, the dance began. They didn't talk too much, sometimes they exchanged a few words when it was time to dance with each other.

-How is your mother feeling? I didn't see a doctor arrive. -She asked, pretending to care. All she really cared about was to get out of that place as soon as possible and forget about this whole evening. She regretted the most that Mr. Thaker was not present to encourage her.

-She's a little ill, but nothing serious. She asked me to carry on with the ball until she feels better.

George, seeing the movements and gestures during the dance, decided to retreat, not intending to interfere in a romance that was emerging. When Scarlett saw Mr. Salvatore retreat and almost melt into the audience staring at the dancers, she knew everything was lost. When she saw the man that this dance was about, it was as if a dagger had pierced his heart, Scarlett's eyes filled with tears. Mr. Wolowitz noticed the eye contact.

-I see Mr. Salvatore regrets not asking for it sooner. -He tried to joke.

-Mr. Salvatore, doesn't matter anymore. -She said with a forced smile, the man looked questioningly, but Scarlett didn't explain.

As a testimony that it wasn't just a man who wanted her to his side, Scarlett pulled her partner, Leonard closer and looked into his eyes as they danced, as if she really cared about him. She hoped that as a result of this incident, George would come to his senses and realise that he should not wait. But on the contrary, her plan failed, Mr. Salvatore disappeared completely from her sight, and his aunt's claims grew stronger in him.

# CHAPTER XLI

On an early Monday morning, Scarlett held a meeting with her employee before they got to work. Doris stood beside her, as usual, but now a few steps away, as Scarlett was guarded by her dogs, her large, spotted friends on either side. Although this breed of dog is basically hilarious and friendly, they say they are not a one-man dog because they are extremely active, agile, and playful, Mr. Meadow has deftly trained them as guards. But he was right when he said they were a sensible, docile, and very affectionate race. They insist on being with Scarlett so much that when they are not with her, it is necessary to lock them up so that no one is attacked, partly because there has already been an example of this.

-I wish everyone a good morning! -Scarlett said with a wide smile.

Many returned good wishes, except for Mr. Meadow, who was the only one who pulled his mouth saying, "*Good, good for you*".

-I am pleased to announce that the crop is thriving, the lands are covered with shoots, all the strong growth has been due to the rains and especially to those who have contributed with their hard work. After all, we all know that sowing began late, so the diligent hands that worked on them deserve praise. But that's not the only reason you're here this morning, even though I didn't call you together at the usual time. What I want to say, here, this morning is that... -Then she thought for half a minute how to continue- I know your children can't get an education, so I want to offer a great opportunity.

People were amazed at Scarlett's offer, and some people commented, saying: "*We don't have the money for that. If we can write and read it doesn't put bread on the table yet. We can't eat books. Our kids will work, they can't waste their time on something like that."*

Scarlett, of course, didn't leave it speechless, she couldn't let go because she knew how important education was to secure a better future for them, and what she regretted most about this topic, was that her nieces were thinking like these people, a waste of time. She knew she had to prove it to everyone to see they are wrong, especially her nieces.

-I know, a lot of you think it's a waste of time. But I insist that they will be able to secure a better and more safe future with this. The other day, I met a very intelligent kid who unfortunately can't count. So, someone else took over the task of counting the goods instead. Do you think it's right that someone else takes part of your job just because you can't count? People can appreciate salary, but why? Because they need it. You know what the money that gets into your hands looks like, but do you know how much you owe, how much goes out of your hands? How many of you have ever thought, that someone could defraud you for such a small thing? Have you ever wondered how a doctor becomes a doctor? Does a priest use only his own words, or does he really read the principles of the Bible during the Mass? How does the banker count that amount of money?

There was a disturbing silence among the people until Mr. Meadow spoke.

-Our kind can never become a banker or a doctor. This is a written rule. -He said with some irony in his voice.

-In my opinion, we are capable of anything if we believe. You all know what kind of life I lived before I came to Gracewith.

-But the Mistress inherited. -The man spoke again, and many nodded in agreement or agreed softly.

-It's true, I came here by inheritance. But here I became who I am now, restarting the farm on my own. It took a lot of time and learning, but I did it and now I'm here. I developed the once deserted and ruined area into a thriving place. Think about it, if one cannot read, write, even count, there is so little chance of getting into a noble house as a governess, butler, cook, or even a maid, just as a fly to make honey. -There was silence among the people again. -Is there anyone else who doubts? -Scarlett looked at the people, but no one spoke- Mr. Meadow? -She looked at the grim man, but he was silent, then someone spoke, she was an older woman, she looked middle-aged, she covered her grey hair with a scarf, and her wrinkles began to become more and more prominent as she stepped closer.

-We don't have money for that. -She said restrained, the others muttered under their noses again in agreement.

Scarlett took a deep breath, looked around again, and saw the frustrated faces of the people. She knew they were telling the truth because they wore ragged clothes and usually if they got any closer to her, they looked like tired workers who had never done anything else in their life, than farming and raising animals.

-Teaching is free of charge. I will teach them the basics myself. And if they want to learn more, then we can talk about that, but we have to see how much they're developing first. Starting tomorrow, at 10 a.m. after they finished their job until 3 p.m. I'll be waiting for them in the barn at Gracewith every weekday. I will also have paper and pencil; they will only have to attend and learn.

People were grateful, everyone cheered Scarlett. Many did not believe their ears, the hope of a better life shone in them, and they all hoped that a better future would come, if not for them, but at least for their children. They trusted Scarlett; they knew she could make a difference in their lives because she had done it so many times. As people began to disperse, Scarlett saw a handsome, large man standing in front of the gate. The man, looking at her grimly, in his gaze was more than tiredness or touched by her speech, he looked much sadder.

-Kwaw? -She said softly, then started toward him.

*

-How did the wind blow you here? -She asked in the kitchen next to a hot tea.

-Miss. Bloom, do you remember when you said you owe me? -He asked, looking deep into her eyes.

-What nonsense is this man talking about? If you will be so disrespectful to my Mistress, I swear... -Doris was furious, but Scarlett interrupted.

-It's all right, Doris, the man is telling the truth. How can I help? -She asked, turning her eyes back from Doris to the melancholy man sitting in front of her.

-My daughter is very ill. -He could barely pronounce those words as soon as he uttered the last word, he cried himself.

*

-Come in, please. -He led the way towards the house entrance, which had neither a door nor a window, covered with sheets and blankets, it was a tiny cold little stone house. There were plenty of people with coloured skin inside, as well as on the streets she had come through. On a narrow bed lay a beautiful little girl, covered from head to toe. -This is what the Whites call the Black Quarter, they talk about it as if some curse is sitting in this place. -Kwaw continued- But if I think about it, maybe they're right, if you look at them, at us...

Scarlett didn't speak, just sat down next to the little girl's bed, she was an oval-faced little girl with wonderfully curly hair that was intertwined in two branches, brown eyes in which, was easy to get lost in if you are not careful. Then she stroked her face.

-It seems like is the same as what her mother suffered from. -Kwaw spoke again, the little girl seemed not to be able to bear the illness anymore, she was barely six years old, when Scarlett thought that the little girl was the same age as Riley she was completely horrified, and she knew she had to do something.

-Has a doctor seen her? -The people around them were all staring at her, but they remained speechless.

-Our kind is not examined by doctors. -Kwaw declared with resentment in his voice.

-Only a doctor should know what's wrong with her.

-Like my wife... -He took a deep sniff though his nose -No one wanted to examine her either. And the reason for all is that damn place.

-What are you talking about? -Scarlett asked, jumping up from the bed, turning back to the child when she started coughing as Scarlett had never heard before in her life anyone to do, she had a feeling as if the child was about to spit out her lungs. But she didn't, instead, she coughed up a lot of blood, the handkerchief in her hand became so full that when she weakly dropped it, it snapped like a wet cloth that hadn't been straightened. Kwaw ran to the bed next to her and started stroking, "It's going to be all right, baby!"

-The Salvatore company. -He said with hatred in his voice.

-I do not understand. -Scarlett said, leaning against the wall, then recalling when George told her that most people get sick by sucking in the cotton.

-They did this, they did it with all of them. -He said, pointing around at the people there, Scarlett hadn't realised how sick they were, many people coughing so hard, that they could barely breathe. -Please promise to help. -Scarlett was afraid to make a promise about such a thing, but she knew it couldn't go on like this, "*I promise!*" she said.

*

Scarlett headed straight for Mr. George Salvatore's company as she left Kwaw's house. She didn't care what was going on between her and George. Nor did it matter what Edith thought of her, the only thing on her mind was to save that innocent little girl. It was as if she had seen Riley with discoloured lips, white nails, and a hand that clenched her chest with all of her efforts as if she wanted to tear out her lungs. With a dry cough in which one can be expected her heart to stop at any time, with bloody spit on every corner of the bed, on the pillow, on the blanket, on the wall, on the child's pyjamas, and on the face as it flows down from her mouth. As she walked angrily along Truro's Streets, the conversation with Kwaw took place in her head.

-We have to hurry, Miss. There won't be much time left if we don't do something... -Then his voice trailed off.

-Please leave this to me, let me talk to Mr. Salvatore. Stay with your daughter.

-She's not eating at all anymore, she can't sleep, and neither can I, as she's coughing, she's in a lot of pain. -He said crying again. -Those damn whites are ruthless, no one helps, I've visited all the doctors in Truro before, I even went to the temples to ask for one last anointing, but they sent me away, saying we are the Satan's people.

Scarlett didn't say anything, she didn't take on her heart what he said, because she hated her own nation for this as well. She hated all people who were heartless and unable to take people into consideration who were not rich, from the same religion, or otherwise different from them. She also knew that if Kwaw's little girl died, it would dry on her soul, as she made a promise, she had a duty to keep.

When she reached the house, the butler opened the door.

-Scarlett Bloom has arrived to see Mr. George Salvatore, please report it. -She said, a little suffocated in a great hurry.

-I'm sorry Miss. Bloom, I'm afraid the gentleman will not receive guests.

-I'm in an emergency.

-As I said, Miss, Mr. Salvatore is busy.

-And I said it is an urgent matter! -She replied, a little irritated.

-Listen, I didn't want that to be the case, but you are not welcome in this house. -Said the butler, completely serious.

-By whom? -She asked, but the man didn't answer, just rolled his eyes. As she looked up and saw Miss. Salvatore watching them from the window, immediately knew who to direct the suspicion to. So, when the man looked up after watching Scarlett for a long time, she burst past him and hurried straight into the salon room, where Edith was still standing by the window.

-Nothing stops you, you are just like her, you have no respect, no shame. -Edith said indignantly but didn't even respect the girl by looking at her, just staring at the reflection in the window.

When the butler caught up, grabbed Scarlett's arm, and began to jerk, saying: -Please, Miss, you don't want me to use violence.

-Don't touch me! -She shouted - You know that everything I said at the ball is true, you can't even look in my eyes, right? -She laughed with pity in her voice. -You know Miranda was better than you at everything. You know you ruined not just a life, but an entire family. Look me in the eye when I talk to you! -She shouted as the butler twitched.

-What's going on here? -George entered.

-I'd be curious about that too! Tell us, Miss. Salvatore, what's going on here?

-Get this woman out of my house! -She shouted as she turned to them, but when she saw them side by side her chest began to tighten, they almost looked like Miranda and O.T.

-No one is going anywhere until I know what this is all about. -George declared firmly.

-Your aunt banned me from this house. Nor did she intend to tell you that I was here.

-Is this true? -He asked in disgust at the whole situation.

-This girl is not for you! A child who is got by all kinds of people. A slut. I appreciate even more the ladies in the brothel. Do you know where she's coming from right now? From the Black Quarter!

George was speechless, unable to add anything to the thing. He looked at Scarlett, who didn't deny it, lowered her head, and took a deep breath.

-Is that true? -Scarlett was in that position she couldn't speak, but she raised her head, her eyes were full of tears. -At least deny it! -He said to her, his eyes were also filled with tears, then leaned against the dresser. -Lie to me, for heaven's sake! -He shouted and shot the dresser, which slammed loudly against the wall. Edith laughed, cheering on the situation.

-She is a pathetic woman. Worse than Miranda herself, she was able to stir up a scandal even in a church.

-I'm not here for this, now. -She sniffed. -I am here because... -But Edith interrupted.

-No, it's right. You are here to stir up another scandal. That's what is your expertise.

-That's enough! -He said nervously.

-One of your workers is seriously ill, and many others too, it is what we talked about last time...

-I can't do anything for them. -He said depressed.

-Yes, you can. They need a doctor.

-They are free people. They take on the job they want. We are not responsible for them. -Interrupted Miss. Salvatore again.

-How can you say that? They are your employee who are dying because they breathe in cotton. -She said, gesturing with her hands.

-As I said, they have a free choice. They can take another job if they don't like it.

-That's not right, they have no choice. Famine is on the rise in Truro, unemployment has become almost a lifestyle. -Because she saw that neither of them respected her with an answer, she continued. -But I see I need to ask for help elsewhere.

-Where will you go? Will you cry between Leonard Wolowitz's arms about the hard life of these poor souls? He probably helps you become a hero in their eyes.

-In his arms? How should I understand that Miss. Salvatore?

-You understand as you wish, but we know very well what kind of woman you are. Where is Mr. Wolowitz, where is that certain Elliot, then my nephew and you able to get below to other levels? -Then she looked out the window at the Black Quarter- Is nothing sacred to you?

-I just want to know one thing. Is that how you see Mr. Salvatore? -She asked, struggling with her tears.

-It's better you leave now. -He said softly.

-Now, I see now what's going on here. -She said, then left.

*"It is funny, how a misunderstanding can break two loveable hearts very easily."*

*

Maybe Edith Salvatore was right about one thing after all, Mr. Wolowitz really was her second chance.

-Miss. Bloom! What a pleasant surprise! -He said as he opened the door.

They went into the house, not only was the ballroom beautiful, but this part of the house was also charming. It was as if you were walking down the aisle of a castle, the arches, which were built with such attention and sophistication as if this building had been built for the queen herself, tasteful wallpapers, beautiful furniture that went well with the colours of the hallway. Mr. Wolowitz and probably together with Mrs. Wolowitz, placed tremendous emphasis on appearances. But since she hadn't had any luck yet with Mrs. Wolowitz, she couldn't say for sure. Leonard appeared in front of her, in stockings, picking up his shirt tastefully, which was also covered with a new level vest, and his hair banded with a blue ribbon, though Scarlett always thought it was a feminine style, it was tasteful for him. He ushered her into a huge room where there were decorative pillows, she had never seen before in her life this kind of it, velvety soft, shacked properly. When she took a seat on the couch, she felt she could fall asleep right away.

-Tea?

-No, thank you. - The man took a seat as well, the silence between them was a little awkward so Scarlett spoke again- How is your mother feeling?

-She is feeling better, thank you. -Then they both smiled nervously.

-You have a wonderful house. -Scarlett said in amazement.

-I guess you are not here to praise my house or take care of my mother's health, right?

-Indeed! I am here for a different reason.

-What would it be then?

*

The garden had a slightly cool summer breeze, tickling through her skin, and the warmth of the sun touched her as pleasantly as if she had been in heaven, Mr. Wolowitz's garden was wonderfully beautiful, full of flowers, and tastefully trimmed hedges.

-So, you're saying that little girl is very sick and no one wants to help? -Scarlett just hummed- And now you are wondering if I can offer my help, right? -Scarlett just hummed again- Would you be impressed if I said I could help?

-Sir, I wouldn't ask for anything you don't do voluntarily, with good intentions. Please, if you would just do it for me... -She couldn't finish when she thought about the condition of that kid.

-I would only do it for you. -He declared, then kissed her hand.

Scarlett took a deep breath and looked at the birds flying in the sky. -Then do so.

-I will write a letter to a doctor in the nearby town tonight. He will be happy to help, I am sure of that. He is a good friend of mine. He will be here no later than Tuesday afternoon.

Scarlett looked in the air wordlessly, knowing what it all meant. In spite of her will, she became indebted to a man she did not know, whom people were talking about badly and looked at with sharp eyes. All for a promise she has to keep.

# CHAPTER XLII

Scarlett was in the barn the next afternoon after the kids left Gracewith. With doors wide open, because of the heat, she began to pack up the place when a man's shadow appeared behind her.

-Mr. Wolowitz, you scared me! -She said slightly frightened.

-I'm sorry. What is this place? -He looked at the seats lined up from logs and hay.

-A school. -Scarlett said a little nervous.

-What kind of school is it, where they sit on tree stumps and haystacks? -He laughed sarcastically.

-My school and if you don't like it, please leave. -She said indignantly, then turned to gather the plates that had cakes on during the morning. She called these reward cakes. It was given to those who learnt well and could say the alphabet or numbers correctly.

-I mean, I don't see a school board. I have no idea how kids can learn without a blackboard?

-Well, I haven't had time to get it yet. It is not even necessary for now; it is enough for them to cram the numbers and the alphabet.

-Visually, I think they would learn a lot more. And they will have to learn to write one day, don't you think?

-Did you come only to make fun of my school or do you want to say something? -She asked impatiently, for which the man just laughed.

-I just want to say I'm coming from Truro. Mr. Kwaw's little girl...
-he said seriously- she's...

-Is her condition worse?

-Well, no...

-Don't tell me, she's dead, please... -She said, cutting into the
man's words, then taking a seat on a log.

-The little girl is fine; she got treatment.

-Oh, thank God.

-Or maybe Mr. Wolowitz. -Corrected her, cheerfully- She got the
treatment, which has to be strictly adhered to, of course, it wasn't
for free, but for that, you don't have to worry. The doctor said he
would come back, but if she had waited a few days with it, she
would be dead for sure...

-I'm so grateful! -She hugged him. She could almost see in front of
her the little girl recovering and regaining the original colour of
her lips, just like her nails, no longer so weak, running and playing
cheerfully. The man didn't know what to do, so he just stood there
until Scarlett stepped back.

The man sat down, Scarlett too. She knew it meant nothing more
than that he still had something to say to her. But she couldn't
figure out what it might be, she didn't even try to ask if he wanted
to say, he would. On the tiny log, as he sat, he propped himself
with his elbows on his knees, then looked at his clasped fingers.

-Why did you eschew me so much at the beginning?

-You know, I didn't know you. They said I'd better keep my
distance. -She said, a little ashamed of the truth.

-People spread a lot of things when they don't like someone.

-Not everyone gets the chance to listen to them. -Scarlett said as the melancholy man next to her looked at the girl. One look was enough to know she is telling the truth. -Rumours are carried by haters, spread by fools, and accepted by idiots.

-So, you didn't...

-No, I haven't heard any of them, I'd rather wait for the protagonist himself to tell this part of his story because no one else would know the truth better than the one who experienced them. Slander may have a basis, but if we know only half the truth, it is no longer true.

The man stood up wordlessly, cast a forced smile at Scarlett, and left.

*

-Doris, you knew what a scandal it would be if I appeared at Mrs. Wolowitz's ball, like that. Why didn't you dissuade me from it? -She asked, rotating the spoon in her cup, even though it was completely cold.

-Well... You are responsible for your happiness. Don't feel bad for making decisions that upset other people. You're not responsible for how they feel.

-So, you think I pushed a person away from me... -Scarlett had to rethink the weight of her words- who was important to me, which came from mere selfishness because I wanted everyone to remember my mother?

-I did not say that. You know it was not about your appearance everything what had happened there. Plato once said: "No one is more hated than he who speaks the truth."

-You must be right. -She got up to leave.

-Oh, I forget, something has arrived for you, it's in the barn.
-Scarlett looked puzzled, then left curiously- I admire people who
choose to shine even after all the storms they've been through.

Scarlett entered the "school room" curiously, as she looked
around, next to the door found a huge, wrapped board, quickly
unfolding it with great excitement. It was a black school board at
least two feet high and five foot long. Scarlett's eyes filled with
tears of touch. She heard a horse whinny so she went to the
window, she saw Mr. Wolowitz sitting on his horseback in the
distance. From the depths of Scarlett's heart, she felt a sincere
smile for the first time in a long time.

# CHAPTER XLIII

Scarlett was enriched in abundance during her first year of harvest. More and more people moved into the village, there were huge festivities during the summer, Scarlett organised a village day where she celebrated with the villagers and her new friend Mr. Wolowitz, who was by her in both happy and difficult moments. Shortly after Christmas, when Scarlett was giving away gift baskets to her workers (full of jam, compote, fresh bread, milk, sweet and savoury cottage cheese, and in which houses children had some candy hidden in them), she found out from some rumours that Mr. Salvatore had travelled to India in advance, as a result of immediate negotiations. She felt as sentimental at the time as a kid whose splinter went into her finger, not even wanting to get out of her room, she lost her appetite, and always had a kind of melancholy mood. One day Mr. Wolowitz visited her and told her how much his life had changed since Scarlett let him get closer. Doris did not look at the events of these visits with a good eye, she did not like Leonard, which she did not deny for a minute. The day when Leonard visited there and offered Doris a bottle of honey, the woman said that she was allergic to honey. Of course, Scarlett chuckled, knowing how much she loved honey but how she didn't like the man and also that Doris had no say in her decisions. The only thing Doris didn't even try to stand in between, was that she was happy to see Scarlett smile again, seeing her in a melancholy mood she looked just like when her mother mourned in the early days of her child's loss. She didn't want to see her like that again, so she didn't even try to speak against the man, but she knew these encounters wouldn't end well.

Scarlett didn't want to celebrate her birthday, though Doris tried hard to talk her into organizing a ball. Scarlett felt she was still unable to mourn her family, especially since she didn't even know if there was one more man to mourn or if Aydan, her little brother was still alive. She had a small dinner that only included her, the girls, and of course Jared. Certainly, she didn't know that Doris had recruited the people of the village, and that evening the people surrounded Gracewith's dining room's window from outside and began singing loudly. Of course, this phenomenon touched her so much that she almost started crying, and suddenly Mr. Wolowitz appeared, which no one expected. Doris far avoided inviting the man in any way. Leonard arrived at her with a bouquet of red roses, she had never thought in her life that such a tiny gesture would be able to touch her heart so deeply. When the man called her for a walk, in Gracewith, Scarlett was unable to say no. Gracewith reached the beach, which also belonged to Scarlett's territory, so they took a long walk. The sun was almost gone when they walked there. It was the day, Scarlett gave new hope for love, hoping Leonard wouldn't feed her with toxic hopes. The beach reminded her of George, of the first day she could see the ocean for the first time in her life, as she ran down the hill like a child to touch the blueness that splashed frothily and wildly on the ground, she remembered the moment when she felt the hiss of the wild wind coming from the ocean and the way it gently and coldly touched her, she also remembered the way George looked into her eyes that evening, she remembered his scent, and the gentle touch she could recall, how fierce, and insane was the desire to kiss him. There was no compulsion towards Leonard. Scarlett remembered what Doris had once told her, standing next to Leonard at that moment, while thinking about George. She understood what she was talking about. "Calm only occurs when the object of our failed desires loses something of its value in our eyes." Scarlett couldn't figure out how his aunt could have poisoned George's mind so much, but it didn't matter anymore. She kissed Leonard on the cheek and then watched the sunset together. When she leaned on his shoulder she felt as if someone was watching them, she didn't want to pay attention to that feeling, but after all, she did, she looked back. A man was sitting on horseback but could not be seen the face, the light of the setting sun had not reached that man's whereabouts, so he was in complete darkness. For a few seconds, the whole phenomenon Scarlett felt didn't even know if it was real or just saw what she wanted to see. She was unable to reveal his existence, but the thought that ran through her covered her in goosebumps. She knew she had to let him go the way he let her go.

# BOOK TWO

# *TURNING TO
A NEW CHAPTER*

# CHAPTER I

-Where have you been?

-I rode out, looked at the estate, discussed with the workers what they have to do while I was away, and visited Lord Quas.

-Has he offered to be an MP again?

-Aunt, how many times do we have to discuss this? -George asked, a little tired of the subject.

-The election will take place next spring.

-We will see what my trip to India will be like and then it will be revealed how I will continue in the future.

-I didn't say a word not to take part in the trial. Let's just say I had to admit I was a little misled when you got back from port last time. Until you said you were late for the boat, I was hoping you choose another career path.

-That day wasn't exactly my lucky day.

-Your career doesn't depend on delaying a journey of a lifetime. -She said ironically.

-It really isn't, but colliding on the street with a man who is Jewish enough in his own way to let the inhabitants of the city know what a villain I am, that I would have let an innocent soul die is, I think, is almost the end of my career, especially that all the people who would support my votes were present in front of Mr. Thaker's office, it sealed a little the life I would have provided for Plan B.

-Jewish?

-It's just a term people use, even though I know his ancestors were Jews. -Edith looked confused- It means he is very headstrong; he always gets what he wants, he is an influential and great businessman.

-Is this about Mr. Wolowitz?

-That's correct. -He said, managing his tie in front of the mirror.

-And what did you do?

-What could I have done? I said it was all a misunderstanding, but I uttered those words just when that vile, worthless man walked up to me, saying, "The Jewish man is telling the truth, he really would have let her die, we asked for his help, and he didn't even listen. Of course, not him, Miss. Bloom was he meant. And if you are happier now, then yes, you were right, for the hundred times. Such is she, the woman I once thought I could make happy, hurried straight into Leonard Wolowitz's arms as she stepped out this door. And if you'll excuse me now." -He said and hurried out of the room.

# CHAPTER II

Scarlett once spent the morning in Beelove at Leonard's invitation. After breakfast in the pleasant early autumn, they took a walk on the man's estate, who was delighted to introduce the woman to the details of his work.

-Tell me, how is it going with Gracewith?

-Not that good, I guess...

-Drought wears everyone out this year, even though I knew it was rare here in England. As a matter of fact, it didn't do me any good either, but I was looking for some way out of the problems, but for those involved just in agriculture, that's impossible.

-I am very disappointed, last year's abundance, which even exceeded the set goal was wonderful, is unbelievable, what happened this year. The sprouts barely survived on the fields, a lot of shoots were dried out, and a few of them remained in some places only, but not enough, my people took buckets to sprinkle them. Not to mention the products obtained by the animals, which became spoiled by the heat. I tried to correct the situation by digging a cellar, but it took a very long time. I don't know what to say to my people, I'm unable to fire them, especially since the number of unemployed has increased even more than last year. I'm afraid to find out what's going to happen in the winter.

-Can I help you somehow?

-I'm afraid not, just divert my thoughts. -She said with a forced smile. The man put a lot of effort into thinking about how he could take the woman's attention, and what he could say to impress her.

-Did you know that the bee lives less than 40 days? -He asked as they walked among the hives.

-Are you serious?

-Yes, during this time they visits at least 1,000 flowers and produces less than a teaspoon of honey. For us is only a teaspoon of honey, but for the bee it is a life.

-It's just amazing! -She said, leaning close to a flower on which a tiny little yellow-black striped bee was bathing in the pollen. Her tiny little body was full of flower dust and her legs were swollen from the pollen she had collected.

-Yes, they're really amazing. -He said, then took the one Scarlett was looking at, picked it up to the sky, and watched it together as it departed.

-And they always go back to the same hive?

-Yes, everyone has a home, just like us. And they have a queen as well, just like me. -He said, looking in the eyes, then kissing her hand.

-What kind of loophole did you find to keep your business going? Since there are a lot of flowers wasted in the dryness, I think that's what you meant when you said it wasn't good for your business either.

-Yes, well, in addition to planting several flowers this year, mostly in pots, which I hung on the lower branches of the trees and placed them under trees to be in a shaded place. -Scarlett opened her mouth to speak, but didn't have a chance to say anything- Do you want to know if this has an effect on honey? Yes, it does. Much weaker honey was made. I was able to sell them at a lower price. But on the other hand, it's still better than not selling anything. This year, in terms of business, is not thriving for me either. But regarding something else... -Then he stepped closer to Scarlett and stroked her face, Scarlett recognized the gesture as soon as the man began to gradually lean towards her.

-Would you show me how you did that? -She asked, but the man looked at her questioningly. -The flower pots hanging on the tree. -She said with a wide smile.

*

She got home late in the afternoon, she had neither the strength nor the mood to go among the kids. She knew they would drain the rest of her strength. So, she sat on a bench on the terrace. Doris stepped out the door, puffing.

-Would you make us a cottage cheesecake? Could give the cups of milk closer? But if they smash a bowl of eggs during their run, who will clean it up? Isn't the nanny... -She said as she spun on the patio- Judas! Miss. Bloom! Apologise, I didn't notice you were here. -She said frightened.

Scarlett just waved with a hand, then looked at the farm at which point it was in sight. It was one of the best things in Gracewith she loved. Everywhere she looked around from her house, she saw the lands, the blue ocean in the distance, the farm, and the village. Gracewith was located on a high hill, almost on a mountain top from which she could see the whole countryside, but this time she did not look at it with pride or joy as she once did. Scarlett was sad, afraid to think about what would happen in the winter. What will happen next year if they write a year like this, full of failure, cost, and fear. She feared that she would have to leave Gracewith so that the future, which belonged not only to herself, not to the children, but to the whole village, would not come true. Disappointed, but not only in the weather, not only because of the promised words she said but also on her own because she can't find a way out, she can't find a way to avoid losing the paradise she once created.

-Would you like to tell me about your life, Doris?

-Pardon? -Doris looked at her in surprise.

-You already know my story. But I don't know anything about you. -There was not only curiosity in her gaze, but a sense of honesty, Doris knew that she was not only asking about it, out of sheer courtesy, but she was really interested in what kind of life she lived before they met.

-What can I say? -She thought how much and what she could say about her life, but there was no real secret- What are you curious about?

-When I came here, you said you were my property. In England, there is no law to keep people in slave labour legally.

-That's right. Whilst slavery had no legal basis in England, the law was frequently misperceived. Black people were earlier enslaved in the territories overseas and then immigrated to England by their owners where they were often still treated as slaves. Many people who had previously been enslaved got baptized, considering this would ensure their independence. Others took the benefit of being on English earth and run away.

-But you're here, you didn't escape.

-Like Nivek and Matilda. -She said with a smile- We worked as slave labourers for your family acquaintance to whom they came on business. We were still kids, all three of us. We were the same age as your grandfather, Henry Bloom. -Then for half a minute she wondered how to proceed- Your great-grandfather, during his existence there, studied a lot of the oppression and misery of the workers living there. One day, my mother, who had to find the ball, which Henry Bloom had scattered, she was looking for at your grandfather's request, the mama, -and then took a deep breath, continued holding back her tears- the mama, served the dinner delayed, everyone was sitting at the table. Including the

Bloom family. When the Lord was furious that the food was a quarter of an hour late... I will never forget the day I was the one who helped her serve the dinner. The Lord slapped the table, shouting: "You are good for nothing! I told you to always serve dinner at exactly six o'clock!". He pulled her towards him by the top of her dress. And there in front of everyone, he started beating her. Your grandfather just stood silent, staring at them. He did not say a word, he did not say the reason why it all happened. -Scarlett squeezed the hand of the crying woman, who wiped away her tears, took another force to continue the story she had started- I wanted to run there and help her, but my mom shouted at me to stay, so I didn't move, I just watched what was happening. It was your great-grandfather who eventually interrupted him, but the Lord was so aggressive that he also hit his own friend and then left in disgust. Mama started begging him to buy me with her last strength. Then she died before my eyes and there was nothing I could do. -Then she broke down again and stared at the ground.

-So, this is how you got here?

-Your great-grandfather made a deal with him. He will sell him all the cargo the gentleman wanted so badly to buy, and he will dispense with this disagreement if he gives me to him. He agreed and then offered to buy Nivek and Matilda as well. When the papers were signed Mr. Bloom was given ownership over us and then brought us here. -She pulled her mouth back to smile, thinking back to what had happened- He said we didn't have to be afraid and offered two choices. Either we stay and work for him or we are liberated (provide us with documents) and we could choose what we want to do in the future according to our free will.

-And you chose the first one.

-We were kids in a foreign country. We stayed. -Scarlett didn't speak because she didn't know what to say- I served four generations in this family. -Doris said, then looked at the stars.

They say if it weren't dark, we would never be able to see the stars. -She continued as she stood up to go in, but she changed her mind and turned back to Scarlett. -Miss. Bloom, I love and respect you very much, but you need to know my opinion, it's really against me, that you meet Mr. Wolowitz. He is not the person you think he is.

-Why do you think that?

-Something is not clear about him. Please, take care.

-I'm not going to be his wife because I met him one or two times. -She said with a laugh.

-I wouldn't take poison for that. -Doris said with a sigh- Just be aware of his intentions so that there is no misunderstanding. Don't give him hopeless hopes.

# CHAPTER III

By the end of November, Scarlett was getting more and more troubled about her wealth, knowing from the cold autumn weather that a harsh winter would await them. She knew the only man who could give advice was Mr. Thaker, the old man who had been by her side throughout her career. The man who supported her all along as a banker, a notary, and as her most loyal friend.

-Miss. Bloom, long time no see! -He said as he entered the library door.

-Forgive me for my recent silence. The farm and the upbringing of the children made me a bit busy.

-Don't worry about that. -He took a seat after Scarlett's gesture as she pointed to the armchair- How are the children?

-Well, Julia and Riley learn French, dance great, and play the piano wonderfully, just as wonderfully they sing. Jared is already a real little gentleman, though he can't communicate in a sentence yet, he can pronounce some words, just like Aliona, who is eerily similar to her mother, my sister Anne.

-Yes, it's amazing how much each gene is inherited. -He laughed softly.

-The human body is truly amazing. -Then she began to caress her dog next to her.

-I'm guessing you called me here because of the farm.

-I confess that's why you are here this evening. My account has dropped a lot lately and as you know I had to take out a loan to build the cellar as well. I received a penalty the other day because I unofficially opened a school for the village children and without a teaching qualification, I taught them. I guess then someone is very happy now that she could hurt me again. I wanted to tell you the reason I slipped with paying my bills.

-What makes you think this person is a *"she"*?

-Mr. Thaker, you don't know much yet. Over the past year, let's say I have made an enemy or two.

-What about the school then?

-Since I have been operating for more than a year, so the penalty is quite high, I am forced to close. Tomorrow, I will announce to the children, as I will have to tell my workers, that because of my difficulties, I am having to send them on forced leave (holiday) for a few months.

-You can't do that to them because they don't have money set aside. They had to repay their deferred rent last year. They won't have anything to eat...

-Yes, I'm aware of that. But there's nothing else I can do; I have to pay my own taxes.

-I hope you know what you are doing.

-Me too... -She replied, then stood up and leaned to a safe hidden in the dresser, then opening it.

The man also stepped closer to view the treasure, there was plenty of jewellery there, necklaces, bracelets, rings, and earrings full of silver, gold, beaded, and precious stones. He reached in to see a piece that caught his attention, a silver ring with a tiny rose on it. The man's eyes began to sparkle at the sight of this jewellery.

-I'm just asking you to keep this one. This is invaluable. -Scarlett herself thought the same, Mr. Thaker convinced her, so she pulled it up on her finger. Daphne entered the room unexpectedly with a book in her hand. Her eyes stopped on the safe full of treasures. Scarlett cleared her throat, which took her eyes off what she saw.

-I'm sorry, I just wanted to put this back in place. -She said, a little ashamed of herself.

Scarlett closed the safe door and sent the girl away. As she straightened, she reached for the brandy on the dresser to fill the glasses.

-Didn't you think about marriage? That would be a solution too.

-You think a marriage of convenience would help balance my bill? -The man was silent, he thought so, but he didn't dare say it so directly- No way until I can pay my bills myself. -She said, a little offended.

-I understood. I will be back in two weeks before the holidays, I have to travel to London for the baptism of one of my niece's children. Please visit me so we can arrange it.

-Certainly.

# CHAPTER IV

Scarlett stood in front of her workers in the morning, who climbed the big hill to Gracewith to listen to Scarlett's speech about how they were to get fired. Scarlett watched those gathered there with a sore heart. When she saw that no one was coming anymore she took a deep breath and started.

-I'm glad you all came. I guess you already know why I called you here, as we watch Gracewith failing every day. This year, as you know, the crop was not sky-shattering. In fact, I can say that this year, we were unlucky. So, I would like to thank you for your work so far. But on Gracewith, unfortunately, we won't need it for a while, so, unfortunately, I am forced to send you on leave, take it as a longer holiday, which will take place in the winter. With a little luck on the farm, we will still need some help so a few people can keep their jobs. -People started complaining unhappily- I know this is hard to accept, but thanks for last year's results and hard-working hands. As compensation, I would like to offer the following unity. Cancelling of all debts that have accumulated over the past few years. -People started shouting out loud, *"That's not fair!" "Please don't do this!" "I have to feed the hungry mouths at home!", "We're all going to starve to death!"* -It is also part of the unity that in these difficult times, I would like to offer that you can live in the rented accommodation for free until everything is back to normal. -People were still tutting dissatisfied with their evil words, but Scarlett knew she couldn't do more for them. -As for the school, I have to close it tomorrow. -People were even more angry about this, hoping that when they would have to starve, at least the children wouldn't have to, because Scarlett fed them every time, it motivated the children to learn more and to be present every time. -I would like to thank you once again for your understanding and wish you all the best. Since it is easier to list the names who can continue to work on the farm, I would like to ask those present to pay attention to the pronunciation of their names. I tried to select these people so that one person from almost every family could be here. The following individuals are still Gracewith workers. -Then she began to list the names, then regretted it again and said goodbye.

*

-Doris. Do you think they wish me to hell? -She asked, sitting at the table in despair.

-I doubt they hate you as much as you think. Just don't think about it. There are times when we are faced with serious decisions. -Scarlett then remembered the Bible verse Otto Tamayo said, that God only places before us the trials we endure. Whenever she thinks of that man, she always has in her mind that she is incapable of seeing him as a loving father after what has happened, neither as a pastor nor as a blood relative.

-I can't imagine what they're going to do in the winter. They think I am a heartless witch. -She said, leaning her head against the wall as a voice came out of nowhere behind her.

-Don't talk nonsense, sister, you can't be hated.

Scarlett looked like someone who saw a ghost, then jumped up from her seat and jumped onto her younger brother's neck, unable to figure out which part of his face to kiss in joy.

-How do you get here? -She asked in surprise.

Sitting at the table, Aydan told her sister everything, all the horrors he saw as he watched his brother and father die. How he hid among the corpses on the battlefield so that the French would not shoot him to death. That he spent a full day and a full night lying motionless in the mud. As the field was cleaned, he was thrown into a wagon, full of corpses, where those who had lost their lives in battle were burned on a so-called death-ground, he fastened his body to the bottom of a carriage with a rope, he was so weak by that time. He ran away so that he could escape and that the soldiers would not shoot him in the head for cowardice. He also said he was fleeing and had to hide because if he was found he would be executed.

-But a peace treaty was signed in the spring. The battle is over, why should you be afraid? -Scarlett asked her question just when Daphne came into the dining room with the kids.

-It's just a peace treaty, which will expire soon, if they can't agree another war will begin. A bloodier war. We need to be prepared. If they find me, I will be executed.

-Uncle Aydan! -Shouted the two older girls Julia and Riley as they saw him and then ran over to hug the young man.

-They've grown well since then! -He said, squeezing them.

Scarlett couldn't think of anything other than what her younger brother had told her. She was looking for solutions, but she had no plans yet.

# CHAPTER V

Two weeks after she fired her workers, she was thinking of solutions for both her workers and her brother. She didn't even notice when Leonard entered the room. In the armchair, she looked in the direction of the window and let the rays of the sun touch her skin warmly compared to the time of winter.

-I'm sorry to bother you! -He said politely.

Scarlett shuddered, then turned to him.

-Don't get mad, I didn't intend to scare you. The butler sent me here, as I saw he was very busy with Miss. Riley Bloom, who asked him to find her lost kitten, so I came myself.

-Mr. Wolowitz! Please take a seat. What do I owe your visit to?

-You didn't respond to my letters and I started to worry. I haven't seen you in almost three weeks, I didn't know if I needed this concern. But as I see it, my intentions were good. What happened?

-Pardon me. The farm tied me up. You know, I just fired my workers and I also had to sell half of the animals.

-I'm sorry to hear that. Can I help you somehow?

-I wish you could. -Scarlett said regretfully.

-And the school? -I thought you were teaching at this time.

-It had to be locked up. Because of an anonymous letter that reached the People's Council. They set a penalty amount. It was also explained to me that I would have to close without proper permission, unfortunately.

-Miss, please take advantage of my offer.

-If you want to offer money for a donation, I have to ask you not to continue. There is no money I can take that is offered from pity.

-And if I could give you some advice? If you could get a small amount from your own earnings?

-What would that be about? -She wondered.

-You know, I looked at your workers... -Doris showed up, interrupting the man as she arrived with the tea, she put on the table then disappeared. -For example, the lady who showed up here... In America, the price of slaves was raised.

-Please don't continue! -Scarlett declared, bouncing off her seat.

-If I saw correctly, there are three of them. If you have paperwork about owning them...

-I can't listen to this anymore.

-Think about it, I have friends who do the shipping. The value of the three is at least $1,500.

-Please don't continue. -She said, depressing, looking out the window, the man didn't even say a word anymore about the subject. They watched Scarlett's brother walk down the garden laughing with Daphne. Riley and Julia were playing chasing each other in front of them. Scarlett had a sudden bad feeling, but she didn't know where to tie it to.

-Miss. Bloom! Can I tell you the second reason of my arrival? -Scarlett hummed in response as she watched her brother and the nanny walking together- I wanted to talk to you about something. You know, I've been thinking a lot lately about ourselves and our time together. You need to know how much you touched my heart... -Scarlett's first thought was a marriage proposal which she felt couldn't be avoided. But she didn't know what Leonard wanted from her after all since Matilda interrupted him. When they both turned to find out what she wanted, Scarlett looked at the ceiling, softly thanking Matilda for the intervention.

-Lady Evelyn Quas has arrived to see you, Miss. Bloom. Oh, I didn't know you had a guest. -She said when she saw the man. Scarlett just looked at the man, waiting for him to say something.

-I was about to leave anyway. -He kissed Scarlett's hand.

When Evelyn appeared next to Matilda, Scarlett's heart began to beat faster. She tried to avoid this moment, but she knew she had to get over it one day anyway. She was very happy when, after Mrs. Wolowitz's birthday ball, she heard that the Quas family would have to travel to London for a longer period of time, for political reasons that affected Evelyn's husband.

-Lady Quas! I didn't know you were back from London already. How was your trip?

Evelyn smiled, then said: -Let's leave the formality. We both know why I'm here.

The smile dried from Scarlett's face, but she maintained her demeanour. She didn't know what to say, so she let Evelyn speak.

-Tell me, how much do you know about my relationship with the man I once loved?

-Pardon? -Scarlett asked, not expecting such a question.

-When we saw each other last time. You said you know everything about me and my lover. Also, about Miranda and my friendship.

-Oh, I see...

223

-And it made my husband especially curious. I had a hard time smoothing it out, I told him that it was a misunderstanding.

-Because it was Lady Quas. I shouldn't have opened my big mouth until I knew the full story.

Evelyn smiled, flashing her beautiful white teeth, Scarlett felt she could breathe again.

-You look too much like Miranda to be just her niece. Am I not right?

Scarlett was ashamed of herself staring at the cup of tea, on the table. -I'm her daughter! -She told the truth; she knew she couldn't hide it from Evelyn.

-I will testify about my right then. Elliot Bloom, who was once your foster father, was the love of my life. About whom I dreamt for years. But he chose your stepmother. But that's certainly not the whole story. When we were young, there were three of us friends. Miranda, Edith, and I, the three of us made up the big trio. But, like all such friendships, there are two best friends and one excluded. Of course, it happened without our attention. I always thought our friendship with Miranda was for a lifetime. We shared everything. She said Otto Tamayo was her first love, of course we were kids at the time, but she let him go when he decided to choose the parish over Miranda, he hesitated a lot between God and Miranda's love. God, how hard this life is... -She said, while Scarlett was as frustrated as she had ever been before, she was now aware that the thoughts about the reverend were true. -I also shared with her that I am in love with her brother. But Edith didn't know anything about it. At a ball, however, she saw the two of us talking, and when she revealed her ideas about the two of us in romance to Miranda, she confessed to Edith how I felt about him. Edith was furious and offended, then all three of us realised what kind of friendship we had. Edith told Elliot how I felt about him, who didn't like the immediacy. It was then when I learnt that a woman should refrain from showing her feelings. Elliot found it more interesting the arrogant, sassy, stubborn... - Then she looked at Scarlett to see if these words didn't hurt her, but she didn't pay much attention to it- Well, um, I guess you know who it is. He broke my heart. And more importantly, I lost my friends. After I found out what she did, I visited her and we quarrelled. After the incident, she spread lies about me to Miranda. I was a victim of slander and I couldn't even explain. Edith is a sick liar. She says things so firmly and turns the words, that I almost believed myself the things she claimed.

-What could she say about you?

-She claimed that I was spreading things in the countryside that Miranda and Otto, well... They did inappropriate things; she was able to pay a maid to lie about these rumours are spreading from my mouth.

-And what happened to Elliot Bloom?

-We met in London a few years ago. He said he was on a business trip.

-I remember that period. He was there for a long time.

-When we met, I told him what happened between the girls. That I don't know anything about his life since then, just what I've heard, rumours in town about him, but I didn't believe them because I don't think it's enough to know half of the story. -Scarlett forced a smile at this sentence- She said there were problems with his marriage and that made him addicted to gambling. He was very unhappy, as I was. I was living in a marriage of convenience with a man I didn't love. So... -She lowered her head in shame.

-So, you comforted each other. -She finished. Ashamed, Evelyn nodded with her head down.

-Do you have any friends? Real friends?

225

-There was only one person, my sister, -she smiled at the thought of calling her that way- I'm unable to think of her as the people who raised me, as a step-sister. After all, if there hadn't been any relationship between us, she would always have been my sister. Her name was Anne. -She said with bitten lips.

-So, you know how I felt when I lost Miranda's friendship. -Scarlett nodded silently with teary eyes. -I can't replace Anne, but I can assure you I can support you in everything. -Then she took Scarlett's hand and stroked it with her finger gently.

-Like a friend? -The woman asked.

-Like a friend. -Evelyn replied.

# CHAPTER VI

-Good morning, Miss! -Doris entered the room with Scarlett's breakfast. Then she looked at the dogs next to her, "*uh...*" she pursed her lips, then avoided the growling dogs from afar.

Scarlett sat up and yawned, stretching out.

-Good morning! Is that the time already? -She asked sleepily.

-Yes, it is, and if you're not in a hurry, you'll miss the Truro's lunch with Lady Quas. Especially if I am right and there is a lot to do before it.

Scarlett began to search under her pillow.

-Didn't you see a little brown diary?

-No Miss. Bloom. Didn't you leave it coincidently in the library? What kind of diary is this?

-A very important object for me. I would have taken poison for putting it under my pillow.

-Do you follow the old phrase? Do you think if you put a written thing, a booklet, or a book under your pillow, the knowledge will come to your mind at night? -Doris laughed as Scarlett joined.

-I've never heard of it.

-Sweet little Miranda has always done that. -Then she looked up at the woman's painting- Whenever she didn't feel like learning the material, the night before the teacher arrived, she always put her books under the pillow.

-And did she know the subject the next day? -Scarlett asked curiously.

-She thought inspiration came from the book, but in fact, she only became confident because she believed in it. She always told the teacher the material they studied before, instead of the one in advance. But she said so well-articulated and confidently that the teacher believed he had missed a lesson, so the pre-eaten reading was learnt together. -She smiled, as she looked at the portrait- Isn't it painful to see this picture?

-It's much more reassuring to see it.

-Didn't you think of exposing your portrait?

-It's like portraying me, and anyway I don't have one. -She laughed.

*

-Miss. Jelon, you're so beautiful every day. Tell me what's your secret.

-Mr. Bloom, please, I will blush. -She put her palm on her cheek- Maybe is because we got another nanny lately and we're working in split roles, I'm with the older girls and she's with the two younger kids.

-What do you say, how did you experience it? Is it true what people say that as they grow, so does the problem with them? -Aydan laughed.

-In my opinion, it is better if they are bigger, they are more expressive and they learn quicker.

-And what do you use to teach them.

Daphne became serious for half a minute, then took a deep breath.

-Everything what's needed.

-Interesting, I thought it was the nanny's job to supervise them only, they didn't have a private teacher? -He asked teasingly as he watched the running children.

Daphne glanced at him, then pushed him gently, saying, "Catch me!" and run away. Aydan followed closely, but she ran in vain, unable to run far from a man who used to run away from the bullets of rifles.

When Doris opened the kitchen window to let out the smoke from her burnt turkey, she saw them huddled on the ground, hugging. She just couldn't run far away from Aydan. They didn't care about the cold ground they were lying on until Julia and Riley turned back to form a pile. Doris looked at Aydan's face as he stood up and then gave a hand to Daphne. As he helped up, he started to approach her, but the girl, turning away, pretended to care that the girls were still rolling in the snow.

-Sometimes you don't get what you want, because you deserve better.

*

-Apologies for the delay, the journey took a little longer than I thought. -Scarlett said as she reached the table where Lady Quas was already waiting.

-It's all right, darling. -She looked at Scarlett, who seemed to be worried. -Is everything fine?

-Of course. -She said with a forced smile and then put her coat down on the chair next on the right-hand side. When she looked at Lady Quas again, she looked like she wanted to make Scarlett feel that she knew she couldn't scam this woman through. -Except I heard rumours, of a person who is kind to me.

-Oh... What would that be about? -Evelyn asked. Unable to tell her first, but something suggested she can trust the woman.

-Do you remember when you visited me last time, you asked who's that valet? -Evelyn looked questioning at first. -A young man half a head taller than me, who was with the nanny, Daphne, I mean governess from now on, as she takes care only to the older children. I feel they spend too much time together lately ... -She said with her half mouth closed. -Well, he is my brother. Elliot Bloom's youngest son, Aydan Bloom. -She said, looking around softly, lest this news gets into the ears of someone who might harm him, but there were hardly a few tables in this part of the restaurant, and most of them were empty.

-This is amazing! -She said with a smile.

-Yes, it is. Except if someone finds out where he is and gives up, he is in huge trouble. -The woman in front of her rounded her eyes. -He escaped the battlefield just before the peace treaty was signed. They searched Bath for a long time after him. If it gets in someone's ear that he is here, he can be executed for cowardice. -She said in a hushed voice as a waiter walked past them.

-And what do you want to do?

-I'm not sure, but before the next war...-But she couldn't finish as she was interrupted.

-What kind of war?

-Shhh... -She muttered before anyone heard it. After taking a deep breath she continued- Aydan said this treat is only to drag the time while the government will make a decision, but he said it will be a bloodier war if it will happen. I wish he could travel out of this time, out of the country, for at least a couple of years until things will smoothen and they will declare permanently dead or a missing person who was lost during the battle and the case is closed.

-I understand. -She said a little thoughtfully.

*

-I've been looking for you. -She said as soon as she saw her brother walking up the stairs.

-Everything's fine, sister? -He asked, taking a few steps back as he walked towards her.

-Yes, I believe so. -Scarlett said, but she couldn't look in the eye as she hadn't explained the plan about his escape to Aydan yet. Then she saw Daphne approaching, so she fell silent for half a minute. As she walked past them, a stunning smile struck the girl's face as she looked at the boy, who was melting like ice in the early spring sunshine. -I just want to tell you to be careful before you reveal your identity, to whom you trust.

-You mean Daphne? She is an innocent soul. -Said the boy pointing backward with his fist closed only his thumb looked in the direction Daphne was going.

-I was serious. -She uttered the words with complete confidence. Then she put her hat on the hanger, where her coat was already, and looked at him again before she left. -Haven't you seen a brown diary?

-No. Why?

-Just asking. -She said, walking up the stairs.

Hiding under the arch of a door, Daphne listened to what they were talking about, and when they got to the end, she quickly flickered out so that no one would notice.

# CHAPTER VII

"*My dear diary, it's incredible that I took you out again. Though I already felt I didn't need to describe my feelings. I thought I was strong enough to crush them before I could put those words down on paper. I haven't written about what happened in my life in over a year. But I will describe what happened in the past another time. I, on the other hand, would like to write about how painful I spend my days now my farm has gone bankrupt and I have no prospects for the future. I don't know if my business will be as full of hope as it was when I got to Gracewith. But what matters more, I can't promise the villagers that they hope for. Please bring anything in the new year, just don't take anyone and anything away from us.*

*As for my brother, one of my eyes is happy and the other is crying. I am more than happy to see him here, but I am very worried. He doesn't know so many people in the area yet, he doesn't have much experience with people. I just dare hope he won't be so stupid to betray himself.*

*About my aunt, Miranda... who isn't my aunt actually but my mother, whom I am getting to know more and more, even she's not present, yet sometimes I feel like she's here. I am so ashamed of myself that I have lost her diary and I even feel more... Frustration, fear, and sadness flow into me as if a vortex was trying to swallow it from within. I am disappointed in myself because I was able to lose an item of this magnitude, I am afraid it will fall into the hands of someone who is not worthy to read its lines and find out those pieces of information, and I'm sad because I couldn't read my mother's last letter to the end. (Which I dare say I actually remembered dreaming about the diary I hadn't been reading for a year).*"

That cold night when Scarlett was writing these lines, Aydan was in the kitchen, thinking deeply about his life. Daphne entered the door in her nightgown, saying she was thirsty. At first, Aydan didn't want to notice her until she lifted her long nightgown, saying she thought something had bitten her leg, and then she began to scratch herself in the area where she felt the little, tiny bite. When she looked at the boy, he was ashamed, turned toward the window. Daphne sat next to him.

-Gracewith is so wonderful at night.

-It really is. -The boy said, looking at the moon.

-Gracewith has a huge area. -She said, then stroked the boy's face. But he just smiled, there was nothing to add. -The field and the ocean are so beautiful. -She continued as she slides closer.

-I think you're beautiful! -He said, holding his arm around her waist. She was leaning closer and taking a gentle breath, touching the boy's skin around his neck and giving him goosebumps from head to toe. They both took deeper and deeper breaths, taking advantage of the fact that there were only two of them in the kitchen, immersed in the foams of feelings.

-And how much more beautiful it will be when it will be yours. -She said, kissing the boy on the neck.

-Unfortunately, it won't happen. -The boy said, reciprocating her touches and tenderness.

-What do you mean? -She pushed away Aydan.

-Gracewith has no other heirs listed. But what does it all matter now? -He asked, trying to lean close.

-It matters. -She said lingering.

-I do not understand you. -Said the boy, looking deep into her eyes- Isn't this just about the two of us?

-Of course not! -She added- Do you think I'm sleeping with all sorts of worthless man? -Then she began thinking- But I can help make it all yours. -She said with an evil smile on her face.

-Are you saying that my sister's property could be in my possession?

-Yes, and I'll tell you how.

-No, stop it now. I don't want my sister's fortune. I don't know what you were thinking. If not so far, now Scarlett will know what kind of person you really are. -Then he started for the door.

-Great, you're sure to be appreciated for your honesty about telling her what you wanted to do in her kitchen. Just as much as you appreciate her for telling you who she actually is.

-I'll warn you if you're going to do anything, my sister... -Then he was interrupted again.

-Your sister? -She began to laugh- Did your sister tell you, she was actually Miranda Bloom's daughter?

-What are you talking about? -Aydan asked in shock.

-You heard it right. Scarlett Miranda Bloom, the little rosebud, is actually the daughter of Miranda Bloom. -She said, looking at her fingernails with complete peace of mind.

-If you don't keep your mouth shut... -He said, pointing his finger at the girl as he stepped closer- I can guarantee...

-What will happen? -She asked as she stepped closer, then grabbed the man's finger- Will Princess Scarlett Bloom fire me from her palace? -She asked sarcastically, then let go of the man and left.

# CHAPTER VIII

-Doris, please make a note, that I will have an appointment with Mr. Thaker tomorrow afternoon at three. I don't want to be late.

-Of course, Miss. Bloom. Will the gentleman come in person?

-No, this time I'm going to Truro. -Then she started searching on the table.

-I understood. -Doris said, but she couldn't take her eyes off the woman as she searched desperately. -Can I help?

-I just can't find my keys that's all. -She said a little angrily, then straightened up, raised both hands, closed her eyes and took a deep breath. -I'll find them when I'm not looking. -Then she started for the door.

-Are you leaving?

-Yes, I'm going to the market. Christmas is here in our heels, I want a little trifle for the villagers, even if I can't buy it yet, but at least I will know what I want.

Doris just nodded, then set off. As Scarlett walked past one of the rooms, she checked to see if Riley had the keys. So, she went in to them.

-Riley would you show me what's in your hand? -The little girl shook her head, looking at her in silence beside Julia, who did the same. Scarlett was used to the girls not talking to her, but now she was impatient with a lot of problems on her head. -I said show me your hand. -Riley held out her left hand and opened her grip, which was empty. -The other one. -The woman said, but she shook her head again. -I said show me. -The same gesture came again and again- Don't make me ask one more time. -Riley shook her head again. -Let me see your hand. -She shouted at the tiny girl, but she just shook her head silently with teary eyes, Scarlett kneeled down and then began to wrinkle her little arm, which she was hiding behind herself.

-Leave her alone! -Julia exclaimed as Scarlett stopped and looked at the little girl who hasn't spoken to her for more than a year. -You're not our mother! You have no right to command us.

Scarlett was just shocked, straightened up, while Daphne went into the room and asked what had happened. Julia said Scarlett wanted to see Riley's hands. Scarlett was still silent; she didn't say anything. Yet she was so eager to say that she was entitled to do it as a foster parent. But she didn't, this was already a development in the relationship between the two of them.

-For what reason? With what do you suspect a seven-year-old? -She asked, pointing at the little girl with a blond-brown curly hair in a blue dress.

-Personal reasons which have nothing to do with a governess. -She was firm.

-Then let's see what's here. -She squatted down and stroked Riley's back from the side where she hid her right hand. -Show me, little one, what's in your hand. -Then Riley held out her hand, opened her grip, and there was nothing in it- Didn't the Miss just look for the air? -She asked indecently.

-With this behaviour, you're not going to impress me, Daphne. -She said confidently, a little sceptical of her.

-Then, how could I impress you, Miss.?

-Be loyal behind my back.

Scarlett said then left. Daphne's eyes gathered in anger, then she looked at the girls and smiled. When she pulled her hand from behind Riley, which she caressed, there were the keys in it.

*

Scarlett sat in the library, with aching in her head, thinking about going to Truro the next day to meet Mr. Thaker and finally recovering her expenses. She was also wondering if it would go straight and calculated that she would have some extras, what would she like to buy for the villagers.

Unexpectedly, Doris entered the room, announcing that Mr. Leonard Wolowitz had arrived. When the man entered the room, he looked much more attractive in Scarlett's eyes than when she saw him last time. Scarlett's dogs started barking loudly until the woman silenced them.

-Miss. Bloom, I am sorry to bother you with the late disturbance. But I couldn't wait long to see you again.

Scarlett stood up and offered the man a seat. She walked to the dresser and poured some drinks.

-Well, there's a lot on my head lately, but I'd love to hear what was so important about what made you ride here at this hour. -Scarlett smiled flirtingly.

-You're not waiting for a guest tonight, are you? -He asked, looking at the door, ironic, referring to a past case. Scarlett just shook her head with a smile. She was completely impressed with herself that she found the man so attractive. She wasn't bothered by any of the negative thoughts he had ever thought of before. -Great. -The man stood up nervously, then began to turn his glass in his hand. -You know, I'm not a man of words. But I want you to know something. You, Miss. Bloom, you touched my heart. Like a woman, never before.

-If it's a love confession now, I'm afraid I don't feel fit for that... -She said getting up from the armchair.

-It's not just a love confession. -He added, as she sighed. -It's a proposal! -He declared, making Scarlett shocked, unable to speak, so she just stared at him. She watched in silence for a few more seconds before it reached her mind what it was all about. But, even so, she didn't want to believe her ears, so she asked back.

-Pardon me what did you say? -She asked back with a forced smile, hoping the question would change.

-You heard it; I want to marry you. -Scarlett just looked speechless again, and when she realised he was serious, she drank the alcohol straight off. -Of course, you don't have to answer right away. I'll give you time to think it over. -The man also drank the liquid from his glass and then kissing her hand, left.

He contributed another degree to Scarlett's headache. So, she decided to retreat to her room and rest. Having lost the keys to the library along with the others, she decided to lock the dogs to make sure the jewellery would be safe overnight.

# CHAPTER IX

Aydan's room was located in a wing on the other side of the house from Scarlett's, on the lower floor. As a soldier, he was accustomed to not sleeping deeply, he got up to the slightest noise. That night, he woke up to a loud noise coming from the girls' room above him. By the time he entered the room, Julia and Riley were already in a deep sleep. But there was someone else in the room. It was dark in the room, just as the world, only the moon was somewhat lit. So, it occurred to him that the person in the room was a woman, a woman wearing a nightgown, Daphne.

-What are you doing here? -Aydan asked.

-That's the same question I could ask.

 -I heard a noise.

-The girls had a nightmare. -Daphne said with a serious expression. Aydan didn't say a word, the moon lit up the room as it emerged from the clouds. Then he saw something, a tiny little glitter under Julia's bed. As he leaned closer, he saw that it was a bunch of keys.

-How did this get here? -Daphne stepped closer than she could take a closer look at the three keys hanging from a hoop.

-Sure, the girls played with it.

-With Scarlett's keys? -He looked at her, but she got nervous and ran out of the room. Aydan hurried after her. As she tried to lock herself in the room neighbouring the one where the girls slept, the boy pushed open the door. -What else are you hiding? -He asked angrily.

-Nothing! -She declared in fear. But Aydan, unbelieving her, looked around, in the single room, barely four by four metres wide, and began to search. Then he found something in the drawer of the cupboard.

-If you're not hiding anything, what is this? -He asked, picking up the brown-bound book.

-You can't understand this... -She said upset in tears.

Then, hearing a loud scream, they both shuddered. There was shouting and clutter in the house.

*

"-You brought shame on the whole family! -Shouted a moustachioed man with a deep voice.

-You can't do anything about it. You can't command me anymore. -Said a young lady.

-I can do anything, I am your father after all!

-If you lock me in here, I'll be on my whole life to escape you. I hate you.

-Please don't say that to your father! -A third person, woman asked for.

*

-Evelyn! -Cried Miranda from one of Gracewith's windows, but in vain, her friend was too far away to hear it. When she had just heard her name, by the time she looked at the window, no one was there.

-I said you can't meet anyone or talk to anyone. -Then hit the girl.

*

At a funeral, Miranda, dressed in black, walked over to her friend and pressed a piece of paper into her hand. As soon as the coffin was lowered to the ground, Miranda disappeared from the scene.

*

-I can promise you one thing. -Said Miranda to her three faithful workers -I will never let him raise his hand to any of you.

*

The next moment she went into her father's room, who was chained to his bed, she took a deep breath.

-Tell me where my daughter, Scarlett, is.

-Never! -Cried the man and then spat on her daughter, his saliva was still drooling on his moustache but it didn't bother her. -You'll never know where your daughter is fucking bitch! You're going to die with me in GracewithHenry.

Miranda took another deep breath as she wiped the saliva from her face. -We will see. -She said, then gently dropped her hand into the powder and began rubbing her father's skin with it.

-What is this? What did you do to me? What is this? -He shouted, squirming in bed. Miranda didn't speak after washing her hands she just walked out the door. -Come back, you slut! What have you done to me? What is this? It's so itchy!

*

-Miss. Bloom, the doctor has arrived. -Doris said.

241

-Just in time. -Miranda replied.

Then they walked up to the room with the doctor.

-Please wait here, he becomes very upset when he sees strangers. -Miranda told the doctor, who nodded in agreement. -No problem dad, I called a doctor who can help you. -She said kindly.

-You're a slut! You haven't called anyone to help me in years... No one can help me! I don't need help from anybody! Just loosen me, I'll kill you with my own two hands! -He shouted as Miranda burst into tears and walked to the door, when she opened it, the doctor took notes there.

-How long is he being in this condition? -The doctor asked, looking at the struggling man.

-Since my mother died. -Cried the woman- Whenever a doctor saw him, they all said he is just getting worse and they can't help.

The doctor took a deep breath and looked at the man, who was completely slackened into wrestling. Shouting: *"It's so itchy..."*

-Dr. Bing, the other doctor who saw him says he has worms... -Would you write something for it? -The man just nodded.

-Here's my report. This must be brought to the notary. From here, it's his job to take over the estate's inheritance list as a priority.

-Thank you doctor!

*

-I want my daughter, I want my daughter back. -Miranda yelled into her pillow as the moonlit up her room.

*

-I'll never forgive you, Dad. I never forgive. -She said, sitting next to the man's deathbed.

*

The villagers gathered to get a job again. Miranda told them the most important things they needed to know about the farm. People adored her, they loved her as much as if the queen herself stood before them. But from one minute to the next she passed out, falling to the ground, the woman in front of them was unconscious.

*

Miranda, from behind a bush, watched as a little red-haired girl played with another little girl. The child looked happy. She was a cheerful, powerful girl, and later three more boys ran there to play together.

*

-Are you feeling well? -Doris asked, sitting next to her bed.

-I don't have much time anymore. -Miranda said sickly, her lips dry and so wet already, because of her temperature. -Please help my little girl find her place in Gracewith. -She told the woman sitting on her bed, who had been by her side all day at her last day."

*

Scarlett was sweaty as she woke up, feeling like she had been burned by a fire while she was asleep. Her skin was as hot as she would be the source of the flame. She felt completely out of her mind when she got up, a little dizzy, she saw a light floating in her room and heard Miranda's voice telling her to "Come". Scarlett, despite being a little dizzy and not seeing clearly, walked after the light. The house was dark, she could not see clearly where she was going just walked away. While walking she accidentally knocked over a vase that shattered loudly. At this sound, she was fully awake and the light ceased to exist, and then she heard loud dogs barking. She set off to reassure her dogs, not wanting them to wake up the people in the house because of a vase.

When she smelled smoke near the library, she started running. When she opened the door, she saw that the room was on fire. Her dogs immediately ran out next to her and Scarlett began to shout for help.

*

After the people in the house put out the fire and Nivek assured them that the danger was over, Scarlett sent everyone back to their rooms to rest. Among them, Daphne, who was watching the events with the children from a safe distance, the two little girls hugged their governess in horror. After everyone was gone. Scarlett stayed in the library, looking around the ruins in despair. The window was still wide open, and next to it was a candle holder stuck in the melted wax. Scarlett knew the room didn't light up on its own, she was sure someone was there and probably escaped through the window. Her brother was in the room too, but he didn't say anything, he didn't want to upset her more. Scarlett then went to the safe, which was hidden in the dresser. When she opened the dresser door and saw that the safe was empty, she fell weakly to the ground. In shock, she had no strength to cry or rage. She was just sitting there staring at the empty room. This was the only chance that secured not only Gracewith, but her freedom as well as her younger brother's escape.

-Now what? -Aydan asked, standing behind her.

-I have to resort to Plan B. -She replied without eye fluttering.

-What would that be?

-I'm getting married.

Unable to answer this, Aydan reached back for the items on the table he had brought back to her. But he decided that he needed to know the truth about his sister, so he just handed the keys over, hiding the brown-bound diary behind his back.

-I found these in the girl's room.

-It doesn't matter anymore. -She said, staring at the empty safe.

# CHAPTER X

The next morning, people tried to continue their lives as if nothing had happened. Except that the captain and his soldiers showed up trying to solve the crime.

-Miss, are you saying, that you were the first who arrived at the scene? -The captain asked.

-Yes, as I said.

-And are you sure you didn't see anyone?

-Absolutely sure. It was dark in the house.

-What was the reason you were walking in the house at that hour? -The man asked in a suspicious way.

-This is my house. I walk whenever I feel like it. -Scarlett replied indignantly.

-Did you hear any noise? -The man asked, taking notes.

-No, as I said, I didn't see or hear anything. A nightmare woke me up and I just wanted to come down for a drink, but since it was dark, I knocked over the vase, after that I heard my dogs barking from the library.

-That was the only time you heard your dogs?

-I don't remember clearly. I was tired and lay down with a severe headache.

-What was the cause of the headache? Did something unusual happen the day before? -The man asked with further interest.

-Yes, I was proposed to.

-Oh, congratulations! -He said, pulling something out of his notes.

-Ahm, I haven't answered yet.

-You mean, you were just asked for marriage?

-Yes, that is what I meant. -She replied, a little embarrassed.

-What was the reason you didn't give an answer.

-This is my own private life! -Scarlett replied a little nervously.

-Miss, I just want to know your background so I can continue the investigation. -He replied to explain. -Who arrived at the scene next?

-Daphne, the governess, and Aydan. -Scarlett pointed to the two young people at the other end of the room, where other officers were guarding the people who had been in the house that night. The captain also set off for them.

-Aydan, who? -He asked curiously.

-He is ohm... One of my valets. -Scarlett said nervously.

-If I understood correctly the miss's name is Scarlett Miranda Bloom?

-Yes, that's right! -She said, a little embarrassed, but she tried to stay confident.

-I'll keep you informed of developments. -He said, his face completely grim, and they headed for the exit.

Scarlett sighed, as soon as the men left Gracewith, Evelyn ran into the room. She looked around in fright, but when she saw Aydan she calmed down, whispering to herself, "Thank God!" Scarlett stepped forward to greet her, but before she did, Evelyn spoke again.

-What happened here? -She asked in surprise as she looked around the room.

-I'll tell you everything, come with me. -She said, then took the woman by the arm and led her.

*

A cold wind blew outside Gracewith's yard, but Scarlett wanted to make sure no one heard them. Walking in the frosty grass, she wore her warm scarf, pulling it up in front of her face because of the cold.

-I can't believe it. So, what are you going to do now?

-I'll go to Mr. Thaker's office and tell the truth.

-You mean about your debts? How will you pay it?

-I haven't planned it yet. -She said, trying not to lie, but she knew she couldn't tell the truth yet. She couldn't say she had been proposed to. Especially since the Captain planted a beetle in her ear of the robes and the so-called "groom". She thought that this could be related to the robbery. Mr. Wolowitz who asked for her hand the night before could be because he wanted to be sure of Scarlett's response. Scarlett looked at the silver ring with a rose pattern on her finger. -It's the only one left from her jewellery.

-It doesn't have much value anyway. -Evelyn added when she saw it.

-What do you mean?

-In the market, gold has a higher price and is much more sought after. -She replied, Scarlett was a little puzzled after what Mr. Thaker had said about the ring, but the thought soon faded, wondering if Leonard Wolowitz might have had something to do with what had happened and if it didn't, what to do about his offer.

-Evelyn. You are living in a marriage of convenience. What is it like? -Evelyn was a little embarrassed to hear that, but then smiled.

-Throughout my life, I thought I couldn't be happy. It was an arranged marriage. My father always wanted me to have a good life, but he didn't know that happiness isn't just about money. -She took a break and then continued. -As you saw Lord Quas is an older man, more precisely ten years older. I never thought I would ever fall in love. Until the night I spent with Elliot Bloom.

-But he was the love of your life. -Scarlett said puzzled.

-It really was him. But, on the other hand, the bond that had developed between my husband and I over the years was very strong, stronger than a love that once burned in me that I thought I was consuming. Elliot offered to meet on occasions. I replied to him that I didn't need that. But he didn't argue, he would have been able to leave his wife and his whole family so we could be together. I had to wake up to the fact that neither love can replace the other, each one is different, special in its own way...

-I don't quite understand that. Can we divide our love, can we love two men at the same time?

-As I said, you can love in other ways. I respect my husband, until that moment I had never been able to notice all the good he was doing for me, for us. He made sacrifices for our happiness and overwhelmed me with his love. He's a man I don't deserve. Many times, a marriage of convenience can also become love.

*

Before meeting Mr. Thaker, she went into her room to get ready. In preparation, she reached into her dressing table drawer to look for her hair ornament, but found the brown leather-bounded diary. She hugged it happily, no matter how much she had to hurry to get there in time, sat down on her bed, and then began to read her mother's last letter. Hoping that she would also write about the desiccation she had mentioned in it, so, she hoped that she still had another chance not to lose her inheritance.

*"So, my dearest daughter, as I couldn't have the chance to raise you and teach you, I can only give you some advice. You have to learn that home isn't a place, it's a feeling. If you get tired, learn to rest not to quit. Stop shrinking to fit places you have outgrown. Be happy not because everything is good, but because you see good in everything. Even a bad day is still just 24 hours. Do never forget, everyone in your life will have a last day with you and you don't even know when it will be. And the last thing I want you to note is that perseverance is what the dream is born of.*

*Never forget your mother loves you more than anything, so does your dad would, beloved Owen Thaker."*

Scarlett, after reading these lines, was hit by another shock. It would never have occurred to her, not even for a minute that the man who had helped and supported her so faithfully throughout her career could be her father.

-Miss. Bloom, if you don't start preparing, you will be late. -Doris said, holding a basket of clothes in her hand that she was just preparing to wash. -Oh, my God! -She dropped the basket from her hand and went into the room and grabbed the hairbrush of Scarlett, who was staring at the window. As Doris stepped closer, she was a little scared that Scarlett didn't even blink.

-You knew it, right?

-What are you talking about, Miss? -Doris asked, still a little horrified.

-That Owen Thaker is my father. -Her eyes filled with tears.

-No, I didn't know. -Then she sat down next to Scarlett on the bed- The only thing I know is that before Mr. Bloom's death, he told the Mistress where the child was. The young woman's father was in great pain in her last hours, afraid of going to hell, he confessed everything.

-How did he die?

-As I know he struggled with heart problems. But the doctor's report also referred to mental disorders.

-This is how my mother got the house papers without Mr. Bloom's consent. Did he really have a disorder of the mind?

-After his wife passed away, he went through a very difficult period. A trauma hit him. He became very aggressive. Interestingly, when doctors visited at our request as if he had recovered, we contacted various doctors, it was very difficult to diagnose him, years passed until finally, a doctor examined him appropriately.

-Didn't he lock Miranda in somewhere?

-Yes, he did. Several times. He locked her in a tower. It was a slightly cooler part and unclean. He kept her there for a long time, at least for weeks. No one could enter, except me and Mr. Bloom. Not even Mrs. Bloom could visit her single daughter. She sent messages with me many times. There were times when Mr. Bloom was not at home, so the Mistress walked to the door and talked to her daughter through it.

-Did you never call for help? Or you didn't have a key to let her go?

-Miss, I prefer not to talk about it. -She said sadly, Scarlett knew it meant one thing, Doris did it, she trying to help her, which had no

251

good results. Scarlett stood up and walked to the window. -A lot happened at that time.

-Do you believe in ghosts?

-I believe memories are ghosts.

Scarlett smiled at her, then looked out at the ocean from her room window.

-Your really are a gift of the ocean.

\*

This time, Scarlett didn't walk as enthusiastically as she usually did to Mr. Thaker's office, which immediately appeared to the man. However, he received her as kindly as ever before.

-Miss. Bloom! I've been waiting for you. -The man said cheerfully, Scarlett said nothing as she walked moody towards the man. The man asked her: -Are you feeling well?

-Oh, Mr. Thaker, if you would only know... -Then she told him everything from the beginning, except the part that he is her father.

-Don't worry about the money. I can still give you a little respite. It is not that urgent. Please don't let it get you down.

-I don't even know what to do. How could I restart the farm, I don't know what to expect from the next year. What do if it gets the same as this year. I have four children to raise. I owe a lot of money. -She said desperately, just as Mr. Wolowitz entered the door.

-Excuse me Mr. Thaker. I didn't know you had a guest. -Scarlett stood up and wiped her flushed face.

-I have to go now, but we'll talk about this again. -She said, then left.

Leonard watched as she walked out. Then he turned back to Mr. Thaker after Scarlett disappeared behind the door.

-All is well? -He asked the man.

-Naturally. The young lady just became sensitive during our conversation.

-How much debt does she have?

-I'm afraid I can't answer your question, Sir. I cannot disclose such information about my clients.

-I don't think you understood completely. I want - then adjusted his vest - to pay Miss. Bloom's debt.

*

Walking through the streets of Truro, she collided with Kwaw. Scarlett didn't expect to see him, but his unexpected encounter filled her with joy.

-Mr. Kwaw, what a surprise. How is your daughter?

-She is well! Thanks to you and Mr. Wolowitz. You saved my daughter's life.

-We're happy to help. -She said on behalf of the two of them.

-Is it true what the people say? That he asked for a marriage?

-From where did you hear that? -Scarlett stopped in the middle of the street, surprisingly.

-You know I've been working for Mr. Andrews who is in partnership with Mr. Wolowitz delivery company since that incident with Mr. Salvatore. So, I heard it there.

-Does the gentleman distribute this?

-Mr. Wolowitz? Oh no! -He began to laugh. -The gentleman is much busier than dealing with such a thing. -Scarlett was a little reassured that she was dealing with a serious man. -Mrs. Wolowitz is the one we've heard from. -But when she heard that, she got a little disappointed. -However, as I see my break is over. -He said then left.

Mr. Salvatore walked out of the brothel with some gentlemen, Scarlett thought for sure they had a business meeting. She didn't know he had returned to town, nor did she know there was anyone in his life. Scarlett continued to watch what was happening in front of the brothel as she saw a young lady step out. She was slender, very nicely dressed, with blond curly hair covered in a powder blue hat. Her face was wonderfully smooth with discrete make-up. She walked over to George with an umbrella and kissed him on the cheek. Scarlett watched this from a small rising where there were bushes, it was near Mr. Thaker's office. After saying goodbye, George walked in the direction of the woman and the others in the other direction. Before he got there, Scarlett tried to hide behind the bushes. But as she squatted down, she stepped aside because of her high boots and rolled straight in front of the man. She lay there for a few seconds when George saw her, he raises his eyebrows questioningly.

-Are you feeling well? -He asked politely.

-Yes, I just stumbled. -She said, then got up, but when she stood up, she collapsed because of her weak ankle, but George caught her again. -It looks like this is my curse. -She laughed with pity.

-That you stumble upon me all the time? -The man asked ironically as they both laughed.

Mr. Wolowitz walked out of Owen Thaker's office when it all happened. The man had a grim expression, nodded, by grabbing his hat, then walked on without a word.

-Some people never changes. -George said.

-Yes, but there are those who do.

-Oh? -The man was surprised.

-I saw there was a lady in your company as well. -Scarlett said with a false smile.

-You mean Winnifred O'Neil? -George looked back at the point the others went. -Aren't you spying on me? -He asked with an expression on his face that Scarlett couldn't decide if he was serious or teasing.

-I only saw it from the ascent when a squirrel ran out in front of me and because of that I stepped aside and fell.

-It's interesting, I've never seen squirrels in the city. -The man said, and Scarlett became serious. -I'm just poking. -He laughed- But if you will excuse me, I have to go now.

# CHAPTER XI

-Miss. Bloom, Mr. Thaker has come to you. -Doris announced.

Scarlett welcomed him, but this time in the salon, since the library hadn't exactly been a hospitality room lately.

-What can I do for you, Sir? -She asked after they had taken a seat in the large living room.

-I've come to let you know that your bills have been settled, all your debts have been paid.

-I don't quite understand that. -She was confusion.

-A charitable person has decided to pay your debts. All £ 8,076.21, in one.

-Pardon me, but before I take this money, I want to know who's behind it. -She said, gesturing stillness.

-You have no say. It was a donation. It doesn't need your permission. Here's the proof. -He said, then handed her a piece of paper.

-But you can tell who this generous someone was. -Said the woman reading the paper.

-I'm afraid not. However, I can tell you, that you can trust this person.

-Well, then I don't know what to say... -She said with a wide smile.

Still, she knew she would need money to make a living, and she didn't want to take out another loan, yet. Unexpectedly, Evelyn stepped in. She was very upset, barely breathing, and her face was completely flushed.

-Scarlett, you need to hurry. You have to hide your brother! -Evelyn declared as she was gasping for air.

As they hurried to find him, they were quite desperate. When they found him, Mr. Thaker said he knew a good hiding place to take him to. Evelyn said they don't have much time left until the soldiers get there. They had to move fast. When the two of them were left, the women sat down to drink tea and bound it to the souls of their workers so that they would not talk about Aydan, and then Scarlett would speak for them if that were the case.

-How do you know about all this?

-I was just in town when a kid ran out shouting after his friend "Aydan Bloom". I asked him what he was talking about, he said his father was the captain and he heard him talk to someone about that he knew where the coward Aydan Bloom was and he was taking it into his hands tonight. As soon as I heard it, I ran here.

Scarlett just nodded and then took her tea from the table, just the moment when armed soldiers entered the parlour.

-Where is he? -The captain asked.

-What are you talking about, please? -She asked the old man with a completely grey moustache.

-Aydan Bloom! -He said, looking around- Your brother!

-I don't understand what you're talking about, my brother has been declared missing for months. -She remained confident- Rather, you should provide such information to me.

257

-I know he's hiding here. Reveal him or I'll find the boy myself. -He said, stepping on his heels.

-As I said, my brother has been missing from the military for months.

-Turn up everything. Find the boy. -Captain Patmore declared to his dogs who hurried away for his first word.

-And do you have permission to do that? -She asked indignantly, but the man wordlessly showed up a letter, he made with such a quick motion that it was impossible to read.

-Your brother has sworn to serve his country, if you reveal him now, he will die a gracious death, which means a bullet straight into his forehead that shatters the brain to pieces. That means he will die a quick death. If you don't, I will find him anyway, but then a hanging awaits him, he will be ashamed before the whole city and die in torment. First, his limbs will be removed from his body, then his truncated body with only his head will be hanged, he will leave in the midst of torment and suffering. Miss. Bloom the choice is yours.

-My brother has been missing for months. -She declared, swallowing the dumpling from her throat.

-Let it be then. Bring in all the people that are in the house!

Everyone was asked around, but everyone stuck to what Scarlett said. Then the Captain got to Daphne. On Scarlett's side were the children who hugged her tightly, fearing the grim soldiers.

-Are you Daphne Jelon?

-Yes, Sir! -She said fearfully.

-Where is Aydan Bloom? -He asked, leaning closer.

-I know an Aydan named boy...

Scarlett pushed the children to Doris, then stepped closer.

-And who is this Aydan? -The captain asked.

-He was a valet. -Scarlett replied- Who you have seen here last week.

-And where is he now? -He asked now impatiently.

-I fired him, he wasn't a good worker, and as you see is dismissal here, I have no money. I got robbed. -She said, but the man pushed Scarlett away and grabbed the girl.

-Where's Mr. Bloom? -Daphne began to moan in pain as all the children were startled, the two younger ones began to cry, while the other two began to shout in defence of their governess to leave her alone. -I'll ask you once again, you rotter. Where is the Bloom boy? If you don't tell me, I'll cut off all your fingers one by one. -Daphne began to cry, already opening her mouth to say something when Scarlett spoke again.

-For heaven's sake, let her go. There are kids here too. -She just uttered these words when a soldier arrived saying everything was clear. They went on with that.

Scarlett ran back to the kids to reassure them, while Evelyn tried to reassure Daphne confidently.

-The captain set up guards around Gracewith until he found Aydan. -Evelyn said, looking out the window. -Do you know where Mr. Thaker took him?

-I'm afraid, no. -Scarlett said sadly. -But I have to do something.

-Do you want me to stay here?

-Not necessary. -She said to the owner of the hand on her shoulder, then stroked it. -Your husband must be worried.

Evelyn just nodded and headed for the exit. When she got to the door, she met Mr. Wolowitz, who was just trying to reach Scarlett, but the guards didn't want to let any case him enter the doorstep.

-I have to meet Miss. Bloom.

-On what matter? -One of the soldiers asked.

-It's personal.

-You know we had to take the Miss. into custody and no outsiders can visit her. -The other replied.

-Great! Because... -he then swallowed the dumpling from his throat- I'm her fiancé.

The two soldiers looked at each other and laughed. Then when Evelyn stepped out the door, they stopped her.

-Where are you going Lady? -Asked the chubby man, who apparently preferred to tease people.

-My husband is waiting for me. I am already late.

-The captain ordered us not to let anyone in or out. -The same soldier replied confidently again.

-Then tell your captain. I say it's better not to getting troubled with my husband.

-Who would be your gracious husband? -He asked, stepping closer to the woman, but he was rolling something in his mouth that made him chews tastelessly, it bothered Evelyn so much, that she pulled away from him.

-Lord Quas. -She replied, and the two soldiers looked at each other, then the moustachioed chewer, nodded on the road, giving way to the woman who had seized the opportunity and then set off, but had to turn back at the soldier's call- Wait! Do you know this gentleman? -He asked her, but since Evelyn was already behind the door when she heard the conversation, she replied, "He's Miss. Bloom's fiancé!". At this, the soldier closed his mouth and then stepped out the door, allowing him to enter. -You know, Mr. Wolowitz, -the soldier said, turning to him- our captain has been waiting a long time to see you hanged. I don't know what's going on in your head right now, but I can assure you, you will not scam us. -Leonard just nodded, letting go of the grim soldier's speech, and walked on.

-Mr. Wolowitz! What are you doing here?

-Shhh. -He stepped closer to Scarlett, who was just holding Jared on her lap, and then looking around at the workers, Scarlett just nodded that he could talk in front of them. He trusted in whom Scarlett trusted, the people were also curiously awaiting Leonard's announcement, especially Daphne. -Your brother is hiding on my property. After I came here and said I was your fiancé they would definitely search my place as well. But you don't have to be afraid, -he comforted, putting his hand on her thighs- he's safe. A boat will go to America in the early hours of the morning, I also told your brother that he could stay on my property there. English law no longer reaches there. You just have to wait patiently. Stay here, please. -He said warningly, then left.

Doris began to sigh. -What are we going to do now, Miss?

-You have to stay here and cover for me. I have to say goodbye to my brother.

-Miss, this is dangerous. -Doris said, leaning softly towards her as she looked at the scattering workers.

-I know, but I have to do this, I was only able to be there with my brother, Elliot, at the time of his death, I was unable to say goodbye to the other members of my family, I can't let him go like that. -Doris wanted to say something, but Scarlett spoke again- Please keep an eye on the others, the traitor is here, only those in the house knew about my brother's presence.

She yanked up her cloak and climbed out a window. Trying to move to the side of the wall so the guards wouldn't notice, she knew if she could get to the hedge from there, she could sneak into Gracewith's little forest and then get down to the farm from where she would go on to Leonard's estate.

-Everyone after me! -Shouted a soldier to those who were guarding the house.

Scarlett felt there was trouble, and it was more than likely that her intuitions did not disappoint. The soldiers headed for Mr. Wolowitz's home. Behind the passing soldiers, she crossed the path to get to the farm, and from there to the estate. She had just reached the hedge when the stocky moustachioed soldier, who had now chewed whatever might have been in his mouth, turned, staring squinting at first, but because of the darkness and the silence that was set in, he decided not to go to the end of the case, so he continued on his way. So, Scarlett got a free path into the woods, through which she cut off her way and got to the farm. There were also soldiers stabbing the haystacks with their bayonets. She tried to run past them, but they heard it. The soldiers tried to approach the barn softly as they stood in front of the entrance, suddenly something huge pushed them up, they didn't even know where they were for half a second. When they looked in the direction of the animal, they saw that a rider was galloping at least 30 metres away from them.

-After the rider! -Shouted a soldier next to the hay, then opened fire.

She was followed by four cavalry soldiers. At first, she took advantage of the forest to try to shake them off, as she knew the trees of the forest relatively well, she knew the path where they could easily ride and where it was difficult. She went out once and decided to explore that part as well. It was one of the most beautiful areas of the forest, with a stream, trees and wildflowers. She also remembered that there was a fallen tree not far from the creek, so she headed in that direction. The riders behind her galloped faster and faster, not knowing what was waiting for them. Scarlett slowed down a little, the soldiers were so close to her that they were sure to catch her, while in an unexpected moment Scarlett jumped over the fallen tree and cut off.

The two who were right behind Scarlett succeeded, however, the obstacle was hidden from the two soldiers in the back, so they stumbled there with their horses. Continuing their journey, she passed through a meadow where the riders following her fired missing the target, as a result of the bumpy hill ground. A chasm in the height of the cliff stood before them. What she always thought was an inability to cross before, it could have been much more than two metres. Before that, when she went there, she always made a quarter-hour detour for that. But this time she felt it was not possible. So, she shook the reins again and sprinted faster and then teased, in the air she felt the risk was worth it, knowing that she would probably see her brother for the last time. She closed her eyes and saw in front of her the happy moment when, as children, they were sitting under the willow tree and telling stories. Carefree childhood when there was no war, no responsibility. Then, reaching the ground, she returned to reality, where she galloped far from the grips of the soldiers.

When she got to Leonard's home, the soldiers took him into custody along with Mr. Thaker. They sat in the living room, drinking. When Scarlett stepped into the room all eyes were fixed on her.

-Tell me, Miss, what are you doing here? I ordered them to keep you under house arrest.

Mr. Wolowitz stood up, waving, struggling to keep his balance, walking to her.

-My dear bride! -He said in a slurred voice with a hiccup. Scarlett was about to drop him when her father, who of course didn't know it yet, Mr. Thaker motioned not to, so she grabbed the man tighter.

-Well, I got a message that my fiancé is not in prime condition. So, I had to see myself. -The captain raised an eyebrow so Scarlett had to keep lying- We have an appointment for the church, tomorrow, and when I heard he was in this condition, I had to come here because we can't set up the papers like this. Don't you think Captain Patmore?

-It's all your fault, if you hadn't fought with me this afternoon, I wouldn't have been like it... -Leonard said, then began to kiss the woman's neck. Scarlett held him off with disgust, as long as Captain Patmore watched the party grimly, Mr. Wolowitz lost his balance, so Scarlett caught hold of him and then smiled at the soldiers with a forced smile.

-You know he is not used to drinking. -She said, explaining.

-The wedding wines. -He said pointing a finger- I had to taste if suitable for our wedding.

-Enough of this circus! -The soldier said as Leonard pulled himself up straight, but after half a second, he fell like a log. The captain slapped his palm on his forehead, then looked at Mr. Thaker- And what about you?

-You know, I brought the wines. It has a really nice taste, it's homemade from Yorkshire, it's very hard to get it... -He said until he was interrupted by the impatiently nervous captain.

-I meant what do you know about Mr. Aydan Bloom?

-Who is that? - Owen asked briefly, looking at the bottom of his glass. -I ran out of wine. Would you be such a nice person, captain? -He said, raising his empty glass toward him.

-I have heard from this wacky that your future brother-in-law, soldier, is unknown and what else has he added? Oh, yes, invisible.

-I told you, Captain, you are bothering yourself unnecessarily, my brother disappeared months ago.

-Captain Patmore! Lord Quas and his wife have arrived with a boy in their hands. -Said a soldier who ran into the room.

-Really? -He asked, looking at the woman, then crossed by Leonard to get to the exit.

In the lobby, there was Evelyn, her husband, and another person covered by the woman.

-Captain Patmore! I have to tell you what joy was that we met today. I told my husband why I was late, so he helped us clear up this little misunderstanding. -The woman said hissing.

Everyone was standing behind the captain, waiting to see how to proceed. The captain frowned, then pulled away the woman and stepped closer to the boy.

-What's your name? -The captain asked.

-Aydan, sir! -He said trembling. The captain looked back to see Scarlett's reaction -But I wonder you don't remember me since we met at Miss. Bloom's home. You also asked who I am.

-You know my facial memory is bad. So, who are you? -The man turned back to the boy.

-Aydan Kelvin, sir! I have been working in the house since the arrival of the young lady.

-Kelvin? -The captain asked back in surprise. -Then why did they claim to be the young lady's brother?

-I have my papers here. -He handed the proof of identity. -I found out the Mistresses brother's is also called Aydan. So, I asked myself, what can it be like to come from a rich family? So, I started daydreaming about it, claiming on a daily basis that I was Aydan Bloom.

The captain pushed the boy's papers back with great rage, with such force that he took two steps back. Through the pride of the captain, he did not speak, just nodded to those present, then left.

-What was that? -She asked, stepping closer to Evelyn.

-I learnt a bit or maybe a little more from Miranda. -She said, shrugging, then hugging her friend.

Then Scarlett turned to Mr. Quas, who gave some money to the young boy.

-Thank you!

-Thank to Evelyn. -He said with a smile, then looked in Leonard's direction, causing his smile to dry.

-And where is my brother? -She asked Mr. Wolowitz.

*

After a quarter of an hour of riding, they arrived at a place Scarlett didn't even know existed.

-What is this place?

-Mines. That's what I wanted to start my career with. But it was loss making. Wait here, is not a place for ladies.

-But... -She wanted to continue until Leonard conjured such a glance that she realised she'd better not insist.

After a few minutes, they both came out of the mine. The boy was very dirty, but it didn't bother Scarlett as she jumped around his neck. And she laughed with joy.

-The danger is not over yet. -He said, then motioned for them to leave.

*

The great farewell began at the port. Scarlett didn't want to let go of her brother in any way. Mr. Wolowitz gave them enough space to make it all happen comfortably. He stopped to talk to the ship's captain and handed him a small sack of money. He, contentedly, lifted it up in his hand, checking its weight.

-Take care of yourself! You will be missed, my little brother.

-Scarlett, I know the truth. But you'll always be my sister. -Then he put his arms around her.

-Everybody on the board! -Someone shouted from the ship.

After Aydan took off, he hurried to the end of the ship because something occurred to him, where he saw his sister waving. Mr. Wolowitz was already with her by then, embracing the sad woman.

-Take care, you can't trust... -He was shouting as the ship departed.

Scarlett began to gesture that she didn't understand. He actually understood the words, she just didn't know who her brother was referring to. By this time the ship was so far away, she absolutely did not understand what name Aydan was shouting.

# CHAPTER XII

It was only a few days after Aydan left. One morning the household barely woke up, when the milkwoman banged hard on Gracewith doorstep.

-What do you want so early? -Doris asked opening the door.

-All of them have perished...

*

A few hours later, Scarlett walked on the farm to assess the damage. As she walked through the animal carcasses, she felt that she has ruined everything, everything this time. If she doesn't act soon, she'll lose Gracewith forever.

-What is your opinion, Captain Patmore?

-Barbarity ... Whoever did this there was not a drop of respect or a drop of dignity in that man. -He said looking at the cow corpses all the way through the cattle pen.

-But how did this happen without anyone noticing?

-Where is the well from which the animals are watered?

-This way. -Scarlett showed the man the well.

-I'll take a sample if you allow me.

The woman nodded wordlessly. After the man took the sample, she turned back to him from the corpses.

-Do you think it was the same person who robbed me?

-It could be possible. Do you suspect anyone?

-Well, there are many people who don't like me.

-More precisely?

-I cannot name anyone who could do such a thing.

-I will come back when I know anything. Until then don't water your animals from this well. -He said looking at the milkman and milkwoman.

-Captain... You didn't know? -The woman asked.

-What should we know about? -Scarlett asked with a serious expression.

- All animals on the farm have died...

# CHAPTER XIII

For days, Scarlett wondered what she could do to restore everything in Gracewith. She was unable to think of marriage. Mr. Wolowitz handled it understandingly in the days after she lost her last brother. Scarlett didn't know who to trust and who she couldn't. Her workers did their work diligently in order to get rid of the animal corpses, and no one dared to say a word about what had happened in this period. Except, of course, Doris, who was constantly trying to comfort her.

-Miss, I brought breakfast. -She sat in her room one morning. Scarlett was sitting awake in her bed, her thoughts taking her so far that Doris's first sentence didn't reach her, but when she spoke again, she dragged her back to reality. -How weird that you don't have your dogs here, I'm used to them so much. -But Scarlett didn't answer, so she tried to get her attention with another topic -And what about Mr. Wolowitz? He went into danger quite boldly.

-What are you talking about? -Scarlett asked, still from a different world.

-I mean, if they would have found Mr. Bloom at his place, he could have been in serious trouble. Nevertheless, he was willing to help.

At that moment, Scarlett jumped out of bed. She felt betrayed. She thought unceasingly of what her brother was shouting from aboard the ship, *"Take care, you can't trust..."* Maybe *"him"*?

-Of course! -She said as she walked to the window. –*"Don't trust HIM"* -She repeated.

-Miss. Bloom, are you feeling well? -Doris asked, a little worried.

-Make sure everything goes the right way today. No one can suspect I'm gone. -She said as she got dressed.

-What? Where are you going?

-To my fiancé. -Scarlett declared ironically.

# CHAPTER XIV

-You're hardly back from India, yet you're already elsewhere.

-I am sorry, Aunt. -George said, swallowing the food that has been in his mouth chewing for minutes.

-You didn't tell me anything about what happened there. -She said, arranging her napkin.

-Well, the trial wasn't what I expected. For the velvet and the silk, the price was raised, but the cotton... -He said, stabbing another piece of meat on his fork. -I am visiting Lord Quas today regarding the post.

Edith smiled contentedly. -What about the cotton mill?

-It's probably coming to an end. We take the work through seasonally and put the last item on the market. After that, I guess you know what will happen.

-What about the workers?

-It's no longer my problem. -He said, putting another bite in his mouth.

-Little red wouldn't think so. -She said provocatively.

-Miss. Bloom is not my problem either from now on. -He tried to close the subject, but his aunt pushed on.

-Do you have another one to pick out? -George put another big bite in his mouth, so he was not needed to answer, his aunt noticing this continued- I don't know if you've met her lately. I heard she has changed. She got more feminine and I heard she got a lot more serious also.

-She was serious before, I thought she was very mature faced her age. And yes, I met her the other day in front of Mr. Thaker's office.

-Are you still interested in her?

-I wouldn't say that. I also met her brother one day. He said she wanted to get married.

-Oh, really?

-Mr. Leonard Wolowitz asked for her hand.

-But did she give him an answer? -The woman asked, which seemed to upset her nephew, who got up from the table. -You didn't answer if you had a picked one.

-As a matter of fact, yes, I met someone along my journey. And this person is the daughter of William O'Neil from the House of Lords.

Her aunt would have apparently jumped out of her skin at the news, but while maintaining her dignity, she hadn't said or done anything to upset George.

George left the dining room, returning to his own office. In the inner garden of the building, he watched as his workers worked hard to reach their daily goals. He thought with a sore heart that they would have to be fired. He was saddened by the thought, so he tried to let go and think of something else. But the first thought that flashed through his head was when he met Aydan at the market. Aydan inadvertently took a step back from a stall, trampling Mr. Salvatore.

-I beg your pardon, Sir. -He said, but at first George didn't answer, just looked through him.

-You look so familiar. -He stepped closer.

-Well, that must be because my sister lives here. We must be similar. -Turned back to the market vendor.

-Who's your sister? -He asked curiously.

-Scarlett Bloom. -He said, hoping the stranger would leave him alone, but on the contrary, it made him all the more interested.

-George Salvatore! -He introduced himself, extending his hand.

-Andrew Bloom! -Aydan said thoughtfully- I remember you, -he said, raising his index finger- I was accompanied that day when you helped her up next to the banker's office, you probably didn't see me I was a few yards away. It was not easy for her that period. She went through a lot. - The boy said a little sympathetically.

-Would you like to sit down for a drink? -George asked, pointing in the direction of the brothel.

\*

-How did you mean that she goes through a lot? -He turned to the boy after placing the order.

-What is your relationship with my sister that you care so much about? -He asked, a little nervous.

-Let's say I'm an old friend of hers. -The man in front of him replied confidently.

-I don't know if you've heard of it, but our parents died. One of our sisters, too, and one of our brothers on the front, Aydan Bloom, -He stressed- and one in front of her eyes, he died in the hospital, suffered a lot, but it was said that thanks to Scarlett, Elliot died peacefully.

-How did you say that? -He asked back.

-Just that he died in the hospital in Bath.

-Not that. What was your brother's name?

-Elliot Bloom. -He said as the remorse fell on George's face. -Did I say something wrong?

-Not absolutely... Go on, please.

-Scarlett, she's in financial trouble. What she thought she could solve. But that's not how it happened. The library was robbed and set on fire one night. So now she is forced to get into a marriage of convenience.

-Could you repeat that? -He shuddered in his seat.

-With some weird man. I don't even know, I think he's American, in terms of his accent.

-Leonard Wolowitz... -He squeezed the tin cup in his hand until it dented.

-Yes, he is the one. -The boy said with a smile that the man understood him, but when he looked at George, he noticed that something was wrong- Are you feeling well?

-Yes, but if you'll excuse me now. I have to go. -He replied, then picked up his coat and left.

*

George realised it wasn't worth thinking about this, so he tried to ignore it as much as he could. His sadness had now turned to anger and panic. He felt that he needed to drink something to eliminate it. After emptying his glass he sat down in his armchair and decided to think of moments when he was happy in his life. But no matter how much he tried to think differently, only the memories he shared with Scarlett burst through at the thought of happy moments. He remembered the moments when Scarlett was as happy with the ocean as a kid with sugar. The moment they rode together as he hugged her to reach the reins and her scent as the lush wind blew towards him. He remembered the time he had the opportunity to tell her how he was feeling, but he didn't. As a result of this thought, he felt as if he were not in his own skin, as if he could not control his body. He got up, ran out of the room, grabbed his hat and coat, then left the house.

# CHAPTER XV

Scarlett reached Mr. Wolowitz's house, rattled its huge gate hard. The butler stepped out, but right behind him was Leonard, who soon let in the confused woman.

-I didn't expect you today. -The man said as soon as they enter the salon- Can I offer you anything? -He asked politely.

-No, thank you. -Scarlett took a seat.

-I think I forgot to apologize for my past behaviour, I was rude. The day we met in front of Mr. Thaker's office. -He said, taking a seat on the couch. Scarlett smiled only forcefully, but her lips trembled. -However, I saw that you had a very good conversation with Mr. Salvatore, who was returning at the time.

-It's pointless to deny it. We met a long time ago and he was so kind to help me up as a result of an unfortunate accident. -Leonard smiled, then opened his mouth to speak, a few seconds past, before he noticed Scarlett wasn't talking, so he tried to say what he thought.

-Did you know that the man was quite unlucky during his journey? -He asked, upsetting the woman.

-He didn't share that kind of information with me. -She declared, then swallowed.

-I've heard he is struggling financially and needs to sell the rose palace. One of his apartments in Truro has been already sold.

-Tell me why are you doing this?

-What do you mean? -He asked, retaining his confidence.

-Is it all just to make sure I'm going to marry you? -Then Scarlett began to tremble with nervousness but tried to keep her demeanour.

-I don't think I fully understand what you're talking about. -He leaned closer to her.

-You are trying to get close to me at first and comfort me when I go through so much, to see if I fall into your arms. Then you save my brother by offering everything which is provided for his escape, you went into it as boldly as if the escape had been planned as if you knew when and where you had to be. Then you humiliate the man, with whom I once had a close relationship just to make a bad impression of him. -The man stood up and stepped closer to the woman, who was now walking up and down. -Then you stole all my assets to pay off all my debts and thus I will owe you. -Scarlett tried to pull away from the man, but he grabbed her arm and yanked her toward him.

-I don't know why you are slandering me. But I didn't do anything! -He told the woman, who was already struggling between his grips.

-Let go of me! -She shouted.

-And I didn't pay any debt. -He said again, still squeezing Scarlett.

-Only you knew about my debt and Mr. Thaker.

-Well, believe it or not. -He let go of the woman. -Whatever I insisted, Mr. Thaker wouldn't let me pay.

-I don't believe you!

-What do I have to do to make you believe me?

Scarlett didn't say a word, just stroked that part of her arm where the man squeezed.

-Whatever I do or say, people always see the bad in me. -He said combing his hair with his fingers- People always tell me there won't be bacon from a dog. –"*Dog*" this word attracted her attention so much, that something occurred to her- Just the way I am condemned for who I am. And how many times do I have to tell people, that I didn't hurt anyone?

Scarlett was a little scared of the man's tone, but it also made her think.

-I have to go now! -She replied, then hurried out of the man's house, Leonard didn't even try to follow her, he just fell into the armchair.

*

When she got home from Mr. Wolowitz's estate, George arrived at the door, he was just about to knock when he saw the woman.

-Good afternoon, Miss. Bloom! -He said, taking off his hat. But Scarlett was very upset, she just ran past him and opened the door. George followed her- We need to talk!

-Can't it wait? I have an important thing to do.

-Nothing is more important than this. -He said, holding her hand to finally stop the woman, which had made its impact.

-What would it be about? -She asked as he closed the door behind them.

-I've heard you want to marry Mr. Wolowitz.

-How do you know about it? -She asked, a little surprised.

-It doesn't matter now. -He said, wiping his forehead in confusion. -I came to stop you.

-If someone, then you should know that I don't take other's opinions.

-Yeah, I know. But you have to listen. He's not a man like us... -He replied, searching for the right words.

-I don't want to listen anymore. -She said as she walked to the window.

-But you have to listen. Do you know what it would mean to marry a man like him?

-What I have achieved so far I will not lose. I can't lose Gracewith.

-I can understand you.

-And you need to know that not a spark cares what others would think. I've tried everything I can to get things right. I used several ways to keep the plants from burning out. But it didn't work. I would have tried to sell all the jewellery my aunt left me. But they stole it. I sold most of my items, furniture, carpets, silver supplies to buy forage for the animals on the farm. Do you know what the consequences were? Everything was unnecessary. All of my animals are dead. I received a letter from Captain Patmore that the water in the well from which the animals were drinking was poisoned. All in addition to someone causing me so much horror and taking away most of my property is also a threat. Not only is my life in danger, but who knows who else's in this house. The maids? The kids? What else will they want to take from me that is important to me?

-Does it matter what I think? -He asked. The woman sighed and then turned toward the man. -You need to know Miss. Bloom; I wouldn't be able to live without you. I love you, Scarlett.

-He declared, tears welling up in the eyes of the woman in front of him.

-Why didn't you tell me all this when everything was different... -She asked, stroking his face. But in the meantime, the kids ran in, with both of their nannies. So, Scarlett stepped closer to them to send them out. But before she could speak, the man had preceded her.

-Wasn't you the one who said love should come first?

-Yes, I thought so. -She replied with her back to the man.

-Then? Say yes. Be my wife. We both know you want that too. You know the truth; you know how you feel about me. You just don't dare to confess to yourself.

-Once I knew... You don't know what you are asking for... Should I give up the commissioner for the uncertain? -She turned towards him- I know what happened in India...

-You always believed in me. You believe in who I am and what I would be able to achieve. You didn't see the impossible. -He said with teary eyes.

Scarlett looked silently at the children at the other end of the room.

-I still believe in you. But maybe you were right. Love is relative. There are times when you have to put something or someone else in the first place, -then she looked at him again with tumbling tears- and just have to hide it in a dark hole.

# CHAPTER XVI

-Mr. Thaker, thank you for receiving me.

-I'm happy to see you anytime. -He offered a seat. -How can I help?

-I came in a personal matter. First of all, I want to thank you for what you did for my brother. -The man just smiled, but he knew she had not finished. -Who paid off my debt?

-Miss, I said it's just a gift.

-Yes, but I'm in a messy situation with this gift. I said almost yes to the marriage offered by Mr. Wolowitz.

-How? -He asked a little angrily.

-I thought the money was from him. After all, he was here the day after the incident, when I met you.

-I can assure you he wasn't that person. -Scarlett was a little confused- Well, all I can say about this person is that loves you very much.

-Well, whoever it was, I'm grateful for. But in the end, I decided to say yes to Mr. Wolowitz's offer.

-Miss, please don't. -He said, leaning closer over the table.

-I have no choice. -The man looked at her understandingly but didn't say anything. -One more thing I came for. That is, to tell the truth. -The man looked at the woman sitting in front of him in surprise, but let her talk- Miranda Bloom was my mother, not my aunt.

-I knew from the first moment I saw you. -He replied smiling.

-There's something else. -But she didn't know how to tell him, she also knew that if she did, she might be limited in her decisions- I know Miranda was important to you because you gave her an invaluable treasure. Which, of course, is not the most expensive at market prices, but in spirit. -Then she handed the ring.

The man took it in his hand, then remembered something, squeezed her hand, then said: -Once your mom came to do this as well, a few years later... -He licked his lips, then continued- our ways apart. I wrote her a lot of letters after we were divorced for about two years. But there was no answer. My father forced me to get married to have a successor so the company wouldn't go bankrupt. But it was never given to my wife and me. Miranda visited me about ten years before her death. She, like the young lady, tried to give it back. And do you know what I said? -Scarlett shook her head- That it looks better on her. -The old man laughed, but his laughter turned into a strong cough. Scarlett quickly ran for a pitcher of water and handed it over. -Who knows, these may be the last days for me too. -He said, wiping his mouth.

-I'd like to ask if you don't mind. Since I don't have a father to accompany me... I'd be so... well... -She searched for the words but couldn't find them.

-Yes, I would like. -The man replied kindly.

*

Scarlett was shopping at the market as Otto Tamayo, the pastor, walked towards her.

-The scandalous redhead. -He said as he took an apple in his hand and began spinning it.

-Can I help you? -She asked, turning to him.

-Yes, I'd like to ask you to never put your foot inside the church gate again.

-Pfff... I'm afraid it's impossible to adhere to. -She said with a smile as the man looked at her in alarm. -Knowing that my future husband is Catholic. -She began to nod with her head left and right, with clenched lips.

-How? -He asked indignantly.

-Yes indeed! -She replied, nodding again.

-Who would it be?

-Mr. Leonard Wolowitz. -She declared with a smile.

-But he's Jewish! -He said, blushing completely.

-You are mistaken, his ancestors were indeed, but through his mother, who is Irish, he was baptized as a Catholic in Ireland; I mean Mr. Wolowitz. -She said, putting her hand on his shoulder- And what's even better. I'm not. So, I have to be baptized first. -The man burst from his nerves- Come on, Sir, or should I call you Father?

-Miss, I guarantee you if... -But he couldn't finish because he was interrupted by Scarlett.

-Oh, please, Father, don't be so overwhelmed. Jesus was also a Hebrew. Didn't you tell us at the Mass to forgive our friends? -She asked, placing her other hand on the man's other shoulder and then whispering in his ear- See you on Sunday!

# CHAPTER XVII

-Miss. Bloom, can you tell me what's going on? -Doris asked hurriedly after the woman, who had entered a small pub in the village.

-Good afternoon! -She said as they entered, as soon as they noticed her the noise subsided.

-Did you just come to offer us a job? -Said Mr. Meadow drunk from the corner of a table. Scarlett stepped closer.

-No, I came to find the person who stole the jewellery from my house. -Everyone was listening- Of course, as I guessed. Would it be better if I showed up with Captain Patmore on my side? -She asked, looking around at the people.

-Miss, you have nothing to do here. Just go back to your palace. -The drunk man in front of her said again, the people around began to approve.

-And what if I said I know who the perpetrator is? -She was leaning closer to the man, then began to whisper. -You are the dog tamer, the only person my dogs don't bark at, besides me. How unfortunate was that you could not escape in silence because you got scared by a broken vase and ignited the library, my library. Tell me where the jewellery is. -She spoke loud again.

-I don't have them anymore. -He said in despair.

-What do you mean you don't have them?

-I distributed them in the village, so we can survive the winter. -He replied, but his voice trailed off.

-And as I see you had enough for a drink as well. Do you know if someone is being caught on red-handed, what is there fate? -She asked, grabbing his hand. -If you don't want me to call the Captain, you'll disappear from the countryside tonight! -She declared, throwing away the man's hand from herself. Then she looked over at the people and knew the man was telling the truth. When she went out into the village, she saw that many of the children had shoes and thick clothes just as she planned to spend her money when she recovered. Seeing this, she was unable to hold anger.

-Where are we going now, Miss. Bloom? -Doris asked again.

-To my fiancé. -She said with a smile.

*

-Miss. Bloom, I was just headed to you. I have to apologize for what happened that day.

-If anyone owes an apology here, it's me. I shouldn't have suspected you.

-You were right about something. I wanted you to know about Mr. Salvatore's background, just to pick me. -Scarlett didn't say anything, just looked silently at the man in front of her and let the thought of this man becoming her husband take over. -You need to know that you are the only one who actually sees me, who I am and I appreciate that. Because it's hard to see the man behind the rank.

-Pride is falling apart silently. -Doris said softly.

-I would like to ask, officially. Miss. Scarlett Miranda Bloom, -then kneel before her- would you give me the honour of marrying me?

-Yes, I do!

BOOK THREE

# *THE TRUTH*

# CHAPTER I

Before the wedding, Scarlett received a letter from Mrs. Wolowitz, her future mother-in-law, inviting her to lunch to get to know her future daughter-in-law better. Scarlett was excited about this, so she decided to put on one of her most beautiful dresses, she knew the first impression mattered a lot, she thought it may seal her marriage. So, she would have to get the best out of this encounter.

-Hmm ... Marriage, it's not going to be a walk in the park. -Doris murmured with her arms folded, leaning against the frame of the door as she watched Scarlett try her dress by placing it in front of her and look in the mirror at how it would stand. It was a green velvet dress patterned with gilded yarn. It was a very elegant piece, one of Miranda's old dresses that matched her size to Scarlett's delight.

-What do you think? -She turned happily to Doris.

Doris swallowed, not mentioning the dress. She stepped closer to help Scarlett try it, then said: -Are you sure in this, Miss?

-Why wouldn't I be?

-I don't know ... Let's say because marriage is a lifelong bond!? -She said with some irony in her voice.

-You know I can't do anything... -The woman replied, a little disappointed.

-And what about Mr. Salvatore?

-We both lost something. He lost me and I lost time. -She was stepping closer in her dress in front of the mirror. She looked

289

wonderful, she was like a real princess in Doris' eyes, but she didn't try to encourage her. She felt that this marriage was out of place.

-So, are you sure? -She asked one more time, looking her in the eye, but Scarlett didn't answer, just looked in the mirror and tried to force her trembling mouth not to cry, to remain straight- The mirror is not a liar. But the pair of eyes that look in the mirror is a liar. -Doris grabbed the woman by the arm and turned it toward her so she could look her in the eye again. -When you are not sure, flip a coin because when the coin is in the air, you realise which one you are actually hoping for. -Scarlett's eyes filled with tears, but she adhered to her principles and continued her activities at the dressing table.

-Miss. Bloom, Mr. Wolowitz has arrived. -Matilda said as she entered the room.

-Tell him I'm done soon. -She replied, then sat down in front of the dressing table to arrange herself before the meeting.

-May your next tears be tears of joy. -Doris said softly as she watched Scarlett sit down at the table.

*

-Miss. Bloom, you look wonderful tonight.

-Thank you! -She replied, entering the parlour door in her mustard-coloured dress.

-Miss. Doris! -He said with a wide smile. -This is yours! -He was handing her a bottle of honey, the best and sweetest of his produce.

Doris took the bottle, then looked at it as she winked at the man: -You know you're not buying me with this, do you?

By the time they both, together with Scarlett, smiled, but when they saw that Doris was serious, both of their smiles dried.

-So, tell me what's your reason for visiting Gracewith?

-I think you got my mother's letter. I planned to introduce you, but I would be out of the house on an urgent matter. I came to apologize in advance for the inconvenience.

Scarlett hoped her fiancé would be present on this important occasion. She was a little disappointed, but she would not let her feelings take over.

-Of course, it is not a problem. -She replied, with a forced smile.

-There's something you need to know about Agatha Wolowitz. -Scarlett then put her hand on the man's hand. -She's a little whimsical, sometimes she says things with which she can hurt people and does...

-I'm sure everything will be fine. -She said with a smile.

# CHAPTER II

Scarlett tried to rule out negative thoughts about her future mother-in-law and instead fill with positivity as she walked into the Wolowitz family's estate. When she got there, the butler led her into the room where Mrs. Wolowitz was waiting for her. The staff behaved more strangely than she could imagine. When he ushered her into the room, he turned on his heels without a word, and left her there, Scarlett waited a few seconds to see if he would return and announce her arrival, but no one came. So, she tried to approach the armchair, which was with its back to her, then spoke.

-Good afternoon! I am Scarlett Bl... -But she was interrupted.

-I know who you are, Miss. Bloom. -A voice said from the armchair. -Come on in. -She spoke again after her words were followed by a long silence. -As if you were at home, -Scarlett was a little emboldened by those words, so she began to approach and then sat down on the couch facing the woman. -anyway, you would soon be the mistress of the house stealing the position from me. -The woman shuddered slightly as she took a seat when she heard these words.

-Thank you for the invitation. -Scarlett cleared her throat.

-You don't have to thank anything. I was just wondering who was so stupid to accept my son. -Scarlett looked questioningly at the old woman sitting in front of her, who was about ten years older than her mother and Evelyn. Her skin looked very worn by life, her forehead much more wrinkled than the sides of her eyes and edges of her lips. From this she concluded that there was no easy fate for the person in front of her, but she was as striking as her obese pug dog, with physically distinctive features of a wrinkly, short-muzzled face and curled tail. The breed has a fine, glossy coat that comes in light brown and black, and the compact, square body with not well-developed muscles to whom she gave a lot of love. The dog was held in her lap and caressed non-stop. This was Mrs. Wolowitz, a grey haired, gloomy-looking lady who seemed to rotate the words well. -I've heard a lot about you. -She spoke again, leaning closer and looking deeply at the woman with her green eyes. -The troublemaker, the red curly haired doll, who was able to cause a scandal at my birthday ball, and worse, did so in a church. So, I ask, why do you think you are for my son?

-Well, Mrs. Wolowitz. I think your son is a great man. And... -But she was interrupted again.

-Are you completely insane? Well, you give nothing to the opinions of others, as I see.

-No, ma'am. I don't care what others think, nor how much you oppose this covenant. -She said in a raised voice, then pulled herself out.

-Hmm... -She leaned closer to the woman in front of her again, then began to stare.

-Mrs. Wolowitz! Lunch will be served in a quarter of an hour. -A young lady of coloured skinned entered, in her sight was something broken as Scarlett examined her. As she looked through on the other side of the room, with her gaze she suggested to Scarlett that she felt sorry for her.

-Didn't I tell you, Marta, that someone could only dare to disturb me if I asked you to? Once again, I can't stand it when you enter so loudly. -She shouted at her.

-But ma'am, you said you are hard of hearing. -She tried to explain out loud, but Agatha felt a great deal of power to interrupt everyone.

-Go back to the kitchen, Scum. -She told her, so Marta left with a courtesy.

Scarlett frowned, trying to ignore what had happened.

-So where were we? -The pair of green eyes turned back to her. -Yeah, yeah... The wedding. -Then she raised her glass and took a sip. -Don't fool yourself, Miss. We both know it's a marriage of convenience, on both sides. As for my son, you don't have to polish in front of me, I think I've gotten him known enough in 32 years. Aside from his minor mistakes, he could be a really great person.

-What do you know about the relationship between the two of us? Why do you think this is a marriage of convenience? After all, what can I give him? -She asked, then looked at the woman, who seemed to be dead. Leaning on the back of the armchair, she lay motionless with her mouth open. Scarlett was horrified as she got into this state from one minute to another. -Mrs. Wolowitz? -She leaned closer, then tried to wiggle in front of her nose with her hand, indeed she didn't even know what to expect as a result of these movements, but she did, Agatha Wolowitz growled as a result, but this movement was even more uncomfortable and even more frightening to Scarlett, the half of the woman leaned out of her support and then snorted. Scarlett waited a few more seconds to see if there was going to be any change, and she did snore incessantly, and she seemed to be in a deep sleep.

*

-Doris believe me it was like I was in a crime novel. From one minute to the next, she went into a state like... like I don't know... -She slapped her thighs.

-And what did you do, Miss? Didn't you report to the servants?

-No, I was scared and I ran away. What could I have done? I thought she was dead.

-Yes, but you know the dead don't snore. -She said a little sarcastically.

-Yeah, I know. Maybe I should go back, and apologise. -She walked up and down.

-Miss. Bloom, Mr. Leonard Wolowitz has arrived! -Nivek entered the kitchen but couldn't wait for Scarlett to answer, the man behind him pushed him aside of his way and hurried in front of Scarlett.

-Mr. Wolowitz. I swear to heaven I didn't do anything. -Scarlett explained.

-Miss. Bloom, we need to talk face to face. -The man said, a little embarrassed, by the time the staff left, leaving them alone, he spoke again: -I felt I shouldn't have let the two of you meet alone.

-How? Did you know this was going to happen? -Scarlett asked, a little outraged.

-I don't deny it. I guessed it would happen. Please listen to me this time. -Then they both sat down at the table. Scarlett didn't say anything, she knew it's better let the man talk, since what could she say anyway? -My mother suffers from hypersomnia. This disease is an excessive daytime sleepiness, it is a condition where people fall asleep repeatedly during the day, sometimes in the middle of eating a meal or during a conversation. The symptoms are, falling into a deep sleep anywhere, without warning. Loud snorting, breathing and snoring. An unusual feeling in your legs. Low mood, little interest in things and feeling irritable. Mood swings that range from extreme highs to extreme lows.

-Did that happen at the ball that night? -The man didn't answer, just nodded. Scarlett just raised his head with her soft hand and smiled at him. -We'll solve it together.

# CHAPTER III

-Georgie, my dear. What's the matter? -Edith asked as she looked at the thoughtful man sitting in the armchair with a glass of whisky in his hand.

-Did I tell you how unfair life is? -He replied, lifting his head with difficulty as if full of lead.

-Are you drunk, son? -She was putting her hand in front of her heart.

-And if yes? And if I say nothing makes sense? -He asked the woman provocatively with a stumbling tongue.

-For heaven's sake, pull yourself together. -She replied, then took the glass from him. -Don't say that it is all because of the red-haired harpy.

-Scarlett! -He raised his voice. - Her name is Scarlett. -Then quietened his tone.

-How could that woman enchant you like that?

-I love that woman! Like no one ever before. But what do you know about love since you remained an old maid?

-It's enough of this disrespect. I am the person who raised you after your parents died. I, and only I, alone was the person who was always by your side and supported you in everything. That woman just showed up in your life and turned everything upside down.

-I'd have been able to leave everything behind for that woman. Including you!

-I can't listen to that not even for a minute. -She replied with teary eyes, then headed for the exit.

-You were the one who ruined everything. -George said softly repeatedly to himself.

# CHAPTER IV

-Nivek, Nivek! -Scarlett shouted impatiently as she ran down the hall.

-Yes, Miss? -He was standing in front of her, confident.

-Did the flowers arrive?

-Yes, we put them in the salon while the cooking items also get here. -Scarlett entered the room, then tore one out of them in desperation.

-No, no, no... I asked for blue hyacinth mixed into the bouquet, not pink...

-Oh, Miss, don't get caught up on that. It's just a flower. -Said a kind voice behind her, then a warm hand weighed on her shoulder.

-You're right, Doris. -She reassured herself and then took the woman's hand. -I'm just so excited. As a child, my sister and I have always dreamt of this moment. Anne should be here to prepare me. -She said sadly- As the whole family should attend this event.

-Keep in mind my dear, sometimes your worst enemy is your own memory, let it go.

-Thank you, Doris! -Doris just waved- I mean it, for everything, you were there for me from the day I came to Gracewith.

-I'm just hoping, Miss, that I'm wrong about your marriage. -Doris said, stroking her hand.

-I hope so. -She said, taking a deep breath.

-Captain Patmore has arrived! -Matilda approached them accompanied by a plump man.

-Miss. Bloom! I bothered you in this lovely environment. Such nice flowers.

-Thank you! They are for my wedding. Which will take place in two days.

-So, you decided to marry that man after all... -He looked disappointed- Anyways I just walked by, and I wanted to ask if you had received my last letter?

-The one in which you let me know about the poisoned well? Yes, I did. However, as you see, I was pretty busy in the last period. I couldn't deal with it. Any developments regarding the case?

-Yes! Unfortunately, I have to declare that in my opinion, is that one of your workers must be the perpetrator. I would suggest you take care with your employee who is in a close position to you. It must be a person who was seen by your dog on a daily basis and worked on the farm as well. Do you have any idea who could it be?

Scarlett looked thoughtfully for half a minute. -No, unfortunately, I can't name anyone.

-That's all right. Since it was a long time ago, it may happen that the person is already over the seas.

Scarlett thought more than sure. Mr. Meadow left a long time ago. She wasn't angry with him, since he didn't keep the money for himself, and thought about the villagers as well and their hard times. She forgave him, even if she had to send him away to keep her dignity. Mr. Meadow was not a mean man, he was indeed a robber, but a warm-hearted robber.

-I am sure I will find that person if you will give me some more time for the investigation. But, it will take a while, especially if the person has already left the county. The question is if you, Miss. Bloom wants me to continue to investigate this case.

-Since I will leave Gracewith, and I will settle down in Beelove, I will be safe. Gracewith is not even in my name. Jared Bloom will inherit it if he grows up, so my wealth is not in danger. Thank you, Captain, for your time, but I would like to withdraw the report.

-Are you sure, Miss?

-Yes, I am.

# CHAPTER V

Scarlett, in her beautiful white silk dress, looked gorgeous as walked along, leaving everyone's mouth open. She didn't really know many of them, but it didn't matter, she knew the presence of these people was important to her future husband. The only person who stood out from the others was George Salvatore, who, when he saw her stand up, but God knows what might have been on his mind at that moment, even Leonard felt his heart had stopped for half a second until Edith Salvatore pulled him back to his place. Scarlett's smile faded and her heart was filled with pain instead of happiness. Owen Thaker escorted her all the way to the altar, then wiped his flowing tears as he turned away so that Scarlett, whom he had looked at as his own child all along, would not see it. Otto Tamayo gave an extraordinary wedding ceremony to the people in the temple, he had never seen such a large number before.

The priest crossed himself and said: In the name of the Father, and of the Son, and of the Holy Ghost.

*Followers*: Amen!

*Priest*: Grace to you and peace from God, our Father and the Lord Jesus Christ.

Followers: And to your soul.

*Priest*: Let us beg! (Then a short silence began). Let our God regard our supplications, and pour out thy mercy upon thy lovers, who now marry at thy holy altar. May they always be steadfast in mutual love! Christ through our Lord.

*Followers*: Amen!

Scarlett stood impatiently in front of her fiancé. She felt that, following the example of Owen Thaker, she too would be crying soon, but she has contained herself. She knew she couldn't let her feelings influence this decision. After the liturgy, the bride and groom stood in front of the altar with the witnesses, who were made up of Scarlett's friend, Lady Evelyn Quas, and Leonard's friend Dr. Jerome Garfield. Evelyn, too, was opposed to this affair, many times she told her friend her opinion, not just Doris, but she knew that her friend was more stubborn than her mother, so she, like many others, could only wish her good luck.

The priest said to the betrothed pair: Dear betrothed pair! You have come here to the temple to seal and sanctify the love of your heart before the servant of his church and the community of the faithful. Christ gives the abundant blessing of this love from our Lord. It enriches and strengthens you with the grace of a special sacrament so that you can take on the sacred duties of your spouses in mutual eternal fidelity. The dignity of the sanctity of marriage requires sincere intent from you. Therefore, answer the questions of the Church.

Scarlett's heart was pounding so hardly and quickly, knowing that they would soon reach the point where they had to take their oath. Uncertainty grew stronger in her.

*Priest*: Leonard Robert Wolowitz, will you vow your intentions before God, that have you come here of your own free will to marry?

*Groom*: I came of my own free will!

*Priest*: Do you promise to respect and love your future wife until death will part you?

Leonard glanced at his future wife, smiled, then turned back to the reverend. -I promise!

*Priest*: Do you accept children with whom God bestows your marriage? -Upon hearing these words, the man sighed, looked down at the ground, and looked at the reverend again.

*Groom*: I accept!

*Priest*: Do you promise to educate them according to the laws of Christ and his church?

*Groom*: I promise! -He swallowed the dumpling from his throat.

*Priest*: Scarlett Miranda Bloom, will you vow your intentions before God, that have you come here of your own free will to marry? -Scarlett was in another world, so a long silence followed the reverend's words until her husband cleared his throat.

*Bride*: Yes! -She said shortly.

*Priest*: Do you promise to respect and love your future husband until death will part you?

*Bride*: I promise! -She replied after a long hesitation.

*Priest*: Do you accept children with whom God bestows your marriage?

*Bride*: I accept them! -She said in a low voice.

*Priest*: Do you promise to educate them according to the laws of Christ and his church?

*Bride*: I do! -She replied softly again.

*Priest*: Dear engaged couple! Now comes the sacred moment when you solemnly declare that you want to be each other's spouses. Turn to each other. Hold hands, and I will bind up your hands together to signify that your marriage will be unbroken before God. -then folded their hands together with a ribbon.

*Priest*: Leonard Robert Wolowitz, make a statement before God and the Church of the Blessed Virgin Mary, do you want to marry Scarlett Miranda Bloom?

*Groom*: I want to!

*Priest*: Say after me: Scarlett Miranda Bloom, before the holy God. I will marry you.

*

*Priest*: Scarlett Miranda Bloom, make a statement before God and the Church of the Blessed Virgin Mary, do you want to marry Leonard Robert Wolowitz? -Scarlett looked at the guests sitting there, especially at George, whose blood had even cooled sitting on the bench. She saw her future mother-in-law leaning against the back of the bench in a deep sleep, and she heard her sigh deeply in her sleep. Then her gaze reached her father and Evelyn, who was just staring silently, but a kind of plea pleaded in their eyes, saying, *"Don't do it!"* Then finally, Scarlett looked at the kids, who were looking back at her in their colourful little princess dresses and suit, smiling.

*Bride*: I want to! -She raised her head towards her husband.

*Priest*: Say after me: Leonard Robert Wolowitz, before the holy God, I will marry you.

*

*Priest*: I now declare your marriage valid in the name of the Church and bless it in the name of the Father, the Son, and the Holy Ghost.

*Followers*: Amen! -They all said in a tone as if they were attending a funeral.

*Priest*: My brethren, who are here, witnesses of this holy covenant, which is incorruptible according to the word of our Lord Jesus Christ: "What God hath joined together, let not man put asunder." (Matthew 19: 6). If anyone opposes this covenant, stand up and speak or forever hold your peace. -The reverend said, and George felt compelled to do so, but Winnifred, the daughter of Lord William O'Neil, sitting next to him, put her hand on his thigh, causing the man's thoughts to turn completely differently, the blonde girl smiling charmingly at him with her pink lips. George felt it was a sign, a sign from God of how to decide not to listen only to his heart but his mind sometimes.

The priest sings the wedding blessing with open arms. -Let us now pray, my dear brothers and sisters, for these spouses, and ask them for God's blessing to help them kindly support them, because they also thank Him for their marriage.

-Creator of the world, our Holy Father, who created man and woman in your image, and you wanted to enrich their community with your abundant blessings. For the new woman, we pray to you with a humble heart who entered the holy covenant with her husband that day. May our Lord and God, your abundant blessing, come upon her and her companion (that in the course of their happy marriage they may adorn their homes with children and prosper your church)! -The faithful began to sing, and Agatha Wolowitz awoke from her deep sleep, and as if nothing had happened, she began to sing. -Let your praise be heard in joy and seek you in times of sorrow, and enjoy your help in their work, and feel that you stand by them when they struggle! -Scarlett felt as she betrayed herself, realizing that all she feared had now come to an end. She was afraid she would never be happy, trying to comfort herself with the thoughts Evelyn had said about her marriage of convenience. -In the community of believers, pray for you, bear witness to you in the world, and reach a beautiful age, and enter into the heavenly homeland with those present, through Christ our Lord. -He finally finished his pastor's speech.

*Followers*: Amen!

*Priest*: Now kiss each other! -He said, clasping his hands apart in front of them. Between minor hesitations, they both began to lean toward the other, Scarlett closed her eyes and then tried to think that it wasn't really Leonard in front of her who she had to kiss. After a brief quick lip touch, they left the temple arm in arm. And they headed for Scarlett's new home, Mr. Wolowitz's estate, Beelove. Where they welcomed everyone who celebrated their marriage with them. As they exited, Scarlett's workers cheered them on, waving ribbons and a cheerful smile on their faces. She returned their smiles, but her heart ached that she could do no more for them. Her husband leaned closer unexpectedly.

-You don't have to worry about them, Honey, I invited them, they too will share in the fun of our marriage, which will be in the Beelove tent, while the nobles will be in the ballroom.

-It's... -She was searching for the right words, but she felt that she couldn't find them. -Thanks. -She smiled at her husband.

-I knew they mean a lot to you, Scarlett. -He said, now calling his wife by name, which touched her heart even more.

*

George approached Edith's room as a maid stepped out, asked about her aunt's activities, and after making sure it wasn't inappropriate to visit, he walked into his aunt's room, watching as she combed her grey hair in the mirror. Edith also saw him in the mirror, but she pretended not to care.

-Aunt, I know you're mad at me. And rightly so, I have no excuse for my behaviour last night. I came to tell you how much...

-Not as much as me. You were right about certain things. It's my fault, I tuned you against Miss. Bloom. And you're also right that

I don't know much about love, -she paused for a few seconds and then continued- about happy, reciprocated love. But I was once young too, and I felt like you now: overwhelmed, exploited, weak, and shattered.

-Aunt, we don't have to talk about this right now.

-Yes, we have to. You need to know that I will not let you make the same mistake as I did. I had suitors, but I always waited for him to come into my life one day, saying he had made a mistake. I'm going to die as an old maid, just like you said. But I'm not going to let you live your life as a bachelor. -George stepped closer, Edith took his hands and continued. -I saw how Lord William's daughter looked at you in the church. The evening is long, we have to get to the party soon. Be strong, son.

*

The ball was amazing with beautiful decorations, great food, and a great atmosphere. Leonard completely impressed Scarlett, who thought it was going to be one of the worst days of her life, but thanks to her husband she felt like she was at a simple ball. Leonard knew how to handle Scarlett's feelings, and he didn't hesitate especially when her emotions wobbled. It was already getting dark when George Salvatore and Winnifred arrived at the party. As they entered the room, Scarlett felt as if she had been stabbed in the heart. She knew that everything she had done was cruel, even to herself. When she decided to talk to George and walked slowly towards them, Doris took her arm.

-Don't make it more painful.

Scarlett hesitated, but she knew Doris was right. So, she set off in a different direction where her husband found her.

-There you are. Come with me. -He grabbed her by the hand and took her to the exit.

During the quarter-hour walk, the couple walked silently side by side. Leonard tried to speak to her, but every time he looked at her, he saw something was depressing his wife, so he decided to keep quiet. They reached a tent where there was merry revelry and people danced like the nobles at the ball would never be able to. When they entered, there became a huge silence. Everyone was watching them, but no one said a word. The villagers, like many, tried to make a good impression, came to this party wearing their best clothes.

-Please, don't stop for our sake. -Leonard said.

-Long live the newlyweds! -Cried little Matt, as several joined, then the music flared up again, people continued to have fun, ate, drank and danced.

Little Matt, a former worker who was now a big boy, would have been just old enough to work on the farm, stepped closer.

-Excuse me, Miss, I mean Mrs. Wolowitz. I would just like to say how grateful we are for what you did for us in the winter. -Scarlett looked at him questioningly- The jewellery you sent, pretty much, saved lives. We've been starving for days until Mr. Meadow arrived with them. We bought warm clothes from it and were able to divide them so that we had enough food for the winter.

Scarlett then realised that the old man's actions were really well-intentioned, how selfless he was by saying that she had sent the jewellery. She smiled at the boy with a forced smile, who then was running back to his friends. Scarlett then finally reconciled to the stolen jewellery. Unable to continue to be angry at the old dog tamer, she knew it was driven by good intentions. But one thing she didn't understand to this day. How did he know where the safe was and its code since it was all described only in the diary? Just as she would have found answers, her husband caught her arm.

-Let's dance!

308

-But I don't know the steps. -Scarlett said, however, it was too late already, she was trying to make some movements in the middle of the circle.

-Me neither! -Leonard tried to shout louder than the music. Then they both started dancing as they could. Scarlett felt much better in this environment than she had ever felt among the nobles.

After they danced till their legs ached, her husband decided to take a seat at a table. Scarlett was fully winded, telling Leonard she needed air. Her husband wanted to accompany her, but she objected, telling him to rest. She then stepped out of the tent. Then she began to walk in the garden, getting closer and closer to Beelove's house, she was deciding to return to the tent when a voice addressed her.

-Miss. Bloom! -Scarlett froze at the place because she knew who that voice belonged to.

-Mr. Salvatore! -Then she looked at him for a while with a forced smile- Tell me how you feel at the party?

-Quite, well! Except I never expected this day to happen.

-Look, I wanted to apologise for the past.

-Please don't. Here, I am the person who owes with an apology. I didn't know you were so determined on this matter. -Scarlett was afraid to admit that she wasn't really, not even a drop. -I hope you will have a happy marriage. -But Scarlett couldn't thank for something she knew wouldn't happen.

When George looked up at the top of the hill where the tent was located, he saw a tall man watching them. He knew Scarlett's husband didn't like when he was talking to his wife, so he seized the opportunity and tried to say goodbye to her forever.

-I'll be travelling to London, probably even moving there.

-Oh? -Scarlett was surprised.

-You know, if Winnifred ... I want to say, Miss. O'Neil, will say yes at my request. We will probably live our lives there. Especially when I get my votes, I applied as an MP. So, in the next few weeks, we will see, if I will be elected and accepted.

-So, you will get married... -Scarlett clarified for which the man only nodded. -Would you move even if it didn't work out? -Scarlett asked as he lowered his head, then looked at her again and nodded.

-I would be unable to be near a person who is the source of my pain. I was glad to meet you, Miss. Bloom. -He replied, kissing her hand.

-You can't escape your feelings. You can't do that; you can't be so selfish.

-Please don't tell me about selfishness. -George said, a little outraged, but kept calm. -You turned the page; I must burn the book. -Then he left Scarlett in tears.

*

Later that night, Scarlett knew what was going to happen, a thing no one had ever prepared her for. After the guests left, she went up to the room. There she prepared and then sat down in her nightgown on the edge of the bed. Her eyes were cried red it was almost as if soaked in blood, she stared into the nothing in front of her and didn't dare to think. Leonard entered the room, sighing once loudly, Scarlett felt aggression, he dropped the bottle in his hand, then stepped in front of his wife, looked over her, and hid in bed. Scarlett looked at him, hoping her husband would stay in that position. He raised his hand, then smoothed her face all the way, Scarlett shivered, her skin was whiter than usual, and then Leonard turned his back, saying, *"I'm too drunk now!"*. Then Scarlett was finally able to breathe, and then she snuggled into bed as well, gasping for air.

# CHAPTER VI

-Ma'am, tell me do we really have to move there? -Doris asked, holding the list she had received from Scarlett, with the things she wanted to move to Beelove.

-Leonard, wants us to live there instead.

-And what about the farm?

-It doesn't matter for now anyway.

-But, but... if we all leave, who's going to take care of the house?

-You don't have to come if you don't want to. -Scarlett told the three staff, Doris, Nivek, and Matilda.

-Don't get mad, but the truth is, we don't want to serve the Wolowitz family.

-No wonder why... -Scarlett replied, thinking of Mrs. Wolowitz, who hadn't even attended the wedding party. -Just promise to take care of yourself. -All three of them smiled and nodded.

-Can I give you some advice for your marriage? -Doris asked.

-You haven't even told me what the fifth etiquette of life is. -Scarlett laughed.

-You will understand everything when the time comes. I want you to note these. You need to know when someone is kind to you that kindness is not flirting. Attention is not love. Silence is not anger and tears are not weaknesses.

-I was hoping it would be something more encouraging. -Scarlett said a little melancholy, then took her bag and smiled at them once more.

-Miss. Bloom! -Doris said again- Stay strong. -She finished as she turned around.

# CHAPTER VII

-Well, we're here on the election day. -Mr. Anderson entered the circle, where Leonard was present. -Oh Mr. Wolowitz. Did you see the applicants? -He asked, and Leonard looked around involuntarily. Seeing George, his anger grew, but he nodded politely.

-It's out of the question for Mr. Salvatore to win. -Replied Sir Limsenhan, there was still some controversy over the applicants, but there was no doubt that George would have few votes only, from the gentlemen around him. Mr. Anderson began his speech regarding his candidate, who was a middle-aged man with a clean background and fine pocket.

-We have been recruiting people for months now and making sure Mr. Shaper is fit for the job. -Said Sir Limsenham.

-I don't think it's a privilege to be far from your homeland anyway.

-What do you mean? -Leonard asked the gentleman who uttered those words.

-For a case like this, the candidate has to move to London. I thought you were aware of its duties and sacrifices of these tasks, Mr. Wolowitz. -He said, a little provocatively.

-Of course, I knew. -He finally realised what this election meant to him now.

-I hope you keep your word, sir, and give your vote, to whom we have encouraged so far. -Mr. Anderson interrupted.

-I adhere to the principle, that I give my vote to the one who is more worthy of this post than to the one who is constantly mentioned like a parrot.

-Now let's listen to Lord Quas talk about his chosen candidate, the President of the Voters said.

-Mr. Salvatore. He is a very fit and good person with great business and decision-making intuitions. -He said his two-lined speeches compared to the two-sided one. -Thanks! -He finished and left, with a little regret, but George patted her shoulder encouragingly. Then the vote began. The nobles went in line and cast their votes, shouting the elected person's name. Meanwhile, after every third or fourth, the name, Mr. George Salvatore was heard. George began to pull away from winning the election. Many were waiting for Mr. Wolowitz to see the Americans who had a great sense of decision making, who will he vote for, they were waiting for this esteemed, influential man with more business associates and co-owners in the room than any people would have voted so far. That's how the vote went on for a while until it was Leonard Wolowitz's turn. He walked over to the table, grabbed the pen, and signed the paper due to minor hesitation. He raised his head and then said the name, "George Salvatore". Then the gentlemen all looked at each other and there was a great disturbance between the speeches and the contradictions. The president of the voters hit the table twice with a gavel, gesturing them for silence, and then the vote resumed, naming the candidates again after signing the paper. Then, at the end of the vote, after a short break, the president of the voters returned with an envelope.

- Gentlemen, please observe the number of votes of the candidates to be declared. Mr. Matthew Shaper: 56 votes, Mr. Gregory Fisher: 42 votes, Mr. George Salvatore: 57 votes. I am glad to announce that Mr. George Salvatore won the election! -He hit the table again. Which again caused a great deal of noise. George gave Leonard a sincere smile as he left the room speechless.

*

-Mrs. Wolowitz! - Scarlett entered the salon - Can we talk? -The woman didn't speak, just pointed to the armchair, Scarlett took a seat, then looked deep into her green eyes. -I have been living here for a month now and no one is considering me, please tell me the reason. Wouldn't I be a good wife enough?

-That's not the reason why. Don't worry. You simply didn't grow to the task of being the mistress of the house. -She said, stroking her pug.

-Still, what do you think I should do to change that? -She asked in a somewhat humiliating way.

-Nothing, we think it's appropriate this way. -She said, muttering to her dog.

-We think?

-Yes, Harold, and I think that's right. Isn't that correct Harold? -She turned to her dog again.

Scarlett rolled her eyes, then walked to the door where Leonard has just arrived.

-How was the election? -Scarlett asked as a valet took off her husband's coat.

-It was great. George Salvatore won. He'll be leaving soon and we won't see him for a while. He said walking with his back to his wife in the direction of the library, then disappeared behind the door. Scarlett took a deep breath and went after him, closing the door behind them.

-Tell me, what should I do to have a good relationship again? -But the man didn't answer, he just arranged his papers. -What happened to us? Everything before the wedding was so different, and now it's been a month since we've been married and you are avoiding me. -Scarlett raised her voice.

-After marriage, a lot changes. -The man replied, then left the room, leaving Scarlett alone.

Nothing explained this strange behaviour to Scarlett. But the first thought that came to her mind was always the memory of what happened the day after their honeymoon. When Scarlett got up in the morning, Leonard was no longer in the room, and the maids came to tidy up the room, after that night with clean sheets in their hands and a curious look in their eyes.

-What's the bedding... -She wanted to ask the moment they took off the blanket and saw the bloodstains.

-Pardon me? -One of the maids asked.

-What is this dark-coloured bedding for? I want something lighter. Get another one right away. -She pointed up at the bedding.

-I'll bring it right now, ma'am. -This was the first time she had been called like this, but she hadn't felt it appropriate yet.

When she left the room and went into the dining room, her husband had finished his breakfast already. Scarlett sat down at the table, and the valets were ready to serve her breakfast. That's when Dr. Jerome Garfield came in.

-Mrs. Wolowitz! What a pleasure to see you. -He said, then kissed her hand.

-Dr. Garfield! Can I ask, what is the reason for your early visit?

-Oh, didn't Leonard mention it? -She looked at her husband. -We spend every Sunday together with our friends, this called the gentlemen day. Leonard got up from the table, then only said to his wife: "*Have a nice day!*" and they left.

This is how Scarlett was left alone on her first day as a wife at the full table with an empty soul.

In the evening when her husband arrived, she was waiting in the room.

-Oh, did I forget to tell you? Scarlett, your room is in the east wing. -Her husband answered when he saw her.

-How? -She wondered. The man rang, and a valet appeared before them. -Mowie, will escort you to your room.

Mowie was a tall, dark-skinned man, but it didn't surprise Scarlett to see another man of colour, since Mr. Wolowitz's staff consisted largely of it. The man led her to the other wing, where a huge room was waiting for her. She had never seen a more beautiful room, but she knew it wouldn't be the place she could call home.

Scarlett's returned to the present at the sound of loud children's mouths. She was finally able to see the children again after a full month. When the kids entered the room, all four of them jumped around Scarlett's neck.

-What is this noise? -Shouted Agatha- Can't you feel relaxed in your own house?

# CHAPTER VIII

-Mr. George Salvatore! -The valet entered the room announcing the man arrival.

-What a pleasant surprise, I didn't think we'd meet for a while. What is the reason you come to London?

-I am proud to announce that I had two reasons to travel here.

-Oh?! -She was stunned as she filled the glasses.

-I don't know if you heard about it, but I became an MP. I decided to move to London.

-This is amazing. I hope you don't do this in the hope that if you're in the company of my dad you can see me more often. -She answered flirtingly.

-Not in the least. -The man stepped closer to her. -The other reason that brought me here was to ask you to become my wife. -She smiled as George knelt in front of her. -I've already got your father's permission; all I need is yours. Miss. Winnifred O'Neil, would you do me the honour of marry me, so I do not just have to see you when you are in the company of your father?

# CHAPTER IX

-They've been here Leonard for two months now, I can't take this anymore...

-Please understand Mom, they are my wife's foster children.

-Wouldn't you do this for your sick mother? Who raised you and gave you everything? Who was there next to you during your toughest hours? -Agatha asked with a palm on her chest.

-Please don't overdo it, they're just kids. They can't be that bad. -Leonard replied just as Riley and Julia entered the room chasing each other. Julia had a huge basket in her hand that was slipping from her grip. Then they stopped in front of Mrs. Wolowitz and dropped the basket. The girls' hands were covered in soot up to her shoulders, as were the lids of the basket.

-What are you about, children? -She asked, leaning closer and then she heard a whimper from the basket. Opening the picnic basket, she saw Harold, her little pug in it. The dog was black from soot, it was as if a completely different animal had been taken into the room, the dog upset the basket and climbed out of it, then she saw that he was wearing a pink needle skirt.

-Ahhh, what did you do, you little monsters to my only darling? -The woman exclaimed.

The children stuck out their tongues at her with a big laugh, saying "Nee-nee-nee-nee" and then running around the woman's armchair twice more, left the room. -I was just talking about this. They are cursed as if they were children of the devil himself. -She over excited herself, her breathing was getting harder and harder. Soon, Scarlett entered the room, gesturing to her dogs in front of the door to sit, who, listening faithfully to their mistress, did what had been ordered.

-Did you called for me, Mrs. Wolowitz? -She asked as she stepped closer than when she saw her husband, whom she had barely seen lately, looking at him in surprise she was amazed: "Oh?"

-Yes, please take a seat. -The woman took a seat next to Leonard. -It would be about the kids. - She looked at them questioningly. -You are aware that we have a say in their upbringing as family members. The girls are very fierce, incomprehensible and bad.

-Mrs. Wolowitz, they're just kids. -Scarlett replied, with her arms outstretched.

-I know this too, which is why it is important at this age to get a proper education. The full cost, of course, is my treat, take this as a kind of wedding gift. Like, step-grandparent, although I hope not only this coat of arms will stay with me for the rest of my life, -she said, clearing her throat as the couple looked at each other and then suddenly elsewhere- my duty to provide the best upbringing and education for the children, for that reason I will send them to London, where they will study at a girls' school.

-You can't do that! -Scarlett jumped up.

-Yes, I can do it and I will do it. -She replied, turning her stick nervously in her hand.

-These kids went through so much, they lost their parents barely two and a half years ago, they have only me, I am their family. Tell her, please, Leonard. The girls need me! -She said looking at her husband and waiting for answers, but the man just sighed and then crossed his legs. -They live with me for a reason, they need to feel cared for, they have to feel that they are safe in a family environment, I won't let you send them away.

-For heaven's sake, Scarlett. -She said impatiently. -Look what they did to my little fur ball. -She pointed with teary eyes at her dog, who was just licking his balls.

-And you have nothing to say? -She asked her husband indignantly.

-As a matter of fact, I think it would be better for the kids to travel. Think of this great opportunity, the years fly by so easily. In London, real ladies will be carved out of them, they will easily find appropriate husbands.

-I can't believe it! -Scarlett was full of rage, she felt like she could hit someone, but she hit something, she ran out of the room, slapping her skirt.

*

She was looking in Evelyn's house for consolation. She listened to her friend's story a little exhausted.

-What are you going to do now?

-I have no idea yet.

-And what about the two younger children? Jared and Aliona?

-They stay with us, but it's a matter of time before they get bored and remove them too. - Scarlett said sadly. -According to them, they are still easy to raise because they are very young. The biggest trouble is that they are disobedient, but who would listen to such a woman, honestly?

-Please don't harass yourself, but she's a very influential woman. I have heard a lot about her and the employees who live there. I've heard she hurts them a lot, the tiniest thing gets her out of her skin and she takes revenge, she pretends she's still living in America and they are still her slaves. I heard that one of them once wanted to escape and was almost beaten to death for it. Please take care with this woman.

-I'm not afraid of her. -Scarlett took a sip of her cup.

-You're just like her. -She was leaning her elbow against the backrest and lowering her head into the palm of her hand.

-After my grandmother's funeral, I know you met.

-Yes, that is. At the funeral, more precisely. She handed me a note. She wrote to me that she needed help regarding her father. We visited with my husband one evening, after a few weeks when we got back from London. When we entered the salon, we witnessed an unexpected moment. Mr. Bloom... - Then she sighed. -He beat his own daughter, forcing her to take off her clothes, shouting her wife's name, though she didn't look as much like her mother as you do, however, there were some similarities. Lord Quas and Nivek separated them. He was then sent to a doctor who found that he was so aggressive under the influence of alcohol, but we knew that was not the whole story. So, we helped Miranda, locked him in a room.

-In a cold, upstairs room that was far away and no one heard. -Scarlett said softly.

-Uhum... More specifically, a tower. God knows what else he did to that poor girl.

-You look tired. -Scarlett said, looking over her friend.

-I'm fine. -She replied smiling- Only my condition weakens me a little.

-How? -Scarlett was surprised as Evelyn laughed- Since when?

-A few weeks ago. -She was stroking her tummy.

-Congratulations!

-Shh... -Evelyn whispered- My husband doesn't know yet.

-How so? -Scarlett asked softly.

-You know at my age it's pretty dangerous. So, I didn't want to tell him until a couple of months passed to be sure.

-It's so wonderful. -Scarlett said, taking her friend's hand.

-We were already starting to lose hope, we've been trying for a few years. Who would have thought that at this age it was still possible? -She said, wiping away her tears- Norman had always longed for an heir. He's such a good man, he never forced anything I didn't want. When I was younger and naive, I always saw the bad side of the marriage of convenience. Though he always gave me everything, it's time for me to give him what he wants too. -She smiled, as Scarlett looked away sadly, not wanting to take away her friend's enthusiasm. -What's wrong, darling? Is everything all right in your marriage?

-My marriage is not like yours. There is only a downside to this, there was a spark of hope on the day of the wedding, but it soon went out after seeing me talk to Mr. Salvatore. He got so cold; we live as if two strangers were living in the same house. We sleep in a separate room. Sometimes I don't see him for days, or we just walk next to each other, we don't even talk to each other. I'm not even talking about how I feel right now that he was in favour of her mother's decision and he didn't even care how I feel.

-Give him time. Your marriage is still so fresh. It took me almost ten years to realise how much I love my husband.

-I don't understand what has changed. When I was out of reach for him, he wanted me more than anything. And since I'm with him, and he could do anything to me, he's throwing me away like a chewed bone.

-Maybe you should have a ball, you should both refresh. You need a little socialization. You've been to places like this for a long time.

-Maybe you're right. -Scarlett thought maybe George would attend this ball as well.

-Mentioning Mr. Salvatore, I don't know if you've heard of him, he is getting married. -She took a sip of her cup.

-What?

# CHAPTER X

"*Dear Diary,*

*I waved goodbye to my nieces during the day with a sore heart. After pouring out my heart to my dear friend, Evelyn, who gave me spiritual support. Although at the moment I felt she would need this kind of support, as expecting a child, at her age is very risky. I'm so happy to find a friend like Lady Evelyn Quas. I know I can always count on her, no matter what. She respects my decisions, although she expresses her opinion and tries to protect me, I know she just wants the best.*

*So, when the kids were gone, I already felt the house is even more empty, I felt like I'm cut off from the world. I don't even understand why I'm still amazed, I knew I was losing my freedom through my marriage. Loneliness grows stronger minute by minute, it's like carrying a bag full of stones, and someone always puts in one and one more.*

*Slowly, I will enter the fourth month of my marriage and my husband hasn't even touched me, but when he saw me, he turned his eyes as if I didn't even exist. It's amazing how much more attractive I think he is than ever before. When his courtship lasted, I always wanted to get rid of the thought of maybe becoming Mrs. Wolowitz one day, I didn't want him to be near, not for a minute. But I'm here now and I wish he would look at me like he did before.*

*I know Beelove is my new home, but I'm thinking incessantly about Gracewith and the two years I spent there. The freedom, the responsibility that went with the farm, the beloved staff, especially Doris, Oh, dear Doris. One of my eyes is crying the other is happy.*

*I would have been so happy if you were coming with me and at least you would be here with me now to comfort me, you always knew what to say, it didn't matter in what mood I was. But it makes me partly happy that you didn't come, Mrs. Wolowitz is so cruel to her subordinates. Evelyn's words were all true, the ones she said about what was going on in Beelove, but I was afraid to agree with her, I was afraid my only friend wouldn't condemn me for marrying into a family like this.*

*One day I was walking around the house in the hallways of my husband's room, when I was looking at the rooms, because of the accommodation of the guests for the ball. When I noticed that one of the rooms was closed. I don't know what might be there, but I'm burning with the desire to find out."*

\*

-A ball? Still, what's on your mind? -Mrs. Wolowitz asked.

-I thought we could celebrate what a great family we have. -But she saw that she wasn't leaning towards the idea. -What a great parent and stepmother you are, by being so generous giving Riley and Julia such a gift.

-Oh, was that their names? -She asked, looking at Scarlett. -All right, I don't mind. -She replied, after Scarlett's strong convictions. -I'll write the guest list.

-Wonderful. I will take care of the accommodation of the guests. I've already counted the rooms. However, the room next to Leonard's one was closed. Yet for what reason?

-It's none of your business. -She said, playing with Harold's ears, but when she saw that Scarlett was still standing there curious, she continued. - Because of bed bugs, cimex lectularius. One of the guests once brought one with him and multiplied so much that it was impossible to enter there. You'd be so kind as not to be curious? I don't want them to spread in the whole house. -She explained.

-Certainly. -Scarlett replied, then left the room.

*

-Marta, please, do you know what's in that room? -She asked the young cook.

-I don't know, ma'am. -She replied just as the tall butler who had shown her new room in Beelove on her second night had entered the kitchen.

He cleared his throat and said: -Mrs. Wolowitz wants to drink tea.

-I'm warming up right away, Mowie.

-Then give me the key and I'll find out. -She whispered to her so Mowie will not hear.

-I don't have a key, ma'am, the only man who has a key there is Mr. Wolowitz.

-But they should use that room when guests come.

-No one has been using that room for years.

-Well, fine. Then tell me who last used that room. -Then Mowie came in again to urge them to hurry up with Mrs. Wolowitz's drink. Scarlett glanced at him, he was tall and handsome, a little older, but still the age didn't affect his look. With a broken look. It was like a soldier standing motionless with his hands held back as the woman walked past him.

*

Scarlett began searching in Leonard's room, as soon as she reached the bedside table, someone opened the door.

327

-Scarlett? -Agatha called her name.

-Mrs. Wolowitz! -She straightened up -I am looking for my earring. I must have lose it on my honeymoon. Did you not see it? A gold earring with small stones in the middle.

-I'm afraid not. -Agatha replied, then whispered something to Mowie.

Scarlett smiled forcedly, then left the room. As she walked down the hall, she reached into her pocket and took out a key.

-Eureka. -She said softly.

*

She visited Gracewith later that day. When she rode towards Gracewith, she stopped to admire it. She looked around the building, but her eyes caught on the wing that had been closed when she arrived due to the danger posed by the deteriorating walls. The wing had a smaller tower that could not be rebuilt due to a lack of money. According to her guesses, this was the room where Miranda had been held by her father. The thought saddened her, so she heeled her horse and galloped towards her previous home.

-Miss. Bloom! What a surprise. -Doris said from a distance as she walked towards her with outstretched arms.

She was not called like that anymore, but she didn't bothered to correct Doris, since she knew, for her, she will always be a Bloom.

-Doris, how are you?

-We are all right. We heard they sent the two girls to London. How are you?

-I'm fine. I hope Mrs. Wolowitz is right and will benefit them.

-Couldn't it have been solved differently? For example, they could come here, to Gracewith and then we would take care of them?

-I'm afraid Mrs. Wolowitz likes, when she's right, right about everything, she thinks she knows everything, even how the other feels.

-Hmm... And who is the nanny of the two little ones?

-She thought they needed a younger nanny who was strong and fresh. That's how we kept Daphne.

-And you, Miss? What do you think?

-I have no say in things. It's like I don't even live in that house. -She lowered her head.

-Oh, that's definitely not the case. Mr. Wolowitz did not marry you, to behave like this. -Scarlett took the woman's hand and smiled at her.

-I've never asked before. But when I rode this way, it occurred to me. What happened to the smaller tower?

-Oh... -She sat next to her- In that room... Well, that room... -She was looking for the words. -Her father kept locked up Miss. Bloom there, it all began at the end of her pregnancy, when she wanted to meet your father, then he tried to lock her away from something else, Lord knows what was in his head. But I've already told you about.

-Yes, I remember it. But you never told me, that he abused her.

-How do you know about that? -She asked with wide eyes.

-It doesn't matter now. I just want to understand what happened to my mother. I would like to know the whole story.

-Of course.

-You wanted to save her, right?

-Yes, I tried once. But after your grandmother died, Mr. Bloom was very aggressive. He was traumatized and he saw Mrs. Bloom everywhere. Even in Miss. Miranda.

-Did he rape her? -Scarlett asked, a little afraid of the answer. She just nodded, biting her lips.

-Just a few days, after the funeral, he locked her up in that tower again and visited her at nights. Destroying that poor girl. Miss. Miranda cried for hours, she cried and cried. She was in great pain, especially since this happened after delivering her child. Once he let her out, the young lady was like a rock unbreakable, never crying in front of us, never showing even a little distress. I remember the day she first came out, my poor girl, she could barely walk, she was full of wounds, bluish-purple spots covered her body, she was dirty and smelled. Mr. Bloom did not let anyone in. I don't know what happened when he let her go, Mr. Bloom locked up himself in his room for hours, crying, completely shattered. I vowed not to let him touch her ever again, even if my life depended on it. Then one night Lady and Lord Quas arrived, I left her alone for half a minute while I let them in. When I went back, he was violently setting about her and trying to undress Miss. Miranda. Fortunately, there were Mr. Quas and Nivek, who separated them. Then Mr. Quas said he was going to get a doctor, so he locked him up before he left. But not knowing that the gentleman has more keys...

-He freed himself... -Scarlett whispered.

-Yes. When he came out with a chair, he knocked Nivek down, pushed Mrs. Quas aside, and grabbed the Mistress, jerking towards the tower. I ran around when I got there, I was already waiting for them with a knife. But Mr. Bloom was stronger than me. I got pushed to the ground and beaten until I couldn't see from the blood. But Miss. Bloom, my Miss. Bloom, I loved her as if she was my own daughter, she picked up the knife, gathered all her courage, and stabbed her father.

-But he didn't die. What did the doctor say when he saw him?

-Nothing. Mr. Bloom was lying on the bed, unconscious when he arrived, not even looking at him, all he said was that the drink brought out this aggression and that he was completely healthy. He was examined by many other doctors, all of them had the same response, trauma, and that this is normal. Many people said he was just drunk and then left. And in many cases, Mr. Bloom seemed so normal that no one accepted our claims. He was a very influential man, and no doctor wanted to confront him when he recovered. After that, Miss. Bloom did to him what he deserved. She tied him up, starved him, tortured him. She promised, lubricating my wounds, that she would never let anyone hurt us. While her father died of exhaustion and heart disease, he apologised for all his behaviour and also told her where to find you. I think he was only afraid that if he didn't apologise, he will burn in hell. But it took us years to get there. She had changed the place's name, GracewithHenry, which contained her grandmother's and grandfather's names along with her father's name to Gracewith. She tried to forget him, all the things he had done to her. So, she threw everything that belonged to him, she only left that painting, because that was the only one on which her mother was on, but after that, she never entered that room. She couldn't even look at the tower after his death, she demolished it. But she did not expect that many weakened walls would cause damage to the wing of the house.

-That's why it was dangerous when I moved in... And what about the paperwork?

-Oh yeah... we were lucky one year a new doctor came to town, Dr. Bing. He didn't know anything about the family, that is how Miss. Miranda succeeded in changing the inheritance documents.

-You didn't tell me how Miranda died.

-Oh... Well, there was no sign of that for a long time. But she died of a sexually transmitted infection one gets from incest. Probably she was too weak after childbirth, her wounds couldn't heal properly, and this is how she got sick.

-So that is why she didn't say anything to anyone, this is the reason why she didn't get married. The reason she didn't tell my dad about me, why she had not visited me before. She didn't even write this down in her diary.

-There are things that people just try to forget.

*

Scarlett went out a night after her mother-in-law went to sleep to try to unlock the door with the key she found. She wasn't afraid that her husband would catch her since it was Sunday night. He used to have fun with Jerome and his other friends on Sundays, and then returns home at dawn on Monday, or no later than noon. Her guesses were true. The key was really for that lock. When she entered, she put down the candle and looked around. On the table she found letters addressed to a certain Elsa Wolowitz as she straightened, her gaze stopped on a painting. She lifted the candle again and took it closer so she could see better. There was a young girl on the portrait with long black hair. She had a beautiful smile, and bright green eyes.

-Bedbugs, huh?!...

-Can I help you? -A voice came from the dark door, Scarlett shuddered. When she turned there, with the candle in her hand, she saw her husband's angry gaze.

-I just... -But she thought it was pointless to give explanation -Who is she? -Pointing to the painting.

-Elsa Wolowitz. -He replied, stepping closer to her- My first wife.

-You never said you were married before. Where is she now?

-The end of the garden. -The man replied, and Scarlett's throat tightened. -She is dead.

-How? -Scarlett asked, but her husband didn't want to answer. -Please tell me, I want to know. I want to know everything about you. -She said stroking her husband's chest, but the man turned away from her.

-You said you don't prejudice. Then please do as you said, once you step out this door.

# CHAPTER XI

Scarlett had planned a ball for the first time, except for the harvest ball for the villagers, but it was different, much different, it couldn't be compared to that. She felt satisfied with the result. The guests seemed to be having a good time. Scarlett, too, until she saw George with his new bride.

-What are they doing here? -Leonard asked.

-I have no idea. -Scarlett replied.

-I invited them. I thought it would be fun. -Agatha said from the chair next to them.

Leonard seemed irritated, but didn't say a word. He started toward the approaching couple with a fist clenched, pulling Scarlett with him with his other hand.

-Mr. Salvatore! -He looked at the man, then bowed to the woman. -Miss. O'Neil! I'm glad the invitation was accepted.

-It was a little long way to travel from London to here. -George replied- But it's better to deliver it in person than to send it by mail. -He handed them an envelope, which Scarlett took. When she reached for it, her hand touched George's and as a result, they were both embarrassed. -Well, we look forward to seeing you at the wedding. -He said after a pause.

-Thank you for the invitation, we're guaranteed to be there. -Leonard replied, taking the invitation from Scarlett's hand, wrinkling it slightly as he squeezed it. They both nodded and then their way separated.

A few hours later, she met at the punch bowl, Miss. O'Neil.

-Miss. O'Neil! -She greeted her bowing, as she finally could speak after getting rid of her husband, who always spoke on behalf of both of them.

-Mrs. Wolowitz! -She stressed, which bothered Scarlett very much. -The ball is great. The atmosphere is surprisingly good. The Wolowitz family always knew how to impress people.

-Why would it be different? -She asked as she filled from her glass.

-Lots of things can be heard about Beelove.

-What kind of things would they be?

-You know... Rumours. -She said with a laugh- They seem to be wrong.

-If you say so, Miss. -She took a sip.

-I've also heard that marriage of convenience isn't very happy. -She told Scarlett, who was turning her back, she was about to leave that part of the room.

-I can assure you, that the rumours are misleading. -She turned back- Now, if you'll excuse me ...

-Oh, of course. Then it's not true that your husband often visits the Black Quarter. Nor is it that people often see him drunk to the ground in brothels.

-I think everyone has privacy that they don't have to report to others. -She left.

Everyone had a great time at the ball. There were plenty of guests present. So much, that extra help was needed, Scarlett called her staff from Gracewith to help cater  for the many guests. More than anyone, the Wolowitz family likes to make a good impression.

-Mr. Thaker, you are here! -She said as she approached her father.

-I wouldn't have missed a Wolowitz ball for any money. Nor to see you, my dear.

-Do you have a minute? -She asked, holding his arm and waiting for no answer she took him to a quiet place.

-What would it be about?

-I know it's not entirely my business. And I said I would keep my cold blood. But I need to know. My husband had a wife, right?

-Yes, that's right. Elsa Wolowitz, whose maiden name was O'Neil.

-Did you say, O'Neil? Was she related to Miss. Winnifred?

-Yes, she was her sister.

-What happened to her?

-I do not know exactly. Many say her husband mistreated her, and some claim her husband killed her because she found out about his secret. But there is no evidence for that.

-What kind of secret? -She asked curiously her question, to which she was not sure she wanted to get an answer.

-Are you sure you want to know it? -The man asked back.

-You are right, better not to know. -She replied on a sad voice.

-They are just rumours, anyway. Does your husband treat you well? -He asked anxiously.

-You don't have to worry, Mr. Thaker. -Scarlett forced  a smile.

When she went back to the guests, leaving Owen Thaker in quandary. A drunken guest caught her and yanked her to dance. Against her will, she was on the dance floor from one moment to the next, but she couldn't turn back anymore because the dance had begun. She went from one dancer to another, people cheered and watched happily as the host also enjoyed the fun. She enjoyed it until the moment she saw that George was among the dancers as well. But there was nothing she could do, it was too late, the steps were one after the other, as were the couples. And at the end of the dance, they could have enjoyed each other's company if the dance had lasted longer, but it finished just as they reached each other. They bowed in front of each other, got serious, and then Scarlett walked out to get some fresh air. George followed, he knew nothing good would come of it, but he did. On the terrace, he found the woman with whom he once watched the moon together.

-There is no reason to sneak, since I know you are there. -Scarlett told the man behind her.

-But your husband doesn't know about it.

-My husband doesn't know much. -Scarlett said sadly.

-How are your married days? -He inquired.

-Do you want to ask, Mr. Salvatore for a preparatory lesson? -She asked ironically, for which George started to laugh.

-Maybe. -He stepped closer.

-Are you sure you want to get married?

-I know one thing. I can't live as a bachelor for the rest of my life. -Replied the man- And you? Are you happy?

-I met Miss. O'Neil. She has a captivating personality and is very sassy in nature. -She said, staring at the moon, then looking at the man. -Now I know why you want to marry her.

-She is really a great woman. -He said, turning his head towards her. -But you didn't answer my question. Are you living in a happy marriage?

-Scarlett! -A voice shouted from the door.

-I have to go now. -She turned to her husband.

*

People started retreating, some went to the room allotted to them to rest, and others went home. Scarlett didn't know if she was expecting this moment or much more afraid of it.

-We need to talk! -Her husband stepped next to her as soon as she said goodbye to a couple of guests.

Scarlett followed her husband, who went to the library. The library was cold and dark, just lit by the moon.

-I can't forbid you who you can talk to and who you can't. But I want you to avoid the company of that man.

-Mr. Thaker? -He is the head of my entire business, my banker, my notary, and even my accountant.

-I didn't refer to him. -He took a deep breath.

-Then the drunk gentleman who dragged me to the dance floor? Well, I don't even know his name.

-Don't play with me woman! -He yelled, then punched his fist in the wall behind Scarlett. She was so shocked, but tried not to show her fear, trying to suppress her feelings so much that she felt she could explode. He swallowed the dumpling in her throat, then clenched her fist. -You know who I'm talking about. – He Leaned even closer to her -I want you to avoid Mr. Salvatore and his bride. -He wanted to smooth the woman's face, but she turned her head away.

-As you wish. -She replied, then left the room. When she stepped out the door, she loosened her tight grip and looked at her palm, in which she had cut bloody-wounded crescents with her fingernails.

# CHAPTER XII

It had been weeks since the ball, and the couple hadn't talked to each other from that day on. Scarlett tried to keep her principles and not beg for anyone's forgiveness. George and Winnifred's big day were approaching. Scarlett always felt like the dagger that stabbed her the day of the ball, when she realised that George Salvatore was getting married, every single minute she thought about it happening soon, this dagger turns in her.

-Scarlett, I'm going to town. -Her husband said as he entered the room- I thought we could go together. People haven't seen us together in weeks, they're going to believe our marriage is getting worse. -He said as he looked at his letters on the table, after more than a minute there was still no reaction from his wife, so he stepped closer. -Do you want me to bring you something? -He stroked the arm of the woman who was standing with her back to him, from her wrist upwards, but Scarlett's reaction was clear. She jerked her arm away and walked out of the room without looking at Leonard.

*

Scarlett later in the day, after returning home from Gracewith, was surprised to see that her mother-in-law was not in her usual place. The armchair in the living room, which was next to the always warm fireplace, with a sleeping mother-in-law and an annoying little fur ball, was empty this time. Marta walked over, at the sight of Scarlett she stopped in front of her Mistress and greeted her politely.

-Mrs. Wolowitz! Good evening! -She said, straightening after bowing.

-Do you know where Mrs. Agatha Wolowitz is? -She asked, pointing to the empty armchair.

-Mr. Wolowitz sent her away. He said he wants to spend the evening with his wife today.

-Are you sure? -Scarlett doubted a little since it was a Sunday night.

-I was there when he issued the orders to us. -Scarlett then realised how wet she was and how embarrassed she looked while they were talking.

-Are you feeling well, Marta? -She asked the woman staring at the ground, leaning into her aura.

-Yes, ma'am. -She smiled.

-Tell me, where were you? -She realised that the young girl was using the front door.

-Mrs. Wolowitz, I want you to know, I had to. -She said, gasping for air as she wrestled with her balance.

-What would it be about?

-You know, I have a son... I raise him alone, I mean, Mom is taking care of him now, but she's very sick. And I had to run home to see if all was well.

-Don't you live in the maid's rooms, Marta? -Scarlett had never seen her leave or just come into the house before, so she was surprised to hear the word "home".

She nodded. -Miss, no one knows about... -She took a deep breath. -A little son was born out of wedlock and is now being raised by my elderly mother, who once worked for the house. But she escaped. I am working now to support them. And I go home at night to be with my little boy, and I come home at dawn before anyone gets up. Will you tell Mr. Wolowitz?

Scarlett knew Marta was honest. She knew that if her husband found out it wouldn't be in her favour, not to mention if Mrs. Wolowitz knew about it. And the fact that the girl's mother had escaped the house and that she was probably, at least Scarlett suspected, secretly caring for her child, would not improve her situation.

-No. -She said with a smile. -I'm not telling him. -She put her hand on the girl's shoulder. -But I want you to know that you can always be honest with me, and if you need anything, let me know.

-Thank you, ma'am! -She answers then left.

When Scarlett reached the room, she was thinking about the girl's fate and wishing she could help her. She was so immersed in her thoughts that when she entered her room, she didn't even notice that a huge box was lying on her bed until she was almost sitting on it. She unfolded it, slowly taking off its top, it was a note she had noticed at first, but she didn't open it. Firstly, she wanted to see what was in the box, when she took it out it was a beautiful azure dress, she measured it to herself, it was just her size. Then she unfolded the note: *"Have dinner with me."* it says, in the lower right corner with Leonard's signature.

Scarlett decided to give in to her husband's will, so she put on the dress she had received, and walked into the dining room, where her husband sat at the table, deep in thought. As Scarlett stopped at the door, the light blue dress caught his eye, which he first noticed, out of the corner of his eye.

-Scarlett! -He got up from the table. -Well, you're here... -He walked towards her- I'm glad. -Then pulled out the chair for his wife, who took a seat and rang the bell.

Leonard sat back and watched his wife. But Scarlett didn't look at him.

-How was your day? -Her husband asked, a little embarrassed, but Scarlett just stared at the end of  the table, leaving her husband's interest in the cold, Leonard waiting for Mowie to put the food down in front of him, and after he left, he looked at his wife again. -Let's not do this anymore. Do you want our marriage to fall apart? People are already starting to gossip.

-Don't pretend it's not already a ruined marriage. -Scarlett replied angrily.

-For heaven's sake. -He slapped on the table- I'm trying to be nice to you and take care of you. Is that how you thank? -He asked, wiping his mouth with a napkin.

-Care? Are you talking about buying me expensive things? That is what caring for someone means? You know what? -With a pointing finger, she began to undress, taking off her newly received dress, and then stood in front of her husband in her underwear. -If this is care for you, then keep it for yourself. -Then she started for the door, but she turned back. -You know, I have no idea why you're treating me like this or what you're hiding from me, but you need to know, whatever it is, I'll find out. -Then she turned her back and left.

# CHAPTER XIII

This day was the second that Scarlett feared the most, after her own wedding. George's wedding was simple but intimate. It was held in London, where Scarlett visited for the first time in her life. She was impressed by the hustle and bustle of the city and the plethora of buildings. What Leonard admired with depth was that she looked like a child who was just exploring the world. As the couple stood in front of the altar, Scarlett became frustrated, which caught Leonard's eye, but he didn't even try to show it to his wife. Scarlett knew she would have to stand in Winnifred's place and say the big words happily, but that wasn't the main reason she was so frustrated. The main thing that hurt her the most was that George didn't even hesitate, he was sure of what he wanted and he looked happy. Scarlett felt selfish for what she thought, but she didn't deny that she wasn't happy about the couple's happiness.

*

Later, at the party following the ceremony, she enjoyed her friend, Evelyn's, company.

-Look how happy they are... -She said, grimacing. -Winnifred... what a name... - Apparently didn't hide her feelings from her friend, who was just smiling silently. –Is she American?

-Yes. But her family moved here when their eldest daughter got married. Her husband was bound here by his work, his customers, the great land. -She said as she looked at the guests.

-Elsa O'Neil. -She whispered.

-How do you know about her? -She turned suddenly towards Scarlett.

-So, you knew her? -Scarlett asked in surprise with a drunken wrist tone, but Evelyn took a sip from her glass. - You never told me about her.

-What did you want me to say? You said you didn't want to know anything about your husband's past. -Evelyn felt Scarlett was blaming her, so she left a little upset.

Scarlett grimaced at her friend, not even noticing that the bride was walking beside her to draw from the punch bowl.

-So, Mrs. Wolowitz, -she stressed her name- how did you like the ceremony?

-It will be an unforgettable memory.

-Which part of it? -Winnifred asked- The delicious punch we served, -Leonard's was standing close, so his attention was attracted to the two women conversation, so he kept an eye on them, this is how he continued his conversation with the business associates- or is it that you realize that the love of your life got married and live his life happily while you live your whole miserable life on the side of a murderous man?

Unable to bear it longer, Scarlett shoved the bride in the white princess dress, who fell to the punch bowl, so from that moment, she got up from the ground in her, now pink dress. George ran there to help, and all the guest's attention was drawn to them.

-You... shag! -She said nervously- Whatever you do, you'll always be the wife of a killer in people's eyes. -She shouted as Scarlett had become more indulgent and prepared for the cat fight, but her husband interrupted in time, catching her and throwing on his shoulder just as Scarlett would have attacked the bride. Then he nodded at George in a kind of *"I'll deal with it"* way.

345

-No one can talk about my husband like that. Nobody! Do you hear? -She shouted, lying on her husband's shoulder as he left with her.

-All right, there's nothing to see here! -George raised both hands to the sky.

*

Later at the lodging, Scarlett sat on the edge of the bed and laughed, saying to herself: -Well, this is what I meant it would be *"memorable"*.

When her husband entered the room, she became a little more serious.

-What was that good for? -He asked, dropping his coat. Scarlett didn't answer, just turned her head. -Listen, I'm just asking you to try to behave like we are a happy couple again. I don't want you to be unhappy next to me.

-To do that, you need to realise that it's not just my fault that we've become who we are now. It takes two to make a fair.

-Then tell me what I should do to make you happy?

-Be honest with me. -She said. The man stood up and turned his back.

-Scarlett, you don't understand much yet. -Scarlett stood up, then stepped closer.

-Then make me understand. -She replied, embracing the man, who turned to her and kissed her on the forehead.

-Lie down. Rest a bit. -Then reached for the coat and walked to the door.

-Where are you going?

-Back to the wedding. After all, we can't let them think we ran away.

-I'm coming too!

-No! -He said showing his palm. -You'd rather stay and relax, you're not in that state.

# CHAPTER XIV

Scarlett spent the day in the company of Evelyn, walking in the city and shopping.

-So, how do you like London?

-Amazing, it's kind of replacement honeymoon for me. After our wedding, we didn't go anywhere. You know, it was just the season... For Leonard is when it comes to his bees as if he had children.

-Oh, it's going to be a great night, tonight! -She said aiming.

-We will see. -Scarlett replied a little ashamed that the matter had turned in her head also.

-Maybe you will have a little heir. -She's been caressing her tummy. -You've been married for months, almost half a year. It is time to. -She was teasingly.

Scarlett just smiled at the thought as she watched with admiration as Evelyn progressed. The idea of how wonderful human beings are, how this process is created and how it takes place. The cycle of life... Wonderful. Scarlett also thought that if she had a child, it might bring light and hope back into her life, she could get rid of this loneliness... Not to mention quenching her desire. After all, a woman who is now twenty-one years old almost, and still a virgin, how would she not desire the tender touch, love, and the pleasure she has read so much about?

-What are your plans for the rest of the week?

-I plan to visit my nieces. I already miss them very much, at first when they came under my guardianship it was very difficult. But by the end, I had learnt to deal with them and understood what they were feeling. Just as they insisted on me.

-I'm glad to hear that.

-Uhm... -Scarlett murmured.

-Go ahead. What happened?

-I want to ask how long you've been at the wedding?

-Oh... I don't know. Maybe we left after midnight. I was a little tired. -She was stroking her tummy again.

-Do you know when Leonard left?

-I've seen you leave together after the punch affair, not since. -She found the incident with the bride a little humorous, so she began to laugh slightly -Why do you ask? -She had to ask as soon as she saw Scarlett's worried gaze. But the woman did not dare to admit that he had not yet appeared in the room when she left in the morning.

-Doesn't matter. -She forced a smile -Do you know what the baby's name will be? -She deflected the subject.

-Not yet. But I want to get some strong name, something that suggests he or she can do anything. That it's capable to realise the dreams, like Scarlett. -She said ironically.

*

When she was prepared to go to bed in the evening, she was a little excited. This was her first night in a bed with her husband since their wedding night. When Leonard entered the door, her heart began to beat so violently that for a moment she thought it would jump out of its place.

-I met Lord Quas today. I found out they were expecting a baby. You sure knew about it. -He said as he poured water into the washbasin.

-Yes, I knew about it.

-It's unbelievable at their age... -He laughed as he took off his shirt.

Scarlett glanced at him and her eyes clung to the man's muscular body. She had never felt such a desire and compulsion before. She got up from the table and then stepped closer to her husband.

-Maybe you want to say something? -He asked the approaching woman.

Scarlett stopped and leaned on the end of the bed. Slightly embarrassed.

-I'd love to visit my nieces tomorrow. -She bites her lips.

-Of course. -He was a little confused, then went to the bowl and began to wash up.

-I'd like you... to come with me. -She said, puttering the edge of the bed nervously.

-I had a lot to deal with tomorrow. -He wiped his face. When he turned, he saw Scarlett's sad face, so he stepped closer -But you don't have to worry, before we go home, we'll visit them together as well. -He said, stroking her face. Scarlett misunderstood the gesture and kissed her husband, more precisely their lips just met, for which her husband pushed her away at that moment. Scarlett embarrassed began to wipe her lips. -What were you thinking? -He asked a little aggressively, and Scarlett shuddered, noticing this, he spoke again: -Forgive me...

-Tell me why did you marry me, if you don't want me? Why do you need me, if you can't look at me as your wife?

-Scarlett you can't understand this... -He said, turning his back again and leaning against the table.

-No, and I won't understand until you explain. Is Elsa O'Neil the reason? Or is anyone else in your life? Were you with her last night lying about going back to the wedding? -The woman burst out.

-Are you spying on me? -He turned to his wife again. But she didn't answer, just tried to keep her tears back with her arms closed.

The man picked up his shirt nervously and ran away half-naked.

# CHAPTER XV

Thanks to the ending warm summer weather, the kids enjoyed a good time outside in the schoolyard. Scarlett first met the headmistress, who was a very witty and kind woman. But it is also possible that she thought so only because all the other people or teachers she had met there so far behaved grimly and disparagingly. She didn't deny that a girl's school needs seriousness and confidence, they really knew how to deal with them. And anyway, what would it be like if they weren't able to restrain so many students?

-Please tell me, they're studying. How are their grades? For no other reason, but they were very bad students at home. -Scarlett intertwined her fingers.

-Excellent. The average for the younger one is now starting to improve. Julia, on the other hand, performed great from the beginning.

-Oh! -She was surprised.

-You don't have to worry. I'm sure you raised them well. But you know your kids need a social life. They probably also benefited from not being in the same class. To tell the truth, it wasn't easy for them at the beginning, but now they're used to it. -The headmistress smiled kindly.

-They fit in quickly or did they need a long time to find their places?

-Relatively soon. In that, too, it was harder for Riley. But Julia was accepted from the very beginning, and she is loved by her classmates.

-You know they lost their parents a couple of years ago... I think it was easier for Julia because she had to play a motherly role when she was young. With a lot of responsibility around her neck.

-I am sure that's the main reason then. -The woman answered, then pointed to the end of the hallway to a door- The girls will spend the afternoon outside, you find them in the yard.

When Scarlett walked out the door, she saw a plethora of girls, all dressed in uniform, with a small straw hat on their heads, or just sliding on their backs held by a powder blue ribbon that matched the colour of their uniform.

-Scarlett? -A voice asked behind her as she walked in the garden searching for the girls. Scarlett turned and saw the little girl with curly blonde-brown hair.

-Riley! -She squatted down next to the girl. -How much you grew... -She looked over her, and soon after, Julia showed up next to her sibling, who was now at least two heads taller than when Scarlett had last seen her. -Julia! -She held out her arms, then pulled her close and they hugged in groups.

Leonard watched them from the other side of the fence. He followed his wife, not because he did not trust her. No, there was no such reason. Leonard knew deep down, everything his wife was doing is rightful because in the opposite case, he would probably do the same. He just felt he knew so little about Scarlett, the woman he had married. He thought that in order to better understand her, he had to see, to see her daily activities, her gestures, her reactions to certain things, as he does now. He was sure his wife was happy at this moment. And he was also beginning to realise that yesterday's incident was because she was lonely. Scarlett is consumed by loneliness in front of her husband's eyes and he does nothing. He knew he had to change all that, but not the way he tried before. Not because others see them and their opinions count, but because he knew Scarlett was a good person and deserved it.

*

Scarlett sat in her room that evening after visiting her nieces and starting to comb her hair. She looked in the mirror as Leonard entered the room and sat down on the edge of the bed.

-I thought you took out another room for yourself. -Scarlett said, combing her hair further.

-Yes, I did. That's not why I'm here now. -He was looking at his wife in the mirror. -Scarlett, -he leaned forward and leaned on his thighs- I know what you think, just like what you do. -Scarlett was a little confused, but she let her husband finish. -You think our marriage is in ruins, which is most likely the case, and you're trying to fix it. -Then he stood up and stepped closer to her, took the comb from her, then began to comb the woman's hair. -Yes, it's hard to get married again. But I want to save our marriage, I want us to have a good relationship. -He said as he watched his wife turn toward him.

-Then let's save it. -She took Leonard's hand.

-I want you to be patient. I need some time.

Scarlett smiled, then nodded understandingly.

# CHAPTER XVI

"*Dear Diary,*

*Today is the last night I spend in London. I am pleased to announce that I feel we have successfully improved our relationship with Leonard. Although we spent the nights in a separate room and I still suspect there is someone in his life. I hope that one day all the secrets he has, he will share himself with me openly and with confidence. I'm not angry at what he's doing because I also married him just to save Gracewith and provide a more secure future for the kids.*

*Nowadays after the conversation when he said that he wants to save our marriage our days were wonderful. We went sightseeing, he accompanied me to the shop, we went to balls and spent the last day with the girls. I didn't even have to mention what I wanted; he knew. We took them to town and we had a great time, we were like a peaceful family with no unresolved issues. At least it's good to pretend we're happy.*

*It's hard for me to admit, but I feel a bond with my husband that I've never felt with anyone, not even George. Every day I look at him, I see a picture of a loving husband. Whatever he does in his free time, I cannot think of him as an unfaithful husband who betrays me. When he is with me, his kindness and tenderness are boundless. I have decided not to pursue any further inquiries, nor to accept false rumours or other opinions. I am happy to say that I feel like the old Scarlett again.*"

# CHAPTER XVII

A few days after returning home, Scarlett heard a bitter cry as she walked down the stairs. When she went to see what was happening she saw Marta hiding her face in her palms and sobbing. -Marta? -She looked through the small door, where they were keeping the tools for cleaning the house, that Scarlett hadn't known about before. Although she had been married for almost half a year, she was unable to explore every nook and cranny of the huge house.

-I am so sorry ma'am! -She got up, then began to wipe her face from the tears.

-Are you feeling all right?

-Mum's very sick. I don't know how long she'll bear it. -She replied, holding back the tears.

-Take me to her.

*

Later that day, Scarlett found herself in the Black Quarter in front of a ruined house. There were sick, skinny and dirty people on the streets. At first, she was afraid to walk in, but there was nothing else she could do, she promised Marta that she would do her best. Every pair of eyes looked at her on the street, for which she began to be frustrated. Walking through, she saw people coughing heavily and lying half-dead in the mud, which made her feel pretty much like she was in a leper colony. When they went into the house, it reminded her of Mr. Kwaw's house, but these people were in a much worse condition, starvation and illness at the same time pulled them down. Anger and hatred burned in their eyes like those who were about to curse the woman before them. A grey-haired woman was lying on the bed trembling with the disease, water dripping down her face while she complained that she was cold.

-Mum, this is Mrs. Wolowitz, she came to help. -Marta said as she sat up and looked at Scarlett.

-What are you talking about, my child? Mrs. Wolowitz had passed away years ago. -She said in a hoarse voice. Marta, meanwhile, hugged her baby boy who was no older than Jared, he had such a mesmerizing look that Scarlett thought she was melting along as he looked at her.

-No, mum. She is Mrs. Scarlett Wolowitz, the lord's new wife.

She didn't believe her ears, so she started laughing.

-Well, someone was so stupid as to marry that man. -She said with a laugh, then lay back in bed.

-Ma'am, I came to help. If you will allow me to call a doctor. -Scarlett said as she stepped closer and sat down on her bed.

-No one can help me anymore. They will bury me and it will be better for me, I will not suffer anymore. -She said looking at her daughter.

-Don't talk nonsense, Mum. -She said, kissing her baby on the forehead.

-I want you to tell me how you feel. In case I can't find a doctor in time, at least I can get the medicine.

-Yet that man, how could he find such a blessed soul? -She said by the time Scarlett smiled- Elsa O'Neil was completely different.

-Did you know her? -Scarlett asked, raising her head.

-Oh yes. -She said amid coughs.

-Can you tell me about her, please? -Scarlett said, but by the time she said the words it was too late to withdraw, she realised she had broken her promise.

-She was a very bad woman. Full of anger and hatred. -She said, frowning- But she might have just adapted to Mrs. Agatha Wolowitz. -She laughed with an open mouth, then Scarlett saw that the woman's teeth were very bad, she knew her illness was very advanced, anything may hurt her. -You know, Elsa was a big city woman, from New York. She has a hard time getting used to life here. One night, she found out about her husband's secret, they got into a big fight, I entered just at the moment when the controversy hit the roof. Elsa threatened her with telling everyone about his illness, then the gentleman killed the woman. After that, I ran away. -Scarlett was goose bumped from head to toe and unable to speak for a few seconds. She saw that the woman in front of her was very ill, Scarlett began to question her further, but she wandered. She explained incomprehensible things.

-The fever has gone up. She's raving. -Said a girl younger than Marta- It often happens.

-I'll talk to Dr. Jerome Garfield tomorrow.

-Please, ma'am, don't do it. He's a friend of the gentleman, if he finds out where my mother is... -Marta pleaded, to which Scarlett understandingly agreed.

-Then I'll try to get some medicine. Stay here tonight with your mother and your little son. I'll take care that no one notices you're missing.

-Thank you, Madam! I am truly thankful! -She said, kissing her hand.

Scarlett was just about to leave, when she stepped out the door, she took a step back when she saw her husband approaching, who fortunately did not notice the woman as he stared at the ground and pondered deeply in his thoughts. After her husband passed next to her, she followed him at a sufficient distance. They walked down the same street she came here to. She tried to sneak, so that the man in front of her wouldn't notice. As he turned to right at the corner, Scarlett breathed. But suddenly she was surrounded by strong hands, first to keep her mouth from screaming, and then her hands were caught and dragged into a smaller alley. She was strongly opposed, but the men were much stronger than her.

-What's wrong, little kitty aristocrat, are you scared? -The number one guy asked, but Scarlett's mouth was covered so she couldn't talk, just whimper.

-Look. How much can this necklace be worth around her neck? -Asked number two.

-A fortune. -The third one replied, taking a look at the string of pearls around her neck.

Then they tried to gag Scarlett's mouth with a piece of clothing, the number three staring at the jewellery, ready to tear it from her neck as Scarlett gathered all her strength and hit her head to the man's head, and spat out the garment.

-You slut! -The third shouted as he got after his bleeding nose.

-Help! -Scarlett yelled- Hel... -She was interrupted by a hand pressed to her mouth. But in a few seconds, the figure who had just walked in front of the alley stepped back and walk towards them.

-Let go of the woman. -Said Kwaw.

-Why would we do that? You're not the cap here, Thomas. -Said number two.

-No, but this woman saved my daughter's life. -He pointed to Scarlett.

-This is your personal business. -Replied the first man.

-This will be yours if I tell your boss why he's running out of goods regularly. -Kwaw said with his hands in his pockets as the men looked at each other, then nodded to the two the third one, in a sort of "*let go*" way. So, they left speechless, they only glanced cunningly at Kwaw as they walked past him.

-Are you well madam? -He looked at the woman.

-Thanks! -Scarlett replied, then began to feel her bare neck.

-What happened?

-My jewellery is gone. -She said, a little frightened.

-It's just a piece of jewellery.

-I got it from my sister, it was a memory. -She said sadly, as they began to walk out of the alley.

-What were you doing here?

-I visited a worker of mine. Tell me how is your little girl? -She changed the subject before the man could get the chance to ask which worker.

-She's well. But really, she is not that small anymore.

-Time goes by so fast.

-Indeed. At one moment they are still babies, and then the man realises that she is almost married. -He said consequently they both laughed.

-Tell me, why do you still live here? Are you not afraid?

-I was just afraid only because of my daughter among those worthless.

-Why aren't you moving?

-It's not like that, ma'am. Unemployment and famine lead to difficult decisions.

Scarlett just nodded in agreement.

-Take care of yourself, ma'am. -He said when he accompanied her to the end of the street. When Scarlett was walking away, he was still standing there looking at the woman, he wanted to make sure she was safe.

*

When she got home, her husband was waiting for her already.

-Where have you been? -He asked as he watched Scarlett hang her cloak.

-I just took a walk. -She said as soon as she felt her husband be in close proximity.

-Where?

-I could ask you that too. I didn't see you all day today. -She looked at her husband, who turned his back and walked away. Scarlett felt that every time she started trusting him, there was always something going on that was whispering "*You can't*".

# CHAPTER XVIII

The next day, Leonard felt his wife wasn't honest enough with him. She didn't say a word to him during breakfast, she just played with her food on the plate, she was more occupied with her thoughts than the real-world moments.

-Does something hurt you? -He asked, a little afraid of the answer.

-No. -Scarlett replied briefly.

-Something just happened?... -He continued curiously.

Scarlett was afraid to admit she had seen and followed him the night before. But she was burning with the desire to find out what her husband was looking for there, but she was also aware that he wouldn't tell her anyway.

-I am thinking about the girls. -She hated to lie, but she realised that this is an adult disease. Adult life, itself is a lie. People say how nice is to grow up, you can do whatever you want, no one can command you. It is the biggest lie to tell your children, especially if you get married and lose your freedom, and the worst thing is that children believe it and they live all of their childhood waiting for the moment, the big moment to turn eighteen and get rid of the school, their parents, their toys... CHILDREN DON'T WASTE THE TIME DAYDREAMING TO BECOME AN ADULT, JUST PLAY, HAVE FUN AND LIVE THE MOMENT, THEY ARE PRECIOUS. YOU CAN'T GET BACK YOUR OLD LIFE, THE YEARS, MONTHS, WEEKS OR HOURS YOU WASTED.

-You miss them, right? -Scarlett just nodded, covering the truth- I'll be going to see the beehives soon. Would you like to come with me?

The woman did not hesitate to say yes, as she knows nothing about her husband's business.

*

They later walked through the hives, and her husband proudly explained the apiary in detail.

-Put this on you. You have to wear it. -He said, giving his wife a protective suit (a cloak), gloves, and a hat, which has a tulle for covering her face.

-What a fashion. -She replied as she arranged the net that hung in her face.

They walked past a hive, where a man, lifting up a bee smoker all around the hive and pulled out a plate full of honey from the hive.

-Doesn't smoke kill the bees?

-All experienced beekeepers use smoke to soothe insects. This method allows you to quickly inspect the hive. By sensing the smoke, the bees take it as a fire alarm and rush to save the honey. In fact, they fill the abdomen so much that they can't pinch for a while. -The man said, then they watched the process as the honey was extracted and put into a bucket, a small piece of the honeycomb.

-And how does that thing works? -Scarlett asked looking at the smoking thing.

-I invented it, before we used only papers, but it burned to ash too quickly, and everywhere you looked there were ashes all over the fields. So, -he started to laugh- I got a teapot, and I burned paper in it, realizing how easy is to deal with the bees this way, I was shocked. Since then, we use this method, of course sometimes we have to lift the pot's lid, to not let the fire extinguished. But it works. -He said happy.

-So, not everyone uses a smoke-pot? Shall I call it like that?

-Actually, it doesn't have a name yet. -He looked at his wife- I mean it didn't have until now. -He started to smile, for which Scarlett blushed- It is unique. I never heard anyone using such thing before. Many people keep the hives inside, like in barns, and they set fire in there, it is kind of dangerous.

-What gave you the idea?

-I don't know. -He shrugged- One day, I was examining a bee, and just tried different methods.

-I think you are a genius. -Scarlett was amazed.

-Come with me. -He said, holding her hand and pulling the woman after him, they stopped next to another hive where the honey had also been collected. Leonard also broke a small piece of it. -Taste it. -He handed it over. - Be careful not to have a bee in it. -He said as she bit into it. -What do you feel?

-It's sweeter. -She said, raising the darker colour.

-They make different kinds of honey. Depends on where their hives are. They are south from the previous hive and collect honey from the field. -He pointed to the beehives from far away at the other side of the estate- Those in the east, gather them from fruit trees and flowering trees. The other is made of lilac flowers. They have their own areas, each bee colony where they go to get nectar, which depends on where the hive is located, the bees can fly up to five miles for food, but the average distance is less than a mile from the home.

-How do you know all this?

-I studied them a lot. In order not to mix the nectar, I divided the areas to always make one kind of honey. We always collect it seasonally. If we say in the lilac garden the flowers are withering, we collect all the honey even before the autumn flowers start to bloom. For example, the orchard is also divided, if the flowers wither before the fruits are ripe, the honey is collected. In every different kind of orchard there are four or five hives.

-You once told me about sugar water, what is it for?

-Sugared water or syrup. Feeding families in the fall is necessary to create enough food for the swarm to continue hibernating. The best solution is honey. Feeding the bees with sugar syrup in fall will help preserve the apiculture product to keep the apiary commercially viable. There are a number of special cases where an upper dressing in the fall is required: The first is the apiary site is far from the honey plants – the insects are supplied with honeydew honey, which is a toxic product. It can be completely removed from the hives by replacing it with a sugar solution. If the nectar crystallizes, the bees do not seal it, it is also removed. And the rainy summer also prevents bribes for insects, they did not collect the necessary amount of nectar to produce honey. The syrup also has its own recipe to make it properly prepared.

-It's not that complicated.

-No, because you don't know yet that bees can get ill too.

-Are you serious?

-Yes, for example: sticky rot, mild rot, blackheads, deformed wing virus, poisoning, or even depopulation.

-Oh, how many diseases…

-And those are just the most common.

-Do they live like us? I mean are there any differences between them?

-Yes, there is always only one queen in the group: significantly different in size from the others. Her main function is reproduction. This bee is considered the main individual in the colony, so the other bees protect and feed her. Then there are the working bees, females, which by number form the basis of the group. They are most often seen in nature. One nest contains about 80,000 individuals. Representatives of the working group look for suitable plants, get nectar, and make honey. Finally, the other members of the swarm are the male drones. The main task is to continue the offspring. Drones do not produce pollen and do not make honey. They are bigger than working bees and need more food. When the drone is no longer usable for the colony, it is simply expelled.

-I remember once you said bees live for about forty days.

-Yes, the working bees. But we can also group their lifespans. The queen bee lives for the longest time, approximately 5–6 years. Because the uterus is fully provided by working bees and protected from hazards, it must give birth to new offspring on a regular basis. Then the working bees. Individuals born in the warm season usually live for a very short time, up to a month. You can blame everything in the high season for the hard day's work. The bees are sometimes born in the fall. In this case, its lifespan is about six months. All such insects must winter and perform their direct function in the spring. Drones live the least. Once born, they fulfil their mission and are soon lost. If the it remains in the hive before the onset of cold weather, they will be driven out by the working caste and will die without a house or food.

-It's still a mystery to me how honey is made. -Scarlett said, a little confused.

-The bees need nectar to make honey, it is a very sweet juice that is selected from flowering plants. The insect collects nectar and it then enters a special organ. The saliva of the bee's contains enzymes that get into the honey stomach along with the nectar and break down the carbohydrates in the juice. Each enzyme performs its function.

-What is the honey stomach?

-As the bee gathers nectar using its proboscis, nectar is passed along the oesophagus to the honey sac, which is a distension of the oesophagus, also called as the honey stomach.

-And what about those who aren't hairy? -She asked, feeling silly about the question.

-The appearance of bees may vary depending on the species. On average, they differ by about three centimetres in size and the striped colour in which yellow-orange and black alternate. Their body is completely covered with hairs that provide protection and function as touch organs. What kind of hairless bee do you mean?

-About those that have a lighter colour.

-I think you're thinking of the wasp. -He answered in not a condescending way which surprised the woman.

-Oh, maybe. I remember one stung me, in my childhood times. What is the difference between them? It has so much of a bee shape.

-Bee collects nectar, pollinates plants, produces honey, and makes honeycombs from the wax produced. While the structure of the wasps was not designed to produce any valuable material. The construction of nests is made of various materials, such as old wood. The wasp diet is more varied, including nectar, fruits, and other small insects. Bee only attacks an opponent if it feels or reacts to a threat and then loses its life after the sting. Wasps are more aggressive, more predatory. They can sting at any time. The structure of the wasp hip is different, so it is capable of an unlimited number of attacks without damaging itself. The wasp can also bite with the jaw.

Scarlett took one on her hand as her husband talked about the difference between a wasp and a bee. Then she began to examine the pollenful little creature.

-How little you are. -She said softly to the bee.

-The distinguishing feature of the bee is the presence of nectar and stray for leakage of taste. The antennas are responsible for smelling, recognizing heat, cold, humidity. Certain parts of the body and legs act as auditory organs.

Scarlett looked at her husband as if she had seen the most intelligent man in front of her. She was afraid to confess to herself, but she felt she was starting to fall in love with the man in front of her. She was unable to wipe her smile from her face as the man explained to her about the bees.

-Have you ever wanted a child?

-Yes. -He smiled at the sky- A little girl. -Scarlett just admired her husband- I wished to name her Beatrice, it means bee. -They both laughed at the irony.

# CHAPTER XIX

-Believe me, Doris, he is not a person like you or anyone else would think. He is kind and caring... He pays close attention to the smallest details.

-Uhum... -She raised her eyebrows at the woman.

-And I feel like I'm getting to like him more and more.

-Listen carefully, ma'am. -She emphasized- I will not say it again, because I did not give this advice either in vain. Are you saying you want the man?

-What's the question now? -Scarlett asked in confusion.

-Yes, or not?

-Yes, he is a desirable man. -Scarlett concluded briefly.

-For sure you were already with him together. -She touched the index finger to the other.

-I wouldn't answer that. -She bounced from the table.

-So not?

-Doris, I said I rather wouldn't comment on that.

-Come on, it is just the two of us. But if the answer is no, I can only rejoice.

-Why would you say that?

-I know too much about that man, what I doubt you know. -She said closing the subject, Scarlett was prepared to ask back, but she didn't- Do you feel a desire near him or stomach cramps, confusion, and fever?

-What are you talking about? He is not sick; he doesn't spread anything. -The woman laughs.

-We can't know that. -She murmured, for which Scarlett frowned. -Love desires nothing that desires something is an obsession.

Those words made Scarlett think, and she wondered how she felt when she was near George. She wished she could get him out of her head. Even for a minute.

-You think about him again, aren't you? -She asked the thoughtful woman, but she didn't answer. -What's done is done. What's gone is gone. One of life's lessons is always moving on. It's all right to look back to see how far you've come, but don't forget to keep moving forward.

-Leonard is a good man. Seriously, I didn't regret the decision I made. -She said a little thoughtfully- At least I don't always mind.

-Hmm... Respect was invented to cover the empty place where love should be.

# CHAPTER XX

Scarlett was walking around town one day when she collided with Edith Salvatore at a stall in the market.

-Mrs. Wolowitz! -Said ironically- What is marriage like?

-Hmm... -She smiled- Nothing has changed since we last spoke.

-Yes, unfortunately, at George's wedding I was too busy with the guests. When I wanted to greet you, -she raised her hands- you just pushed my daughter-in-law into the punch bowl. Tell me, how does it feel, the knowledge that George has found his soul mate? -She asked with her arms closed in front of her.

-Miss. Salvatore, people say that our envy always lasts longer than the happiness of those we envy. And that doesn't apply to me, because I'm really happy about Mr. Salvatore's happiness. -She nailed the topic down, then headed in the other direction when she remembered something, so she turned back: -Forgiveness is the scent that the violet spills on the heel of the shoe that tramples it. I will forgive you.

-You rather hide behind fictional words, while real words hurt you.

Scarlett wanted to speak back to the woman in front of her sharply at the time, but she remembered what Doris had once told her, "Only about the uneducated man can be known when he's in a bad mood. Discipline yourself". She knew she could apply that now, she looked around at the people in the market who were staring at them, so she just smiled politely, while bowing in farewell.

# CHAPTER XXI

Scarlett chatted with Evelyn one afternoon, telling her how wonderful her days were in London, also admitting how much she missed it, she felt really close to her husband and that she longed to return.

-Maybe you need to organise more trips. -She laughed.

-Yes, that's possible. -She smiled too. -Tell me, how do you feel? How is your condition?

-Fortunately, nowadays, the morning nausea disappeared, it has been very common in the first weeks, but now I feel less and less weak, I am starting to regain my strength. However, my tummy is getting heavier. -She caresses her round tummy in a circle. -But I only have five months left. -She said enthusiastically.

Scarlett's smile disappeared as she began thinking.

-Not even now...?

-No. -She couldn't talk about such things, so she falls quiet. Evelyn realised it, she didn't even try to continue with the subject, she wanted her friend to feel comfortable, however what occurred to her knew that it may upset her.

-I need to tell you something. -Scarlett looked at her friend curiously. -I know you had a strong relationship with Mr. Salvatore. That's why I feel you need to know about it. Mrs. Salvatore is seriously ill.

-What had happened?

-No one knows, a new kind of disease has attacked her body.

Marta entered the room with an ear touching smile on her face.

-I'm sorry, ma'am. I didn't know you had a guest. -She said as she would turn around to leave.

-Marta, just say it. - She turned and walked in front of them and looked deeply at Evelyn- You can trust her.

-Mom is better, she's been out of bed for the first time in weeks, and imagine she's so well recovered that there's no sign of the disease. Thank you very much, ma'am. I made this for you. -She handed over a braided bracelet.

Scarlett smiled as she looked at the gift. So, the girl happily left the room.

-She is a kind soul.

-Indeed, she is.

A few minutes later, Daphne entered the room with the children.

-What a busy day. -Evelyn mentioned smiling.

-Please, don't be mad ma'am. But they insisted, they wanted to see you.

Scarlett hugged both children.

-Did you do something with your hair?

-Yes, ma'am. I made it shorter.

-Very cute. You'll surely conquer every man with this look. -Scarlett complimented the girl.

-I just want one. -Daphne replied, a mischievous smile on her face.

-I'm going to London this weekend. -Evelyn said.

-I'm going with you.

-What about your husband?

-For sure, he won't mind. I'd like to visit... -Then noticed the curious eyes on the girl in front of her- the girls. -She smiled.

-Great, I'm going by stagecoach in the morning.

\*

-London? -Her husband asked -What would you do in London?

-I'd like to spend some time with Evelyn, you know, if the baby is born, she won't have too much time, and I'll be there to visit the girls as well.

-All right. -Her husband replied with a smile, then stroked her shoulder.

Leonard began to cough strongly, he pulled out his handkerchief and then began to cough loudly again.

-Are you feeling all right?

The man looked into his handkerchief, it was full of blood.

-Yes! Of course, I am. I just caught a cold, that's all.

-But is it? -Scarlett tried to ask.

-Nullness. -The man closed the subject, then put the handkerchief in his pocket with a quick motion.

Then Daphne entered the room.

-Oh, I am sorry. -She looked through the shirtless man who was ready to start washing up. -Marta said you were getting ready to go to bed now, so I thought you would like some warm water to wash. -She said, raising her steaming pitcher.

-How thoughtful. -Scarlett praised her, she walked over to the washbasin and poured the warm water. As she turned, she stopped in front of Leonard as if to say something to him, but she just began to admire his shirtless upper body. -You can leave now. -Scarlett said with a forced smile. When she left, Scarlett gave her husband a contemptuous look, then walked toward the door.

-Scarlett! That's not what it seems. -But Scarlett just left without a word.

As she closed the door behind her, she looked down the hall, then opened into Elsa's room, which remained open since the last time she was in there, hoping to find the letters she had seen before. She began to search, but the letters were all gone. Tired of searching, she sat on the ground. Then she saw a white circular shape under the bed. Scarlett reached for it and then took it out, unfolding it started reading. After reading it, she stood up to leave, then looked back at the nightstand, which showed that a corner had been broken. It smoothed that part all the way through, but surprisingly it wasn't the colour of wood, it was like it was painted and even darker than the rest of it.

# CHAPTER XXII

Scarlett had nightmares the night before the trip. In which her husband Leonard's ex-wife was featured. The woman spoke to Scarlett, calling on her name, saying, "It wasn't his fault, the world needs to know." Scarlett got up in the middle of the night, but she was afraid to go back to sleep, fearing Elsa would return. So, she got out of bed early the next morning.

When she walked into the salon in the morning, she found Mrs. Wolowitz warming up herself by the fireplace.

-Good morning! -She said, but the woman just muttered under her breath something. -I wanted to talk to you.

-About what? -She asked, covering her dog with her poncho.

-About Leonard. Is he feeling well? He coughed so hard last night.

-Just a little cold.

-But he has had it for a long time.

-He will be fine.

-Had a doctor see him?

-I said he would be fine. -She replied impatiently.

-But it's about your son who is coughing up blood. -She was anxious.

-He was sick as a kid as well. The doctor came to him every week. He'll be fine. -She repeated.

-Why? What caused this?

-Maybe me. I made him who he is now. -She said, very depressed-
He was always there next to my skirt, I pampered him. He will be
fine; my little boy will always be fine. -She said again.

Scarlett decided to leave her alone, just got up and left the room.
But she stopped when she heard her mutter again. -He'll be fine.
Everything will be fine. My little son will be fine.

# CHAPTER XXIII

Scarlett firstly visited her nieces in London. Then with a full basket of fruit set off for the Salvatore house. Where the valet opened the door and guided her to Winnifred's room.

-Mr. Salvatore is not here. But his wife is very ill. Do you want me to hand over the basket?

-I came to see her. -She replied, then opened the room.

-Mrs. Wolowitz... -She looked weakly at the woman- Did you come to watch me die? -She asked in a hushed voice.

-Where are the staff? You must have a fever; you are so flushed and wet. -She said dropping the basket, then dipping the cloth in the water, began wiping Winnifred's face.

A few hours later, Winnifred woke up, and Scarlett pulled the chair closer to her.

-Are you still here?

-How are you feeling? -She asked, wiping her face again.

-What do you want here? -She took her hand.

-I just wanted to visit you.

-Lie. You came for some reason. Do you want to comfort my husband if I die? -She started to laugh, but she was so weak she couldn't do it long.

-No, as a matter of fact, I came because of my husband. I brought something I found in Elsa's room. -She handed over the crumpled letter.

-What is this?

-Elsa wrote, addressed to you. On the day of her death.

Winnifred started to read.

> "*My dearest sister,*
>
> *Today I found out a terrible thing that seals my marriage. I know why my husband never touched me during our marriage. Why I can never be the mother of a Wolowitz heir.*
>
> *Oh, my dear sister, the truth is so awful. I will suffer for the rest of my life; I will grind my sorrow over my husband's illness. He will never be mine, nor I will be his. As much as I would love, this will remain platonic love forever.*
>
> *But I will stay by his side as a faithful companion to the end. Because I love him more than anything.*
>
> *You need to know that compared to a marriage of convenience, he is doing his best, he is kind and caring. I know he would never hurt me on purpose. That's why he denies me from himself. That's why he doesn't give me the only thing I want.*
>
> *But please don't judge him. He is a good man.*
>
> *I will love you forever, my dear sister.*
>
> *Elsa W."*

*

Winnifred cried out after reading these lines.

-It's her handwriting. -The woman said putting her hand in front of her mouth. -Please keep this letter. Testimony that your husband is not a murderer. -She handed back the paper- Dear Scarlett.

-I'll get some water. -She went to the table to water the sick woman.

George entered the room with a surprise seeing Scarlett there.

-Mrs. Wolowitz. What are you doing here? -He asked, looking at Scarlett, but the feeling of seeing the man again shocked her.

-Scarlett helped. The nurse left sooner; Scarlett arrived just in time when I was at my worst. She took care of me while I was asleep. -She said, almost in a whisper because of weakness.

-I'll leave you alone now. -She said, walking toward the door.

-Scarlett... -Said the patient- Thank you, for everything. I will not die with anger in my heart.

Scarlett didn't say a word just walked out. She had just reached the exit, putting on her cloak when she heard a loud shout. So, she ran back into the room. As she entered, she saw George leaning on his dead wife's body crying, "Don't leave me my dear". Seeing George's suffering, tears began to gather in her eyes, then dripped silently.

*"Tears are the silent language of grief"* – Voltaire.

# CHAPTER XXIV

When she got home the first night, no one expected her to arrive so early. That's why it touched Daphne so suddenly, as Scarlett walked to her husband's room to announce her arrival. Daphne was just walking out of Leonard's room, ashamed she walk past Scarlett silently. Scarlett stared in confusion for a moment, then turned on her heels and left.

Shortly afterwards, when she was combing her hair into a nightgown getting ready to go to bed, Marta burst into her room.

-Apologies, ma'am. -She said desperately.

-For heaven's sake. What happened? -She asked in horror.

-Mum... is dead. -She said, crying.

Scarlett stepped closer, then began stroking her shoulder. -Don't water the mice, calm down. Go home and I'll cover for you, stay as long as you feel it's needed.

-Thank you, Madam! -She left.

*

The next morning, Mrs. Wolowitz searched for Marta.

-Where's that damn girl? -She asked herself the moment Scarlett entered the room.

-Oh, I sent her to the market to shop. -She said, opening her book in front of her.

-Scarlett, are you back already? -She asked in surprise.

-Yes. It was shorter than I planned. Leonard hasn't woken up yet.

-I haven't seen him yet.

Daphne entered the room with the children, she had seated them at the table to teach them.

-I would like to talk to him about his evening visitor. -She said by the time they both looked at her, but Scarlett didn't continue, she just left the room.

# CHAPTER XXV

Leonard was in a deep sleep as his door slammed shut. Someone walked in on soft steps, into the darkness of the night in the man's room, who had become very tired during the day, so he fell asleep quickly as soon as his head touched the pillow. She climbed on his bed first, then began stroking the man's naked chest with her fingers. The man didn't get up for it either, he was so overwhelmed by the dream. Then Daphne, seized the opportunity and climbed on him. She began to caress the man when she saw that he liked it, she leaned closer to his face, and kissed him, the man got up. He pushed the woman off so suddenly that she fell straight to the ground.

-What are you doing here? -He asked the girl.

-I'm just... -She tried to explain.

-Get out of my room! -He growled as he pointed toward the door.

She started and then turned back in front of the door.

-I saw how you looked at me. Don't deny what you really want. -Then she left.

# CHAPTER XXVI

Scarlett was walking down the hall as Marta walked towards her in a hurry.

-Good morning, ma'am. -She said, not waiting for her mistresses to return her greeting, she just walked away.

-Marta! -She said after the girl, who turned back but was still slowly stepping back to where her original path had taken her. -Would you please unpack my luggage? It is in the dressing room.

-Of course, ma'am. -She replied, then hurried away.

Scarlett looked at her in surprise, then continued on her way. Unexpectedly, she collided with her husband at the junction of the hallway.

-Scarlett, I heard you came back. You didn't come to me when you arrived.

-Maybe I would have greeted you if you hadn't had a visitor last night. -She said fiercely, then prepared to go on, but her husband prevented her with his arms outstretched.

-Honey, you get it wrong.

-Oh, did she only bring you hot water again, but this time in her nightgown?

-Scarlett...

-I won't listen to another lie for a minute. I'm tired of it...

-Honey, I never lied to you. -He said kindly.

-But you didn't tell the truth either, I'm groping in the dark for a man I don't know anything about.

Leonard then took Scarlett's hand and they entered Elsa's room. She looked at Elsa's portrait again, which was much more beautiful in daylight. Compared to the fact that Marta's mother had described her as the devil, she didn't seem so bad. She had a kind look, a gentle smile.

-Do you want to know the truth? I killed Elsa. -He said, standing with his arms outstretched in front of the window.

-But that's not the whole truth. Isn't it?

-You don't want to believe the fact that I am a murderer. Do you?

-I would like to know the whole story.

-Well, -Leonard said sadly, sitting on the edge of the bed -As never before during our marriage, we had a fight, she was arguing with me about a certain thing. Elsa went completely insane, she was crying and attacked me, I was afraid she would hurt herself as we were here. Right in this corner, next to the window. -He pointed to the right corner with a huge window- The space was small as she frantically insanely, pulled the curtain, causing the rail to tear off. -He pointed to the window, which was barely four metres from the bed. -I wanted to protect her, so I pushed her away, -his tears began to gather in his eyes- but I killed her instead. -He cried as he looked at the bedside table.

-She banged her head... -Scarlett said, looking at the darker corner that was truncated. Scarlett realised what had happened, sat down next to her husband, and took his hand. -Leonard, it wasn't your fault. It was a simple accident. Please, don't punish yourself for it.

-But it shouldn't have happened! I confess I didn't have a perfect wife, she had flaws, as I had. But I know she loved me.

-And you loved her too.

-She wrote a letter to her sister, Winnifred. Which broke my heart even more. She never said anything bad about me. Even though I didn't give her what she wanted most. We were similar in this thing and only in this one thing. I hope you know, Scarlett, honey, -he stroked her face- that I would never hurt anyone.

Scarlett knew, and she also know that he was telling the truth.

-I want us to always be honest with each other. You need to know something... -She was about, to tell the truth about the letter, but didn't know how her husband would react if he were to find out that she spied on him and search his ex-wife's room- Winnifred, err, Mrs. Salvatore passed away a few days ago.

-How? -The man was horrified.

-From an unknown disease. The number of people infected increased throughout London, but it only affects women.

# CHAPTER XXVII

Marta hid her little boy in the kitchen closet and he crouched in silence there. She gave him an apple and then suddenly closed the door when she heard someone approaching. Daphne entered the door.

-Marta? What are you doing there with that boy?

-Nothing. -She began to hurry at the table.

-Who is that kid? -She pointed to the kitchen cabinet.

-Daphne, you have to keep this a secret, please. -She begged her.

-Very well... -She said with her head held high. - But you will owe me a favour.

-Of course. I have a lot to do... and I even have to unpack my mistress's luggage. -She complained aloud.

-If you want, I'll unpack it. -She said with a half-smile on her mouth.

-Would you really do it? -She asked cheerfully- But no, it can't be. She asked me to. -She replied, returning to her vegetables.

-Just trust me. I'm happy to help a friend. -She said, wiping her smile down as she turned away.

# CHAPTER XXVIII

After a few days following her trip, Scarlett felt very weak. So, she stayed in bed all day, and several days after. Leonard hurried anxiously to his wife, whose condition was getting worse by the day.

-Scarlett! -He said when she finally opened her eyes. -How are you feeling?

-Water... -She said weakly, Leonard immediately jumped to refill the glass and then helped his wife, who didn't have the strength to hold the glass. -I'm leaving for Jerome. -He said, jumping off the bed as Scarlett drank enough of the water.

-Please don't leave me alone. -She said softly.

-It won't last long, please endure it. -He kissed his wife on the forehead, then ran out of the room, down the hall, then to the exit, where at the door he met his mother.

-Does the princess want attention? -She asked, with Harold in her arms.

-Please do whatever you do, but don't go in there. -He said, pressing the doorknob, then looking back at his mother and raising his index finger. -No woman can go to her.

And outside the door, he collided with George, who was standing sadly in front of the door. George buried his wife a few weeks before and then decided to return to Truro, unable to live in the house where he had lived happily with his wife so far.

-George! -Leonard was surprised- What are you doing here?

-I came to see your wife. So far, I have been unable to do so. But I owe her a debt of gratitude for caring for Winnifred that morning when I couldn't be by her side.

-What? -He asked indignantly.

-Can I see her?

-Scarlett is sick. -He said with a sigh.

George pushed Leonard aside from the way and ran into the house. Leonard followed and instructed his yawning mother as he entered the house to send for Dr. Jerome Garfield. Leonard watched from behind the door as George knelt beside Scarlett's sickbed, stroking her face.

-Scarlett... please get up. -Her hair was now falling wet on her face, he combed with his fingers- You can't leave. I can't lose you too. -But Scarlett didn't move, lying motionless with her eyes closed, just in the position she stayed while begging Leonard not to leave- Scarlett, I love you!

*

-Can we talk? -Dr. Garfield asked his friend.

Leonard left the room with him without a word, leaving George alone with Scarlett.

-Fortunately, the lungs aren't damaged yet, so it's easy to get air. But as for the fever...

-Please don't spare. -He said, placing his right hand on the man's shoulder.

-Here's the medicine, give it to her every three hours. I guarantee nothing, if the fever doesn't go away... -He said hesitantly to express his opinion- I don't see much chance of surviving the morning. But I pray for it.

-Thank you, my friend! -He told the man, who smiled with an encouraging smile and then walked toward the exit.

Leonard walked back into the room, then sat down in his chair and watched as George was next to his wife.

-I never hated you. -Leonard told him.

George turned around.

-I know. -He said as he stroked Scarlett's hand. -Did you tell her?

-No. -Leonard replied briefly, then stood up and walked in embarrassment, wiped his lips, then said: -I haven't been able to tell her the truth yet.

-She needs to know why you got married. -George interrupted, a little frustrated- She doesn't deserve this...

-I know.

*

Leonard walked into the kitchen to pick up Scarlett's dinner himself, knowing that she had barely eaten for days. When he entered, Marta nursed a small child in her lap. When she saw Mr. Wolowitz, she was shocked, then jumped up on her feet, hiding the child behind her skirt.

-Mr. Wolowitz, I can explain...

The man waved with his hand in silence, raising his palm toward her.

-No need. My wife is dying. I'll deal with that later. -He said sadly, then picked up the tray on the desk and left.

When he returned to the room, George wiped the woman's face with a damp cloth.

-You know, Leonard... That's how we re-evaluate what we have. -Then looked at the man- I wasn't with Winnifred when she was sick, I could have told her so much and thanked her for everything she gave me. The happy moments.

-George...

-No! -He interrupted- If your wife hadn't been there to take care of her, I might not have been able to say goodbye to her. -He glanced at the sleeping woman- This is not the year to get everything you want. This is the year to appreciate everything you have. -Then kissed the woman's hand- Scarlett is an angel.

After that, a disturbing silence settled between them until Scarlett broke it. But no one understood what she was talking about, she was strongly opposed to someone, which also affected her bodily reactions.

-I have to go with you... please let me go with you.

-She raves... -Leonard said, stepping closer to his wife's bed.

-Miranda! -She cried- Miranda... -She whispered.

-Scarlett, I'm here, honey. -He said, kissing his wife.

-Dad doesn't know yet... He doesn't know... I have to tell him! -She shouted as she sat up, then opened her eyes wide, and after a short time she fell weakly back into bed.

-Scarlett! Scarlett! Please look at me! -George shouted, shaking her head.

-She's not breathing... -Leonard murmured, then began to undress, climbed on the bed over his wife then started cardiopulmonary resuscitation. Followed by mouth-to-mouth breathing, Scarlett didn't respond, so Leonard continued- You-can't-leave-us... -He said pleadingly as he pressed the woman's chest- Please... -Her husband said almost crying, just as his tear rolled out, Scarlett began to breathe again, which made both men calmed down.

George wet the cloth again and wiped the woman's face. Leonard was completely exhausted and after a few minutes when he ensured that Scarlett was still breathing he went out for a drink.

When Scarlett opened her eyes, George was the first person she saw.

-You again? -She asked weakly. -There's no way I can get rid of George Salvatore.

-Scarlett! -He kissed her hand crying.

-Every time something happens, I close my eyes to rest, -she said with a sigh- when I open it... -But she couldn't finish because she was interrupted by strong cough.

-It's familiar whenever Scarlett Bloom gets in trouble, I'm always the lucky one to be in the right place at the right time. -He laughed.

-George, I have to say something... -She tried to get up but fell back weakly.

-Shh... Just relax. -Then he kissed her on the forehead.

Leonard listened behind the door to what was happening in the room and on his shattered heart as if another crack had formed. Sadly, he propped his head against the door, then took a deep breath and entered. By then, Scarlett was asleep.

-The fever subsided! -George said with delight- Would you mind if I stay?

Leonard thought, then shook his head, knowing his wife was much happier with George's company than his.

*

Agatha Wolowitz sat angrily in front of the fireplace as Leonard walked into the room.

-The fever subsided. -Leonard said reassured as he watched the sunrise.

-I am glad. -She replied magnanimously.

-I would like to know why you don't like Scarlett.

-Who said I didn't like her?

A child of coloured skin, about twelve years old entered the room with a bowl of cookies and a glass of milk. He put it down next to Mrs. Wolowitz, then looked enviously at the cookies in front of them for a while.

-You're that worthless Marta's brother, aren't you? -She asked.

-Yes, ma'am. My name is Akita, the gentleman has allowed me to serve here.

-Yeah, I've heard of it... another lifeless nobody in this house.

-Mother... -Leonard murmured.

-Would you like one? -She asked, lifting a cookie into the air. The boy began to nod shyly. The woman began to stretch toward him as the child held out his hand to take it, she jerked it back, bit it, and handed it to the dog on her lap.

-Mother! -He shouted at the woman. -Would you be able to listen here? -But the woman was not frightened, however, the child ran away.

-Son, did you see that kitchen scum even bring a kid here? What are we here the beloved service?

-They got my permission. And now, if you'd listen... -He put his hands together- Scarlett is a good soul, and if you can't be happy with me about her improvement, I'd ask you to go back to the house in Truro.

-Do you want to send your own mother away? The woman, who raised and supported you?

-Enough! -The man said nervously- Don't try to manipulate. Scarlett is my wife and the Mistress of this house. -Then he left his mother there in doubt.

# CHAPTER XXIX

George was talking to the doctor in the hallway when Leonard got there too. The maids walked one after the other doing their jobs. When Daphne got there, it was too early, the kids were still asleep, so she was alone.

-As I see Mrs. Wolowitz starting to recover, the fever is still on and she's weak, but she will soon regain strength. You have a very strong and wilful wife, Leonard. -The curious eyes of Daphne silenced the doctor. -Hmmm... Maybe we could go to a quieter place, is a little busy here this morning. -He looked down the hall.

-Of course! -Leonard said, then leading the way.

As the gentlemen disappeared at the fork in the hallway, Daphne looked around and opened the door into the sleeping woman's room. She walked to her bed and stroked her face.

-You're so beautiful... But I can't comprehend what they like about you so much. You climbed out of the filth! -She said out loud as she snatched the pillow from under her head and pressed it to her face. -I could be in your place, with a rich, upscale, influential husband or lover. But as long as you are alive, you will stand in my way! -She pressed the pillow harder onto the objecting woman. Then she heard a voice from behind the door, it was George's voice searching for his watch. Daphne had to hide somewhere, she looked around the room, then she saw a wardrobe. Quickly she hid in there.

George entered the room, then took the pocket watch on the dresser. As he turned to look at Scarlett, the woman was completely red, lying unconscious on the bed and her pillow lying on the floor. He ran quickly after the doctor, shouting his name. Daphne took the opportunity and ran out of the room. Around the corner, Marta watched the people running in and out of her Mistress's room, but she knew it was dangerous for her as a woman to be so close, so she went to deal with her own business.

*

-What do you think? -Leonard asked Jerome.

-I don't know... -The doctor replied nervously- I would say it could have been a respiratory disorder or a seizure. But that wouldn't explain how her pillow got to the floor so far from the bed when she was so weak, she could barely open her eyes.

-Tell me, George, was there anyone else in the room beside you? -Leonard asked.

-No. I am afraid I haven't seen anyone. I was alone. However, I had a feeling like someone was watching me, but I didn't see anyone.

The wardrobe's door opened with a crack, blew by the fresh air entering the room through the open window, which had blown it. The three of them got their heads there and then approached it slowly. George and Leonard simultaneously opened the doors of the closet with a sudden motion. But it was empty, something pierced the doctor's eyes, he wanted to take a closer look, so he stepped closer. The clothes at the bottom of it were trampled. There were no traces of shoes or dirt, but deep pressings were left on it.

-The person has to work in the house. I'm sure. -Jerome said as he looked at the rainy weather and the muddy garden.

*

The children, Jared and Aliona, were supervised by one more nanny, many times Mowie looked at them to make sure the

396

perpetrator hadn't targeted them either. Mowie was one of Leonard's most trusted workers, whom he could entrust with anything. Scarlett was unconscious while George was trying for days to figure out who might have been in the room. But it was almost forgotten when Scarlett regained consciousness. Everyone was very happy that the woman was starting to recover. Not long after, the men suspected that it was Scarlett's nurse, as he was the only one who could enter the room who took care of Scarlett. But they had no evidence to suspect him, so when Scarlett got better, he was fired, as was the temporary nanny, who was looking after the children.

-I'm so happy, honey, that you're finally feeling better. -Leonard said kindly.

Scarlett just smiled.

-Yes, this is what I missed to cheer me up. -Leonard said with a smile.

George felt superfluous in the company of the couple, but at least he was distracted by caring for Scarlett of his deceased wife, so when he saw that the time was here, he was slowly retreating. He visited less and less until he was gone. Scarlett missed the man whose presence gave her strength, so she asked about him every day, one day she got the answer that George had returned to London and taken his place back as an MP.

# CHAPTER XXX

Three weeks after her illness, Scarlett regained her strength and was feeling as if she had been reborn. One day Captain Patmore arrived. When he went into the parlour, he found both mistress's of the house there, but the lord of the house was missing.

-Actually, I came to Mr. Wolowitz to discuss an urgent matter.

-Well, my husband is out of the house. But as his spouse and most trusted companion, you can share with me or pass on a message through me.

-And I'm his mother! -Mrs. Wolowitz interrupted.

The captain sits down in a nearby armchair without being invited to.

-Very well then. -He said- Tell him, an important letter is in my hand, I believe he needs to know about it, it must be very disturbing that such a personal object is in my property. -Then he took a cake from the plate.

The two women looked at each other, but neither of them said a word.

-Where is Leonard Wolowitz? -He asked with a serious expression.

-He has travelled on a business matter to London and from there to Netherlands. -Agatha said.

-Do you know when he's coming back?

-Maybe in a few weeks, but it could take months. -Scarlett replied.

The captain said nothing. Scarlett thought all along what kind of letter might it be, but she didn't want to ask while Agatha was with them, she was afraid it was about something that if it would get into her ear that would easily cause a heart attack for an old person like her. The captain stood up and said goodbye to the women politely.

-Wait, I'll accompany you. -Scarlett said, then walked after the man. Akita, Marta's younger brother, ran down the hall, in front of them, at whom the captain looked sharply. She tried to forgive him for this and remained calm. When they got to the door, she finally asked what had caused her tongue to itch. -What kind of letter it is about?

-Letter from his ex-wife. This will help us find out the truth about your husband, not only regarding the murder of his wife but also prove that your husband has a secret, this is something serious and I'll find out what it is.

-This can't prove anything.

-Of course, it can. The husband is keeping a secret. His wife found out and he killed her for it. So far, only rumours have been circulating about this whole history, but now there is evidence of it.

-Could you tell me what's in that letter?

-The fact that your husband has a serious illness. If this is what I think it is attached to, gallows await him and will burn in the fire of hell in his eternal life.

Scarlett's suspicions grew stronger and she feared that what she thought would come true.

-Tell me why you hate my husband so much? -Scarlett began to despair, but she tries to cover it.

-I just don't like otherness.

-We can't be the same.

-No, but we must remain as the Lord created us. We cannot give in to the temptation of the devil. Think about it, if they multiply, what will happen in our world?

-You, the embodied devil, how could you slander an innocent man? -She tried to curb her aggression.

-Soon it will be revealed how harmless your husband is. Good night! -The captain replied, then left.

-Marta you, dog! Where the hell are you? -Agatha shouted from the parlour. Scarlett remembered something and then closed the door and just stared in the emptiness.

-I'm already here, ma'am! -The girl ran in, carrying a huge tray.

-Ah... what are you doing, you, stupid girl? -The woman shouted- You scalded me...

-Please forgive me, it was an accident! -Marta's cry was heard in the hallway, where Scarlett fell weakly to the ground by the door.

-That's why I will whip you, you wretched! -Said the woman- Get out of my sight you, scum!

Scarlett sat on the ground, raising her head to see Marta running out of the room with the face hidden in her palms. Something occurred to Scarlett, so she got up. Then she hurried to her dressing room. As she hurried toward the room, Daphne walked there with the two children.

-Good evening, ma'am. -She bowed before her as she passed them.

Scarlett ignored them until Jared, who had just begun forming sentences a few months ago, spoke.

-Daphne is taking us on our last journey. -As he said that Scarlett paused for a moment and then turned back. She wasn't sure what she had just heard. Then she looked questioningly at those passing by as their nanny tugged them.

-Can I help you, ma'am? -Daphne asked with an impeccable smile.

Scarlett looked at them in confusion, she heard a voice that sounded familiar to her. She was avoiding Daphne and the children for a while if she still had a chance, she did not want to infect them, but she felt something was wrong. When she turned again to walk up the stairs and was far enough away to not hear it clearly, Aliona said "We will die", but this time she didn't turn back again, she was convinced she was starting to fall back and only her imagination was playing with her. So, she didn't stop all the way to her dressing room. Where her first thing she did was to find her luggage, which was empty by then, she decided to look among the clothes she had been in London with, when Winnifred died, but she couldn't find what she was looking for.

*

-Marta! -She burst into the kitchen for which the young girl shuddered. -Didn't you find a letter in between my clothes?

Marta wondered the question. What would a letter do between the Mistress's clothes? -No ma'am. -She wiped away the tears Agatha Wolowitz had caused.

-I see... -Scarlett said, a little desperate- I've searched everything. I've checked my empty luggage three times in the dressing room.

-Should it have been in your luggage? -Marta asked thoughtfully.

-Yes. -Scarlett replied as she was about to leave.

-Ask Daphne. -Scarlett turned back then and looked at the girl in surprise- She was so kind as to take on this task, as I was delayed with my kitchen duties. You know how delicate Mrs. Wolowitz is. -She said as she let out a deep breath as the large pot was transferred from the table to the stove by her.

-Are you saying Daphne unpacked my belongings?

-Yes, ma'am. She must have been in your room a few weeks ago when you were so ill in this matter. I think she knew it was important to you and wanted to give it to you. Did you check in that room as well, Ma'am?

Scarlett paled at these, and Marta was horrified that she said something she shouldn't have.

-Ma'am, did I say something wrong? -She asked, a little shaky.

-Daphne... well, of course, that's why her voice was so familiar... -She said to herself- It was her all along...

-Are you feeling well?

-I got back on my feet *today* and Leonard is on his way today. That means...

-What does it mean, Madam?

-The kids are in danger with her! -She ran out of the kitchen.

She met Mowie in the hallway, who watched in surprise as his mistress ran in the house in alarm at a speed he had never seen her run before.

-Are you feeling well, Ma'am? -He asked the desperate woman.

-The kids are in danger. Where is Daphne?

-She took them for a walk. -The tall man replied.

-Bring the dogs! -She shouted.

A few minutes later, she sniffed one of Aliona's toys with his dogs. Then she jumped on horseback and followed her spotted dogs. The dogs ran through the bee field and then through the orchard and a meadow. Until they reached the mines, which were Leonard Wolowitz's first investment. Daphne stood beside the deep pit leading to the mine, holding both children's hands tightly. The dogs sensed the danger so they started barking loudly.

-Daphne, don't do it, they're just kids.

-Kids, huh?! ... Do you know how is to take care of these little monsters twenty-four hours a day? Do you know how to bathe, get to sleep, feed or even change the nappies? Of course not. Since you have nothing else to do but look good, go to balls and have fun.

-Daphne... You don't know what you're talking about.

-Oh, of course, I don't know. Mrs. Perfection, do you think I would be reluctant to take your place? I tried to cross your way so many times... -She said gritting her teeth and looking at the sky.

-Well, Aydan was talking about you then, not to trust... -She said softly to herself.

-Louder! So that I can hear too. -Cried the girl from a few metres away.

-You gave Elsa's letter to the captain just because my husband didn't want you... You tried to kill me that afternoon... You betrayed my brother too... You turned the girls against me, so they hated me... You were the one who stole my jewellery... Not Mr. Meadow! You did all this awfulness... -Scarlett said in frustration.

-You are mistaken, "Mr. Meadow" stole the jewellery, or we might just call him my drunken uncle. I was just guiding him... -She said thoughtfully- No, I'd rather straighten his path. He was a very stubborn man and extremely loyal to you, so I had to threaten him, I said I would kill the kids, I knew how much he loved the Bloom family. But that damn man betrayed me, he shared all the wealth with the villagers. This task involved really hard work, who would have thought stealing the journal was so risky, luckily it had the safe code in it, which I, fortunately, found where it was. And the key... not to mention that's when I almost failed... but I also figured it out, it was so hard to teach those stupid girls... -Daphne replied proudly of her work.

-What else did you do?

-Let's see... I attracted the foxes so you had to buy dogs. In order to hire me, you had to give a better position to my uncle first... -She said raising her hand in an explaining tone. -I was the one who told the authorities about the school, so you had to close it, actually, I didn't have any plan with that, I just played, it was fun seeing you so depressed about the poor little muddy monsters. Well, I told Captain Patmore about your brother. I had to get rid of him, he annoyed me so much... He also found out about the journal and the key. You had already lost during that period a lot, your farming did not work due to the drought, you sold your animals and furniture. So, I knew in order to get into Beelove with of course you... I had to kill all of your animals, to make sure this marriage would happen and then I could occupy my place next to that handsome man as the mistress of the house.

-Daphne, you hate me! Please let the kids go, they're innocent. -Scarlett said nervously.

-Yes, you're right about that. I really hate you. Do you know how it feels to serve a woman who has climbed out of the filth? To call her Mistress, a woman with the same age as me!? Watching as she wears a different outfit every day, wears gems, goes to balls? Do you know how it feels to go to bed and get up thinking that I could be in your place?

-Daphne, we can find a solution. Just let go of the kids... -She said, taking a few steps.

-Stay there or I'll jump. -She said with clenched teeth.

-All right! All right... -Scarlett gestured to calm.

Her dogs barked and growled more and more, the woman felt like she was starting to lose her confidence until she saw a small log on the ground just lying at her feet, then it occurred to her. Scarlett whistled softly twice, which, before her first hunt, Mr. Meadow had taught her to instruct the dogs. She knew they had a much stronger sense of hearing than a person who was more than three metres away. That's when the dogs started approaching them growling.

-What did you do? What do these bastards want from me? -She asked, a little terrified, watching the dogs.

-Daphne! -Scarlett shouted. When Daphne looked, a log was flying towards her. -Catch it! -Scarlett said again as she reflexively caught it. Then Scarlett didn't hesitate, seeing the children's hands free, she ran to her with quick steps, then pushed her. Daphne crashed straight into the deep black pit. She knelt down and quickly grabbed both children so they wouldn't overbalance and follow Daphne. -All right, you're safe! -She said, hugging the kids as she looked at the black hole where she saw nothing in the darkness of the night.

*

Scarlett, along with her mother-in-law was waiting in the house, Agatha Wolowitz was more frightened by the thought than Scarlett, of living with an assassin under one roof. As soon as Doris heard what had happened, she hurried straight to Beelove, where Scarlett welcomed her most trusted worker and very good friend warmly. As Doris entered the room, Agatha Wolowitz looked at her in surprise.

-Ma'am! -She opened the door panting- Are you all, all right? -She walked over to Scarlett, then took a seat on the couch, took the children on her lap and began to cherish them.

-We are all well. -Scarlett replied briefly as she watched her dogs warming themselves by the fireplace on the cold autumn night.

-What do you think? -The younger woman looked at Doris, though Doris didn't look as old as Agatha, thanks to her beautiful smooth skin, one or two grey hairs flashed in the light.

-What do you think? These children were traumatized. -She replied aggressively.

-Scarlett, how can you let this woman touch the kids? -Her eyes widened.

-What are you talking about? -Scarlett asked in surprise. Agatha just pointed at Doris, but she couldn't make a voice.

- You know, Mrs. Wolowitz, yes, I will let. In fact, I'm appointing Doris as the new nanny for the kids.

-How? -She asked as she felt her chest was tightening.

-Yes, as you heard. Who else would be better suited for the job than the most reliable person I've ever known? -Scarlett asked with a smile.

-But she can't walk around here like she's one of us! This is outrageous! -She said nervously- I've never heard about keeping a black nanny.

-Oh-Oh-Oh, Ma'am. I didn't even say I would like to work for a white chick. -Then Scarlett made her quiet, before she would be tortured for what she said.

-Do you know what's outrageous? The fact that even after such an incident, you are able to attack with such things. The fact that this racism still persists, that you are still unable to look at me like the mistress of the house! The inability to change your mindset. -Then she took a deep breath- But that's changing now, because, I'm going to be the Mistress of the house from now on, I'm Leonard Wolowitz's wife, and you will be only second.

Scarlett felt a little firmer with the woman, who was looking at her in frustration, speechless. Scarlett's thought for half a minute that she had had a heart attack, until she started blinking after almost a full minute when Scarlett had finished speaking. Captain Patmore entered the room, after searching for hours for the girl Scarlett claims had crashed into the mine.

-Mrs. Wolowitz... -He was taking off his hat.

-Tell me is she dead? -Scarlett asked, almost feeling the answer, but she was afraid, no matter how reassuring it would be, if the answer would be yes.

-We didn't find anyone! Are you sure she should be there?

-Do you want to call me a liar?

-No Ma'am, we've been searching for hours for her. Maybe it would be more helpful if Mr. Wolowitz were here, he knows the mine.

-Yes, but Mr. Wolowitz left this morning, even if we send someone to get him, he will reach him in a few days. Then we run out of time. -Agatha replied.

-Mrs. Wolowitz, do you know where the maps of the mine are?

-Well, yes, for that matter. But there are also three mines, it is important to know which is the one where it all happened. -She raised herself slowly from the chair.

-It was the East one. -Scarlett said, following her.

They went to the library, where the woman took out a couple of maps that belonged to the eastern mine.

-These would be, but we need this one right now. -She said opening a larger one- No one has been there in years, more precisely since it collapsed.

-It collapsed? -Scarlett asked in surprise.

-Yes, that was the reason Leonard shut it down, people lost their lives there.

-Was it profitable?

-It was, but less by the end. Leonard thought human life was more valuable than some copper.

What Agatha said to Scarlett, her heart pounded.

-She only fell four metres from the entrance, she could have easily survived it.

She tried to let go of her kind thoughts about her husband. She had a hard time waking up to what Agatha explained, who told everything exactly about how the levels were and if she got to the 43rd floor she would find an exit to the shore.

-We have to stop her. -Scarlett told the captain.

-I'm going now! -He grabbed her arm- I'm sending a guard to the other exit. -He reassured her.

-I'm coming too! -Scarlett replied.

Ma'am, a mine is a very dangerous place, it could collapse at any time.

-I take the risk. -Scarlett said, grabbing the map.

*

When they climbed down four metres deep to the point where Daphne should have fallen, they walked a few more feet where they found candles and matches. There was a burnt-out match on the ground, so they knew right away that the girl was alive. After a few hours of climbing and searching, Scarlett was completely exhausted but didn't give up. They also reached the 43rd level, where as soon as they got there, the rising sun illuminated the floor. They knew they were late. When the soldiers met them, they said they saw no movement.

# CHAPTER XXXI

"My dear diary,

It's been months since Daphne was gone, luckily everyone is fine and she hasn't shown up since. But my concern is growing. We haven't received a single letter from Leonard in weeks. He said he had to travel to Germany on business. I wrote him many letters, which I guess he hasn't received. I am afraid he would get in trouble when he gets back. Captain Patmore is a very wilful man who, if he hears when my husband returns, he will keep an eye on him.

The famine is growing, I try to help the villagers as I can, but I can't give them the bread from my plate... People are already rebelling in the city. People don't dare sell in the market because they are being attacked and plundered. The other day I heard that four children had died of malnutrition in recent weeks, including little Matt. The thought depresses me when I remember what he said the day I first opened the school. He said he wanted to be a doctor, to be able to help people. Why is life so unfair?

I want to help them with all my heart. I try my best to make sure people don't have to starve.

I hope everything could be as simple as in the novels I read..."

*

-Dear Scarlett, what are you thinking about?

-I was thinking of reopening the farm. After all, spring is here, we need to act.

-And if this year will be like the previous ones? -She tried to lean slowly toward the table to take her cup, but her tummy blocked it, so she had to turn sideways a little.

-If the sowing starts to sprout in the spring, I will continue to feed hope.

-Yes, but it didn't snow enough to protect it from frost.

-I know, but after the summer heat, there wasn't as much frost this year as before. -She said positively.

-Well, if you think there's a chance, I'll fully support you. -Said her friend kindly. -But you also need to be aware that this does not put bread on the table of every hungry person.

-Yes, I'm aware of... -She said a little thoughtfully. -That's why I want to open a mine as well.

-Are you joking? -She asked with a laugh, but Scarlett didn't join- No, you're not joking... -She said this time seriously- But that's very dangerous...

-I am aware of. But I have ideas. I've been to the mine, I have so many plans.

-What do you mean?

-Well, as we searched for Daphne, we went into a floor that had collapsed before, that's why the workers didn't go back. Walking through the ruins, it was noticeable that the wall had a different colour in the light of the candle.

-Scarlett, you can't be sure...

-I'm not. That's why I will go first and take a sample.

-I can't stop you, because you're very stubborn. Just be careful.

-I will be that. -She replied, smiling.

-Is there any news about your husband?

-I haven't received a single letter since he travelled to Germany.

-For sure he is fine. -She stroked her friend's knee.

-I know, -she said, turning to Evelyn- I am afraid of what will happen when he would be back.

-What are you talking about? -She was surprised.

-I have no idea what he's hiding. But Captain Patmore has ideas and has suspected something that even I don't know about, but he said he will keep an eye on him.

-Oh, Scarlett...

-Maybe I should go and ask Mr. Thaker for an opinion regarding the farm and the mine.

-Mr. Thaker? Haven't you heard of it? -She asked in surprise, however, knowing that her friend hadn't come out in months.

-What should I know?

-Mr. Thaker is seriously ill and has been in bed for a month. The doctor diagnosed him with thrombosis months ago, which turned into a pulmonary embolism. It's a matter of days, maybe he has hours left.

# CHAPTER XXXII

There was a knock on the door of the man's bedroom. He said weakly from his bed, "*Come in!*" Then Scarlett walked into the room.

-Miss. Bloom! -Scarlett didn't correct him, because she had enjoyed hearing that name- Come in. -He tried to sit up on the bed, but Scarlett interrupted.

-Just stay. -She said, sitting on the chair next to the bed, so the man lay back. -Mr. Thaker, I came because I have to confess something.

-Tell me, dear. -The man said in a bronchial voice, his breathing getting harder and harder.

-I should have done it a long time ago. But I was afraid you would have stopped the wedding if you had known.

-What would it be about? -He looked questioningly, and after a moment of silence, his eyes widened. -Mr. Wolowitz isn't treating you well?

-No, nothing like that. You know... -She searched for the right words, but couldn't find them.

-Feel free. -The man encouraged.

-Mr. Thaker, you are my father...

Then they both fell silent, the man staring silently at the ceiling and Scarlett was looking at her hands.

-How long have you known? -He asked, still staring at the ceiling.

-Too long. -She replied briefly as she rotated the rosy ring on her finger. -She wrote everything down, also wrote an apology letter and... -She wanted to hand over the brown-bound diary, but the man pushed it away.

-I believe you... -He said, then turned his head toward her. -My dear child, my little girl... -He cried- My little Scarlett... -He then kissed her on the hand.

Strength faded out of the man and he spoke more and more softly. Smiling, he repeated, "My little daughter!" and then slowly he began to turn his head until he faced the ceiling, then he fell silent. Scarlett knew what it all meant, she cried as she held her father's hand. She stood up, then looked into her father's sky-blue eyes from which life came out, put his hands on each other's on his chest, and the rosy ring between them, then kissed him on the forehead.

# CHAPTER XXXIII

Doris was looking after the children as Scarlett entered the room.

-What condition is he in? -She asked as she nursed Aliona.

-He died. -She said, falling on the bench.

-I'm sorry, darling. -Doris said sympathetically.

-When I finally find my family, the person who created it is leaving me.

-Don't be that hard, the kids are still here. -She stepped closer with the little girl in her arms.

-You're right, they're still here for me. What would I do without them? -She said as she took the little girl in her lap.

-I'm sure you'll still make it. -Doris replied confidently- You are a strong woman.

-I'm worried about the girls. What if she goes to London?

-Aa-aa-aa, -gestured with her finger- Don't even think about that.

-And what if she did? No one has seen her since then. -She said depressed.

-If she tries, they are protected at school, they are surrounded by a lot of teachers. They are supervised, there is no chance. You have instructed them that only you or a member of the Wolowitz family can visit them.

-I know, and you're right ... Maybe I am overthinking. Maybe I shouldn't have kept them away during the holidays because of such paranoia.

-It's logical that you're so afraid, after what had happened.

Scarlett stood up handing over the child, then Akita and Marta entered the kitchen. Marta said Mr. Wolowitz allowed them to live in one of the maids' rooms. Scarlett listened with pleasure that Marta did not have to return to that dangerous place, nor did her brother and her little son. Akita promised to be a funny good-natured child, hardworking and helpful. Scarlett liked them very much, which is why when they were alone with Doris again, she asked her to take care of Marta's little boy too so that Marta could perform at work more easily. After seeing how tiring this double work was, it seemed impossible to reconcile motherhood with work. Doris accepted this task with pleasure.

-Ma'am, I forgot to tell you how much I have missed the clean well water since I moved into Beelove. I know they get water from a spring, but it's so far from here that it takes so long for that poor little kid to carry it here. -She meant Marta's brother, Akita- Not to mention how much water a kitchen need...

-I've never thought of that before. You're right, I will resolve it. -Scarlett said with a smile.

# CHAPTER XXXIV

Scarlett spent half a day in the mine, starting with a small hammer and a large iron nail on the 26th floor. She heard loud bangs, then a small piece of rock hit her forehead.

*

-I'm looking for Mrs. Wolowitz.- George stood in front of the door as Doris opened at his third knock.

-Mr. Salvatore! -She said in surprise- Which one?

George began to laugh as Doris smiled too.

-Of course... The Mistress is gone, she said she needs to see something at the mines, but I haven't seen her in hours, I'm worried about that.

-At the mine? -He asked in surprise, too, but as they both knew the woman and knew she probably had something in her head again, he quickly took the reins from the stableman and jumped back into the saddle, then galloping his horse straight toward the mines.

*

Scarlett kept climbing and climbing, but she felt it could collapse at any moment. But it didn't happen. She soon saw the sunlight. As she took her last steps up the ladder, a hand reached for her, grabbing her and helping her up so easily.

-For heaven's sake. What are you doing? -George asked angrily.

-I was just looking around. -She replied, sweeping the dirt from her clothes .

-After not dying from a deadly disease, you think you're trying to get lost in a mine alone?

-Oh, men are all the same, maybe you are afraid that women will take power over you? -Scarlett said upset.

George wanted to say something spicy, but he looked down at the sweaty and dirty woman from head to toe, then changed his mind, knowing whatever he could say, she would explain. So, he took out a handkerchief and handed it over. Scarlett looked questioningly, not knowing what to do. Then George stepped closer and began to wipe the wound on her head.

-I've already lost someone important to me. -He said as he gently wiped her forehead. -I don't want to lose another one. -Scarlett just swallowed- Please promise you'll take better care of yourself. -A long silence fell between them until George broke it. -Reminders of our first meeting. You were dirty from head to toe as you tried hard to tear down the slats nailed to the door. I will never forget that moment.

-Nor me -Scarlett smiled as they leaned toward each other. Then she reached into her pocket, pulling out a piece of stone that has copper in colour.

-What is this?

-I found it downstairs on the 26th floor when a piece of stone fell on me. -She said as she handed it to the man.

George stared with round eyes.

-What do you think?

-It seems so, but it needs to be examined by an expert to make sure. I'd love to take it with me. Of course, if you allow me.

-Would you do it?

George just nodded and then got on his horse, but he waited for her as well. He didn't want to leave her alone, knowing it would get dark soon.

# CHAPTER XXXV

Marta looked for an opportunity to talk to Scarlett and when she finally found the right time, she caught her in the hallway.

-Mrs. Wolowitz! -She stepped close to the woman.

-Can I help you, Marta?

-I just want to thank you for taking care of my son while I work.

Scarlett took a deep breath, then tried to explain so she wouldn't misunderstand kindness.

-Your son was born in a free country and will not be owned by anyone as you know it. But I can only help temporarily while your child is so young. Once he reaches the appropriate age, he needs to get to work or go to school. -Scarlett said as the girl nodded understandingly.

-I know it's just, you know, a white man... -She thought for a moment- Don't be mad... -She said, glancing shyly at her- I didn't mean it like that. What I want to say is that no one has ever done such a nice thing for me before.

Scarlett just smiled, then when she was about to leave, she turned back because for a fleeting moment it was as if she could see the girl's arms were wounded as she lifted them up gesturing. But when she turned back, Marta was already standing in front of her with hands behind her back.

-Marta... -She said, holding out her hand.

She handed her own, Scarlett pulled up the sleeve of her dress, then she saw the wounds on her arm again.

-Where did you get these?

But all Marta said was that she still had a lot to do, so she set off on her way straight into the garden. Although Marta did not tell, Scarlett knew the truth, she knew who is also responsible for all this.

# CHAPTER XXXVI

-Well, I'd love to get over it soon, no matter why you called me here. -Mrs. Wolowitz walked through the library door.

-You need to see this. I did some research and found out that we could safely reopen the mine.

-Mines would never be safe.

-Could you just look at it?

-Not a word... -She raised her hand.

-You haven't even listened to what I want to say...

-I won't even care about such a nonsense thing. People lost their lives there. -She said closing the case.

-Don't pretend to really care about the lives of others. -Scarlett said, opening another debate. -Nothing matters to you and no one, but that little snubbed-nosed cat... -She pointed to the woman's pug running against the wall continuously.

-I lost faith in people, after... -But she didn't dare to continue.

-How can you look with a better eye at a fur-ball than a man?

-This fur-ball has never done anything to offend me. Harold never talked back. He is more loving and caring than any human being ever could be.

-I'll tell you what, you are the most hated and stubborn woman I ever met. No one loves you... Did you ever think about why? You are the most racist and a narcissist witch I ever knew. You don't care about others, not even about your son. I don't know what he has ever done to you to behave like that...

-You will find out everything in time and believe me, your angle of seeing the people will change, on an arc degree.

-You will never be loved if you don't change your attitude, you have to see good in people. You are judging people by their appearance, you don't even try to know them, who they really are inside. You can't just walk around and whip everyone whose face is not sympathetic for you. A dog is a friend for life, I have dogs myself. But you will never be a valuable woman if you love more a dumped dog than the people around it.

-How dare you? -She asked indignantly. Unable to decide if it was worse the way she was talking to her or the way she was about her dog. Harold began again to lean to the side to reach his balls and began to lick them.

-I will tell you how. No one, but no one in your life has ever given their opinion, no one was ever honest because they were afraid. But let me say something. I am not afraid. Sit down and listen. -She pointed to the chair on the other side of the desk.

She took a seat without a word, after which Scarlett handed her a few drawing pads and notes.

-What are these? -She asked, exchanging papers in her hand.

-Plan B.

-What kind of plan B? What is plan A?

-The A is my private business. I'm restarting the farm.

-What did Leonard say to all of this? -She interrupted her.

-Gracewith is my property, whether we are married or not. If you hadn't seen the papers I had written before my marriage and Leonard had agreed to the terms, and signed them. He does not inherit anything through our marriage. I parcelled out the lands and distributed them among the children, and Jared, as the only Bloom boy, who will carry this name, inherits Gracewith. This means Leonard has no say in running the farm.

-You harpy! -She said, drumming angrily with her walking stick on the ground.

-Would I be? Yes, I am also glad that such an extremely rare and marvellous resembles me. Did you know its beak and claws were very strong?

-Yes, it just showed up. -She said ironically.

-Let's go back to Plan B. Plan B is the reopening of the mines. But this time, it will be done much more carefully, much safer. -She squeezed the pencil.

-And you want to do it all with some helmets and slats? -She laughed as she tossed the papers in her hand on the table.

-As you said. - added Scarlett- Helmets, if you take a closer look at the drawing, are made of metal, if anything falls on it, people's heads will be protected.

-Of course... They'll be deaf if something falls on them, especially if their heads are empty. It will also be very harmful and painful. You are talking nonsense. -She said grimly.

-Not if this is inside. -Then handed over another drawing, the drawing showed something in the helmet.

-What is this?

-They will be stuffed with wool that will be covered with cotton linen.

-And won't it fall off their heads?

-No, under the filling, there will be a thin belt.

-And that building? Where did you get it from?

-I read about it in a novel, so I want to realise it, I drew it.

-So, it's just a writer's imagination of something that doesn't even exist... Brilliant... -She laughed again.

-I've improved. These will require great effort to bring out the copper and stones. The way they did it before was not the safest, wasn't the fastest either.

-What are you talking about? -She stood up from her chair.

-Sit back I'm not done yet. -She said aggressively, then put a copper stone in front of the woman. -So far, they have been carried in buckets to the jack that people had to pull up, which is a very bad technique. People were tortured like that. Therefore, their roles will be taken over by the donkeys, we will buy more donkeys that to be replaced every four hours and we will change an 80kg lifting place up to 200kg. As for the stone, I saw a lot of stone was not removed, which was left in place unnecessarily. We can also benefit from these. In a simpler way. We're building a slide.

-What?

-A drop-down slide, where the stone and excess pieces of rock flow straight to the lower exit to the shore. We will then sell them as building materials.

-We haven't thought about that before.

-And as for carrying stones and copper, it is difficult for people to always carry them up to six or seven metres in a bucket. I thought we could do it differently. I read once...

-Those stupid books again.

-What can be of great help to us. A two-wheeled little wagon which is barely a metre long and half a metre wide to fit in even tight spaces would be suitable for this purpose. As for the roof falls, more support beams will be needed, and I thought we could put some planks over the beams that will hold them when it collapses, because I think is a very weak and cheap solution if only a few beams are erected. If not for a long time, but to gain time, so people can get out sooner if that happens.

-But it's more time and money.

-Safer and more efficient. There will be less chance of collapse and injury or death.

-Are you sure this will work?

-America wouldn't have been discovered if Christopher Columbus hadn't set off.

-From where do you want to invest so much money in all this?

-From the farm's profits, apiary profit, and the orchard profit.

-Why are you so sure you're going to make a profit at all?

-I can only hope the bear doesn't see his shadow this year. -She said, but since her mother-in-law looked incomprehensible, she closed the subject.

-Tell me why is all this so important to you? Don't you have everything?

Scarlett looked out the window at Gracewith, responding: -But others don't have.

# CHAPTER XXXVII

Doris was in the yard with the kids, some snow-covered Beelove, taking advantage of it to take the three kids out to play. The kids happily built all sorts of things with snow: shaped it, squeezed it, tossed it.

-They don't even know they're the happiest right now, at this age. -Doris said looking at the children.

She heard horse whinny in the distance, she saw Mr. Salvatore watching Beelove on a horse back from afar.

-In the embrace of winter, he knows how precious summer is, for in vain a huge flame burns in his heart, if no one ever warms by it... -She said softly.

It was then that she saw Scarlett stepping out the door, looking away at the man who was raising his hat and then heeling his horse galloped away.

-So many good-hearted people don't have a mind... -She muttered as she looked at both parties.

-Doris! -Scarlett said from afar and began to walk towards her. -How are they behaving? -She asked looking at the laughing cheerful children.

-As a matter of fact, compared to that their nanny was such a beast... Pretty good.

Scarlett sighed, then turned on her heels, but looked back at Doris's request.

-As for the well... Thank you!

-Thank it, when it will be done. -She smiled then she took two steps, but had to turn back again because she remembered something- But one day of the week they will be unable to work, as I know they found water, which is now already waist height, so they will have to slowly resort to another way, so they will stop work until they get the right materials.

# CHAPTER XXXVIII

-Scarlett! -Agatha said as she walked past her.

Scarlett took a deep breath and then turned to her mother-in-law.

-I was thinking. -It was immediately in Scarlett's mind that this was already starting bad. -I decided that... -She was trying to find the right words - you should share this wonderful idea with Leonard.

-Pardon me? -Scarlett wondered, she was far from expecting this. -I don't think I understood you, you mean you are not against my idea?

-No, not in the least. -She said with a smile, it was the first time she saw the woman smile, which freaked Scarlett out.

Scarlett's words stalled; she couldn't utter anything. So, she just looked at Akita who was sneaking towards Agatha's dog. He started playing with the dog, who was barking merrily. Agatha turned back, then hit the child on the head with her stick. Now Scarlett was sure it was the old Agatha.

-What do you think touching Harold with that filthy hand? -She asked the child who was rubbing his own head, unable to give a single explanation, he just ran away. It occurred to Scarlett for half a minute that her mother-in-law had changed, but apparently, she hadn't, she just rewarded the idea that's all. -Aa, a letter has arrived from Leonard.

Scarlett began to read the letter she had found on the fireplace, to which her mother-in-law had pointed out.

*"Dear Scarlett,*

*I want to let you know that the company is booming. My trip to Germany was a success. Mr. Wolfred decided to buy half of the honey container. We can also expect additional orders and we have signed a contract for one year. But in order to maintain the business chains in London, Amsterdam, and Berlin, I have to travel to France to buy more hives.*

*My trip to France will take a little longer than I could promise, I have to say that frustrating words have come to my ears that will scare you too. Mr. Wolfred said the Anglo-French peace treaty had expired and the French were already recruiting their people. Another war will break out. You can expect my arrival in a month.*

*Please take care of yourself, Honey, and of the household!*

*Sincerely,*

*Leonard R. Wolowitz"*

-No letter has been received from him for more than a month, this boy is on his way all the time. It would be so good if we could write to him, that he knew what was going on around the house. -Scarlett was completely lost in the letter, so Agatha cleared her throat and spoke again- What did he write?

Scarlett was thinking about if it would be a good idea for her, for the mother-in-law, to know the truth or not.

-Just that he will return in a month.

-Is that all what he wrote in a letter?

-He wrote about his journey. The business is booming; he had a lot of orders.

# CHAPTER XXXIX

Scarlett watched the kids play by the window. She heard Doris as she loudly warned them not to go near the well because it was deep and full of water. She could hear Doris stepping into the snow with her full body and it crackling under her feet. She heard her dogs start whining when Aliona hugged them. She heard the chirping of the robin, the blowing of the wind, the laughter of the children. She felt she had found her peace of mind. She does not think of the past, only the present. She remembered what her mother had once written in her diary: *"Don't cry because it's over! Smile because it happened!"*. She did so. She smiled deeply and then hid in her book so she could continue reading her novel in harmony.

Doris played with the children in the snow. The kitchen door was open to let out the smoke from the burnt dinner, for while Marta was roasting the chicken, she was much more preoccupied with watching her child's merriment. When Marta tried to take it out of the oven quickly because she was running out of time and didn't want to get into another fight with Mrs. Wolowitz, she was so hurried that she forgot to grab the baking sheet with her kitchen towel. As a result, she burned her hands. She shouted loudly and was in a lot of pain. When Doris heard it, she started running, leaving the children outside. As soon as she ran through the door, she accidentally kicked the support at the door, and then the wall shook with a sudden click. The broom that was used to sweep the snow away, which was leaning against the wall fell into the gap between the handle and the door, which blocked it.

-Let me see. -Doris said, then ran for the bandage.

The kids played merrily in the snow until Marta's little son accidentally playfully shoved Jared into the snow. There was silence for a few seconds, then the kid started laughing, he got up and pushed the little boy as well, who also started laughing, so they played like this, always taking one step at a time. Aliona sat among the dogs, took a handful of snow in the palm of her hand, then blew it into the dogs' faces, so she played until the dogs began to bark and then growl. From this, the little girl shuddered and stopped playing.

Doris froze in the doorway when she returned with the bandage as she looked out the window at the yard. One of the dogs began to scratch the door while the other next to Aliona barked violently. Marta, noticing the phenomenon, got up with great difficulty as she turned to see what was happening, she saw the children standing at the edge of the well pit. Marta's child pushed the white boy in front of him, who laughed and stood up, holding both hands to his friend ...

Scarlett was pulled out of the imaginary world that the book had painted before her, thanks to the chaos. She looked out the window and saw the two children playing next to the pit, Marta's little son standing at the edge of the pit as Jared pushed him. A three-year-old boy who was almost lost like a little ant in the darkness of the pit.

Marta ran to the window and then began to bang desperately, hoping the kids would notice and pay attention to her, but in the heat of the game and the hilarious moment, they didn't care. Jared pushed Marta's son into the pit, unaware of the danger awaiting his friend.

-Nooo! -Marta shouted as if she had been stabbed in the heart.

Doris banged the door, then tried to break it. But in vail, she could not break through the obstacle in any way.

Jared overbalanced as he watched the boy drowning in the water. So, he tilted towards the depths, just a hair's breadth away from death. One of Scarlett's Dalmatians, the moment Jared tipped out

432

of balance, grabbed the child's coat between his teeth and yanked him back.

Scarlett ran down the stairs as best she could as Doris and Marta ran to the front door to save the little boy. But in vain, it was a waste of time to run around Beelove. The little boy was floating above the water. Marta's eyes filled with tears as she knelt beside the pit. She jumped into the pit and took his little lifeless body in her arms. Scarlett got there the moment the woman cried loudly, mournfully, mourning her only child. The only person who shed light on her in her darkest hours, the only person she endured all the pain her mistress, Mrs. Wolowitz, had caused her. The torment, the smacks of whips, and the cracking of her skin.

# CHAPTER XL

-Why is your nose watching the ground? -Mrs. Wolowitz asked.

-Marta's little son, we can now say that he is a real angel. -Scarlett said sadly.

-Angel... -The woman laughed- These are all creatures of the devil; you can be sure of something he must not have gone to heaven.

-I will never understand you...

-And if it weren't that woman... Your so-called "confidential" worker...

-Don't you dare say anything about Doris.

-How can you protect her kind so much? You're sorry for them like they're one of us... I'll tell you, they're not. And let them perish, for it is not a pity for them.

-How can someone be so heartless? -She said, then continued in a slow arc turning to her. -Of course, we are... -But she stopped when she saw that the woman was already in a deep sleep. Her dog, Harold, jumped out of her lap, then walked past the woman's skirt, stopped beside it, then lifted his leg and give her warm sprinkling. -all equal... -Scarlett finished, in a disgusting way by what she had seen.

*

-Ma'am, I'm so sorry... -Doris lamented as she caught the woman walking down the hall.

434

-So am I. -She said, but she didn't stop.

-It was my fault...

-Doris. -She stopped by the crying woman. -It wasn't your fault; it wasn't anyone's fault. It's an unfortunate accident. -She wiped away her tears.

-I want to be there when he is sent for his last trip. I want to be there so much... -she cried louder and louder- But there is no one who can be left with the children, of course I understand if you would never trust me again...

-Don't talk nonsense. -She said, opening the parlour door where Agatha was sitting in her armchair and the children were playing in front of her. -Mrs. Wolowitz will take care of them. -She pointed to the ones inside, where the two children were rolling the ball towards each other, and then for a moment Agatha kicked it so far away that it rolled straight under the chest of drawers, Harold followed it and ran to the chest of drawers with so much force that his pressed face became even flatter, as a result, the children began to cry- Or maybe not. -She said, closing the door in front of them- Dress them up and you should change as well. See you in an hour in front of the carriage.

Scarlett reopened the salon door, but now she walked in, with Doris at her heels, who took the kids' hands and left soon.

-Where's that damn girl with my tea? -She murmured to herself.

-I didn't tell the whole truth about the letter. -Scarlett confessed, but she was so busy with her thoughts about tea that she hadn't even heard Scarlett words.

-I hope she remembers that I was asking for mint tea. -She peered toward the door.

-I've been worried about Leonard, it's been two weeks since he went to France, but I haven't received a letter.

-Where's that worthless Marta? I will skin her. -She asked now louder.

-She had been preparing for her son's funeral, if you hadn't noticed, others have more serious problems than a silly tea! -Scarlett snapped, then heard a slam of the door behind her as she turned to see, she saw Marta with a huge tray in her hand, standing frozen, then weeping she dropped the tray and ran out.

-Do you see what you did? -She pointed to the tea set on the floor and the spilled tea. -Are you happy now?

*

Few people gathered at the funeral, most of them coloured, as did the Reverend, and even Scarlett and the adjoining Jared and Aliona were the only white people.

Although Scarlett never had a child of her own, she was just trying to feel what Marta was feeling. But she was unable, since what could it feel like to have your child buried sooner than you, to have your only child buried underground where is dark and cold? She knew the loss was painful, but she couldn't feel it with all her heart. Who could understand this if not a person who had already gone through all this? Nobody else. It was even more painful to see a tiny coffin brought to the excavated place.

People start singing, worshiping, while the coffin was slowly lowered into the ground. Marta hadn't cried so far. When the coffin hit the ground, Marta kissed her white flower and threw a handful of earth on the coffin with it, her eyes soaking in tears. When, on the other hand, people sang about the ascension and she heard the handful of earth she had thrown into the pit, bang on the small half-sized coffin. She began to cry more and more loudly and painfully. She made the children cry too, but so bitterly that Scarlett took Jared from Doris's arms. Then Marta looked at Scarlett, pointed at Jared, she shouted, *"You killed my child! You killed my little boy, The only man I've ever loved"*.

# CHAPTER XLI

After the funeral, Doris visited Scarlett anxiously one day.

-Ma'am, forgive me for disturbing you.

-Come in. -She told the woman standing in the doorway.

-The kids are asleep. Now is my chance to be alone with you. -She walked toward the woman who was taking notes, leaning over the desk. -You know, I'm worried.

Scarlett then put down her pen and raised her head in Doris's direction.

-Master Jared doesn't eat properly and doesn't even play with Miss. Aliona.

-Does it affect Aliona as well?

-No, not yet. But I've been observing this since... Well, you know... -She aimed.

-Yes. I understand. Is that all? -She asked, taking the maps in her hands.

-Ma'am? I do not understand.

-What? -She asked, raising the mining manual in front of her.

-That you are not interested.

-Doris, -she said with a sigh, -I didn't say that I didn't care. But the war has begun, I also have to care about the farm, not to mention

438

mining, which would be a good opportunity for so many people to get a job in these difficult times. Now, I'm just not able to deal with that too... -She finished finally realizing what words she had uttered.

-To deal with that... -She said at once with Scarlett- I didn't know all of this was more important than your family, a traumatized child who wakes up at night and hides to cry.

-Doris... -Sighed again- I'll call Dr. Garfield for him.

Doris hummed loudly, then walked out, lifting her head.

In the hallway, just around the corner from the kids' room, she collided with Marta, who was apparently upset. She walked past her silently, staring at the ground. Doris didn't say anything either, since what could she say to a grieving mother?

# CHAPTER XLII

Marta grabbed the opportunity that the kids were left alone after seeing Doris go into the library, she hurried to the kid's bedroom. There the two children slept peacefully, looking at Aliona, who blushed in her sleep, pulled the blanket over, to make her more covered. She then went to Jared's crib, who was also sleeping soundly, indicating that there were traces of wrinkles on his skin. Marta took a cushion from the armchair next to her, holding in her arms tightly around, and then began to rock like a baby, after which she sang a few lines from some American lullaby.

-You know, Master Jared ... I had a little boy too. -She said, looking at the child. -I rocked him just like this and I sang this song. -She said with a smile at the thought, then the smile was suddenly wiped off her face. -But you took him from me! -She said in a raised voice, lifting the pillow over his head, then suddenly toward the crib, then to Jared's head, a very little parted the child's head from the pillow when Marta heard a noise, more precisely a key rattle. Then she threw the pillow back where she found it, then whispered in the ear to the child, *"Sleep well, you little murderer."*

# CHAPTER XLIII

-Mrs. Wolowitz! -Jerome said as he entered the door after knocking.

-Dr. Garfield! -She put down the book in her hand on the table- Well, what did you diagnose?

The man set his bag on the table and then began to pack his things.

-The child is in shock. Specifically, he was traumatized. I've already told Doris what to do, but I'll tell you as well.

-Needless, Doris will tell me everything. -She closed the topic.

-What are you working on? -He asked, looking at the drawings.

-On a better future. -Scarlett replied briefly.

-Did you create them all?

-Yes, with some novels help.

-These are brilliant! -He exchanges them in his hand- How will the helmets be stuffed?

-At first, I thought of cotton, but 'I'm thinking more and more of wool, it will be pressed, it will be pressed or worn anyway, though wool provides the same protection and is cheaper.

-Wool is a good choice. And what are these on top?

-Well, I just started this, but it would be a candle holder or a smaller flambeau holder. I thought it was a lot more effective this way because it sheds more light on what's in front of them, and they don't have to hold in their hands.

-Brilliant! -He looked at the drawing- Does Leonard know about it?

-I'm afraid I haven't had a chance to tell him yet.

It occurred to her that Jerome was one of Leonard's closest friends, who was also a doctor.

-So, Jerome, you're a doctor. What can bloody sputum suggest?

-Well, it can refer to many things, including Pulmonary embolism, Digestive system (haematemesis), Cardiovascular system (this includes aortic dilatation, left ventricular failure, valve defects), Haematological problems, bleeding (Often caused by improperly adjusted blood thinners increased bleeding by bloody sputum), Abnormal bleeding tendency, Autoimmune diseases, or sexually transmitted diseases experienced during this symptom. Such diseases. Why do you ask?

-I was just curious. Mr. Thaker was said to have had such symptoms as well.

-Well, yes, he had a pulmonary embolism.

-My husband was a little sick at the same time... -She pointed out indirectly, for which the man looked a little upset.

-Well, Leonard was a sick type as a kid as well.

-In other words, there is something wrong with my husband. Is it curable? -She took a deep breath.

-This... Ma'am, please don't do this. -He said, looking into her eyes.

-I would like to know.

-No, it's a completely different kind of disease. No one has yet explained the cure. -There was a disturbing silence between them for a few seconds.

-Such old friends. Huh? -She asked, releasing the tension as the man did not say a word.

-As a matter of course, yes. We grew up together.

-Oh, he never told me.

-I will never forget, his mother was always afraid, he was always under supervision until he was an adult. And even now. -He leaned toward her, whispering half to the edge of his mouth. -If you know what I mean... -He continued, nodding toward the salon room, and they both laughed.

-But I wanted to ask. When will your husband return?

-Within a few days. -She said with a smile.

-I'm glad. Did you receive a letter?

-As a matter of course, these days. He mentioned he was boarding on Monday.

-Wonderful. I can't wait to tell my wife. She will be happy with the news. Then we have to have dinner together.

-In any way. -She replied kindly.

-If he gets home, would you send him to me immediately, I have to talk to him about something important.

-What would it be about? -She asked as she escorted him out.

-Tell him that Captain Patmore visited and took an interest in him.

Scarlett just watched the man as he left the house, wondering what it might be about...

# CHAPTER XLIV

Doris was bathing the kids one night when Marta showed up in the room. A jug of steaming water was in her hand.

-I brought some hot water. -She said in a low voice trembling.

-That's great! Thanks! Just put it on the table. -Doris replied, pointing to the table, then began wiping Aliona's little body with a damp cloth.

-As if I heard, when I came this way, that the Mistress was searching for you. -She said nervously, playing with her fingers.

-Oh... -She said, leaning heavily up, due to her old bones. -Would you take care of them for a moment?

Marta nodded silently. When Doris left the room, she spoke softly.

-Just as you took care of my son. -Then kneeled next to the children- Go and warm up by the fire, whatever you hear, do not turn around. -She told Aliona, lifting her out of the water and wrapping around with a towel. -Do you remember what happened to my little son Master Jared? -The little boy just looked at her silently. Marta let the child down on his back slowly, until the child completely was covered by water from head to toe. -You will play in heaven with my little treasure.

But she was unable to keep him down for long, but not because she felt sorry or would have been unable to kill a child. No. Because suddenly Doris showed up behind her. So, in a moment, she lifted him out of the water, the child began to cough loudly and took deep breaths.

-What did you do? -Doris asked, taking the child in her arms and shushing him.

-I just washed the soap off him. -She said, staring at the ground.

-This is how you wash the soap down? -The woman quarrelled with her- And why is Miss. Aliona so close to the fire?

-I told her. She's already done bathing.

-If I knew you weren't able to do a job like that, I wouldn't have trusted you with it. -She took Aliona's hand and led her away from the flames.

Marta left soon, but Doris was unable to take her eyes off the woman.

# CHAPTER XLV

There was a loud knock on the door, which was then repeated three times until someone finally opened it. Doris looked at Thomas Kwaw standing in front of the door, then frowned.

-What do you want? -She asked briefly.

-I came to see Miss. Bloom.

-She's Mrs. Wolowitz now.

-Is she at home?

-Yes, but she's very busy. -Doris closed the door, more precisely she would have closed it, but he put his hand there to prevent it.

-I've been trying to visit for days, but they always send me away. Would you mention to her that I was here? Please!

-Wait... -Doris felt sorry for the man.

She returned a few minutes later.

-Come. -She said, leading the way.

Walking down the hallway, Kwaw was amazed at the magnificent palace. "Much bigger than the other..." he muttered under his breath. Doris took him to a door. Then she asked him again to wait. She went into the room and reappeared within half a minute, letting the man in.

-Mr. Kwaw! -Scarlett said, standing up from her desk to greet the man.

-Mrs. Wolowitz! -He took off his hat.

-What can I owe the visit to? -She inquired.

-I just wanted to bring this back. -He said, handing her the jewellery she had received from Anne.

-How did you get it? -She asked cheerfully.

-Let's just say I won it. -He put his hands in his pockets.

-How can I thank you? -She asked, turning the jewellery in her hand.

-If you mention that... -The man replied shyly. -I've never begged for a job before...

-Mr. Kwaw, what would that be about? -She frowned.

-It was a layoff a couple of weeks ago... No one gives me a job and the trouble are that our kind took to the streets. We cannot pay the rent. We're hungry.

In other words, you are not here just because of you... -She replied softly.

-No. Please hear me out... -Scarlett watched silently- A lot of people died, sick and cold. The majority of whites could have enlisted as soldiers because of the French occupation. But we're not hired for that either. We can't feed our children and there is no roof over our heads. Many are hiding under bridges. At least they are protected from the cold there...

-Not a word... -Scarlett gesturing to the man.

-So, you won't help... -He said, turning slowly toward the door.

-I did not say that. -Scarlett replied, and the man turned back- Although I restarted the farm and I have enough workers. But I have a Plan B... -She said softly.

-What kind of plan B? -Kwaw asked curiously.

-The mine. I'm going to start the mine.

-Ma'am, what are you talking about?

-Mr. Kwaw, what do you know about mining? -She asked, jumping up from her chair.

-Well, one thing and another. My father was a miner.

-Great. What are your opinions about these ideas? -She asked, pointing to the drawings.

Kwaw picked them up and began flipping through.

-These are wonderful ideas.

Then Mrs. Wolowitz entered the room, looking at the man in front of her in surprise. He greeted her appropriately, but she just kept staring.

-What is this... what's this man doing in my library? -She asked with her stick pointing in the direction of Kwaw.

-You forgot again that this is my library too. And the gentleman is Mr. Thomas Kwaw, he will be the manager of the Eastern Mine.

-What? -She asked indignantly.

-So far, I've been thinking about selling stones as building materials, but now I have a much better plan. -The man and the woman looked questioning- We are building a village in Beelove, people will be able to move here instead of the Black Quarter and get a job in the mine.

-Thank you, Mrs. Wolowitz! I knew I could count on you! -He said happily, but a bang interrupted him from his further words. They both looked in the direction of the voice where they saw Mrs. Wolowitz lying on the ground unconscious.

# CHAPTER XLVI

*"Dear diary,*

*For a while, I feel like the world has been on top of my shoulders again, and is pressing me. Continuous work and a lot of worries at the same time hit my life like lightning in a tree.*

*Doris may be right; I pay too little attention to the kids and myself. But it matters a lot to me to provide work for those in need who are hungry. I don't know if it was a good idea to allow them to move to the Gracewith hay barn, where I keep all of my goods. But I couldn't leave them on the streets. At first, I planned to move them into Gracewith's house, as no one lives there other than my employees, but Mrs. Wolowitz talked about it, or rather threatened to sue and delete Beelove's legacy from my name if I let them live there. All this would not have stopped me because my mother-in-law is a real mouth hero, but since she is a very influential woman and let's face it, if something is annoying her, she doesn't realise what she says, given how hateful and bad-tempered she would have probably been.*

*The villagers despise me for what I did, but they couldn't stay on the street. I provide them with food, the work has already begun, they are diligently carrying the stones and building the houses. Luckily, I still have some money left on the farm for the time being and Lady Evelyn also helped take care of the workers. They work for free for just a little food, so I can provide them with the least. I hope this sacrifice is worthwhile, I plan to move families with many children, together with the elderly to the first houses to be built, because they have priority. I also handed over the papers to reopen the mine, I had to organise it in advance, I couldn't wait for Leonard to arrive, no matter how angry I made my mother-in-law. Mr. Kwaw helps a lot, I was able to correct the plans thanks to him, who is already more experienced in practice than I am. Hopefully, we will be able to try out the new system soon and people will be able to get to work. If we succeed with this mine, we will hopefully be able to open the other two soon, giving people more opportunities."*

-Can we talk, Madam? -Doris entered the room in silence.

-Of course. What would it be about?

-About Marta. -Scarlett looked at her questioningly- Didn't you experience anything unusual about the girl's behaviour?

-What do you mean?

-The other day while bathing the kids, when I thought I was called... -Doris thought about her next words- I am sorry, I don't know if I can dare accuse her. Marta stayed in the room with the kids until I got back, Miss. Aliona stood by the fire, near the flames fluttering in the fireplace that could have easily scorched her. And Master Jared...

-Doris, you know my dear, she didn't take care of children before... Her mother had raised her son. Maybe she just doesn't know how to deal with the kids.

-Please, hear me out this time.

-All right. Go on. -What about Jared? -She asked the woman, who was suddenly left without words.

-He almost drowned in the bathing tub.

-Where was Marta during this time? -She stepped closer to Doris and put her hand on her shoulder.

Doris took a deep breath and swallowed what was in her throat.

-By the bathing tub. -Scarlett looked at the woman in surprise- And kept Master Jared under water.

# CHAPTER XLVII

Scarlett was in the mine with Kwaw to try out the new structure. First, a few small pieces of rock and stones were rolled down the slide, and then the first rolling cart was tested, packed with earth to take to the hoist, which they wanted to try to really withstand the weight they had set. Scarlett pushed the cart as she accidentally stepped on her skirt, then stumbled and fell to the ground, laughing, then she let Kwaw help her up.

-You have to be more careful, you're very dirty already.

-It's just a dress. It can be washed. -She replied with a laugh.

The man was not fully aware of his strength so he yanked her off the ground as if he was preparing to lift a large heavy sack. With her lightweight, Scarlett flew as if a feather had been picked up by the wind. Because of this, when she was already on her feet, she was unable to keep her balance, so she fell towards Kwaw, who pulled her closer to keep from falling again.

-I am sorry... -Kwaw said.

Scarlett stood silently, leaning on the man's muscular upper body. She looked up into the man's eyes and saw the glitter in it, it was like the glitter she saw in the villagers' eyes the first year she arrived in Gracewith, what she saw in George's eyes when he looked at her, knowing that this glitter was nothing but the light of hope. Scarlett took a step back, then smiled forcibly.

-It is all right.

When they went up to the entrance to the mine, they looked at each other. They were both impatient, waiting to see the result. Scarlett slammed the donkeys, who pulled a huge wooden wheel around as if they were in a mill. Kwaw lowered the lever, making sure to do it at the right time so as not to jerk and tear between the loose rope and the donkey-wheel. They both looked into the pit, watching as the hoist full of soil grew larger and then slowly rose to the surface. They both laughed when they saw that their plan was working.

After that, they hurried along to see if each stone has rolled down, Scarlett began to count, all had.

-It worked... -She said softly once, then turned to Kwaw. -It worked! -She shouted, jumping around the man's neck. Then, realizing what she had done, she took silently a few steps.

They later talked as they walked along the shore.

-Morgan is very happy to have got a job in the blacksmith shop.

-He deserves it. He is a very nice man and hard-working.

-Yes, he's a really good worker. Half of the helmets targeted are already forged. Women also work hard to get the liners done in time.

Scarlett smiled.

-What is it? -The man asked smiling as well.

-Just that, I probably wouldn't have succeeded without you. If you didn't improve the ideas and give an opinion... Then I would have foolishly made the slide so narrow that the stones were stuck.

-There is still a chance, but less. At first, I didn't understand why you wanted it that way, why it couldn't just be taken out with the jack. But now I understand the rocks would be too heavy for the donkeys, you didn't want to torture them.

-And you understand why I didn't want to lower the earth here?

-You didn't want to confuse the two?

-That is one of the reasons. Although the air is very dry on some floors, down here the humidity is very high, if it gets wet it easily clogs and involves more work.

Then they both watched the workers carry the soil.

-You are the most intelligent and determined person I have ever met.

# CHAPTER XLVIII

Scarlett was walking into the library when she heard a noise, not knowing what to think at first, she looked around. As she walked closer, she saw a tiny little foot hanging out from under the desk.

-Yeah, I made sure someone was still in the room... But I don't see a single soul as I looked around. -She said kindly, then she heard the child sobbing, so she just bent down. Jared crouched under the desk, hugging his knees, was rocking himself.

-Jared? -The woman asked, but there was no answer, the child stared in the nothing in front of him and repeated a sentence, "I didn't kill him! I didn't kill him!" Scarlett reached for the child and took him out, pulling him straight into her lap, sitting on the floor with Jared in her lap, and shushing him. Jared suddenly shuddered as if he had just woken up from his sleep. He looked at Scarlett and said:

-Aunt Scarlett... She said I was a murderer, that I killed her son. But it isn't true, right? -He asked with teary eyes- Am I a murderer? Am I? -He repeated, crying.

-Of course, you are not, my dear. -She pulled the child's head into her chest so he wouldn't see the tears and be unsure. -Of course, you are not.

Doris entered the room anxiously looking for Jared. When Jared saw her, he got up from his aunt's lap and ran out the door next to Doris.

-Ma'am are you... -She wanted to ask her question, but Scarlett stood up and motioned for silence.

-You're right, Doris. I don't spend enough time with the kids. -She wiped away her tears. -Call Dr. Garfield.

*

Later that day, Scarlett walked past the kitchen when the door was a crack open. Doris went the other way, hurrying to the front door to let their guest in. Scarlett watched as Marta sang and smiled as she prepared milk in two cups for the kids sitting at the table.

-Wait here, I have to get Mrs. Wolowitz's tea off the stove, too.

First, she put a bowl of cookies on the table, then headed to the other side of the kitchen for the milk. She was firstly preparing the tea, which she put next to the milk cups. Where she took a small vial from her pocket.

-Mrs. Wolowitz! -Captain Patmore greeted her. -I'm here for your husband's matter.

-Not now, Captain. -She said, pushing the door.

-Your husband hasn't returned in months. I am waiting for answers.

-I said not now! -She shouted, bursting through the door. The kids lifted the cup to their mouths and were ready to drink when Scarlett burst in, with Doris, Mrs. Wolowitz, Captain Patmore, and two other soldiers behind her, and then Akita showed up behind them as well. Scarlett slammed the cups from both kids' hands, which smashed to the floor with a big crash. -You wanted to poison my kids! -She shouted with her index finger pointing at the girl.

-I did not do anything. -Marta said with teary eyes.

Mrs. Wolowitz walked to the kitchen counter, where her tea was prepared on a tray with a vial next to it.

-Then what is this? -Mrs. Wolowitz asked, showing what she had found. Captain Patmore took the small bottle from the woman and smelled it.

-Get this woman under arrest! -He ordered his soldiers who were holding her by the arm.

-I'm innocent! -Marta shouted repeatedly, but no one took note. Akita watched freaked out as his sister was dragged away, but there was nothing he could do, he pulled up against the wall.

Dr. Garfield also arrived at the scene, where he entered the room in surprise, inquiring about what had happened. Scarlett, hoping she was wrong, handed the half-empty vial to the man, who smelled it.

-Poison? -He asked in surprise. Scarlett became aware of the woman's action, no matter how much she didn't want to believe it.

# CHAPTER XLIX

The rope was already hanging around Marta's neck, but she knew it would soon be the other way around and she would hang on the rope. She looked through the people, then saw Scarlett in front of her. She knew her mistress would never wish her harm, but she couldn't help her anymore, as the captain thought he could prove her guilt. She remembered the day it all happened, as she was standing on a log that could be kicked out from under her at any minute.

Marta was in the kitchen that particular day and she put the bowl of cookies on the table. Jared looked at her with sparkling eyes saying: "You're not mad at me, are you?" as if she had only seen her own child before her eyes, her little boy asked always like this when he done something bad with the same tone. She forced a smile, then went to the kitchen counter to prepare the tea, took out the vial, then took another glance at Jared, "You don't deserve this…" she said, then poured half of the vial into the tea, leaving the other half in the small bottle, "I'll be soon with you, my little boy" she told herself. She picked up both cups and took them to the kids. That's when they entered the room.

She once talked to Doris about death.

-What do you think it might be like? Are you afraid of it? -She asked the woman.

-No. I think when we die, we have to think about the place where we want be the most and the person we want to be with and that will happen.

Marta did this, conjuring a peaceful place in her head that, if the living people would see it, they would rather die, and then she imagined her little boy's face. She was so immersed in this imaginary world that she was no longer afraid. She didn't even hear the verdict being handed down.

-This woman tried to kill two innocent children, which resulted in her being brought to justice. They made a verdict, -he said to which people began to shout- so I pronounce it. The court ruled the woman here... as guilty! -The voice of the people was heard again- Therefore, on the rope she will fight for her life until life leaves her. -He declared, and in a moment the log under the woman was kicked out.

Scarlett watched as Marta suffered, her heart was aching as she tried to intervene, but there was nothing she could do about it. When it was over and she knew, her body was hanging lifeless, Scarlett turned to leave, before the crowd did, she saw Akita standing at the gate, as their glance reached each other, the child ran away, and Scarlett followed. She caught the child under a bridge and hugged him tightly. Akita cried bitterly.

-Akita, please look at me. -She said raising his head- Your sister is at peace and can be with her child.

-I know it's not your fault, you just tried to protect the kids like any normal mother would... -The child said crying. -I also know you talked to Captain Patmore for Marta. I know... I know...

\*

That evening, Scarlett was sitting in the salon with her mother-in-law, who was very disturbed by the woman's seriousness.

-Scarlett, you aren't usually like this. Is it because of the stupid cook girl?

-Marta wasn't stupid. -She looked out the window.

-But she wanted to kill Jared and maybe Aliona as well. She was a killer. We were lucky to have here Captain Patmore on the spot and her actions have been proven, who knows she could have gotten free at the end if the captain had not been witnessed it.

-She was a broken woman. -Scarlett said keeping up to the subject.

-Don't worry for a minute, it was for the best. Better for the world without them. I don't even understand why you're so compassionate, you carry their destiny so much in your heart. If it were up to me, it would be genocide.

-I'm convinced you're wrong, Mrs. Wolowitz. A woman who has lost her own child is expected to crumble. -She said, looking at the bracelet she had received from Marta.

-I will repeat, she intended to kill the children, at least one of them for sure. And she tried many times before.

-Why do you think she meant to poison him and not you instead? -Scarlett asked, but there was no answer, so she turned. Her mother-in-law fell into a deep sleep and snorted with her head tipped back towards the ceiling.

# CHAPTER L

Scarlett, returning home one night from Gracewith find out there is an unexpected guest who was waiting for her in Beelove. Her guest enjoyed the company of Mrs. Wolowitz, who reported how selfishly she decided on everything without her husband's consent. Scarlett opened the parlour door, then saw Mrs. Wolowitz chatting with her son, Leonard.

-Leonard! -The woman rejoiced- Welcome home! How was your trip? -She asked her husband kindly.

-My mother reported everything you did in Beelove.

-Yes, I have a lot of plans to improve it, for example, I would like to replace the ropes that are attached to the hoist with chains over time, and I was also thinking about water drainage because of the flooded floors, not to mention the slide...

-Scarlett enough of this. -The man said, silencing his wife. -How could you do all this without my permission? -He asked angrily, then took his coat on the armchair and hurried to the exit. -I'm leaving now, and we'll talk about that tomorrow.

For a minute, Scarlett didn't realise what was happening around her, just staring incomprehensibly at her departing husband. She looked at her mother-in-law, who proudly leaned on her walking stick in front of her. Then something flashed to her mind, so she hurried after him.

-Leonard, wait, you don't know everything that happened in your absence! -She shouted after the man who was now being cut off, then ordered the stableman in front of the entrance to saddle her horse as well.

-What are you doing? -Her mother-in-law asked.

-I will save my husband because as I see you forgot a little detail about what happened in his absence. -Then Agatha realised the danger too, while Scarlett was trying to take her coat, she helped her to put it on.

-Where is Leonard? -Jerome stepped in, fully flushed in hurry.

-You just missed him. -Scarlett said in preparation. Then they both jumped on their horses and galloped after Leonard.

Arriving in Truro, they tied their horses next to the brothel, where Leonard's horse was also tethered in front of the drinking trough. Scarlett was about to go into the building as Jerome took her by the arm and yanked her back.

-Not there. -He said, then pointed in the direction. After a while, they walked through the Black Quarter, but it wasn't as busy as it was before, the last time she was here.

The streets were empty for a long time until they heard footsteps just around the corner, Jerome grabbing Scarlett's mouth and pulling her into a dark alley where they hid. Scarlett was glad this time that Jerome had acted so quickly as she was unable to speak, even though it evoked a bad memory in her. After the soldiers passed by, they also continued on their way. They hid around the corner again and watched the light of one of the houses, soldiers were standing outside protecting the entrance, there was a sudden loud noise once, and both of them shuddered at the gunfire.

-What was that? -Scarlett asked in horror, but Jerome didn't answer, just kept watching. The captain came out alone and walked to the next house where his soldiers were following him.

-We need to go. -Jerome said.

-No! If my husband is in danger, I want to know about it. -Scarlett said stubbornly.

-Fine then, come with me. -He held her hand, then continued to walk through the streets until they saw two figures in the darkness of one of the small alleys opposite between the houses. There was an intersection in their path. Scarlett looked at the two men, one man was an unknown-coloured person, and the other her husband, Leonard.

-We don't have much time! They're close! -Leonard told the other man, then pressed against the wall.

Scarlett knew her husband was in big trouble. She also guessed what nationality there might be in the background since it was not in vain that Mrs. Wolowitz had an opinion of them. Scarlett was afraid they would attack each other and her husband would be hurt. Both happened, the two men fell to each other and began to kiss fiercely and Captain Patmore found them too.

The soldiers were looking in the direction of the two men, so they did not notice the people behind them. When Leonard turned to them, he almost ignored them, looking straight through them at Scarlett's disappointed face. Two soldiers forced him to his knees and then began to punch him hard.

-We need to go! -Jerome said, jerking Scarlett away from the place as she was struggling with a stifled cry.

# CHAPTER LI

The judge and the other members of the court entered the room. Everyone was waiting for the judge to take a seat, when this was done the other people could take their seats as well. Leonard was chained and taken to court. Evelyn squeezed Scarlett's hand hard.

-Did you talk to him? -Scarlett asked in a whisper.

-I tried, but when it comes to his work, he can be very stubborn. Be strong darling. -She stroked the woman's arm. -The truth will prevail anyway! -She said, not knowing the whole truth, since how could Scarlett talk to anyone about it?

-Gentlemen of the jury, we see before us today, one of the most disgusting and vile men we have ever known, Mr. Leonard Robert Wolowitz. He was caught doing an indecent thing with someone from the same sex as him. -Said the barrister.

People started to jeet and utter strong, evil, terrifying words to the man who silently endured the humiliation.

-The honourable member for this justice, Judge Norman Quas in the case of Mr. Leonard Robert Wolowitz calls to the stage Captain Patmore. -Said the speaker of the court.

Captain Patmore marched in to testify.

-What can you say about the evening when this incident happened?

-The suspect was in a small street the night he hid in a dark cul-de-sac with his lover, Mr. Ergon Wendoz. -Then the captain looked at those present, his eyes caught on Scarlett and Mrs. Wolowitz, then continued. -The two men were in warm proximity to each other.

-It must be cold that night! -A man shouted, and many began laughing at it.

After a while, George Salvatore arrived late in the room, trying to sneak in and take his place unnoticed by the other MPs, but Scarlett noticed. She watched in surprise as George attended the justice, then turned her gaze to her husband, who was constantly watching his wife.

-Their lips touched and their hands were in an indecent place. -The captain continued.

-Thank you, Captain Patmore. -The judge said.

-I would ask Ergon Wendoz, to be put in front of the judge. -The man showed up to testify too, many people began to shout and insult him, the man looked at his rival, Scarlett, and then took a seat.

-Could you tell me what happened that particular night? -The barrister asked.

-I met Mr. Wolowitz. -He replied softly.

-It says here, -he looked at a paper- that Mr. Wolowitz bought a property in that neighbourhood and then signed it over to your name. Do you deny that this had happened?

-I don't deny it. -He said confidently.

-What did this man ask for, -he pointed out at Leonard- in return for all this?

-Attention. -He said, staring at the floor.

People spoke again and, in the room, became great chaos.

-Lie! -Cried Mrs. Wolowitz.

-Order, order! -The judge struck his gavel and everyone fell silent.

-Can you tell me what happened that particular night? -The barrister asked again.

-I met Leo... Mr. Wolowitz. He wanted to see me, he came to my house, but since I wasn't home, he set off, it was only a few minutes since I left home. We ran into each other on the street. -The man fell silent, so the barrister felt he had to speak again.

-Why did he want to see you?

-He was upset. He felt he needed to talk to someone. He said his wife had decided on things without his consent. -Then fell silent again.

-And you say that he had to discuss such an intimate thing with your kind? -The man just looked up from the floor at those standing in front of him, but he didn't speak. The barrister went to court. -This man claims that Mr. Wolowitz wanted to discuss his personal problems with him, which would indicate nothing more than that the two men had a close relationship with each other.

-It doesn't prove anything! -George shouted.

In the room, people began to whisper, which bothered Scarlett so much, this situation became more and more confusing, she felt as if she was only physically present, her mind was in a completely different place, which was like she was squirming in a hurricane until she returned on the gavel's bang, back into her body. The judge exclaimed: "I close the sitting! Next week, I'm asking for the two soldiers' statements, who were with Captain Patmore." When the judge stood up everyone followed suit, waited for him to leave the room, and then they, too, began to flee. Scarlett stayed, just sat on the bench, and watched as her husband was dragged in away, chained as if he was some kind of animal.

-Come on, darling. -Agatha said after Leonard disappeared from their sight.

Scarlett stood up and followed her mother-in-law, they left the room and then the building. A huge crowd gathered outside and everyone gave them a contemptuous look. Suddenly George showed up next to them as they walked down the stairs.

-Mrs. Wolowitz, I'm sorry about what happened, I hope the matter will be solved. -Scarlett just glanced at him before she opened her umbrella. -If I can help you with anything, please let me know.

-If you could do anything, I would have already asked you for. -She said, lifting the umbrella over her head and walking away.

# CHAPTER LII

Walking past her father's office, Scarlett was in a nostalgic mood, full of memories, memories of the first day she arrived in Truro, when she first visited her father's office, and other memories. She had a feeling for this tiny building opposite a brothel she never thought she would feel. She wished Mr. Thaker would walk out to her, with his slow old footsteps, to see him once more as the wind catches his white hair, if she could look him in the eye again and feel the support, he had given her always, she wished he could be by her side again to give her some advice.

-Are you coming or what? Should I be waiting for you? -Mrs. Wolowitz asked, heading for the market.

-I'll be right there, give me another minute. -She told her mother-in-law, who just waved and went on.

Agatha walked through the market, people stared at her, insulted her, and there were some who spat in front of her. She didn't notice but Akita was also at the market that day, Marta's brother, who had come to get away from Beelove and its household for a while. As he walked closer to the apple stall, he saw Mrs. Wolowitz walking towards him, so he hid behind it, not wanting to get a whipping for leaving the house without permission. People pulled away from Agatha as if she had leprosy, the woman pulled herself together against this behaviour, raised her head, and so walked through the crowd, who looked at her as she was a circus creature or something. Once a woman's voice stood out from the others.

-You raised your son, to be like that! -She shouted. Agatha didn't want to notice it, so she continued on her way until someone poked her shoulder. When she turned back, someone has splashed something in her face. Agatha fell to the ground, screaming in pain.

-It burns... I can't see! I cannot see! -She shouted bitterly.

-You needed it! You deserve it! -Some of them said, and then people began to disperse.

Agatha was still writhing on the ground, no one wanted to help her. Akita was already squatting at the stall covering his ears, unable to listen to her suffering, so he jumped up from one moment to the next and ran towards her.

-Come! -He yanked up from the ground, pulling the woman's hand, which covered her face with the other hand, and yelled painfully. Akita led her to the nearest drinking trough and then began washing her face with cold water. Soon after, Scarlett got there too, helping the little boy.

-What happened?

-Someone splashed her.

Scarlett took off her poncho and pushed her head completely into the water. She then placed the poncho on her head to protect Agatha from the cold, and to cover it in front of people who were staring.

Later that afternoon, Jerome arrived to examine his dearest friend's mother. After this happened, he went to the salon from the woman's room to talk to Scarlett, where she was stroking Akita while the child was drinking milk. Seeing Jerome, she stood up and hurried in front of him so that they would not be within earshot of the child.

-So? -She hoped for an encouraging response.

-Mrs. Wolowitz is in critical condition. The acid with which it was watered has damaged her vision so much that it is almost certain to cause blindness.

-Almost certain? -Scarlett asked back.

-Most likely. -He took a deep breath- There is very little chance of even seeing vaguely. I bandaged her wounds, well, her burns were very bad, as you know around the face and eyes, especially at her age, the skin is the thinnest with very little muscle and fat, so on some places, it burned to the bone. Scarlett put her hand in front of her lips in horror. -At first, I thought she wouldn't survive, but Mrs. Wolowitz is just as stubborn as you are. -He smiled at her. -If you visit, don't be surprised I had to bandage her whole head.

-Didn't it only affect her eyes? -She asked in surprise, unable to take a single look at her mother-in-law in the heat of the moment.

-Well, it was washed off pretty late, so I think it splashed her over the forehead when watering, which caused serious hair loss and slipped down her face, and her hands burned a little as well.

-Jesus, with how much was she splashed with?

-According to my guess, half a litre, a quarter. The point is, -he gestured to her to remain calm- since I just gave her sleeping medicines, her wounds are too fresh and she's been suffering a lot, I'll leave her for you, she will sleep now for a long time, if she wakes up and asks for it to give her, you can give any time after she has eaten, had a drink and been to the toilet. -He handed her the vial- Just put three drops in her drink. It is important to give her mashed foods so that she does not have to chew too much or talk too much, it is terribly painful when the skin on the face is stretched after such an incident. I will come to change the bandages every day. -He said, then turned to the door. -Oh, and something else, always be with her, someone should always be watching her. If she wakes up and has pain, or the wound feels itchy after a while, it's important not to let her touch her face, if she needs to be tied up to the bed don't hesitate to do it.

-I got it. -Scarlett replied, then let the man leave.

As Jerome left, Scarlett walked past the kid who was eating a cake, warming himself by the fireplace. She sat down next to him, watching for a moment. Gathering her strength, asked the child. -Tell me, Akita, did you see who did this to Mrs. Wolowitz? -The kid started scratching his ear.

-No ma'am, there were a lot of people around.

-I understand. -She said, stroking the child.

# CHAPTER LIII

-Mr. George Salvatore! -The butler announced George's arrival.

-Show him in! -Lord Quas says- What a surprise! -He told the man walking towards them- Have a tea with us. -He pointed to his wife, who was smiling.

-Thank you, but I'm not staying for long. -He said, looking at his hat. -I've come about an important matter.

Evelyn had a hard time getting up from the table, she was afraid to hit her big belly on the edge of the table, and then walked beside her husband, who kissed her on the forehead.

-I'll leave you alone. -She said, walking toward the exit.

Lord Quas walked to the drinks table, picking up two glasses.

-If you don't want tea, I think you'll accept a drink. -He said, filling the glasses with whisky. -I didn't know about your arrival in Truro, have you relocated? -He asked, handing over the glass.

-They transferred me temporarily at my request but I am only an observer, I will report afterward in London. When I heard what happened, I knew I had to travel here.

-I understand. -The man replied, sipping from his glass. -And what would you like to talk to me about, my dear friend?

-I'm glad you asked the question like that because as a friend I would ask for something.

-Oh? -The man was surprised.

-I arrived in the case of Leonard Wolowitz. -The man sitting in front of him was serious. -I have no evidence of that, but I know the man is innocent. You shouldn't condemn. People say a lot.

-There are eyewitnesses to prove his actions.

-Didn't you think those people were lying? Mr. Patmore has hated the man since he lost his niece and slandered Mr. Wolowitz with murder, for which there was no evidence. Let him go home to his wife.

-So that's what it's about? -He slammed on the table. -Mrs. Wolowitz, I knew she took your mind... But I can't do anything, as I told my wife. If you were so convinced of his innocence, you wouldn't have come here to ask for it. We both know what led you to see me today.

-Fine, then just gain us some time. Delay the justice, until we can find some evidence to be able to show. -He said, putting his hand on his friend's shoulder, who nodded in agreement.

# CHAPTER LIV

-Mrs. Wolowitz, can I serve the lunch? -One of the maids asked.

-No, thank you! -Scarlett replied- I have to leave soon to see my husband.

-Mrs. Wolowitz! Mrs. Wolowitz! -Akita shouted as he stormed into the parlour. - She woke up!

They both rushed into the woman's room, where she was still lying incomprehensibly. Trying to recall what happened.

-Mrs. Wolowitz, I am here! I am here! -Scarlett said, taking her mother-in-law's hand. -You slept through more than a full day. -She stroked her bandaged hands. -Lunch will be brought soon, you must be very hungry.

-Where is? -Asked hoarsely- Where is that child? Who saved me? -She asked half-mouthed painfully.

-He is sitting next to me.

-I can't see anything. -She said painfully, touching the bandages on her head- I can't see...

-The doctor had to cover your eyes, they were seriously injured, it is very sensible for the light. -She took the woman's hands and tried to keep them from touching her wounds. -You'll have to stay that way for a while. -When she saw the woman begin to despair, she tried to calm her down, but she was inconsolable. Then Akita stepped beside her bed, taking the woman's hand.

-Everything will be fine; you will see ma'am!

476

-Is it you? The kid from the market? What's your name?

-Aaa... -Then he looked at Scarlett, who was looking at them. -llan. My name is Allan.

-Nice to meet you, Allan. -She said softly, sighing as she tried not to move her mouth. -Tell me, would you stay here with me for a while?

-I'll leave you alone now, I have to go. Lunch will be brought soon and the doctor will be here in half an hour.

*

Scarlett visited her husband in prison for the first time, even though he has been kept inside for two full weeks. When Scarlett first went into the cell, she didn't even know what to expect or how to react. All the way across the hall she went along, then turned the corner where she saw the guard's table, she thought about what to say to her husband, but she couldn't say anything when she saw him.

-I know what you think of me now. -He said to his wife without even looking at her. -And you're absolutely right. I'm a nobody, a dishonest, disgusting, nobody...

Scarlett sat down in front of her husband at the table. She looked at him, then took his hand, at which point Leonard finally looked up at Scarlett.

-We'll work it out together! -She stroked his face with her other hand.

-Oh, honey. I never deserved you! -Tears welled in his eyes. -You should be with George. -Then he cried.

-You could have told me.

-You would have been unable to understand.

-Do you love him? -She fought with her tears.

-Yes. -He said softly- I love him very much.

-As I gave my heart to someone else. We are both equally at fault in this marriage.

-But I ruined it! -He shouted, upsetting the table in front of him, and then walked to the window. -I'm guilty and I'll get there. -He looked at the gallows.

-You have to have faith! -Scarlett replied as she walked beside her husband, then hugged him from behind. -Have faith... -she repeated.

*

-Dr. Garfield! I didn't know you were still here. -She said, colliding with the man in the hallway.

-Your mother-in-law was in critical condition because of her wounds.

-Is it that serious? -She asked anxiously.

-I'd rather call it a hysterical seizure. -He corrected himself- Either way, she'll be fine.

-How much more time does it take to recover?

-Well, the incident happened a week ago. I'll give her another three weeks and we can take the bandages off. The first week and a half are heavier, the wound is blistering with cruel pain, but we will slowly get over this phase. After that, she will still have to wear a blindfold for a while. -He arranged his hat on his head in front of the mirror.

-Can I ask a question?

-I didn't visit your husband. No one other than family members are admitted.

-It wouldn't be about that. How long have you known?

Jerome took a deep breath. -I suspected it when we were teenagers, and then we didn't meet for a while. I moved away, when he came here too, after that we got together more and more.

-Did he tell you?

-No, he would never tell anyone. I found out for myself... -He said sadly then suddenly raised his head- Don't get me wrong, not like that... -Scarlett just nodded.

-It's a good thing you tried to defend him, that you supported him. I guess on Sundays you just came, so I wouldn't suspect it.

Jerome couldn't say anything about that.

-Now, if you'll excuse me... -He said, walking past her, then turned back. -Don't be surprised by what you see upstairs.

*

Scarlett walked to her mother-in-law's room door, where she lay tied up to the bed. In a chair by the bed, Akita read a book aloud. But with reading errors.

-Then the bee-a-are...

-Bear. -Says Mrs. Wolowitz softly- We pronounce it "Ber".

-Then the bear ate a-all th-the ho-ho-honey.

Scarlett closed the door softly so as not to disturb them.

# CHAPTER LV

Scarlett had brought food to Gracewith for the people still living there. She decided she had to go in person so she could occupy herself and divert her thoughts. By the time she got there, she saw the soldiers who were lining up and aiming their guns towards the people living there.

-What do you say, Kwaw, is your life important? You are already in a lot of trouble. -The captain said, looking deep into the man's eyes. -Just testify, tell the judge what your neighbour has done and we will save you and your child's life.

-I have not seen anything! -Kwaw said firmly- Then one of the soldiers knocked him down with his gun, and then the two of them began to punch and kick him. Kwaw's little daughter shouted a few steps away desperately.

-What are you doing? -Scarlett hurried over.

-Nothing for which you should get involved. -The captain said, looking back at the man lying in front of him.

-Given that this is my property and one of my employees is being beaten, I do have a say! -She declared out loud. -Do you have permission to be here? -But she continued not waiting for an answer. -Then get out of here!

The soldiers just looked at each other, Captain Patmore took a contemptuous look at Scarlett, then waved at his soldiers, who had laid down their guns. He looked at them for a while, then turned around and left with his soldiers.

-Are you in one piece? -She asked the man, who was holding his bleeding head. -What did they want?

-To betray you, ma'am. -Said a woman from the background.

Scarlett didn't dare ask what they had done, just looked at the man's bleeding head.

-You don't have to worry, ma'am, we didn't say anything. -Said an older man from the background.

-I will testify regarding your husband on the next day.

-What?

-I will try to prove that he is innocent.

-You can't do that...

-Why not?

-You know why. You have no proof, which means you have to lie.

-Does it matter? Your kind believes anyway that I will rot in hell... -Scarlett was just about to replay something spicy, but she heard something.

-Shipwreck! -Ran a child screaming- Shipwreck.

Everyone raised their heads for this. But they remained motionless.

-It could have food products on it. -Said Kwaw.

-Hurry up fast! -Screamed Scarlett realizing. -Tell the villagers before the soldiers return, bring all the wagons and people who are strong.

*

When they reached the shore, they saw the French flag.

-We have to be careful, if there are any survivors, they could have weapons. -Scarlett said.

Most people saved the cargo, while Kwaw and Scarlett searched the bodies, to make sure if they were dead or alive.

-This one is alive! -Kwaw said, turning him with the toe of his shoe onto his back. -What will we do to him? -The young soldier lay unconscious in the sand. Full of wounds and having difficulty breathing.

-Leave him here. He won't last long. -She said, looking at him and walking on.

-What? You can't do that.

-Of course, I can. Our country is being attacked by these people. My family has been slaughtered and you ask me to save this man?

-Yes. -The man answered seriously- I hated all white people until I got to know you. -Then he stepped closer to the woman. -Maybe I wouldn't have done it before because I only have bad memories of your kind, but now I know not everyone is the same. Nor is he fighting because he feels like that, the government obliges.

-We found a few more French alive! -A woman hurried in front of them, then ran away to help others.

-Kwaw, if they find him on my property, not only I will go to jail for it, but I'll hang for home treason...

-Would you do it for me? -He asked seriously.

-Kwaw...

-I was standing up for you, and I will, always. -He grabbed the woman's hands- Every life matters.

-Ship! Ship in the far distance! -Someone shouted.

-All right. Look for survivors! -Scarlett shouted, then turned back to Kwaw. -You know where the basement is hidden, right? Take them there.

-There's one here too! -Cried a man.

*

A half an hour later, the English soldiers arrived at the shore of Gracewith, where people stumbled drunk and packed the cargo found.

-What's going on here? -Captain Patmore asked as he arrived too with his soldiers on horseback.

The other soldiers arrived in a boat and approached the woman.

-What kind of question is that? -Scarlett asked.

-Don't have fun with me, Mrs. Wolowitz! -He said impatiently, looking at the woman who was lit by the moon.

-I have the right to steal the cargo found on the shore. This beach belongs to Gracewith and from there to Beelove. Owned by my husband. -She pointed over the beach.

-This is true. -A soldier said softly.

-And what's your plan with the products? -The captain of the ship asked as he walked over.

I give it to the starving villagers. They need it more in this misery. -Scarlett replied with a smile.

-And the French soldiers? -The captain asked.

-They're dead, we checked them.

-All of them? -He asked back.

-Whom we looked at, was all of them.

-I'm only interested in one man. Francis Toussaint the ship's captain, son of August Toussaint, who re-launched this war.

-I haven't even heard from him. -Scarlett shrugged.

-We can't find him, Captain. -A soldier arrived who was also examining the corpses.

-Maybe he drowned. -Scarlett gestured with her hands.

-He was a good swimmer. -Captain Patmore says. -Once he swam around lake Geneva.

-I doubt he could do it if he was wounded... -She replied again.

-Is there any chance that he got free?

-Of course, there is. But not in our presence. -The woman answered- We found the shore as how it is now. -Then they all looked along the beach. -Except that there were more objects lying here and there then.

-Inspect the houses and all the buildings around the shore, all the places where they can be! -The captain of the ship gave the order.

Scarlett went to Gracewith with them, where the house was inspected first, then the hay-barn.

-What are the gentlemen looking for? -Kwaw asked, jumping down from the rung he was sitting on. The captain frowned, then looked at the elderly and children present.

-They have to be here! Search every nook and cranny! -The captain shouted, then turned to Kwaw. -Why isn't a strong man like you at the beach?

There was a silence for a while, then an older woman stepped forward, grabbed the man's shoulder, and looked at the soldiers stabbing the haystack with their guns.

-You know, the poor boy has a soft brain. -Then looked at Kwaw. -Requires constant attention.

Kwaw looked after Captain Patmore, who was far away approaching from Gracewith's house. He turned his head to the side and spoke.

-Why are you lying on a side?

The captain looked at Scarlett first, then at the old woman.

-You know, a mother's life with such a boy is not easy...

-All clean! -The soldiers shouted.

The captain gestured, taking another look at Scarlett, and they left. Once they were sure the soldiers were far enough away, people started packing their haystacks into another set. After removing the appropriate amount, the trapdoor was opened. Scarlett and Kwaw looked at each other, then both climbed down. They were able to rescue five soldiers, two of them were in critical condition, one was a fuller older soldier with a white moustache and the other had a similar age as Leonard, same height and body structure.

-Who are you? -Asked the youngest, with a French accent.

-Your guardian angels. -Kwaw answered.

-We bring food and bandage, just stay here. -Scarlett looked at the young man with several badges- Francis Toussaint himself, right?

-Yes. -He said weakly.

-You have to promise that you stay here until the danger will pass. Can you do that? -The man just nodded.

# CHAPTER LVI

-I would call the two soldiers to the stage, who were present at the scene at 7:10 that evening. -Said the speaker of the court.

-Could you please tell me what you saw that evening? -The barrister asked his question.

-We can't say anything other than what Captain Patmore had said. -One of them spoke up.

-Do you want us to repeat it? -The other asked.

The Speaker of the court brought the Bible in front of them, and they both laid their hands on it.

-Do thee swear, in the name of the Father, Son, and the Holy Spirit, that everything you saw is the same as Captain Patmore's testimony, and not a single word, no dot, no comma differs?

-We'll swear! -They said at once.

-I'd like Thomas Kwaw to come to the stage. -The judge said.

Kwaw walked up, then took his place to testify.

-Mr. Kwaw, would tell us why are you here today? Why did you volunteer to testify?

-Good afternoon, Your Honour! -He spoke politely- I came here, to confront you because I am convinced that Mr. Wolowitz is innocent in this matter. -He declared, for the people's surprise.

-Why would you be so sure? -The barrister asked.

-Ergon Wendoz was my neighbour, although Mr. Wolowitz visited him, sometimes. They always remained outside the house, did not enter, and did not spend much time, their meeting was always in the public. You also need to know that Captain Patmore visited me the other day, pointing a gun at me and my child.

-Why would he have done that? -The barrister asked.

-He wanted me to lie at the court, to say things that aren't true about these two men. He threatened me with death, as he did with my child. -By the time there was another noise in the room.

-He threatened... -Scarlett said to herself.

- Order! -The judge hit his gavel.

-We can't believe this man. -The barrister said, this is slander that could involve hanging.

-Slander... -Scarlett said again as she caught Evelyn's attention.

-Are you well, my dear? -She asked.

-Whatever this man claims we can't take into account. -Said the lawyer.

-Why because I am not a rich, influential person? -He jumped out of his chair- Or because I'm black?

Then George also got up from his seat so he could speak.

-I see no reason for this man to risk his life and toss in words that would affect his child. After all, who would endanger their own child's life? Thanks! -Took his space again.

-Mr. Wolowitz is a good man! He saved my daughter's life. -For this sentence George caught after his head, knowing the danger Kwaw was dragging with it after him.

It became another confusion.

-Order! Order!

-Threat, slander, threat, slander... -She said to herself, then got up from her seat- Let me say a few words.

The judge just gestured to her after Kwaw was removed from the chair, Scarlett occupied it.

-I know it's not my turn. But you need to know something. -She said.

-Just be quick, Mrs. Wolowitz. -Lord Quas, the judge said.

-Captain Patmore showed up in my husband's absence, more precisely when he was on a business trip. Threatened with a letter, more specifically a letter from Elsa O'Neil. Mr. Kwaw is not the first person to be slandered, so he can be released. -She said, looking at the man in the soldiers' arms. -He said that whatever my husband's secret is, he will reveal and take care of it.

-As we know, Elsa O'Neil was Captain Patmore's niece! -George stood up again.

-Sit down, Mr. Salvatore. -The judge said.

-Yes, she was. -Scarlett said, unaware of the matter. -He's been determined to see my husband in a cell for a long time, but all the more so on gallows.

-Is that all you want to say? -The judge asked.

Scarlett looked around. -Yes!

-The sitting is suspended! -He said beating the gravel again. -In the next session, Captain Patmore will be asked to approach the stage again, asking for the maids working in the house and then the gentleman's mother.

After leaving the room, George hurried after Scarlett.

-What was that good for? Do you think it was a good idea?

-No. But I have to gain time until I figure something out. -She replied.

-Mrs. Wolowitz! -He said, taking her arm- I have to tell you something. I know about your husband's secret. -He said seriously.

-What? How? -She didn't even know how to start with her questions.

-Once, more precisely, at a ball. I saw him with a man, but it was a long time ago.

-And he knows about it? -She inquired in surprise.

-Yes!

-You never told me.

-You never wanted to hear me out.

-I didn't understand for a very long time what my mother-in-law said at our first meeting that this was a marriage of convenience for both parties. I understand now. -She said thoughtfully in a sad way- Why do you help then?

-I do everything for you. -He said as he stepped closer to her- Everything, Scarlett. For your protection, but if I knew that paying your debts wouldn't help... I would have done things differently.

-Are you saying that you were the generous donor? -She was surprised- I have to go now... -She said, pushing the man away from her, then hurried away.

# CHAPTER LVII

Scarlett hurried to the soldiers in the basement, when she arrived saw the trapdoor was wide open. The elders there, who were unable to work, just shook their head and gestured wordlessly that they don't know where they went. Scarlett ran out in search of the French soldiers but didn't have to go far, she found Francis Toussaint washing at the well behind the hay barn.

-Did you miss me already? -He asked in his own charming way.

-You shouldn't be here, they can see. -She said angrily.

-I'm sorry I dared to come out from the rat hole for a minute... Where we've been kept in the dark for days. -He said, turning to Scarlett. She was ashamed of herself, but she could not deny that she found the man attractive, especially half-naked.

-Soldiers can still search for you. -She tried to look away, but she kept feeling compelled to glance, so her eyes were like a pendulum clock. -Not only you, but you can endanger everyone.

-How long do you want me to hide here? We've been here for more than a week... One of my soldiers is so sick that I don't even know in which hour he will die...

-Just as long as necessary. Until I find a way to get rid of you safely and secretly with your people.

-What's going on here? -A voice asked from the background.

-It seems Madam it won't be a secret after all. -He whispered to Scarlett, leaning over and walking on.

-Mr. Salvatore... -She said, reaching for her head.

After explaining everything, George was unable to say a word at first, and then was unable to stop arguing with her.

-How could you do that? Do you know what all this means? How endangered you are... Your employee, your family, but most of all you...

-I am aware of. -Scarlett said, closing the subject, at least trying.

-I can't believe you did that and what if everyone will be executed during the night?

-Injured, sick soldiers. They are incapable of doing so. And what could they do anyway, there are hardly a few men in Gracewith and Beelove, most of them are seniors, women, and children.

-You haven't seen a single war in your life, you only live in the stories of your novels. Where everything is beautiful and good. But real life is far from that. They don't care about them. Why do you think your mother and sister were killed?

-How can you say that? -Scarlett asked upset.

-You can't see the wood from the tree, Mrs. Wolowitz. Wake up at last! -The man quarrelled with her.

Annoyed, Scarlett left George alone in Gracewith and returned to Beelove. She walked angrily down the hall, until Mowie's request to stop.

-Ma'am... Forgive me, I'll only bother you for a minute.

-Yes, of course. -She said, covering her emotions.

-The trial is tomorrow, we've been notified... Uhm, that we have to attend... Tell me, what do you want us to say at the court?

Scarlett just stood silently in front of him, then realizing that tomorrow would be another day when they will try to prove her husband's guilt. She felt like she couldn't breathe as if her throat was tight, she fell to the ground instantly. It was as if she had just been hit by everything. She felt everything was ruined, her marriage, her family, her life. She just sat there, leaning weakly against the wall, gasping for air. Doris showed up at a moment as she began to wipe the woman's foaming mouth, stroking and reassuring her confidently. For Scarlett, Doris was like oxygen underwater, whenever she felt drowning, it was Doris who exhale life into it.

-I'm here, ma'am! I'm here! Everything will be fine. -Hugged and caressed- My dear, I am proud of you and you should be too, for getting through all the storms that failed to crush you. -She raked hugging her. When Scarlett got air again, she looked at Doris- Flow like the water and you will find your way through any rock.

# CHAPTER LVIII

The day has come for another trial. Where all the workers at the Wolowitz House were interrogated. First, Mowie was called, who looked at his mistress before his confession, Scarlett with an encouraging, albeit forced a smile. Mrs. Agatha Wolowitz was also present, sitting not far from Scarlett, holding the child's, Akita's, hand tightly, (known as Allan) when she heard the speaker of court speak, announcing the case and the arrival of the guilty Leonard, her grip tightened. She didn't see, but she could feel the tension in the air, she could hear the clanging of the chains and the deep breaths, she knew her son wasn't showing his fear, but he was just as terrified as she was.

-Mr. Albert Mowie, the well-known butler himself, who runs Beelove's house.

-That's right! -The man replied.

-Did you have any suspicions about the man's double life? -The barrister asked.

-No, sir. I was busy running the house and running everything else perfectly as you knew the Wolowitz family is a very system-loving family.

-Have you noticed anything unusual in the couple's life? Were there any indications that the couple did not interact at all?

-I knew Mr. Wolowitz travels a lot on business matters and regularly he is out of the house, I always came to the conclusion that it was all about the honey industry.

-Thank you, Mr. Mowie! -The judge said.

The speaker of the court spoke again: -Since not all of the maids have arrived, I would call Captain Patmore on stage.

-Captain, do you have any explanation for the allegations made by Mr. Thomas Kwaw and Mrs. Scarlett Miranda Wolowitz? -The barrister asked.

-I brought the letter from my niece, Mrs. Elsa Wolowitz, alias O'Neil, which she wrote to her sister, Mrs. Winnifred Salvatore, alias O'Neil, before her death.

-Would you please read aloud this letter so we can continue to pass judgment?

The man stood up and then began to read the letter aloud. After reading it all the way, he wiped his eyes and then sat back down.

-The man has a specific secret. Which is also referred to, by his wife, who died suddenly, shortly after the discovery of her husband's secret that evening. This proves nothing more than the murder of Mrs. Wolowitz; This man killed his wife so that no one else would know the secret.

-Mr. Leonard Robert Wolowitz, do you have anything to add? -The judge asked, looking at the man who was shaking, leaning against the railing, and looking down, no one knew where his mind was at that very moment, but he certainly was not in this world, somewhere far from hearing the man speaking.

-I have! -George stood up.

-I'm protesting! -Cried the captain.

-Objection overruled! -The judge said, banging with his gavel.

-As you know, Winnifred was Elsa Wolowitz's sister and my wife. I would like to inform you, although the letter did not reach her, they maintained a good relationship. The two girls told each other everything, my wife, God rest her soul, never complained about the mistreatment of her sister. Nor as described in the letter.

-The man still has secrets; he never touched his wife because he was attracted to his own gender! -The captain shouted, causing another noise in the room.

-Order! -Lord Quas shouted.

-Let me speak, not as a man's friend, but as his doctor! -Jerome stood up.

-Sustained! -The judge said- Mrs. Agatha Wolowitz, please come to the stage!

Akita led the woman to the chair and then took a seat not far from her.

-Thank you, Allan! -She said softly.

-Mrs. Wolowitz, I only ask one question. Did you know about your son's illness? -The lawyer asked, turning to the blindfolded woman, she was unable to speak, there was silence.

Scarlett began to say to herself, "Just be strong now! There is only one question...", Evelyn took the hand of her troubled friend, who began to squeeze it. Agatha was unable to answer when the lawyer asked her again, she began to tremble and burst into a strong cry.

-That was a clear answer! -Said the barrister.

Akita led his mistress from there. She was then replaced in turn by footmen, cooks, kitchen maids, and other kinds of servants, who all gave ambiguous answers. Most talked about the disappointment and danger they had experienced regarding Daphne, citing it as an interesting thing they had experienced in the house, others mentioned Marta as well. At a time, one of the young maids was called to the interrogation chair, who started working at the time when Scarlett first came into the house.

-Tell me, Miss. Adele Winter, if I'm not mistaken. There was anything you found strange about the couple's relationship. -This maid was the only one who was asked this question, so she didn't know how to answer it, she knew the truth was the purest thing.

-Well, as a matter of fact, the mistress and the gentleman sleep in a separate bedroom. Except for the wedding night. It was the only time Mrs. Wolowitz spent the night in her husband's room.

-This is another affirmative response to Mrs. Elsa Wolowitz's letter that her husband did not touch her at any time, which I suspect he did not do to her second wife either. -Said the lawyer, turning to the council.

People started talking again and insulting Leonard loudly until the little hammer knocked on the table again.

-Oh, no. I was the one who changed the bedding the next day. My mistress was bleeding after the honeymoon. -She added.

-That's not proof, my lord! -Said the barrister- It could have been animal blood, paint, or even a trace of fruit or vegetables.

-Why would they have done that? -The maid asked.

-So that workers in the house did not suspect that their wedding night was not consummated. In other words, the honeymoon didn't reach the marital. -The lawyer said again, making another noise.

-There's no evidence of that! -Scarlett shouted.

-Order! Order!

The lawyer turned to the woman again.

-Have you ever seen this man in the house? -He pointed to Ergon, Leonard's lover.

-I've never seen him in the house before.

-But somewhere, -he said, inferring from the woman's words- I'd like you to tell me where.

She took a deep breath and said softly what she saw.

-He's been on the estate a long time ago. Where he approached my brother, in a way. -She said, ashamed.

-Is your brother here? -The woman nodded- Where? -Then she pointed among those present.

-I'd ask Mr. Winter to come in front of the court. -The judge said as the man swapped places with his sister. He was young and very upset, afraid of the consequences.

-Tell me, Mr. Winter. Are your sister's claims true? -The barrister asked.

-They are true. -The man replied shyly.

-Would you tell us what happened?

-I was working among the bees when he showed up behind me unexpectedly. He said he was looking for Mr. Wolowitz, but he was out of the house, so he decided to look around on the estate. He walked behind me and kept praising me.

-What did he say?

-He said... He said, I was attractive in shape, he also praised my work, my strength in lifting buckets full of honey... He also said, well... -The boy scratched his forehead in confusion- That he would love to see me without clothes. After that... –But he paused, afraid to tell the truth.

-What happened next?

-He grabbed my lower half. -He said, completely blushed.

-And what did you do?

-I pushed him away and then hurried into the house, fearing that he would come after me and dare to harass me.

Scarlett raised her hands in front of her face, afraid to see her husband's reaction.

-I would ask Mr. Ergon Wendoz to stand up, the court will make a verdict, returning shortly with the answer. -Then the trial jury withdrew. She finally looked at her husband, who was watching his beloved partner in despair. They returned soon after -Have you reached the verdict?

-We have, my Lord. -One of the parties stood up.

-Do you find Mr. Ergon Wendoz guilty or not guilty?

-Guilty, my Lord! -He declared, as Ergon crashed to the ground and began to cry loudly.

-Do you wish to make a final statement Mr. Ergon? -But the man just cried lying on the ground.

Lord Norman Quas put the black cap on his white wig over his head and then said it out loud.

-This man, standing before us, called by his name Ergon Wendoz. You be taken to a place of execution, there you will be hanged by the neck, until you are dead.

Ergon was very difficult to remove from the room, the soldiers first had to prise him off the floor to be able to pull him straight back into his cell, from where he could just leave for execution the next day. Leonard held on very tightly, though inside he was completely shattered, yet he didn't show what he was feeling, but his grip tightened on the barrier.

-I close the meeting. Next time, I will question three people in court, Dr. Jerome Garfield, the defendant's doctor, Mrs. Scarlett Miranda Wolowitz, his wife, and Mr. Leonard Robert Wolowitz, the defendant himself.

After the trial, Scarlett hurried to the doctor, where he changed Agatha Wolowitz's bandage.

-...and I'd ask you, Mrs. Wolowitz now, I know it's not easy, but try not to cry. -Jerome told the old woman.

-Dr. Garfield, can we talk for a second? -Jerome stood up, entrusted Akita to take care of his mistress, and hurried to Scarlett.

-Now what? -She asked in dismay.

-Mrs. Wolowitz, please calm down. I can't say everything will be fine, as I don't know. All I can advise is to keep a cool head, the most important thing is to stay calm. We must not show our fear.

Scarlett sniffed, then nodded in agreement. George walked past them, then saw in the arms of Jerome the woman he loved.

# CHAPTER LIX

-My darling, you have to calm down. -Evelyn told her kindly, pulling her head over her shoulder, at this moment her husband entered, who, as soon as he saw the red-haired woman, turned around on his heels and was about to leave.

-Norman! -Called his wife.

-No! Whatever you want to say, no! -Her husband said aloud.

-You have to listen to Scarlett.

-I cannot do. -He said seriously- You know, I cannot.

-Just listen! -She said firmly. Then the man walked over and sat down next to them.

-I warn you that if you try to manipulate or speak out against the law, I will accuse you of contempt of court and breaking the law, which can lead to severe imprisonment.

-Sir, I just want to report that my husband testified about his wife's death. What happened after a dispute, Leonard pushed Elsa, but it was an accident. My husband would never have hurt Elsa.

-Why are you telling me all this?

-I hope that a murder charge will not arise regarding my husband's act.

-There is a chance for it... -He said as he watched his wife take deep breaths. -But now the situation is more serious, there is evidence of your husband's guilt, eyewitnesses say what happened.

-But you can surely do something regarding... -But their fierce start was interrupted.

-Ma'am, please understand that there is nothing I can do. -The man shouted- Don't even try to... -But his wife, who was in such pain, shouted too loud, so he wasn't heard out. The man ran to ring the bell. -Someone, call a doctor! -He shouted.

*

-Where is the doctor? We've been waiting for him for hours! -Lord Quas asked angrily, walking up and down the hall.

-Dr. Bing is here. -The butler announced. The doctor hurried to the room, where Lady Evelyn was in labour under Scarlett's supervision.

-Dr. Bing... -She said weakly.

The man examined her and then left to exchange a few words with Lord Quas.

-Scarlett! -She sat up weakly- My dear friend... Promise me, if I won't be here, you will still be the godmother of my child.

-Don't say that... -She wiped her friend's sweaty face with a damp cloth.

-Damn, I'm so big! As a hippo... You can't believe how much under my ribs hurts, my ankles are swelling like they will bursts, and my head aches like hell I can't even see clearly, it is like everything is covered by mist. Honestly, I cannot recommend it to anyone. -She said as she got her hand to her mouth. -Forgive me, I didn't mean like that.

-No problem. -She reassured her- I'm starting to get used to the idea that I will never have a child.

-You're not saying that now because your husband is in prison, right?

-No... -Scarlett said in despair.

-You've never been together, have you? -She asked in the midst of suffering.

Scarlett just nodded silently, a nurse walked into the room, Scarlett stood up and kissed her on the forehead. -Now I'm leaving you alone, try to relax a little. -Then she left.

In the hallway, she collided with Dr. Bing and Lord Quas. Where later, Mr. Salvatore also joined by accident, unaware of what had happened.

-I am sorry. I didn't know Lady Quas... -He tried to find the right word, but he couldn't -Do you want me to leave?

-No. Just stay my friend. I'd be happy to have you here when it happens. I'd be happy to share my joy.

-Dr. Bing, what was your diagnosis?

-Everything is fine. The baby is on the way to childbirth. -The man replied calmly.

-By "everything" you mean for her age? I mean, others have normal pains as a strong young woman, but Lady Quas has a very hard time bearing it. -The man didn't answer just looked. -Would you allow me to call Dr. Jerome Garfield here? He is an expert and yet it would be better to have two doctors present.

-Lady Quas is perfectly fine, I see no complications here. Yet what's needed here, Mrs. Wolowitz, is knowledge of childbirth, he doesn't have to come here as a decoration.

-I still believe the presence of two doctors does not affect. Does it?
-Then the doctor looked at Lord Quas, who seemed to support Scarlett's idea.

-If it makes you reassured, of course, I have no objection. -He said with a grimace.

*

-Dr. Bing thinks the room would be too crowded. -Scarlett said, looking at George, who walked into the room wordlessly, then looked at his glass and took a sip.

-Has Dr. Garfield arrived yet?

-Yes, he is examining Evelyn. -She replied briefly, then silence settled between them for almost a full minute until the man spoke again.

-About what happened last time...

-Don't apologise, -she said, turning the glass in her hands- you were right, I did a very dangerous thing.

-If they find the French soldiers, which I've heard they're looking for, they're not only sentencing your husband to death, but you will be threatened with treason, which I think you know what consequences drag with it... -Scarlett took another sip from her glass.

-You know, we don't have to act like enemies, at least as long as we're here, don't resent each other.

-Isn't it still be a better idea to leave Dr. Garfield out of all this? -A voice came into the room- Yet he is so young and inexperienced. -Said Lord Quas.

-I think it's safer. -George said, raising his glass.

-You don't just think that because this woman's opinions matter a lot to you? -He pointed to Scarlett, who took it a little offended.

-Aren't you just afraid you'll be indebted to one of Mr. Wolowitz's friends?

Lord Quas could not answer this, even if he wanted to, as the two doctors arrived in the room arguing, not knowing that they had company. They were so engrossed that they didn't even look around in the room.

-Dr. Bing you have to understand me. It is most likely that she may be endangered by eclampsia. This means we must act as quickly as we can.

-I will say for the thousandth time, calm down doctor. There is no danger. Taking my experience into consideration, Lady Evelyn is perfectly fine, she is behaving normally.

-You don't consider the baby too tiny, smaller than a normal one?

-No, I haven't. And don't even ask me about the bloating of her body parts, because I saw how you examined her. She has thick ankles and big hands, that's all. Many women have. Look, doctor, people differ, we are not the same, some of us are thinner, some of us are plumper. Childbirth differs as well, some of them make it easier, some of them have more pain. So, as for the children, I saw so many babies born at only 2,000 grams and less, and I saw above 4,000 grams as well.

-Considering her body structure and knowing her since before she was with a child. She does not have a problem. And what about her eyesight? She says she can't see clear!

-For God's sake. She is in labour! Of course, she can't see clearly. The pain takes away her attention from everything. In case you still wish to stay until the baby will arrive. You must stay silent! This is the first and last warning!

-What is going on? -Lord Quas intervened.

-Nothing is going on. -Said Dr. Bing.

-There is something you must know Lord Quas...

-There is nothing to be told. -Dr. Bing reassured.

-Then give me the latest sample of her urine, I have to test it.

-For God's sake...

-Give him the sample. -Lord Quas said- To give him the chance to calm down.

*

-Another hour has passed... -Scarlett said

-It'll be over soon. -Said, George.

-I've been here since this morning; it's been almost 12 hours since she went into labour... -Scarlett worried -I need to see her. -She bounced up and went toward the woman's room, where Jerome was also present.

-How is the mommy? -She asked as she walked to the woman's bed, but Evelyn couldn't answer, she was just staring at the ceiling in pain, stroking her tummy, and trying to control her emotions.

Then Jerome walked past them.

-It'd be better to leave now. -He told Scarlett, who got up sadly from the bed.

-Am I all right, Dr. Garfield? -Evelyn asked, but the doctor stared at her in confusion -I don't feel like if I was fine, I wouldn't be lying here right now then.

-You are absolutely fine. -The doctor said reassuring the woman, who probably hadn't heard the man because of her moaning and hyperventilating. Evelyn soon after the conversation with the doctor started vomiting, Jerome handed her a bucket and stroked her back. As he walked out, he hurried straight to Lord Quas, where Dr. Bing had already overtaken him. -Your wife is not fine. -He said nervously. -I hold on to the belief that Lady Quas is in danger of eclampsia.

-What are you talking about? -Lord Quas asked.

-A very rare disease. -Dr. Bing said in a low voice, looking at Dr. Garfield in front of him as if a court fool were standing in front of them.

-From which she is definitely not suffering. Eclampsia affects around one in every 200 women with preeclampsia. (one in 2,000-3,000 pregnancies). The condition follows a high blood pressure disorder called preeclampsia. She can't be that one.

-She is confused with bad eyesight, she even vomited, and the baby is a tiny mite, smaller than a normal baby. -Declared Dr. Garfield- And in her urine, I found too much albumen, (protein). The fact is, we must act fast.

-Which means? -Lord Quas asked.

-The hospital... -He said softly- We must take her there. The baby has to be delivered by caesarean section.

-Are you insane? You are not thinking about the risk that should come with it? -Dr. Bing quarrelled.

-Isn't that safe? -Scarlett asked.

-Would you be able to expose a mother and her unborn child to such a risk? In a public hospital... there is a big chance that she could pick up any kind of infection.

-Don't you understand that this is our only chance in this situation? This is the appropriate thing, the only possibility to avoid seizures caused by the trauma of natural birth.

-Even if she would be at risk of eclampsia... Caesarean is too risky. It could kill any of them or in worse cases both of them.

-Why don't you let Lord Quas decide? -Scarlett interrupted.

-Could you guarantee that both of them will survive? -He asked desperately.

-No. But if she stays, she will surely die. If you hesitate, the chance will flow away, we should be already on our way.

They heard a loud moan by the time the debate was interrupted. Everyone ran to Evelyn's room. The two doctors went in, the others were waiting outside. Shortly afterward, Dr. Bing opened the door, wiping his hands.

-A daughter was born! -He declared happily.

Everyone walked cheerfully into the room greeting the child. Jerome watched the phenomenon from the other end of the room. Lord Quas happily took his child in his arms, though he felt like a grandfather by her side, it could be said from his expression that he was the happiest "grandfather".

*

After everyone went their room to spend the night there. People went to rest. In the middle of the night, on the edge of Scarlett's bed George sat, he shook Scarlett's shoulder, and dragged her out from the most beautiful dream into reality.

-Wake up! Wake up! It's about Lady Quas...

After that, they too hurried to the woman's room, where she was writhing in bed complaining of a severe headache. She began to pound her head and shouted loudly how much it hurt. The bed was surrounded by all five of them.

-Do something! -Lord Quas shouted, but the two men stood helplessly next to the woman's bed and watched the process.

-My head... My head... it is soo... Ahhh... -She screamed as almost the walls began to tremble.

-What's happening? -Scarlett asked desperately.

-This is eclampsia... -Dr. Garfield said.

-Why aren't you doing something? -He asked, clutching the hand of his wife, who continued to wrestle.

-I'm afraid it's too late... -Jerome said.

Dr. Bing stood silently by the bed. Evelyn began to gasp and then tried to speak, but not a single voice came out of her throat.

-Dear, just stay with me! Stay with me! -He kissed his wife's hand.

Evelyn just yawned like a fish, but was unable to make a sound. Suddenly her neck twitched and she pushed her head deep into the pillow, while she continued to writhe with the rest of her body.

-It's like... -Scarlett said.

-She cannot breathe... -George finished.

-Dr. Garfield! Please! -Lord Quas pleaded crying.

-I'm so sorry... -He said sympathetically.

She growled for a while and gasped for air. It was like a fish thrown ashore. Her neck veins were strained, her face completely reddened. Then in a sudden moment, the chaos was over. Her body relaxed and she fell lifeless on the bed. It was like a stove that blushes from the heat from a moment to the next and then suddenly loses its colour due to the extinguished flame. Her body was snow-white and her temperature gradually cooled. The baby cried out loud feeling her mother's death, her crying was much more bitter than that of any new-born.

-Not my love! Please breathe! -He said as he leans on his wife's body crying, saying softly- Breathe! Breathe...

# CHAPTER LX

They sat in the salon in the morning, waiting for Lord Quas to leave his wife's room and join them. Everyone was there, except Dr. Bing, who left in a hurry after the death of Lady Evelyn Quas. Soon Lord Quas walked into the room, holding his child tightly in his arms, his eyes crying red and he was still in his pyjamas.

-Lord Quas, if there's anything we can do for you... -Scarlett said, but she was interrupted.

-Evelyn was the most beautiful, wonderful, and kindest woman I have ever known, I can proudly say that I was honoured to call her, my wife.

-What will be her name? -George asked.

-My dearest wife wanted Mrs. Wolowitz to be the child's godmother. Which I strongly opposed. I never understood why she insists so much on it. -He said looking at Scarlett, whose expression had become even sadder. -Until now. Mrs. Wolowitz, you have been a very good friend to her, and the only one since I knew her, you have been here by her side all along. We would be honoured to have you as our child's godmother. Will you accept this position? -Scarlett nodded in surprise. -As one of our family's dearest friends and my child's godmother, would you name her?

At this sad moment, Scarlett did not know how to cover her happiness so as not to offend Lord Quas, who has exposed her to this great task.

-What about Beatrice?

-Beatrice... -He mumbled, then smiled at Scarlett. -I love it. -Looked at her baby and said while babbling. -Hello, little Beatrice Evelyn Quas!

-Lord Quas, if you'll excuse me, I have to go. -Jerome stood up.

-I have to tell you, Dr. Garfield, despite your young age, I admire your talent. I would like to ask you to be the new family doctor for the Quas family, if you accept.

-I am honoured. -He said, shaking hands with the man, then left.

-Norman, if you have a moment. -He aimed for a two-person conversation with the man.

The broken man handed the baby to Scarlett, then left with George. They returned a few minutes later, but it was as if the host was not the same, as if he had become much more free. It was as if a stone had fallen from his heart.

-The funeral will be on Friday at 10:00 a.m.

But Scarlett and George said nothing. Scarlett handed the child over and then they were about to leave.

-Mrs. Wolowitz, you need to know something. -He said after her, for which they both stopped.

-After the next trial, as a result of the maid's confession and the letter... The members decided... -He didn't know how to express himself. -Of course, we'll take your testimony into account... But considering you only got married once and you're so young...

-What are you saying? -Scarlett asked impatiently.

-They have never seen you with a man after your marriage. If you say at the court that your wedding night was consummated, we will have to make sure, so it is mandatory for a midwife to examine you.

-How? You can't do that. - George became nervous- Is there anything I can do?

-I am sorry George, you can't do anything as an observer, only if you improve your testimony, but the verdict will be the same. Everything proves against the accused; the court is sure that it was not finalized. Of course, if you admit it, and tell them that nothing happened, no one will examine you.

-Can't this be avoided somehow? Is so humiliating. -Scarlett asked desperately.

-I'm afraid my hands are tied. I can't do more for you.

Scarlett looked at the man understandingly and then left. George was right at her heels.

-Scarlett, wait! -He shouted after her from the distance.

-Mr. Salvatore... I didn't notice you. -She wiped her eyes -What did you tell Lord Quas that he had become so calm.

-Just my experience of when my wife died. I told him I sympathized deeply but he has to be strong for his daughter. I also told him what helped me get over it.

-And what was that? -She asked, hurrying.

-The love. -He grabbed her arm as Scarlett stopped, then slowly began to pull toward him. -I thought more and more about the person I love the most.

-You suggested thinking of his daughter...

-Yes. -The man replied briefly, then leaned closer and closer to the woman in front of him until their foreheads met. -I thought of you, Scarlett.

Scarlett felt that she never heard kinder words before, but she couldn't think of anything other than the next trial. She pushed the man away from her, then walked away. -I'm sorry!

-What did I say wrong? -He asked, walking after her.

-You didn't do anything. Only in the present situation, I am unable to think of anything other than a trial.

-What are you afraid of? The maid testified that she found blood. You have nothing to fear.

-Oh, Mr. Salvatore... -She cried.

-You want to say, that you...

-No, no... it didn't happen. Don't you feel the weight of the consequences? If I confess it happened and the midwife examines me...

-You endanger yourself with this.

-But I wouldn't be able to say we didn't. That my husband never approached me and that he never touched me. I have to save him... -She stepped closer.

-What do you want to do? -The man asked, afraid of the woman's answer.

-I can't do anything else... -Scarlett cried.

-But you can't just give yourself to a complete stranger.

Scarlett was thoughtfully for a moment, then wiped her tears and become serious.

-No, not to a complete stranger. -She said, looking at the man, who frowned at first and then looked at her with widened eyes.

-No, we can't... -George started to object.

-Please, didn't you say you loved me and you would do anything for me? Don't you want me? -Scarlett asked, walking toward the man backing away from her.

-Yes, of course. But...

-Don't you understand? If it turns out that my husband is guilty, I will be sealed forever and no one will ever want to marry me... I will not remarry and people will point at me with their fingers.

\*

After a few hours, Scarlett got home, but she felt she had to take another walk before she got home to clear her thoughts. When she arrived, she opened the parlour door and looked in, where Mrs. Wolowitz was sitting on the floor with Akita playing with the dog.

-Harold is my dearest friend, he has never let me down. -She said, stroking her dog- I wish I could see him again...

-You will! -Akita replied- I'm sure you will, just have faith.

Agatha began stroking the child's face. -I hope you're right, dear Allan.

Scarlett walked on, in silence. After meeting Doris, she asked for a hot bath. After a few hours, she lay speechless in the tub, hoping the hot water would suck out all her negative thoughts, so she just lay there and tried to think of nothing. After a while, as the sun went down almost completely and the room became dim, Doris entered the door.

-Forgive me, ma'am, I had to ask Emanuela to take care of the kids. -She said in a hurry to light the candles, but there was no answer from Scarlett. Then she went there and saw how hot the woman's water was. -It starts cooling off, I'll get some more hot water. -Then she started for the door.

-Doris, I have something to say.

-Yes, Ma'am. -She walked back from the door.

-I found out that after my confession, a midwife would examine me to make sure my answer was true...

-Why would they do that if you say that you didn't sleep with your husband? -Scarlett then glanced at the flames in the fireplace, from which Doris deduced the answer. -You want to say that, right?

-There's only one solution, but I'll need your help.

-You mean... to be with another man? -Doris was surprised.

-That's the only thing I can do to save him...

-This is out of the question! -She jumped up from next to the woman's tub.

-Doris, you have to understand...

-You are insane. No, ma'am. I can't let you do that and if you cannot handle the truth then don't ask others to be honest with you.

-Doris, this is about me, too. If it turns out my husband is guilty. There will never be a good future waiting for me, wherever I go they will not accept me.

Doris just sighed.

*

517

A few hours later, when the household was at rest, Doris hurried to the back door, also known as the maid's entrance. She waited outside for a while, but it was too cold, so she went in. Soon after, someone started knocking.

-Shh... Everyone will jump out of bed, are you completely out of your mind? -She asked the man in front of her, then let him in. -And be clear with the fact, because I'm helping doesn't mean I think it's less of a bad idea. In fact, it's a complete lunatic idea, I'm against this little alliance.

She led him to Scarlett's room, where she nervously waited for the man to arrive. She was sitting on the edge of the bed, playing with her fingers clasped.

-Ma'am, he's here. -Doris declared.

-Let him in. -Scarlett replied, getting up from the bed.

A few seconds later, George entered the door. At first, he just stayed with opened mouth, he didn't know what to say, and then he finally spoke.

-You look wonderful tonight.

Scarlett smiled only forcefully, then stepped closer to the man, who took off his coat and hat, which he then threw on the armchair. She grabbed his hand and pulled him close, leaned close, and kissed him on the cheek.

-Thank you for coming! -She said, whispering softly in his ear.

George was just as embarrassed as the woman in front of him, he didn't know where to start, even though it wasn't the first time he'd been with a woman. Scarlett swallowed deep, then slowly began to undress the man. She began to unbutton his vest, one by one. George took a deep breath and looked straight at the bed through Scarlett, hoping it would help him relax. After taking the vest off the man, she slowly began to pull his shirt out of his pants, leaning closer, she aimed at George's neck, which she covered with the kisses of her soft lips. George then took another deep breath and looked at the ceiling, his skin completely engulfed in goosebumps, he didn't need much time for the man's instincts to start. As soon as Scarlett reached under his abdominal part to pull out his shirt, George picked up the woman in front of him and threw her on the bed. He took off his shirt, which he threw to the floor with quick movements, then tore open the woman's silk nightgown with full force, which opened entirely on her upper body, scattering the buttons to every corner of the bedroom. George leaned closer, feeling Scarlett's temperature rise. He gently kissed the rose-scented woman's skin, starting from her neck, then gently slid lower and lower, caressing her with his hands. Scarlett felt like being in a completely different world, far away from her problems, excluding everything that happened around her and focused only on one thing, George. George reached for her breasts, stroked them gently, then slid down again. Scarlett took deep breaths, more and more often, feeling the man's touch was tickling her body, but in a completely pleasant way. Until suddenly it stopped. Scarlett sat up, closing her nightgown in front of her.

-Don't be mad... -He said all sweaty- But I can't.

-But the trial will be tomorrow morning. -She said, a little confused.

-I know. -The man replied sadly.

-I thought you wished for it. I thought I was the one you wanted. I'm here now and you can have me. -She pointed at herself.

-But at what price?

# CHAPTER LXI

Scarlett visited her husband in the cell the morning before the trial. Leonard had climbed onto his bed to see out of the little window. When he heard the cell door open, he turned and climbed down to his wife.

-Scarlett, honey! -He grabbed his wife's hands. -I thought I'd see you only at the trial. You can't imagine how happy I am to see you here. -Tears welled up in his eyes.

-I have to tell you something. -Then she looked at the soldier, who walked on and then started slamming with his gun the cells and insulting the French soldiers inside. -After my confession, a midwife will examine me, I brought some money to see if I can bribe her...

-Scarlett... -He tried to silence his wife.

-I didn't dare go to the bank, but I found some at home, not too much. But I added a string of pearls I received from my sister.

-Scarlett! -He said firmly this time. -Please don't do anything stupid.

-But this may save you... -She said softly.

-I'm not asking you to lie for me. Look at me... -He raised her face towards him- You've already done a lot for me. -The woman was silent and looking at her husband. -I'm proud you became my wife. I never deserved you. Please promise me something, -Scarlett looked into the man's eyes again- be happy when I won't be with you anymore.

-I don't want to hear anything like that. You're not going to leave me here!

-Scarlett, we must be realistic, that's what's waiting for me. He pointed to Ergon's body, which had been rotting there for a few days, on the gallows. -People will be gathering tomorrow at this time to throw food, insult, and see me as I die. Scarlett, you need to know something. I have to tell you before I die how proud I am of all you have accomplished. For whom you are! -He stressed- The opening of the mine and your plans are great. Please never give up on your dreams!

Scarlett cried as her husband hugged her tightly. Then the soldier knocked on the bars, shouting: "No contact."

-I'm going to die soon, and you would deny me from embracing my wife for the last time? Don't you have a heart?

Embracing her husband, Scarlett was facing the bed, where she saw a bunch of bloodstains and a bloody handkerchief that scared her a little, but tried not to show it.

*

Scarlett walked into the building as she entered, at the other end of the room she saw George, whose presence made her feel uncomfortable. When she turned to go further, she accidentally collided with Jerome.

-Mrs. Wolowitz! Good to see you. We have to talk.

-As I wanted to talk to you, Dr. Garfield.

-It would be about your mother-in-law. Mrs. Wolowitz has recovered a lot and is in excellent condition to remove the blindfold from her this week.

-Great. -She closed the topic.

-Is there a problem? -The man asked the woman, full of anxiety.

-What I want to talk about, is much more private. -She said grabbing his arm, then pulling him to a quieter place, looking around. When she saw that there were only two of them within earshot, she began to explain her plan to Jerome.

-Paying a midwife is complete madness... -He said softly.

-But I have no choice.

-Mrs. Wolowitz, you can't do that. It is dangerous. And Leonard... -He didn't know how to confront the woman in front of him with the truth.

-Dr. Garfield, I have to do this. If they think we've consummated our wedding night, he still has a chance to survive.

-Listen to me very carefully, Leonard is sick, I have to prove this now so that both of you can preserve your dignity. You asked about the bloody sputum... If they find out that you did it and still condemn your husband, he will die, and you... -he stopped for a moment- you will never remarry.

-Lie! -She shouted.

-No, that's the sad truth. Leonard, like this or not, will die, he won't be alive for long... Your husband's fate is already sealed, someone just has to say the verdict.

-Don't you have a drop of hope? -She asked sadly, then hurried away.

Killing even that little spark of hope in Scarlett, Jerome sat in the interrogation chair, then looked at the woman. After their eyes met, Scarlett quickly looked in another direction. They also brought in Leonard soon, who was worn out by this whole situation, just dragged himself along and then had to lean on the railing to keep himself from collapsing. So far, he has been doing so well, confidence was shaken in few people seeing him. Scarlett looked at the empty space next to her. Evelyn was no longer by her side to encourage and support her. Not far from her sat Agatha, on the other side with Akita, whose hand she was holding. Scarlett slid on the bench next to her mother-in-law, then took her hand.

-Dr. Jerome Garfield! -Cried the speaker of the court.

-Tell me, Doctor, are you here as a friend or as a doctor for the defendant? -The barrister asked.

-I'd speak as the man's doctor. -He stood up from his seat and then began to speak confidently. -I'd talk about Leonard Wolowitz's illness! -He pointed at his friend. -One day, this man visited me. It was a rainy, cold autumn day, many, many years ago. He turned desperately for my help. Saying he caught the disease. After I examined him, it turned out that this man was suffering from venereal disease. Which is spread by sexual, body fluids, or mother-child (pregnancy/breastfeeding). Many individuals develop an influenza-like illness or a mononucleosis-like illness for 2–4 weeks after exposure while others have no significant symptoms. Symptoms occur in 40–90% of cases and now commonly include fever, large tender lymph nodes, a rash, headache, tiredness, and/or sores of the mouth and genitals, throat inflammation which can lead to heavy cough and bloody sputum.

-Your Honour Judge, that means only one thing... -The lawyer said.

-I didn't finish yet! -Dr. Garfield said aloud.

-Sustained! -Lord Quas hit with his gavel.

-Syphilis has had a large impact on society, both as an illness and as a source of discrimination. I believe that letter that Mrs. Wolowitz wrote about this secret of her husband, was about this disease, which was the reason that Leonard, my friend, did not touch his wife.

-So, you married both of your wives because you didn't want your secret revealed and be discriminated? -The barrister asked, people all whispered softly and adapted to the situation sadly.

-That's right, Sir.

-Then would you rule out that he didn't get this particular disease from a man? Are you saying it only spreads between men and women? Although scientists have proven that the virus is most prevalent among homosexuals. -The people nodded in surprise.

-Order! Order! -Called Lord Quas, trying to look strong.

-Yes, but that doesn't prove anything. Mr. Wendoz was hanged, even if you still have his body, his blood is already clotted, you are unable to examine it. It could be only proved if the man had the same symptoms. -Jerome shouted.

-I'd ask Mrs. Wolowitz to the court! -The judge shouted.

-I'm not finished yet! -Jerome shouted.

-Objection Sustained! -The judge shouted.

Scarlett glanced at her husband, who leaned weakly against the railing. Then she walked down slowly. As their gaze met as she walked past her husband, Leonard was completely shattered, Scarlett knew if she could at any place now she would be where she could scream out loud, getting rid of all the awful pain.

-Mrs. Wolowitz, I would like to know what your relationship was like with your husband. -The lawyer asked.

-He was always kind to me; he was understanding and very attentive.

-Tell me were there difficulties in your marriage?

-There were milestones, of course, as in any marriage.

-Is it true that you sleep in separate bedrooms?

-We agreed on that at the beginning, yes. Because this is my first marriage and I need some time to get used to it... -She said with a sigh.

-This is not a specific reason. How could you get used to a marriage without even sharing a room?

-So, why, would that be a specific reason if I say that my husband snores louder than a mule or sweats heavier than a horse, or he is warmer than a bear's fur? -Scarlett asked indignantly.

Then all those present laughed out loud, and even Leonard smiled.

-I'd like to ask only one more question. -Said the barrister.

Then two soldiers walked in, one handing something to the judge, who passed it on. Lord Quas asked something of the soldier in front of him, who withdrew after his answer. Scarlett was so immersed in the phenomenon that she hadn't heard what the lawyer had asked her.

-Would you repeat that, please? -She asked softly, staring at the judge, who did not provide any promising sight, he looked disappointed.

-I asked if you had consummated your wedding night. -He repeated.

Scarlett looked at the man, then turned her gaze to George, who bit his lips, then to Jerome, who shook his head, then to her husband, who looked down at his wife. Leonard's eyes soaked in tears, as did Scarlett's. She turned back 360 degrees in front of the judge, stood up, and answered the question with minor hesitation.

-No, we didn't. -Then she could almost hear all three men sighing.

There was a silent silence in the room, many did not expect this answer or were just hoping on this one.

-But as I said, we slept in a separate room because of me. My husband respected my decision and understandingly waited for it to happen, when I was ready for it.

-Thank you, Madam! -Lord Quas said sadly, then hit his gavel.

When Scarlett stood up, the lawyer was unable to hide his joy, looking back at them with a wide grin.

-I would call the defendant himself!

-Then Leonard pulled himself together and looked at the court. -I recently received news that... -Then he took out the piece of clothing the soldier handed him- this handkerchief belonged to Ergon Wendoz. -In the material in his hand was a smaller piece of clothing that was stained with blood. -The guard testified that he had a strong cough, often so much so that they thought he would not see him die on the gallows, but drowned in his cell. Is there anything you would like to tell us, Mr. Wolowitz?

Leonard took a deep breath. -I can't say anything that would convince you.

People were outraged and then began to shout until they heard the gavel. Then the trial by the jury withdrew. It was a small break for the people, but they barely got up from their chairs, they came back.

-How is that possible? They barely left for a few minutes. -Jerome asked George.

-I'm surprised, too. -The man replied.

Then the judge asked: -Have you reached the verdict?

-We have my Lord. -Replied one of them, who remained standing.

-Do you find the defendant guilty or not guilty?

-We found him... -He said pausing, putting tremendous pressure on everyone- guilty!

Leonard almost collapsed when he heard it. There was more chaos, which this time was also silenced by the gavel. Agatha began to cry out loud, whom Akita was trying to comfort. Scarlett tried to stay strong, wishing Evelyn was there to reassure her.

-Does the prisoner wish to make a final statement? -The judge asked.

-I just want to say that love is not a sin! -He declared out loud, and people spoke again, insulting the man in front of them.

-It now remained for me to declare... -The judge said as he put the black cap on his head again. -The formidable sentence of the law. Which would be... -He took a deep breath. -that you will be taken to a place of execution, where you will be hanged by the neck, but not until death... as an aristocrat, and a very influential businessman, you will get a far worse experience than a man like your "lover". -He stressed- You will be cut down and your bowels taken out, cast into the fire before your face and your head will be taken off. -Then slapped with the gavel.

Agatha began to cry even louder, Scarlett watching her husband collapse in front of her.

-All rise! -The speaker of the house said as the court left.

-I never heard such a sentence, during my career. -Said George- I regret there's nothing more we can do for him.

*

Returning to Beelove, Scarlett watched as Mowie ushered in his mistress, who stumbled from one side to the other like a drunk, helplessly after realizing that her only child will be on the gallows, she was this once uninterested in the brightness, in the wealth, the perfection, not interested in the name Wolowitz being shamed in front of in society. The only thing she saw was the flame in her that provided the life had begun to extinguish, leaving not a single spark of embers, the only thing left was just the grey ash. Accompanied by Akita, they reached the salon where her dog, Harold, was waiting. The naughty puppy was full of energy to play, but Agatha kicked him with her foot aside and just walked past him.

-Ma'am, can we serve the lunch? -The head housekeeper asked.

-No, I'm not staying. -Scarlett replied- I have to clear my head. -Then she walked away.

Unconsciously, she headed for Gracewith, just staring into nothingness, thinking of nothing, just letting the late winter cold bite all her thoughts out of her. She had been walking slowly for half an hour until she suddenly fell weakly on the field and then roared.

Soon after reaching Gracewith, she looked around the lands where her workers were working diligently. She just stared at them for a while, not really knowing what she was doing here, what brought her here at all. It was as if she didn't even control her footsteps, she just walked and walked and walked. When she turned, she unexpectedly met the French lieutenant and also the captain of the ship, who was wearing his uniform. He was standing behind her with some of his soldiers.

-Mr. Toussaint! -She said frightened.

-Ma'am... -He bowed politely.

-Are you about to leave? -She asked Francis in surprise.

-Yes, we are. I was in town today where I met one of our spies. The two countries have signed another peace treaty so the French are free to leave English soil. The ship will leave the port of Truro tomorrow at dawn.

-That, um... Where is a soldier? -Scarlett asked, looking at the men. -I remember there was a tall soldier with you as well.

-Oh, yes... He passed away unfortunately during the night. My people are already digging his grave, I hope it's not a problem if we bury him here.

-No, of course not. I'm almost used to seeing you here. It all came as a surprise.

-We have already been to Falmouth; we are visiting Truro Prison tonight to free our detained comrades and return to our homeland. So, you will not see as for long.

-The jail? -She asked thoughtfully.

-Yes, that's correct. I wish I could thank you for everything you did for us. -Francis Toussaint said.

-As a matter of fact, there would be something... -Scarlett said thoughtfully.

-What's going on? -George arrived on horseback.

-I will save my husband!

# CHAPTER LXII

It was late at night, slowly hitting midnight as some drunk soldiers walked to the gates of Truro prison, with strong drinks and some empty bottles in their hands, with Francis Toussaint in the lead. The soldiers sang some kind of French song out loud, there were six in all, the lieutenant standing in front, two other soldiers behind him, and three more in the back, where two were holding one in the middle because he was unable to stand on his own two feet.

To the loud knocking and singing, the prison guard, whose office was up a corner away, hurried in front of the door.

-What do you want? -The prison guard asked at the door, looking out the peephole.

-My name is Lieutenant Francis Toussaint and I came to free my soldiers. -He said, holding out a piece of paper to the guard.

-At this time? Why didn't you come sooner? -The man asked- There will be a change of guard soon. Come back after that.

-It's just a few minutes all over. -And then he showed the time on the silver pocket watch in his hand. -We still have a full quarter of an hour. -The guard hesitated- And our ship will leave in a few hours...

-All right... -He said, then let them in.

As the soldiers walked in, Francis's eyes were caught on the keychain which the guard hanged on his side on a hook that was fastened to his belt. Then he started leading them along. They passed the small office of the English prison guard, which consisted of a small table and a chair, with a book and a pitcher on the table. The guard unhooked his key, then took two metres in the narrow small hallway, then stopped in front of a cell.

-These are French soldiers here. -He said, then opened the cell door.

-Hey... hey, you! Do you want some booze? -One of the drunk soldiers asked the man in a cell a few feet away from the French's, to whom he spoke as if he was just babbling to his pet.

-Hey, you! -Cried the guard- You rather leave him!

The soldier straightened up and then winked at Leonard. The guard, after releasing the soldiers, headed in the other direction, straight toward his small resting corner, next to which was a staircase leading down. Then he stopped abruptly at the three drunken soldiers who had been cheering so far, then began to stare at the one in the middle, causing the soldiers to look at each other.

-For the sake of... -The guard said aloud- You soaked yourself well in alcohol dude, you stink like a ferret... -He began to fan with his hand the air in front of his nose.

The soldiers began to laugh out loud, then sipped from their bottles again and began to sing. When they reached the stairs, the guard stopped abruptly, hearing the tower bell.

-You bastard! You said we still have a quarter of an hour! -The guard shouted.

Francis looked at his watch and spoke half-mouthed.

-Hum. Yeah... The watch seems to be slow. -He said shrugging, then they heard a knock on the door.

-Wait here! -He said, then ran away.

The moment the guard turned around, one of Francis' soldiers unhooked his key from his side at a glance. When the guard disappeared at the corner, the soldier threw the key to Francis.

-We have to hurry! We barely have three or four minutes! -Francis shouted in French.

One of the soldiers stood around the corner and looked down the hall. Francis opened the cell door in the blink of an eye. While the other soldiers who had just been released stared in confusion.

-Who are you? -Leonard asked.

-No time to ask! -Francis said, then helped the other two soldiers drop the one in the middle onto the bed.

-Are those my clothes? -Leonard asked.

Francis took out his pocket watch and tucked it in the lying man's pocket.

-And that is my watch... -He said, pointing a finger.

Francis pressed a bottle into Leonard's hand, pulled out the cork with his teeth, and began watering the bed. One of the soldiers began to unpack the medicines on the table which he took out from his pocket.

-What are you doing? -He was puzzled.

-We are saving your ass. It doesn't matter to him anyway. He would be happy if he knew, that we are using his body for a noble purpose. -One of the soldiers replied.

After the bottles were emptied, Francis picked up the hat on the ground that had fallen off the head of the corpse.

-Hurry up, they're coming! -In French he shouted in a whisper the soldier around the corner.

Francis put the hat on Leonard's head to cover his face, then dabbled the man's face with spirits. One of the soldiers quickly closed the cell door. Francis could already see the shadows approaching. He turned back to Leonard, arranging his hat.

-Pretend to be drunk.

-What?

-Just do it! -The French lieutenant ordered.

-I'd swear for my life it was here! -The guard pointed to his side, utterly desperate.

When they returned, the soldiers were standing in the hallway. The guard looked at the small table, where the bunch of keys lay.

-How will you long make us wait? If I remember correctly, I mentioned that the ship will leave in a few hours...

-How the hell did it get here? -He was lost.

-You put it there after you released the soldiers. -The lieutenant said, the man already starting to point with his finger when Francis started to speak again. -I'm drunk and you don't remember what you're doing? Ch-Ch-Ch... Can we go? -Francis started for the stairs and took a few steps down, then he turned back. He saw the guard was staring at one of the soldiers again with an interesting expression. -What do you think, wouldn't be a better idea if my soldiers would wait outside? Just look at them, you don't want them to climb down like that, do you? -He pointed at his tilting soldiers.

-I'll accompany them! I'm leaving anyway. -The guard said who was in the previous shift to the other.

His colleague nodded in agreement, then headed down the stairs following Lieutenant Francis. The drunk soldier, who offered a drink to those in the cell, fell on the guard's neck and began to whisper in his ear. Then a soldier next to Leonard's cell struck a match on the sole of his boot, setting it on fire, and then walked in the footsteps of the soldiers advancing outward, throwing a piece of burning match through the bars, which set the cell full of spilled alcohol, on fire.

*

When they were almost back upstairs, the guard started sniffing.

-What's that smell? -He shouted, then ran over the next few steps.

He ran to the flaming cell, then, hesitating, not knowing what to do, finally began to run in a direction, grabbing a bucket of water next to the table in which drinking water was kept, and then sprinkled it on the cell. When he saw that it wasn't working, he started ringing the bell at the table as he put his whistle in his mouth and began to blow loudly.

-I told you that the English are a strange population. -Francis said with his arms folded, then turned his back, along with the soldiers.

*

After a few hours, Scarlett, George, and Jerome also arrived at the scene, all three in nightgowns.

-Would you please, tell me why we were alerted in the middle of the night and dragged here? -Jerome asked.

-They didn't even give me enough time to put on something normal. -Scarlett said.

Captain Patmore led them into the cell, which smelled of alcohol and the burning smell of the human flesh. Ash settled in the cell and everything was burned.

-What happened here? -George asked.

That's when Lord Quas arrived at the cell, who was also surprised by the sight.

-I hoped, one of you will tell me. -Said the captain.

Scarlett approached the burning body lying on the bed with slow strides.

-Is it? -She asked in the midst of a bursting cry, and by the time everyone started walking there. -Tell me he doesn't... -The woman's tears streamed.

-His height matches... -Jerome said, reaching for the object sticking out of his pocket and taking it out. It was a silver pocket watch engraved with "Leonard R. Wolowitz".

-My husband's watch. -Scarlett picked up, then cried, George without hesitation quickly hugged the woman.

That's when the guard of the previous shift arrived.

-Tell me, what happened here? -Captain Patmore asked the arriving man.

-I have no idea. -The man declared.

Jerome walked to the table, where he kicked into something, when he picked it up, he saw a small vial. He took it to the captain and handed it over.

-What is this?

-Sleeping pills. -The doctor replied. -It's so strong it could knock three bears out.

-Would anyone tell me how it got here? -He lifted the vial.

Then George took a step closer, but he kicked into something too. Everyone's eyes were on the subject. The captain walked closer, then picked it up, smelled it, then suddenly jerked his head, as he smelled the strong smell of alcohol through the glass's mouth.

-Could you tell me how these items got here? -The captain asked the two guards.

The one who was on duty at the time began: -Maybe it was brought here by the drunken French. -He said shyly.

-French? -He asked in surprise.

-Yes, they came to release the detained soldiers by order. -The older man said. -You know they've been here, they arrived so suddenly that I even lost my keys. -He confessed.

-Did you lose your key? -Captain Patmore asked as he approached him

-Yes, but only for a few minutes, and I found them after all.

When Scarlett heard this, she began to cry more bitterly, hiding in George's shoulder.

-When did this happen? -The captain asked.

-During the change of guards, but realizing the mistake, I had to run back to find them. And I did.

-I have to go after them! -The captain hurried out the door where Lord Quas stopped him.

-Leave them. -He replied, holding his hand on the man's left collarbone.

-But Lord Judge, they broke the law, supplied one of the convicts with drinks and drugs. If I'm in a hurry I can still catch them at the port.

-I said leave them. -The judge repeated himself, then looked at the corpse. -It doesn't matter anymore. -He would then walk up to the man's bed to examine him.

The captain saluted, then left the cell, escorting the other three parties still assigned here. When they left and the judge was left alone, he began to laugh nodding his head.

\*

Scarlett and the other two men hurried to the harbour. Where Francis and Leonard stood in front of the ship on the pier.

-Leonard! -Scarlett jumped around his neck, pulling her husband close, then walking in front of Francis. -Thank you, Lieutenant! -And kissed on the cheek.

The lieutenant smiled blushing, then nodded his hat.

\*

Captain Patmore hurried straight to the brothel, where he went to the room in the building that faced the harbour. As he burst into the room, the naked couple huddled on the bed rolled down to the foot of the bed.

-What do you think? -The stranger asked indignantly.

The captain silently pointed his gun at him, and they wrapped the blanket around them and ran out of the room. The captain opened the window, then took out his spyglass and opened it to look around. He moved to the right and to the left with his upper body, then suddenly stopped. "Ahha, I caught you, you dratted!" he muttered, then pointed at them by the time the soldier aimed his gun at him.

*

-We don't have much time; dawn is starting to break the night. -Francis replied.

After saying goodbye to his best friend Jerome, Leonard walked over to George and held out his hand to him. George slapped it away, then hugged him, tapping his shoulder. He then walked in front of Scarlett.

*

-Captain, is that a good idea? If we shoot him, they may think we have tried to assassinate the French lieutenant and another war could break out, disregarding the peace treaty.

- Aim for him! -He shouted.

-I've taken aim, Captain! -Cried the soldier- I'm waiting for the order.

The captain didn't answer, he was just staring at them for a while.

*

-Thank you for everything! -He told his wife, then kissed her on the forehead. -You have given me a chance for the rest of my few years.

-We have to go! -The lieutenant stepped beside them, then they walked aboard together.

*

-Captain, they're anchored! -The soldier shouted again, keeping his finger on the trigger. The captain just stood still. -They're getting away! -The soldier spoke again. -5, 4, 3, 2, ... -Recounted back, slowly pulling the trigger- 1... -then silence. - Captain, the measured target is out of range.

But the captain just turned around and walked out of the room.

# CHAPTER LXIII

Scarlett was walking in the Truro cemetery with a huge bouquet of wildflowers in her hand. She stopped in front of Evelyn's grave, which was full of beautiful flowers, more and more expensive bouquets. Scarlett smiled, then took a small bouquet out of it and placed it on top of the many flowers. She stroked the tombstone, then kissed her hand, which she pressed onto the tombstone. Then she stood up, took a few steps, and stopped at Leonard's grave. Seeing it, she smiled and took another bouquet on the barren fresh ground and placed it on it. Now as only her bouquet decorated it, she walked on, until she reached her parents' grave, where she was greeted by an unexpected guest. Edith Salvatore stood in front of Miranda's burial.

-Dead people receive more flowers than the ones who live, because regret is stronger than gratitude. -She said as she walked beside her, as she stopped beside Edith, she began to wipe her eyes.

-Miss. Bloom, I am so sorry. I didn't notice you... -She said, then took a step back.

Scarlett split the remaining bouquet in half and placed it on the two graves next to each other, one on her mother's, Miranda Bloom's, and the other on her father's grave, Owen Thaker's. She straightened up, then turned to the woman, bowed politely, and was about to leave.

-I'm sorry! -She said after the woman. -Everything I've done to you. Now I learnt that I couldn't stand in the way of love. -Then she looked at the two graves. - None of them.

-Sometimes it's too late to regret certain things. -Scarlett replied and walked on.

After she reached the cemetery gate, she saw a woman who was very familiar to her. She hurried after her. Noticing that Scarlett was following her, she walked faster and faster until she started running. However, she was wounded and was limping, Scarlett couldn't gain on. She entered an alley, a narrow little deserted street where she could not see a soul, the woman disappeared as if the earth had swallowed her.

When she turned, it was as if she had seen a ghost. He stood tightly behind her, as if he came out of nowhere. Kwaw called on her name: -Mrs. Wolowitz! Forgive me, I didn't intend to scare you.

-Mr. Kwaw, what are you doing here? -Scarlett was surprised.

-That's exactly what I wanted to ask you.

-I just think... -She thought about her words. -It was like seeing an old employee of mine. -She said, stroking her forehead. -Doesn't matter, it must have been a mistake. -She took a few more steps toward the man to return to his vicinity as she jumped in fright, from where they went on together.

-Do you still remember this street? -He asked.

-How can I forget? -She laughed as they reached the corner.

As they turned, the homeless sat in line by the wall. As Scarlett walked past them, she threw a small amount at each person's small collections, and people began to be grateful except for one person. As the woman passed by them conversing cheerfully with Kwaw, the ungrateful homeless woman looked up and looked at them. Daphne watched as Scarlett and Kwaw disappeared into the crowd.

# CHAPTER LXIV

-We greet everyone who took the time to come to the opening of the mine! -Scarlett stood beside the mine. -This day is not just a day for a new beginning, it is a day that opens up new possibilities for us. Opportunity for a better and more secure future. As you know, I will run three industries, farming, beekeeping, and mining. This triple force provides liberation for all of us, liberation from famine and poverty. I would like to offer everyone a job opportunity to make it all possible for you. My dear friend... -She pointed to the man standing next to her. -Thomas Kwaw will lead the mining, he will be the manager and in charge of the mineworkers. -Some people were a little upset to hear this and it caused confusion. -I want equality and harmony among my workers. I want everyone to respect each other regardless of gender, religion, race, or rank! -Then a lot of people started applauding. -This mine got its name from my late husband, Leonard Robert Wolowitz. I am pleased to announce, -then pulled the sheet off the board- that I will open "Leo", which means lion. The first mine opened in Beelove for a decade and we will hopefully be opening its other two brothers as well. -People applauded and cheered.

Later, Scarlett returned to Beelove, where a carriage arrived, and two little girls jumped out of the carriage cheerfully and ran toward her. Doris was standing in the doorway, but when the two younger children, Jared and Aliona, saw Riley and Julia running towards Scarlett, they also began running, making it difficult for Doris to guard them. When they got there, they all hugged their aunt in a group.

After that, they all cheerfully entered Beelove house, where Scarlett decided to make another announcement to Agatha. Jerome was waiting for them in the parlour. Everyone entered the room and they sat around her.

-All right, Mrs. Wolowitz, and now I'm taking off the blindfold and examining your vision. -He said, then took off the blindfold, the children looked a little strangely at the face of the burnt woman sitting in front of them, who was wearing a wig to hide the bald spots caused by the acid, Jerome stood in front of her first, then turned her head to the light, the woman started to squint at first.

-God... -She said softly -My dear good god... -She repeated.

-Are you feeling well? Don't you feel a pain or a sting? -He asked in surprise.

-I can see... -She said in surprise, then began to repeat happily. -Although a little vague... but, -Then she looked at the kids and started pointing at them again: -Jared, Julia, Riley, Scarlett... -She smiled. - Aliona -She then glanced at Akita and she felt her heart start to tighten and got her hand on the chest. -Allan?

-Actually, I'm Akita, Marta's brother. -Replied the little child shyly.

At first, Agatha looked like she had a seizure, but she began to cry.

-Are you well ma'am? -The boy asked, placing his hand on her shoulder.

-Call me mommy! -She then hugged the child with such a violent motion that her wig almost fell off, Akita had to adjust it.

Everyone in the room started laughing and started talking cheerfully. After a while, Scarlett stepped aside to discuss some things with Agatha.

-Mrs. Wolowitz, I know we didn't always have a good relationship. But I decided to leave Beelove.

-What? Where would you go? -She asked in surprise.

-I have decided to move back to Gracewith, giving back your position as the mistress of the house in Beelove.

-Don't be silly. My son left it all to you. This is all yours.

-Dear of you, but then what's left for you? -Scarlett asked, but she just waved.

-Don't mind me, I have my own property. I plan to return to America; I have had enough of the English land. I'll take Akita with me and then raise him as my own. And of course, there is your brother, to whom someone needs to pay attention. -She pointed with a finger.

-How do you... -She wanted to ask, but it was at that moment when Akita arrived, "Mama! Mama!" shouting after Agatha and then grabbing her by the hand, he dragged her back among the people.

-I'm coming, I'm coming. -She said, taking small little quick steps- How about a nice English name?

-What kind of English name? -The child asked.

-I don't know what if you choose one for yourself?

-Can I be Susan? -The child asked, and she laughed out loud.

-What about Allan? Allan Wolowitz?

-You were serious... mother? -The child was surprised.

Scarlett smiled and walked on.

*

A few hours later they arrived in Gracewith, where Matilda and Nivek were already waiting for them, the children returned cheerfully into their old home. Scarlett felt like she had returned home every time she crossed the threshold.

-Madam, we'll serve the dinner soon! -Matilda announced.

-Thank you, Matilda.

Scarlett walked into the library, which she hadn't seen for a very long time during her long absence, even if she had been there, she had never entered this room. The room was the same again as it used to be, there were plenty of books on the shelves and even the furniture was the same.

-Nice right? -Doris asked, sneaking silently behind her. -Mr. Wolowitz renovated it, commanding it before his long journey to Europe, which was completed in the meantime. That dear man didn't even see it.

-I thought you didn't like him. -Scarlett said with a smile.

-Not in the least ... -She said with a pause- But over time he grew to my heart.

-I hope I don't disturb the conversation. -Said another voice behind them.

-Mr. Salvatore... -Scarlett said in surprise.

-Not in the least, I was just getting ready to go. -Doris said, then walked out.

-It was a nice speech. I mean, at the mine.

-Thanks!

-And what are you going to do now?

-If I guess I'll continue my busy business life. My husband has signed some contracts with European companies that will kick-start the honey industry. I have a lot of orders and new hives that will need to be inaugurated. The farm is also doing well for the time being, although it is maybe too early to say it in early spring. And of course, there's the mine... -She said with a smile.

-You're a miracle. -He said as he stepped closer.

-And you? What are you going to do? -Scarlett asked the man almost half a metre away.

-It depends on your answer.

-I'm afraid I don't understand what you're aiming for. -She said, blinking profusely.

-If you say you are going to be my wife, I'll stay in Cornwall. My wife will be a wonderful businesswoman. We may have one or two children and maybe I will open the cotton factory again or a school, either or both. And at the side of my wonderful wife, we will create great things. -He took one step further.

-And what if I say no? -She asked with a deep breath.

-Then I will go back to London, taking my place in Parliament as MP, and at best you will never see me again. -He said with a forced grin- Well, what's your answer?

Scarlett took a deep breath and walked toward the window.

-I'm afraid you have to plan your trip to London. -She said, turning her back on the man.

George walked out of the room silently, stopped at the door, then looked back, hoping the woman had changed her mind. When he was sure Scarlett was sure of her answer, he walked away.

Doris hurried into the library nervously with quick steps.

-Miss. Bloom are you crazy? Would you just let him walk away like that?

-You know how it is. When a man makes money, he feels like he wants more women, but when a woman makes money, she feels like she doesn't need a man.

-We both know, you love him and you want him.

-Why would I? I'm a strong woman. I don't sit around feeling sorry for myself nor let people mistreat me. I don't respond to people who dictate to me or try to bring me down. If I fall, I will rise up even stronger because I am a survivor and not a victim. I am in control of my life and there is nothing I can't achieve.

-That is a good point. -She stopped to think for a moment, then shook her head. -But we both know that he never tried to bring you down. The one who tried was his aunt, but she cannot control him anymore. Especially if you are next to him.

Scarlett began thinking, then looked out the window and saw George playing with Jared throwing a ball.

-I've been married once.

-You know what you want... Don't deny from yourself. Time is like a river. You cannot touch the same water twice, because the flow that has passed will never pass again. If you don't go after him now, you might lose him forever. Here is my fifth lesson, before you die, dare to live.

Then Scarlett ran, ran out of Gracewith's door, and hurried into the garden, where the early spring air and fresh floral scent covered everything. The trees and bushes bloomed wonderfully. George walked slowly through the rose bushes, then tore a rose that pierced his finger, he put the bleeding finger to his lips, then raised his head and saw the woman running towards him. The man began to walk back toward her, then stopped at the willow tree where he met Scarlett.

-You can't go to London.

-Why can't I? -He asked putting his hand in his pocket.

-Because you can't leave me here. I can't lose you again... I love you, George.

George didn't believe his ears at first, so he laughed. When he realised that she was serious, he hugged her tightly and then kissed her firmly. After a while, Scarlett pushed him away.

-And I want three kids. -She said seriously, then the man handed over the rose.

-With this single little rose, I wish you a Happy Birthday, dear Scarlett! -He then grabbed her in his arms again.

**To be continued...**

CPSIA information can be obtained
at www.ICGtesting.com
Printed in the USA
LVHW101357030922
727403LV00005B/121